A-LEVEL
AND AS-LEVEL

BUSINESS STUDIES

Martin Buckley, with Barry Brindley and Malcolm S. Greenwood

LONGMAN A AND AS-LEVEL STUDY GUIDES

Series editors
Geoff Black and Sttuart Wall

Title available
Accounting
Biology
Business Studies
Chemistry
Computer Science
Economics
English
French
Geography
German
Government and Politics
Law
Modern History
Mathematics
Physics
Psychology
Sociology

Addison Wesley Longman Limited,
Edinburgh Gate, Harlow,
Essex CM20 2JE, England
and Associated Companies throughout the world

© Longman Group UK Limited 1992
This edition © Addison Wesley Longman Limited 1997

First published 1992
Sixth impression 1994
Updated edition 1997

British Library Cataloguing in Publication Data

Buckley, Martin W. (Martin Wilfred), 1943–
  Business studies. – (A-level revise guides)
  I. Title II. Brindley, Barry III. Greenwood, Malcolm IV.
  Series 658

  ISBN 0-582-31652-9

Set in 10/12pt Century Old Style
Produced by Longman Singapore Publishers (Pte) Ltd
Printed in Singapore

ACKNOWLEDGEMENTS

The authors are grateful to the following Examination Boards for granting permission
to reproduce past questions.
  Associated Examining Board
  Northern Ireland Schools Examinations and Assessment Council
  University of Cambridge Local Examinations Syndicate
  Edexcel Foundation (London)
The Examination Boards bear no responsibility for the example answers to questions
taken from its past papers which are contained in this book.

CONTENTS

EDITORS' PREFACE

Longman Study Guides are written by experienced examiners and teachers, and aim to give you the best possible foundation for success in your course. Each book in the series encourages thorough study and a full understanding of the concepts involved, and is designed as a subject companion and study aid to be used throughout the course.

Many candidates fail to achieve the grades which their ability deserves, owing to such problems as the lack of a structured revision strategy, or unsound examination technique. This series aims to remedy such deficiencies, by encouraging a realistic and disciplined approach in preparing for and taking the examinations.

The largely self-contained nature of each chapter gives the book a flexibility which you can use to your advantage. After starting with the background to the A, AS-Level and Scottish Higher Courses and details of the syllabus coverage, you can read all other chapters selectively, in any order appropriate to the stage you have reached in your course.

Geoff Black and Stuart Wall

NAMES AND ADDRESSES OF THE EXAM BOARDS

Associated Examining Board (AEB)
Stag Hill House
Guildford
Surrey GU2 5XJ

University of Cambridge Local
 Examinations Syndicate (UCLES)
Syndicate Buildings
1 Hills Road
Cambridge CB1 2EU

Northern Examinations and Assessment
Board (NEAB)
Devas St
Manchester M15 6EX

Edexcel Foundation
 (London)
Stewart House
32 Russell Square
London WC1B 5DN

Northern Ireland Council for Curriculum,
 Examinations and Assessment (NICCEA)*
29 Clarendon Road,
Belfast BTI 3BG

Oxford and Cambridge Schools
 Examination Board (OCSEB)
Purbeck House
Purbeck Road
Cambridge CB2 2PU

Oxford Delegacy of Local Examinations
 (ODLE)
Ewert Place
Summertown
Oxford OX2 7BZ

Scottish Examination Board (SEB)
Ironmills Road
Dalkeith
Midlothian EH22 1LE

Welsh Joint Education Committee (WJEC)
245 Western Avenue
Cardiff CF5 2YX

*Shown as NISEAC in this edition

CHAPTER 1

PROJECTS, CASE STUDIES AND EXAMINATION TECHNIQUES

GETTING STARTED

All of the examinations covered by this book include a paper with essay questions. Most also include projects and responses to case studies as part of their scheme of assessment. The aim of this chapter is to provide guidelines on how to deal with each of these assessment areas.

Much of your success will depend upon your efforts in the examination room. In a very short period of time you will have to show the examiner your mastery of the subject. There is, however, no short cut to mastering this, or any other, subject. Success will be achieved by revision, not just in the few weeks prior to the examination, but consistent revision throughout your course. Many students claim to do this, but in reality the number is far fewer.

As part of your preparation for the examination you should be practising answering past examination questions. Chapters 2–21 of this book summarise important information on specific topic areas and provide recent examination questions from different examination boards. The questions have been carefully selected to illustrate the various kinds of questions which might appear in a topic area. You should develop your own *outline answers* to *all* the questions set on topics within your syllabus (see Table 1.1). This will help you to revise the topic as well as giving you practice in answering questions. Indeed, nearer the exam you might practise writing *full answers* in the same time you will have in the exam itself.

Each of the questions at the end of a chapter has an answer provided. These answers are not definitive and there may be occasions when an entirely different approach would be equally acceptable. However, by comparing your answer with the one in the text you should be able to assess the correctness of your approach and note any errors and omissions. This will help you to learn from your mistakes.

Amongst the answers in each chapter you will find a *student answer* with examiner comments. Study the answer and the comments carefully; it will give you a good idea of what the examiner expects in an answer. The *tutor's answer* in each chapter will help you to see what a full answer to the question might look like. The other questions at the end of each chapter will have rather more brief *outline answers*, commenting on the main points which might be included in an answer.

ESSENTIAL PRINCIPLES

THE SYLLABUSES

Table 1.1 shows how the chapters in this book relate to the various examination board syllabuses.

CHAPTER AND TOPIC	AEB	CAMB	CAMB O/S	NEAB	NISEAC	SEB	ULEAC
EXAMINATION BOARDS							
1 Project, Case Studies and Examination Techniques	✓	✓	✓	✓	✓	✓	✓
2 Forms of Business Organisation	✓	✓	✓	✓	✓		✓
3 Structure of Industry and Commerce	✓	✓	✓	✓	✓		✓
4 The Economic Micro-Environment of Business	✓	✓	✓	✓	✓		✓
5 The International Economy and Business	✓	✓	✓	✓	✓		✓
6 The Political, Social and Technological Environment	✓	✓	✓	✓	✓		✓
7 Management and the Organisation	✓	✓	✓	✓	✓	✓	✓
8 Management Style: Motivation and Leadership	✓	✓	✓	✓	✓	✓	✓
9 Communication I	✓	✓	✓	✓	✓	✓	✓
10 Communication II	✓	✓	✓	✓	✓	✓	✓
11 The Market	✓	✓	✓	✓	✓		✓
12 Marketing Strategy	✓	✓	✓	✓	✓	✓	✓
13 Marketing in Action	✓	✓	✓	✓	✓	✓	✓
14 Personnel Management	✓	✓	✓	✓	✓	✓	✓
15 Industrial Relations	✓	✓	✓	✓	✓	✓	✓
16 Financial Accounting	✓	✓	✓	✓	✓	✓	✓
17 Analysis and Interpretation of Accounts	✓	✓	✓	✓	✓	✓	✓
18 Management Accounting	✓	✓	✓	✓	✓	✓	✓
19 Sources of Finance and Investment Appraisal	✓	✓	✓	✓	✓	✓	✓
20 Production I	✓	✓			✓	✓	✓
21 Production II		✓		✓	✓	✓	

Table 1.1 Syllabus Coverage Chart

PROJECTS

“A definition.”

We can define a project as some kind of investigation undertaken by an individual student. It will relate to an issue, topic or management problem on which the student is required to collect data, undertake analysis, draw conclusions and make recommendations. It will be presented in a report format.

Most of the examination boards include a project as part of their assessment criteria. The phraseology may differ, it may be called a project, dissertation or assignment but it combines those elements outlined above.

CHOOSING A TOPIC

Projects provide you with a chance to select a topic that you are interested in. This should mean that motivation is less of a problem than in other parts of your course. Selecting an appropriate topic is very important. A lack of thought at this stage may affect the successful outcome of the project.

Past project material may be available within your school or college. You should ask your tutor whether it is possible for you to look at a representative selection of these projects. You should also ask your tutor to discuss the projects with you. What did he think were the good and bad points in each? What difficulties did individual projects face?

“Look at past projects.”

Most examination boards insist that you submit your proposed title to them for approval – some ask for rather more detail, but even if they don't you would be well advised to do more than just 'think' of a title. You should discuss with your tutor:

- the aims of the project
- potential sources of information
- methods of investigation
- criteria for assessing project results (as this will reduce the chance of misunderstanding between you, your tutor and perhaps the examination board about what you are hoping to do)

In determining your project title you should also consider the following points:

Does it conform to the course requirements?

Some examination boards insist that the project considers a work-based problem. Others may suggest that it covers more than one functional area of the organisation. If in doubt, check with your tutor.

Is it tackled from a business studies angle?

The aim of the project is to show that you can apply business studies concepts and techniques to a given situation. Thus it follows that projects may fail because:

i) they deal with a topic in an incorrect manner. For example, whilst 'the ethics of advertising' is not legitimate, 'evaluating the effectiveness of XYZ Co.'s advertising campaign' would be.

ii) the project is merely descriptive and fails to use the appropriate concepts or techniques. Thus in a project 'Should ABC Co. invest in new machinery?', the concept of opportunity cost should be introduced, as should the various techniques of investment appraisal.

Is there a clear question to answer?

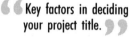

Key factors in deciding your project title.

In submitting their project titles, candidates are encouraged to ask a question. Experience has shown that titles such as 'Personnel policy in ABC Co.' or 'The advertising strategy of PQ Charity' will result in a project which is too descriptive to gain high marks. However, in many cases the general area of research is perfectly acceptable, but by asking a question the research is focused, analysis undertaken and conclusions drawn.

Is it feasible?

Due to the constraints of time, money and student ability, students are often recommended to limit their area of research. Thus a study of a large organisation is legitimate but so large and complex that the end project is likely to be very descriptive. Far better to tackle one problem within a particular department of that organisation.

An attempt should also be made at the outset of the project to see if the information needed is readily available. Where the information has a value to the organisation itself or its competitors it is unlikely to be available for student use. If in doubt, ask the organisation whether information will be available – be specific – indicate precisely what you will need.

Can high marks be gained from undertaking this project?

You should be aware of the assessment criteria against which your project will be judged. Generally speaking, a large proportion of the marks will be given for higher level skills, e.g. analysis, evaluation, conclusions and recommendations. Once more we emphasise – avoid purely descriptive projects as you will deny yourself many potential marks. It is far better to undertake some investigation into a practical problem within an organisation.

Some boards allow candidates to base their project on secondary (desk) research. In such circumstances candidates are expected to use a variety of sources (not just textbooks!), draw together that source material and undertake some form of critical evaluation.

In choosing your topic area, the following comments by examiners might prove helpful.

EXAMINERS COMMENTS ON SPECIFIC PROJECTS

- **The implications of EMS for the UK**
  'You must avoid a purely economics project. Why not concentrate your research on a

specific firm or industry and analyse the impact of EMS on that firm/industry. Try to avoid mere description and don't overstate the political aspect of the subject.'

■ **The impact of the Single Market on local firms**
'This project was severely hampered by the unwillingness of local firms to provide information' (examiner comment on moderation).

■ **An evaluation of the services offered by X bank for small businesses**
'Avoid a purely descriptive account. There is a need for primary research to establish a) What services small firms require; b) What the bank (claims to) offer(s); c) are small firms satisfied?'

■ **The effect of 'green consumerism' on the product range and marketing policies of specified supermarkets**
'This is a valid and interesting topic. However, (1) be sure to approach it from a business studies angle with reference to objectives, costs, benefits, sales, profits, etc; (2) why not reduce your research from 5 to 2 supermarket chains?'

■ **A study of the equal opportunities policy in XYZ firm**
'This, as it stands, may end up being too descriptive – ask a question, investigate an issue! You should also check whether the detailed information you require is available (n.b. avoid basing your project on "bland" public relations statements).'

■ **Does consumer protection work?**
'Far too difficult a topic at this level. It is likely to end up as a description of the legislation and examples where it didn't work.'

SUCCESSFUL PROJECTS

Here are some titles of projects which have been submitted to examination boards.

■ Would it be feasible to open a sports shop in Weybridge?

■ How can AB Hotel solve its staffing problem?

■ How should XY record shop adjust its marketing strategy in the light of increased competition?

■ An evaluation of the selection methods used by a manufacturing company.

■ A critical appraisal of the financial results of NM garage for 1988–90.

■ Should FG Co. computerise its accounting system?

■ How effective is the promotion strategy of AC Engineering Company?

■ How can AM golf club make more effective use of its resources?

■ Can the induction training of a supermarket be improved?

■ A critical assessment of the success of the merger between two small engineering firms.

■ How can a superstore company improve its stock control?

■ To what extent can a Blackpool hotel improve its trade in the off-season period?

■ An investigation to determine which of two speculative investment projects should be undertaken by a firm of builders.

■ An evaluation of communications in a local factory.

■ An assessment of the different wage payment systems in two local companies.

■ Should STN Co. have its own transport or employ local carriers for delivery purposes?

■ An evaluation of a local supermarket's flexible working practices.

■ How should a local boutique decide upon its pricing policy?

■ Should RTO Company relocate to a 'greenbelt' site?

■ Would it be an economic proposition to open a town centre restaurant on Monday nights?

■ Should PQR Company lease or buy its new computing system?

■ Should STU Engineering Company relocate its premises?

■ How should a company introduce a 'no smoking' policy?

DEVELOPING A PROJECT SCHEDULE

You have already been advised to draw up a statement regarding your project which identifies its aims, sources of information, methods of investigation and criteria for project evaluation. Quite apart from clarifying what you hope to do, it moves you forward to the next important stage – developing your plan of action or project schedule.

The aim of the project schedule is to break down a relatively complex task into a number of much more manageable tasks. It is also the means by which you can check your progress and ensure that you finish the project on time. In order to draw up your project schedule you will need to:

- decide how much time each week you will allocate to the project. Be realistic! There are many other activities you will undertake in a typical week including formal classes, private study, recreation, etc., etc. You will be surprised at how much time these other activities take up, which is why it is so important that you allocate a definite amount of time each week for the project. Even better, if you can allocate part of a definite day or evening each week to the project (n.b. let friends and family know that this time is reserved for your project – and you will not welcome distractions). As a general guide, you should be allocating a minimum of 6 hours per week (over 20 weeks) to a typical project of 6,000 words.

- determine the individual tasks which need to be carried out. These will probably include:

    1 obtaining background information on the organisation of your choice;

    2 making sure you understand theoretical knowledge relevant to your project (e.g. product life-cycle, elasticity);

    3 undertaking practical investigations (e.g. devising and implementing a questionnaire);

    4 analysis of results;

    5 drawing up conclusions and recommendations;

    6 writing up (and possibly typing) the project.

    For each of these tasks you should estimate the time you will need to complete. You will also need to work out a rudimentary critical path identifying those tasks which have to be completed before others start and which ones can be carried out concurrently.

> Identify the critical path.

- obtain the date by which your project has to be finished and submitted for marking. Then working back from that date, calculate the number of weeks which you will need to complete the project. You should, in practice, plan to finish a few weeks before the deadline so that unanticipated difficulties do not prevent you from meeting that deadline.

Once a project schedule has been drawn up you should make every effort to work to it. It is all too easy with the pressure of short term deadlines for essays etc. to ignore the project schedule. In practice, leaving project work until near the deadline is one of the major reasons why students obtain low marks on this component.

Many students will also reach a stage in their project when the initial enthusiasm wanes. This may be caused by an unanticipated set-back, or from realising how much routine work has to be undertaken before the interesting part. In these circumstances talk to your tutor or a friend on your course. You will certainly not be the only person experiencing these difficulties.

PRESENTING YOUR PROJECT

All four examination boards who use projects as part of their scheme of assessment require presentation in the form of a report. NEAB coursework assignments are not required to be submitted in a report format but would benefit from such presentation.

Despite reports being a common form of written communication in business and government, there is no one agreed format. Try to obtain examples of past projects and study the report structure. You may find considerable variation. Select a report structure that you feel happy with and which suits the kind of project you are undertaking. One logical format which has been used by students for many years is given below:

" A typical project format. "

Project Title
Table of Contents
Introduction
Findings
Conclusions and Recommendations
Appendices

We will look at each of these points in turn.

Project Title and Table of Contents

These first two items provide basic information for the reader. It informs him or her of the area of study and how the report on that study is structured. The Contents page is particularly important as it enables the reader to find his or her way quickly round the report. A well thought out structure, as illustrated by the Contents page, will immediately make a good impression on the reader.

Introduction

The Introduction sets the scene for what comes in the main body of the report. This is done in a number of ways.

First you should describe the nature of the project to be tackled, amplifying the main aims and defining the points of the project.

Secondly you should provide such background information as is necessary for the reader to understand what is written in the main body of the report.

Finally you should explain your plan of action, including the techniques and methods of enquiry you tend to adopt. (It is also useful to explain why you may have rejected certain lines of enquiry.)

Obviously the length of the Introduction will vary between reports but as a general rule it should not be more than two or three pages long. Examiners often comment that poorer candidates tend to produce overlong and very descriptive introductions. (For example, ask yourself whether the history of the business since 1910 is relevant to the report.)

Findings

In this section, the body of the report, you will use those techniques and methods of enquiry outlined in the Introduction to generate your findings. This is normally the longest part of the report. The details should be logically arranged and where different points are being made or techniques used, this section should be divided into sub-sections. Careful editing is necessary to ensure that the points you are trying to make are not obscured by too much information. If necessary, use Appendices for additional information.

Conclusions and Recommendations

In this section you will:

1 briefly restate your Findings;
2 draw Conclusions from those Findings;
3 make Recommendations based on your Conclusions.

There are several points which are worth noting here.

First no new material should be presented in this section – you are merely summarising your findings.

Secondly your conclusions should relate to the facts. You should avoid unsubstantiated conclusions nor should you let personal prejudices cloud your judgement.

Thirdly, this section gives you a chance to evaluate critically what you have done. For example, the sample size may not be sufficient to be sure of your conclusions, or cash flow figures may be suspect. It is better to let the examiner know you are aware of these shortcomings rather than let him believe you are ignorant of these problems.

The Recommendations are the final part of your project. As they are supposed to be acted upon they are essentially practical points. At all times avoid vagueness. It is not sufficient to suggest 'something should be done' – it is your responsibility to suggest what that 'something' should be. It is also advisable to avoid suggesting that 'further investigations' are necessary, as this implies that your investigations are flawed. Finally you should consider the impact of your recommendations. Thus if the introduction of new technology is likely to displace staff, you need to indicate (at least in general terms) how this may be overcome.

WRITING STYLE

It is not only the collecting and planning of material that has to be considered but also the actual writing of the report. You should consider the following points:

1 Each section of the report should be numbered and have a clear label. Major areas within each section should also be numbered and have sub-headings.
2 Pay attention to the way you present statistical information. Your aim should be to enable the reader to assimilate that information as easily as possible. The use of tables, diagrams and figures can be a very appropriate way of presenting information. Make sure, though that the material doesn't precede the first reference to it in the report. Large volumes of statistical data may be best included as an Appendix to the report, with a summary in the report itself.
3 Write in a straightforward manner using short sentences, as these improve clarity.
4 Avoid technical jargon where possible or be prepared to define it clearly.
5 Use a dictionary to avoid mis-spellings and a thesaurus to avoid repetition of words and phrases.
6 Your report is a record of past events – use the past tense.
7 Use the third person style throughout the report. Avoid the use of words such as 'I', 'you', 'me' and 'us'.

EXAMINATION TECHNIQUES

" Major reasons for failure. "

Good examination technique is essential for every student. In a time-constrained examination, the ability to utilise that time effectively must be achieved well before sitting the examination. Poor examination technique, e.g. not answering the correct number of questions, not allocating time properly or misreading the question is the single largest reason why candidates fail to perform as well as expected. This is the reason why candidates in most schools and colleges are given at least one set of 'mock' examinations before the real thing. The aim is to let you practise those techniques which are relevant to your examination. Errors in technique can then be identified and put right before the real examination.

REVISION

Revision should be a continual process throughout your course. It should not be left to the 3 or 4 weeks before the exam – though by this time it should have increased in intensity! Although the amount of revision undertaken will vary from candidate to candidate we would recommend you start getting organised three months beforehand. For your revision you will need:

- *A complete set of notes.* Get hold of a syllabus to see that all topics have been covered. Fill in the gaps that are identified.

- *At least one standard textbook.* There will always be times at which you wish to improve or check the accuracy of your notes. You will find the following textbooks useful:

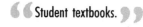
" Student textbooks. "

M. W. Buckley	Structure of Business (Pitman)
D. Dyer & J. Chambers	Business Studies: An Introduction (Longman)
P. Fearns	Business Studies (Hodder & Stoughton)
S. Hammond	Business Studies (Pitman)
B. Jewell	An Integrated Approach to Business Studies (Pitman)

- *Past examination papers.* These will give you valuable information on the structure of the examination – how long it is, how many questions, compulsory questions, the number of questions to be answered, etc.

- *Model answers.* These show the way experienced teachers in business studies would answer a particular question. This book contains a number of questions and model answers which you should work through.

- *Examiners' reports.* Sadly, candidates tend to make the same mistakes year after year. Examiners' reports highlight these failings and also indicate in general terms what the examiner was looking for in a good answer.

To revise effectively you need to plan. Try to identify times in each day when you will be able to revise. Draw up a revision plan based around these times. However, don't forget those 20–30 minute gaps – for example in the bus on the way to school each morning – as these can add significantly to your revision time. It's a good idea to let your family and friends have details of your revision plan then, with a bit of luck, you won't have too many interruptions during your revision periods.

Your revision plan should also indicate precisely what you are going to revise in each session. It is a good idea to break each syllabus down into topic areas. You will find that you need to allocate proportionately more time to those topic areas that you find difficult or uninteresting. Try to revise the whole syllabus. Candidates who try to spot questions or generally limit revision to, say, 10 topics often come unstuck because their "bankers" don't come up – or come up in a form they are unable to answer.

HOW to revise is a very personal matter, but very often this valuable time is mis-used. For example, don't revise passively. Mere re-reading of your notes is pretty boring and concentration is easily lost. Try rewriting your course notes in a more concise form – use headings – make lots of points. If these summary notes are put on index cards they are easy to carry round and revise from at odd moments.

The average person's span of concentration is relatively short – certainly no longer than an hour. You are well advised to give yourself a 5 minute break each hour – make yourself a cup of coffee or just chat to someone.

You can also break up a revision period by changing to different activities. For example in a two-hour revision period you might start by condensing your notes on a topic onto index cards, continue by outlining an answer to a typical examination question on that topic and finish by getting someone to test your knowledge of that topic's key facts and figures.

THE EXAMINATION

Your preparation for the examination should start the night before. Check to make sure you know where the examination is held. Gather all necessary materials together (e.g. pens, pencils, rubbers, calculators, spare battery, sweets etc.). You may wish to do some last minute revision but this should be no more than two hours – it's far more important to have a good night's sleep than to revise into the early hours of the morning. Finally make sure you allow plenty of time for getting to the examination – public transport is sometimes delayed.

Once in the examination room read the exam paper carefully, including the rubric. In reality, the rubric should be familiar to you through your study of past examination papers, but it is possible that the structure of the paper has been changed in the last year. Read through the questions carefully, making notes in the margin as you go along. For each question underline what you consider to be the key words. These key words give you three kinds of information:

- the subject matter of the question
- verbs which instruct you how to use this information (e.g. 'analyse', 'critically assess' or 'compare and contrast')
- any special requirements (e.g. 'write a report to')

Only after you have analysed all questions in this way should you select your questions for answer.

ESSAYS

Once you have decided what questions you are going to tackle, you can start to plan your answer. As a general rule essay questions carry equal marks; consequently you should plan to allocate an equal amount of time to each question (and also ensure you answer the required number of questions). Remember – it is always far easier to move from [0/20] to [5/20] on a new question than to move from [15/20] to [20/20] on a question that is already well answered.

Planning your essay

Your essay should have an introduction, core and conclusion. The introduction should be brief and to the point. Any technical terms which are used in the introduction should be defined. It is also useful to indicate the stages that will appear in the core of your essay.

In the core of your essay you will be developing the major points. It is important that these points are developed properly or you will lose many marks. Many examiners' reports

Develop your points.

criticise students for merely listing rather than developing points.

You should also consider the order in which you make your points. The most important points should be made first of all. Leave the least important points until last (just in case you run out of time). Thus in a question on why a sole trader may consider company status, if you believe limited liability is a key consideration, it should be mentioned first.

It is also important that you write a conclusion which summarises what you have said. This allows you to punch home once again what you consider to be the important points. In some cases the essay title actually asks a question, in which case your conclusion should actually indicate what your answer is.

Finally, in writing your essay you should take care that you produce a logical and coherent answer. Try to

- write in short sentences. Long rambling sentences can easily lose their meaning.

- ensure you make only one point in a paragraph. To include more than one destroys the impact of both points.

- avoid using abbreviations. They may not be known to the examiner! Alternatively they may have dual meanings for example – plc!

- allocate time for checking your answer. It is easy to omit points that are relevant, but equally easy to include points that are irrelevant.

CASE STUDIES

You will have encountered *case studies* many times on your course. Your lecturers will have used them to:

- illustrate good or bad management practice
- provoke discussion
- develop skills in problem identification and analysis, decision making and communication (e.g. oral presentations or report writing)
- role play an event and thus develop an understanding of interpersonal relationships.

Case studies are also used by all the examination boards as part of their assessment strategy. These cases may be distributed before the examination for you to study or be issued on the day in the examination hall. In the former case you will be able to study and analyse the situation at leisure, but with the unseen case paper you will have to rely on the techniques of case analysis learnt during your course. These techniques are detailed below.

CASE ANALYSIS

Getting started

On receiving the case you should first read through the case quickly. Don't stop and ponder. The aim of this first reading is to familiarise yourself with the general situation before undertaking a more detailed analysis on the basis of the questions set.

Assessing the situation

You are now at the stage where you need to become more familiar with the information in the case study. This may be done in a number of ways. The most popular way is highlighting those aspects of the case study which are considered important. This certainly does have the advantage of drawing your attention to important points. All too often though, so many points are important that highlighting loses its impact. The rule should be to use your highlighting pen sparingly.

Another method which students often use is to index information. This is done by selecting key ideas, for example marketing or production, and indicating by the initial M or P in the margin of the case study any point relating to marketing or production.

This method of grouping information under headings such as marketing, accounting, production, or personnel can be used as a more detailed framework for studying the case. Thus if you were studying a case where the emphasis was on marketing you would be looking for information on products, prices, promotion and place. Of course, the framework could be considerably more complex, for example:

ACCOUNTING	MARKETING	PRODUCTION	PERSONNEL
Accounting system	Marketing organisation	Location	Personnel organisation
Finance	Products	Production methods	Manpower planning
Gearing	Product life cycle	Production planning/	Recruitment
Profitability	New product	control	Wages/salary policy
Liquidity	development	Maintenance	Training/development
Budgeting	Buyer behaviour	Purchasing	Welfare, health and
Investment appraisal	Market structure	Stock control	safety
Asset control	Pricing policy	Quality control	Industrial relations
Employee motivation	Promotion	Work study	Worker democracy
	Distribution	Employee motivation	Employee motivation
	Market research		
	Employee motivation		

Table 1.2 A useful framework for approaching case studies

This framework has the advantage of forcing you to consider the most important facets of the function(s) you are interested in and also revealing what information is missing.

Not all the information in the case study will be of the same quality. For example there will always be a certain amount of irrelevant information. More importantly though not all information has the same degree of precision. Some information will be very concise, for example:

> 'the company was founded in 1962'

Other information though raises as many questions as it answers, for example:

> 'many of the workforce were well trained'

You might ask yourself 'Exactly how many?' . . . . or . . . . 'Why not all the workforce?' Alternatively you might ask yourself whether this is fact or opinion. However you finally interpret the statement it should always be used with caution.

Identifying the problems

(This is of limited importance in an examination situation as the questions will identify the problem areas to consider. It is included here for the sake of completeness.) You will, by now, be very familiar with the case material and will already have identified some problems. You should now:

1 List all the problems you have identified. Many will be stated explicitly in the text. Others, though, will only be identified by the careful analysis you have just undertaken.
2 Ask yourself whether any of the problems are connected. For example, high absenteeism and high labour turnover may (but not necessarily) be connected. Equally you may find that one problem is the cause of another. Thus low profitability may be caused by poor stock control.
3 Ask yourself – are the problems stated the real problem or the sign of a more deep-rooted problem. Thus high labour turnover may merely be the outward manifestation of low morale.

Generating alternative solutions

Having identified the problem and its cause, we now need to generate alternative solutions to that problem. In doing so we need to be clear exactly what we are trying to achieve. If we are unsure what our end objective is (the ideal situation) it is unlikely that our solutions will succeed. You should write down your objectives, i.e. 'what am I trying to do?' and 'what results do I expect?' These objectives should be kept in mind at all times.

Generating solutions is probably the most difficult stage for students. For each problem we have identified we need to generate a number of different solutions. The more alternatives we have to consider the better the final decision is likely to be. There are three main sources from which we may obtain potential solutions.

1 The subject matter of business studies which you have studied will have provided you with a whole range of principles, analytical tools, strategies and tactics which have been used and found successful in real-life situations. It would be most unusual if you were not able to apply any of this information to the solution of the problem(s).
2 Past experience may also help you. You may have come across a similar problem before. You will be able to draw from the alternative solutions considered then. In practice this is the most common source from which managers generate alternatives.

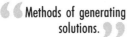
Methods of generating solutions.

3 You may also have been taught a technique called 'brainstorming'. At the root of this technique is the instruction to suspend judgement. You should note down every solution to the problem that you think of, however preposterous it may seem. You will find that one idea generates another. It is only at a later stage that these ideas will be evaluated and, perhaps, discarded.

Evaluating the alternatives

The key question to answer is 'how well does each alternative solve the problem?' In practice you will find that all solutions have good and bad points. None will solve the problem perfectly. You should list the 'pros' and 'cons' for each alternative solution before making a decision. You may find the framework introduced under 'assessing the situation' helpful in this situation.

In making a decision between alternatives you will have to assess the impact of each solution on the whole organisation. It is important to realise that the solution which is best for one department may incur high costs in the rest of the organisation. It may be necessary, therefore, to select a solution which is less than perfect for that department in order to minimise costs elsewhere.

Communicating your decision

In an examination you will be told how you should communicate your answer. The two most important formats are:

- a straightforward essay;
- a report.

Both have been discussed before in this chapter and you should now return to those comments.

The following case study will help you see the type of question which might be set in this part of the assessment.

CASE STUDY EXAMINATION

Kent Ltd.

Kent Ltd. is a manufacturing company employing 230 people in a predominantly rural part of South-Eastern England. Apart from one other large engineering firm it is the major employer in the area. The firm, which specialises in the production of high quality motor cycles on a job or batch production system, was started by John Kent in 1945. Direction of the business passed to his son-in-law, David Richards, in 1967 and at that time the majority of shares were held by members of the Kent family.

The business has been run very much as one big happy family. Labour turnover has been low and trade union activity non-existent. A staff association has negotiating rights, but has been considered generally rather ineffectual. Most of the employees have been with the company for many years. Kent's policy of promoting from within the firm has resulted in four of the six senior managers each working over 35 years with the firm. Moreover, as there is no formal Personnel Department, getting a job has often been dependent on knowing people who work at Kent's – and their personal recommendation.

Employees have been given considerable latitude at work. Office employees operate an unofficial system of flexitime. Starting late, finishing early, or taking long lunch hours has been acceptable to management as long as work efficiency was maintained. Production workers chose their own group members and organised how the work was to be done. Traditionally they have been set a weekly target to achieve, and often decided to schedule work so as to finish on Friday lunchtime. Private work has often been brought into the factory or office to be completed in work hours and the management has also taken a relaxed attitude to employees borrowing production tools, word processors and similar equipment overnight and at weekends.

Managers have always maintained good interpersonal relationships with their subordinates and are often seen working as members of work groups and socialising with them outside workhours. These links were encouraged by David Richards as a means of improving communication within Kent Ltd.

Until recently Kent concentrated on four major segments of the motor cycle market –

mountain (or off road), military, police and courier. Since 1980 Kent has experienced a significantly higher level of competition in both home and overseas markets. Kent responded by cutting prices – in the case of military motorcycles by as much as 15% – but this did not have the anticipated impact upon sales. Consequently, in 1985 the firm withdrew from the mountain motorcycle market which was more affected by the early 1980's recession than other markets.

Since 1985 Kent has invested heavily in new plant and equipment, financed by bank loans. It was anticipated that this borrowing would eventually be financed by a flotation of the company on the Unlisted Securities Market. Unfortunately the company made a loss in 1989 (see Appendix 1) and its financial advisers felt that Kent's plans to raise money in this way would have to be deferred.

In 1990, as in previous years, the company produced about 3000 motorcycles per annum for the three remaining markets. Approximately 70% of this output has been for the military market where a small number of customers are responsible for a major proportion of Kent's production (see Appendix 2).

In the police and courier motorcycle markets there are no dominant customers, orders tend to be small and the specifications unique. Kent Ltd. has been very reliant upon the technical expertise of David Richards the present managing director and chairman. As a graduate engineer he has a wide research and development experience in the motor car and motorcycle industries. He is also a motorcycle racing enthusiast whose individualistic and pioneering designs have allowed Kent Ltd. to stay ahead of the competition in the police and courier motorcycle markets. Generally the company enjoys a high reputation for quality, but several important customers have criticised Kent's occasional inability to meet delivery schedules.

In July 1990 Kent Ltd. was approached by Amakusa Motors, a leading multinational motorcycle producer and competitor. The company, which has manufacturing bases in Japan, North America and Brazil proposed that the two companies should combine the manufacturing and marketing of their ranges of motor cycles. The proposal also included:

a) the promise of a £12 million cash injection into Kent Ltd. by Amakusa Motors. In return Amakusa would be allocated 51% of the enlarged share capital and three seats on the five person board of directors, and
b) an arrangement for the exchange of senior managers between the two companies.

After a stormy board meeting, in which David Richards argued against accepting Amakusa Motors' proposals, the family decided that the proposal offered the best possibility of future success. As a result of the agreement, which has now been concluded, Andrew Giles–Kent's Production Manager has switched positions with his opposite number in Detroit–Alison Paul.

Since arriving at Kent Ltd. Alison Paul, with the concurrence of the managing director, has introduced a number of changes. For example, production workers now have to clock on and off, and they may not leave work early without the permission of their supervisor, or production manager. In addition, daily work schedules and a system of inspection have been introduced, in order to ensure that schedules and quality levels are adhered to. Letters have also been sent to production workers informing them that it is company policy not to allow private work to be undertaken on company premises or company property to be borrowed.

Since these changes were introduced, bad feeling has developed between workers and management. It has been noted that despite the introduction of stricter controls, output and quality have declined. Moreover, accidents and absenteeism have increased; and for once Kent Ltd. is finding difficulty in replacing skilled production workers. Some production workers have approached the National Union of Engineering Employees to represent their interests. It is thought that the Union may have recruited about 20% of the production force, and that many more would join if the Union was given negotiating rights.

Last week it was rumoured that from 1992 Alison Paul was planning to introduce a new flowline production system; and production would be concentrated on military motorcycles. She will neither confirm nor deny these changes (although other plants within the group are organised along similar lines), and as a result there has been a walkout of production workers.

At present the firm is at a standstill and David Richards has called an emergency board meeting for next Thursday.

APPENDIX 1

Financial Information

Year ended 30th June	1988	1989	1990
	£M	£M	£M
Turnover	25.5	28.5	34.5
Net profit (before Tax)	2.1	(1.8)	1.5
Net Assets Employed			
Fixed assets	11.1	13.5	18.6
Current assets	10.5	11.1	12.3
Less: Current liabilities	(3.6)	(5.4)	(9.6)
	18.0	19.2	21.3
Financed by			
Share capital and reserves	13.5	12.0	12.3
Bank loans	4.5	7.2	9.0

APPENDIX 2

Kent–Military motor bikes

No. of customers	% of orders
2	35
8	65
12	90
15	100

Total World market sales: 28,000 units p.a.

1 a) What arguments could the board of directors put forward to support the merger with Amakusa Motors? (15)
   b) For what reasons do you think that David Richards is against the proposal? (10)
   c) How might the government view a merger such as this? Give reasons for your answer. (10)

(*Total 35 marks*)

2 a) How would you describe the style of management at Kent Ltd. prior to the merger? Explain your answer. (6)
   b) To what extent could Alison Paul have avoided the problems which have beset the production function, whilst still achieving her aim? (14)

(*Total 20 marks*)

3 You have been appointed to the recently advertised position of Personnel Manager at Kent Ltd. The Managing Director has asked you to prepare a suitable report for next Thursday's board meeting outlining the factors which need to be considered before deciding the firm's attitude towards the unionisation. Prepare the report in a suitable form. (25)

4 How will the change from job and batch to flow line methods of production affect the different functional areas within Kent Ltd? (20)

(ULEAC 1991)

OUTLINE ANSWERS

Question 1

1 a) The problems which face Kent include:

lack of strategy	over reliance on Richards for R & D
increase in competition	inability to raise finance
low profitability	management inability
poor marketing effort	management succession

A merger would enable many of these problems to be overcome, e.g. reduction in competition, less pressure on profits and the benefits of Amakusa's marketing, R & D, finance and managerial skills. Both Amakusa and Kent could benefit from economies of scale. To obtain high marks you should link problem and solution in your answer.

b) You should cite two groups of factors. Personal factors would include loss of status, power, security, work he likes. You could also argue that opposition arises from a concern for 'his' workforce or the desire for a quiet life. Organisational factors to be mentioned could include the different management styles, production systems and company cultures – all leading to possible problems on the integration of the two firms.

c) Governments wish to ensure viable competition in all markets because of its beneficial effect on prices, efficiency and innovation. You should discuss the impact of the merger on these variables.

   In this particular case there are also 'multi-national factors' both positive and negative to be considered, e.g. impact on the balance of payments, economic growth, employment and training, industrial policy and government revenue.

Question 2

2 a) The style of management could be described in several ways. For example:

Democratic:	Lewin
Theory Y:	McGregor
Human relations centred:	Mayo

You should explain the term you have used and draw from the case study at least two examples to substantiate your selection of management style. For example you could argue that the ability of employees to choose the members of their work group or determine the scheduling of work illustrates a democratic management style.

b) There has been a significant change in management styles and work practices. It is unlikely that major change could be introduced without some unrest. However, such changes could be introduced with fewer problems if:
   - a proper manpower plan is developed
   - changes are introduced gradually
   - planned changes aren't kept secret
   - people participate in the change process
   - disturbance of work groups is kept to a minimum
   - any guarantees, e.g. retraining, are communicated to workforce as soon as is practicable.

Question 3

A rather fuller answer is provided to this question.

To: D. Richards, Managing Director
From: J. Smith, Personnel Manager
Date: 13th June, 1991
Report on: Factory Unionisation

Terms of reference
On the 6th June, I was instructed by D. Richards to prepare a report for the Board of Directors on the factors which need to be considered before deciding Kent Ltd.'s attitude toward unionisation of the workforce.

Points to be considered
1 The introduction of trade unions into the firm would limit managers' right to manage. At the present time, managers have to justify their actions to the Board of Directors alone. This would change with managers being challenged by worker representatives on decisions they have made.
2 The introduction of trade unions may result in higher levels of conflict between Kent Ltd. and its employees as worker representatives highlight and exacerbate employee grievances. Worker representatives, in some ways, have an interest in generating conflict because it justifies their existence. This may have a negative impact on employee morale and motivation, increase resistance to change (through strikes, go

slows, work to rules) and increase labour turnover.

3 Trade unions force employers to incur extra costs. These extra costs range from increased managerial time spent on consultation with the workforce/worker representatives, the need to formalise personnel policy and procedure and the provision of an industrial relations framework. It is also possible that a trade union-backed workforce may negotiate higher wages and better conditions of work than we would wish to concede.

4 Trade unions are a means by which information can be passed to the workforce. Many of the problems we have experienced recently have arisen because we have no formal channel of communication with the employees apart from their line manager. Trade unions provide an additional formal communication channel and are a means of avoiding the problems of inaccurate information conveyed by the 'grapevine'.

5 Trade unions are a means of resolving disputes. Disputes are likely to occur even in a well managed organisation. It is to our benefit (cost wise) that we can negotiate with one body and be assured that they represent the workforce. Moreover, discontent at a 'poor' settlement may be directed at the trade union as well as ourselves!

6 Workers may be less unsettled if they see their interests are being handled by a trade union (rather than the staff association – which has been rather ineffectual).

7 The trade union challenge to managerial decision making has positive as well as negative aspects. Management, concerned about how the workforce will receive their decisions may:

    a) consider their decisions more carefully

    b) improve communications with workers

Conclusions

The decision to accept or reject unionisation of the workforce on the above arguments is finely balanced. Unionisation will certainly limit our managers' freedom of action and impose extra costs upon the organisation, but on the other hand could lead to improved decision making and better communication with the workforce.

[n.b. you were not required to make recommendations]

Question 4

Here is an actual *student answer* to this question, together with examiner comments.

> Under job method of production a task or
> work is completed by an individual or a group of persons. The
> whole process is done by an individual or a group and it carries
> a greater degree of satisfaction for workers of seeing a
> completed work.
>
> Under batch production a group of similar items or a batch of
> items is worked on by a single worker or a group before it
> carries on to the next process of production. The whole batch is
> first completed under a single process before it is passed on to
> the next process.
>
> Under a flowline production the whole process of production is
> broken down into several processes and each worker contributes a
> small proportion of the work as it flows on an assembly line.
>
> The change in the method of production from job and batch to a
> flowline system would affect each and every functional department
> of Kent Ltd.
>
> It would change the whole structure of the production
> department. More equipment and machinery would have to be
> purchased. All the machines would have to be set in a systematic
> manner and each process would have to be linked through conveyor
> belts. Production methods, designs and operations must be clearly
> laid out in order to have the maximum advantage of this method.
>
> The marketing department would now have to be active and
> effective in boosting the sale of military motorcycles, as under
> this method production will be concentrated on military
> motorcycles. Price cutting should not be used as its demand is
> not price elastic. With the merger of Amakusa the possibility of

❝Clear, concise understanding of production methods.❞

❝Explain how!❞

exports have increased as the firm can now serve the North and South American markets.

Personnel dept has to change its plans for acquiring labour. More semi-skilled and technical persons would be required in future. Existing employees would have to undergo an extensive training program so as to adapt and learn the techniques involved under flowline production. Moreover supervision and control would be easy and statistical techniques have to be adopted to detect any defaults.

The Accounting department would have to change its methods of labour and overhead costing as remuneration methods and working hours would change.

The Finance department would exploit sources for long term capital to purchase any additional machinery but need for short term finance of working capital would decrease.

Thus the switch of production methods would tend to revolutionise every functional department of Kent Ltd. The efficiency and productivity of the workers would be enhanced and capital resources would be efficiently utilized, thus overall profitability of the company would be increased.

Abbreviations/spelling! – check work!

This may be true, but needs to be developed.

Explain why!

Tutor's comment

There are numerous good points made; some, however, need to be developed further in order to realise the full potential of this answer.

2

FORMS OF BUSINESS ORGANISATION

GETTING STARTED

Within a mixed economy there are many organisations which have been created to satisfy society's demands for goods and services. Thus, in the UK there are over 2 million organisations. In this chapter we will examine the different structures and objectives that these organisations adopt.

Historically the UK evolved as a market economy, with the government playing a passive role, allowing the forces of supply and demand to determine what was produced and the prices charged. However, over a period of time the state has intervened to remedy deficiencies of the market economy so that today, alongside a large private sector, we have an important public sector.

ESSENTIAL PRINCIPLES

OBJECTIVES

Firms in the private sector are owned by individuals. Many individuals rely on the profits generated by these firms for a substantial part of their income. Without profit these individuals would look elsewhere for employment and investment opportunities. For all firms, therefore, profit is an important objective (see Table 2.1), but it is not, as classical economists would argue their sole – or even their most important – objective. Many firms do not seek to maximise profits. Owners may be content if profits are sufficient to give them the life style they desire or to provide employment for family members. Others may decline opportunities for expansion and profit growth so as to maintain control of the business or to avoid unacceptable risks.

> In a mixed economy profit has a number of functions:
> - it is a reward for risk taking
> - it provides the resources for business expansion
> - it encourages efficiency and innovation
> - it ensures that businesses respond to consumer wants.

Table 2.1 The functions of profit

Managerial theories point to the 'divorce of ownership from control' as another reason why profits are not necessarily the sole, or even the most important, objective of firms. Executive directors and managers in control of the day-to-day running of the business may, subject to a minimum profit constraint, pursue their own objectives. These may include security of employment, power or personal status and prestige.

"Profits are not the only objective. "

Behavioural theorists suggest that to consider managers as one homogeneous unit is wrong. In practice there will be numerous groups of managers each with their own interest. These interests may reflect a functional specialism, e.g. accountancy, or a particular position within the hierarchy of the firm. The precise objectives which the firm adopts reflect the power of each group and the necessity of compromise.

Finally, others suggest that in a complex and changing environment business objectives will also change to reflect the dominant pressures on the firm at any point in time. These may be as diverse as control of pollution, consumer protection or governmental relationships.

THE SOLE TRADER

This is the simplest form of business unit and tends to be found in industries where personal service is important, where there are few advantages in large scale production and where little capital is needed to start up the business. The sole trader provides the capital to run the business, bears the risk of loss, enjoys the benefit of any profits and makes his or her own decisions. There are few legal formalities necessary in order to start business as a sole trader.

Table 2.2 outlines some of the widely recognised advantages and disadvantages of operating as a sole trader.

ADVANTAGES	DISADVANTAGES
■ receives all the profits	■ has unlimited liability
■ makes all decisions	■ lacks help and works long hours
■ his or her own boss	■ may lack business skills
■ good relationships with staff and customers	■ no continuity of business on death (or ill health) of owner
■ can maintain privacy of business	■ expansion limited by lack of capital

Table 2.2 Advantages and disadvantages of the sole trader as a form of business organisation

PARTNERSHIPS

As a form of organisation partnerships are commonly found in those professions (such as accountants and solicitors) whose rules may prevent members from forming companies.

Many of the problems associated with sole proprietorship may be overcome by forming a partnership. Thus responsibility for finance, risk and work is shared.

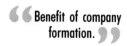

A definition.

A partnership is defined as 'the relationship which subsists between persons carrying on a business in common with a view of profit'. Unlike companies, partnerships are not a legal entity. This means they cannot own property or sue or be sued in their own name. Like sole traders, partners have unlimited liability for the debts of the firm. In practice this means that partners are legally responsible for both their own and their co-partners' actions. They must choose their partners with care. Another potential difficulty can arise from having to obtain the agreement of co-partners to a course of action.

There should always be a written contract.

The terms on which partners conduct their business are known as the partnership articles or agreement. It is not necessary for these terms to be written and in many cases the courts have had to infer contractual terms from what the partners said and did. Such a situation is obviously undesirable and a written contract detailing the rights and responsibilities of partners should always be drawn up. However, where no partnership agreement exists, the Partnership Act of 1890 lays down that:

- partners will share profits and losses equally
- decisions relating to the nature of the partnership business require unanimity
- decisions relating to the day-to-day running of the business may be settled by majority vote
- all partners are entitled to be involved in the management of the business

COMPANIES

There are over 1.3 million companies registered in the UK. They vary in size from the very small with only 2 shareholders to the very large multi-national enterprise in which thousands of shareholders have invested. Companies fall into one of 3 categories:

- Companies limited by shares – the most common form of limited company and may be divided into public and private companies.
- Unlimited companies – with no limit to the shareholders' liability. Such companies are rare.
- Companies limited by guarantee – the company's constitution states that each member will contribute a specified sum on winding up (if necessary). Liability is limited to this sum.

Public and Private Companies

Any registered company is deemed to be a private company unless:

- the memorandum of association states that the company is a public limited company and the name includes those words (or the abbreviation plc)
- the memorandum must conform to the requirements of the Companies Acts
- the company has a minimum share capital of £50,000

Private companies' major disadvantages are that they cannot advertise the sale of their shares or obtain a stock exchange listing.

Compared with sole traders and partnerships, companies have the following *advantages*:

- incorporation creates a new legal entity, independent of its shareholders. The company can own property and can sue or be sued in its own name.

Benefit of company formation.

- shareholders have limited liability; thus they know in advance that their liability is limited to the amount they have invested.
- the company has continuity of existence and is unaffected by the death or retirement of one of its members.
- it has greater opportunities for raising capital for expansion.

However against these advantages must be put a number of possible *disadvantages*:

- the ability of the company to contract is limited by the 'objects' clause in the memorandum of association (though in practice such clauses are very widely drawn).

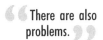

■ there is a legal obligation to disclose certain information; for example contractual powers, rules relating to the internal conduct of the business (e.g. election of directors, calling a shareholders' meeting) or annual accounts.

■ there may be a divorce between ownership and control.

■ internal procedures may prevent the company from adapting quickly to changed market conditions.

■ close relationships between the company, its customers and employees are often precluded by size.

THE PUBLIC SECTOR

The public sector provides goods and services for consumers through:

■ owning shares in a company, which is financed and operated in the normal commercial manner.

■ local government and other statutory agencies. These services are funded by the government through taxes and borrowing.

■ public corporations.

PUBLIC CORPORATIONS

The essential feature of a public corporation is that the assets of the industry have been taken over by the state so that the industry is owned, managed and controlled by and on behalf of the community. Objectives of public corporations reflect not only a desire on the part of management to provide goods and services efficiently and achieve a target return on capital invested but also the government's wider economic and social objectives. Thus at different times the government has required public corporations to sell products/ services at prices different to those which would have been chosen by management, to retain inefficient working practices, to purchase products from uncompetitive sources and to change capital investment plans. It is consequently often difficult to evaluate the performance of public corporations solely in commercial terms.

Like a company, a public corporation has a distinct legal personality as a result of the Act creating it. The Act also lays limits on the trading activities the corporation can undertake. Other features which distinguish public corporations from companies include:

■ a government minister supervises the public corporation and is able to give general direction to the industry on matters of public interest

■ the minister appoints people to the corporation's board. These individuals' background may be in the industry itself, the private sector or trade unions

■ additional capital requirements are traditionally provided by the government

■ the interests of the consumer are protected by consumer councils who may make representations to the board and the minister and, additionally, by the Monopolies and Mergers Commission which may carry out efficiency audits

THE NATIONALISATION AND PRIVATISATION DEBATE

Nationalisation

Nationalisation is not just a UK phenomenon. For different reasons and in a variety of ways many Western European countries have 'taken over' large parts of the energy, transport and communications industry. During the period 1945–50 the Labour Party pursued a wide-ranging programme of nationalisation. The major arguments for nationalisation are put forward below:

1 Some goods and services would not be provided if left to the private sector, for example, many of the commuter services around London are uneconomic. Nationalisation guarantees the supply of these goods and services at fair prices.

2 Typically nationalised industries are capital intensive. It is doubtful whether adequate investment funds could be raised privately; particularly as the profitability of these industries was often poor.

3 Nationalisation can also enable economics of scale to be achieved through the use of larger more efficient production and administrative units.

There are also problems.

Public corporations' objectives.

4 In the case of 'natural monopolies' nationalisation avoided the problems of wasteful duplication of resources as well as consumer exploitation.

Socialists also have political motives for nationalisation, believing that economic planning necessitates control of vital parts of economy and also facilitates a programme of fairer wealth distribution.

Privatisation

The term privatisation has been used in three different ways. It encompasses the idea of:

- selling state industries, e.g. British Gas or Powergen
- deregulation, which exposes the public sector to market forces, e.g. the private generation of electricity
- contracting out of services, e.g. local authority refuse collection or health service cleaning and catering

Deregulation and contracting out increase competition, whereas the transfer of state industries from the public to the private sector does not do so unless the organisation is split up.

Many of the arguments for the privatisation of state industries are synonymous with the problems of nationalisation. Thus:

- the creation of monopoly state industries results in a restriction of consumer choice
- diseconomies of scale may occur as a result of the difficulties of co-ordinating and controlling such large organisations
- lacking competition, public corporations may be run less efficiently than firms in the private sector (remember that competition is admired for its beneficial influence on costs, prices and innovation)
- government objectives may be imposed on, and conflict with, the efficient operation of the state industry

Nationalisation's problems.

Aims of privatisation.

The primary reason for the privatisation of state industries in the 1980s has been the government's belief that this will result in an improvement in efficiency. However, the sales have also helped the government to keep within Public Sector Borrowing Requirement (PSBR) targets and assist monetary control. Additionally, the extension of share ownership amongst employees and the public generally is intended to increase their commitment to the firm and free enterprise.

OTHER FORMS OF ORGANISATION

CO-OPERATIVES

Co-operatives may be either 'retail' or 'worker'. In the UK the most common form of co-operative enterprise is the Co-operative Retail Society. Worker or producer co-operatives flourish outside the UK (e.g. Spain – Mondragon) but are not so popular or successful here. In the UK, worker co-operatives have failed to obtain managers of the right calibre or sufficient finance. Most successful worker co-operatives (e.g. Scott Bader Company Ltd., John Lewis Partnership) started life as some other form of enterprise. Underlying co-operative organisation are the following principles:

Some co-operatives are very successful.

- the workforce owns and manages the business
- the workforce determines the co-operative's objectives
- profits are divided amongst the members

FRANCHISES

In recent years franchising has emerged as a major segment of retail business. In 1988 it was estimated that franchises accounted for approximately 10% of the UK retail market. For many people who want to own and operate a small business it offers the greatest chance of success.

A definition.

A franchise can be defined as 'a concession given by the owner of patents or trademarks relating to goods or services to another person allowing them to produce and sell those goods or services'.

In a typical franchise agreement, the *franchisor* agrees to:

- assign an exclusive sales area to the franchisee
- allow the franchisee to use its (the franchisor's) trade name
- provide nationwide advertising and promotion of the trade name
- provide a specified amount of management training and support
- provide goods to the franchisee at a price
- give advice on business location, layout and decoration
- offer financial assistance or advice

In addition, the *franchisee* agrees to:

- operate the franchise according to rules and procedures laid down by the franchisor
- invest a specified amount of capital in the business
- pay the franchisor certain royalties (e.g. percentage on sales)
- make purchases from the franchisor or other specified supplier

> **Franchising has many benefits.**

Franchising is attractive to the franchisor because it enables them to expand their sphere of influence without any more capital investment (they may even receive a capital contribution from the franchisee). The franchisor will also receive contributions towards overhead costs, e.g. advertising, from the franchisee. Against these points must be put the fact that it is difficult to control franchisees and that an unsuccessful franchise arrangement is the worst advertisement the franchisor could want.

To the franchisee – often having little experience of running a business – it offers a well known product/service, training in all aspects of the business, proven standard operating and administrative procedures and, in some cases, financial assistance (since most small business failures are attributable to lack of business knowledge these features are highly beneficial). However, the franchisee may feel that the constraints placed upon him in terms of what he can sell, pricing policy, hours of work – in reality the ability to run the business the way he wants to – are extremely irksome.

EXAMINATION QUESTIONS

1 How far do you agree with the view that in the analysis of business behaviour, profit maximisation is the over-riding objective?   (AEB 1987)

2 Seven out of ten people who set up businesses on their own fail within the first five years, whereas nine out of ten franchises survive. Examine the reasons for this.
                                                                                 (AEB 1987)

3 Describe and comment on the process of privatisation in Britain to date.
                                                       (London – specimen exam paper)

TUTOR'S ANSWER

Question 1

Traditional neo-classical economic theory of the firm states that all firms, despite being organised differently and working in different environments, have a single aim – that is to maximise their profits. This is done by producing to the point where the cost of the last unit of output is equal to the revenue obtained from that unit and setting a price as high as the market will bear.

However, profit maximisation as the sole objective of the firm may be criticised in a number of ways.

In arguing that firms seek to maximise profits, economists have made a number of assumptions. For example it is assumed that firms have perfect knowledge of market conditions and that the situations which face them are predictable. In practice, few firms know how elasticity of demand at different prices will affect their products, their competitors' future marketing strategy or what their future investment plans will be. Profit maximisation in these circumstances is impossible.

Another assumption which economists make is that firms have only one objective (which is, of course, profit maximisation). Yet if we take the small firm sector with its large proportion of owner-managed firms (and this is the nearest to the economists' idea of an entrepreneur) we find that whilst profits are an important objective, they are not the only one. Thus doing work which he likes may be more important to the owner-manager than expanding the firm and earning greater profits. Moreover, greater profits may require the owners to assume greater risks, work longer hours or give up control of the firm, any of which could be unacceptable. But not only does research into the small firm sector tell us that owner managers have a number of objectives rather than just profit maximisation, it also suggests that these other objectives are inconsistent with maximising profits.

The idea of profit maximisation as the sole or over-riding objective of firms also seems unrealistic when we consider large businesses. In many we see a divorce between ownership and control of the firm. A large firm will have thousands of shareholders who appoint professional managers to control the firm on a day-to-day basis. Yet there is no reason to assume that professional managers, who have little or no shareholding in the company, should have the same objectives as those shareholders.

Managerial theories of the firm suggest that, in practice, shareholders have little control over the activities of the professional managers, and that this latter group have the power to pursue their own objectives. Thus in order to improve their security, status or pay within a firm managers may try to maximise sales revenue or achieve a specified annual rate of growth rather than profits. Such a policy would, however, be subject to a minimum profit constraint in order to keep shareholders happy.

Behavioural theorists on the other hand, argue that the objectives of the firm reflect the interaction of various groups of managers within the firm. Thus future investment plans are a result of the negotiations of accountancy, personnel, marketing and production specialists. The firms objectives are, therefore, a compromise between the interests of these different groups.

So far we have ignored the impact of the wider environment upon the firm and its objectives. There are numerous groups who are likely to make demands upon the business including employees, consumers, government and the local community. The demands of these groups – it may be for improved working conditions, better after sales service or pollution control – place a constraint upon profit maximisation as an objective and may even in certain circumstances become an important objective in their own right.

In conclusion it can be seen that a firm is likely to have a variety of objectives which reflect not only the interests of the shareholders but also the managers and other groups within the environment. Yet we can say that because profit is a reward for risk taking and provides the resources for business expansion it must remain an important objective for any private sector enterprise. Other objectives will only be pursued in the longer term subject to a satisfactory level of profits being achieved.

STUDENT'S ANSWER

Question 2

> Small firms are an important part of the UK economy. Over 95% of all firms can be defined as small, and they make a significant contribution to employment and output. Small firms may be defined as having less than 200 employees and, additionally, these characteristics:
>   1 the size within the industry is small
>   2 the owners are also managers of the business
>   3 it is not part of a larger organisation
>
> Most franchises would come within this definition.
>   The rate of business failure amongst small firms is high. Although there are over 160,000 business start ups each year there are also 130,000 businesses which fail. There are many reasons for this.
>   Many small businesses will fail quickly because the idea is

Good, links the two parts of the question.

Good, sound knowledge of basic facts.

poor, and inadequately researched. Before entering business it is a good idea to draw up a business plan. If it is necessary to borrow money from the bank the businessman will probably be required to do this. The plan will answer questions such as what goods/services are to be produced, where are they to be produced, where will they be sold and what finance is needed. Finally a projected cash flow forecast and projected final accounts will also be required to assess the overall viability of the proposal. Without a plan, weaknesses in the business proposition will not be identified and businesses will open that are doomed to failure from the start.

Once in business the major reason for small firm failure is lack of management experience. The business person needs not only a technical expertise, but also ability in accountancy, marketing, personnel and general administration. For example without accounting knowledge it is all too easy to fail to see the danger signs relating to cash flow or credit control or to obtain the necessary long term capital. Yet the reality is that most owner managers have little more than their technical expertise. This problem would not be so serious if owner managers would take professional advice. Unfortunately for many small firms the cost of these specialist services is prohibitively high.

Managerial inexperience is also the reason why many small firms fail to plan for the future. They don't realise that the environment is changing and that although sales are buoyant this year, next year may not be so good because of increased competition or changed consumer tastes. Additionally they fail to identify the opportunities which could be their lifeline.

One particular example of a change in the environment which has affected small firms particularly badly is the recession. As economic conditions have changed, rising interest rates, bad debts and falling sales have squeezed profits. Many small firms faced with mounting losses and lacking reserves of larger firms have gone into liquidation.

Another reason for the poor small business survival rate relates to the commitment of the owner manager to the business. The growth in the number of small firms during the 1980s owes much to the decline of other employment opportunities. Setting up a business, often financed by redundancy pay, was seen as a more acceptable alternative to the dole queue. Moreover many were quite unprepared for the long hours and other poor working conditions which are often associated with small firms. When employment opportunities emerged they were happy to give up self employment.

Let us compare the situation faced by the small firm with the franchisee. A franchise is an agreement where one person — the franchisor — the owner of patents or trademarks gives another — the franchisee — the right (to produce and) to sell those goods or services to the public.

Broadly we can say that the franchisee is in a much more secure position compared to the typical owner of a small firm. In the first place he is purchasing the right to market a proven product or service. The franchisee will obtain sales through the reputation of the franchisor's trademark.

Secondly, the level of help available to the franchisee before start up is normally much greater than for other small businesses. Help will range from site selection and site design to the training of the owner and his staff. At this stage the franchisor will also screen the potential franchisees to ensure they have the right qualities and commitment to run the franchise

" This is an excellent concise summary of reasons why small firms fail. **"**

" Good points — see chapters 4, 5, 6. **"**

properly. A poorly run franchise is a very poor advertisement for the franchisor.

Quite apart from the training which enables the franchisee to overcome his business inexperience, the franchisor has a standard operating procedure which covers personnel administration, basic book-keeping, financial planning and stock control. Moreover, through the bulk-buying power of the franchisor, the franchisee can enjoy cost reductions on materials used in the business as well as advertising and promotion.

As can be seen from the points made above, franchising provides a far greater chance of being successful to those people who want to own and manage a small business.

" Could be extended. "

Tutor's comment

This is a good answer. The basic information is well covered and presented clearly. 'A' grade material.

OUTLINE ANSWER

Question 3

Privatisation is the process of returning state industries to the private sector. You should distinguish it from deregulation and contracting out giving examples of each.

The UK privatisation programme started with sales of about £400 million in 1980. By 1989 sales were running at £5 bn. State industries privatised include some very large businesses, e.g. British Telecom, British Gas. With some large concerns the method of sale has been to offer shares to the public. Others (e.g. Girobank) have been sold directly to another business (the Alliance and Leicester Building Society). A third method has been to allow the managers and workers to buy out the government's interest.

You should consider the reasons for privatisation including restriction of consumer choice, diseconomics of scale, lack of competition and government interference, contribution to PSBR and wider share ownership. You should also make brief comments assessing whether privatisation has had the impact which was desired on, for example, consumers (lower prices, more choice, better service) or the industry (more competition, less government intervention, greater efficiency), the workers (security, changed working practices, motivation through share ownership).

It will always be difficult to assess the impact of privatisation overall, and whether it has been successful, not least because we have no idea what the situation would have been without the change. It is also made more difficult because the nationalisation-privatisation debate has political overtones.

FURTHER READING

Buckley *Structure of Business* 2nd Edn Pitman 1990:
   Chapter 2 Structure of Business 1
Jewell *Business Studies* Pitman 1990:
   Chapter 2 Business Enterprise
Neuberger (Ed): *Privatisation* Papermac 1987
Hawkins *The Organisation in its Environment* OUP 1987: Block 2 Organisations and the Private Sector Block 3 Organisations and the Public Sector

CHAPTER

THE STRUCTURE OF INDUSTRY

SMALL FIRMS

THE GROWTH OF FIRMS

MULTINATIONAL CORPORATIONS

MANAGEMENT BUY-OUTS (MBOs)

GETTING STARTED

One outstanding feature of UK industrial development during the last century has been the growth in the size of the firm. Concentration ratios suggest that the large firms dominate many industries. Yet small firms continue to exist.

In this chapter we will be looking at why small firms continue to survive and why they are considered to be an essential feature of our industrial structure. We will also be considering the reasons why firms grow and the problems associated with large multinational corporations. Finally we will look at Management Buy-Outs as one particular way in which large firms correct past investment mistakes.

ESSENTIAL PRINCIPLES

SMALL FIRMS

There is no one authoritative definition of what constitutes a small firm. The Report of the Committee of Enquiry into Small Firms (The Bolton Report) stated that generally a small firm was one which employed less than 200 people and had three additional characteristics:

- a small share of its market;
- owners who worked and took a personal interest in the firm;
- not part of another organisation.

This definition was however, modified for certain sectors. Thus a construction firm was considered small if it had less than 25 employees.

An alternative definition though can be found in the 1985 Companies Act (S247). Here, for accounting purposes, a company is considered small if it satisfies any two of the following conditions for each of the last two years:

- turnover under £2 million;
- net assets under £975,000;
- an average of 50 or less employees.

WHY SMALL FIRMS EXIST

Economic theory suggests that due to economies of scale large firms should be more efficient than small. However, small firms have continued to survive. There are many reasons for this including:

- Small firms often supply a small market. The market may be small geographically as in the case of the corner shop. Alternatively, the firm may be producing specialist goods for which total demand is small.

- Small firms provide opportunities for would-be entrepreneurs, or people who find employment in large impersonal organisations unattractive. Moreover, small firms maintain better relationships not only with staff but also with customers.

- Firms may remain small as a result of a conscious decision on the part of the owner, who may not want the additional risks associated with growth or may want to maintain control of the firm. Alternatively the owner may just not think of trying to expand the market or product range. Finally small firms suffer from a number of problems which may prevent growth (or even threaten their existence). These include:

  - lack of managerial expertise
  - inability to afford professional help
  - lack of financial support
  - high level of competition
  - inability to survive recession
  - government bureaucracy and the complexity of legislation
  - impact of government monetary and fiscal policy

> **❝Reasons why small firms exist.❞**

- Small firms often provide a personal and more flexible service. Large firms often have no interest in this. Thus there are large firms who specialise in building housing estates (e.g. Barratt) who wouldn't be interested in building garages or loft extensions. The market has been segmented so that they do not compete with one another.

- Large firms often find certain work uneconomic. In these circumstances they will sub-contract the work to a smaller firm. Although there may be little profit in this sub-contracting work for large firms, they undertake it so as to maintain consumer goodwill and encourage the customer to return to them in the future with other work. The process of hiving off specialist work to small firms is known as vertical disintegration.

- Small firms will always exist where growth confers no economic advantage, e.g. hairdressing, window cleaning.

- Small firms are the traditional 'seed beds' for new industries and market leaders because:
  1 they are important innovators in products, processes and services
  2 they respond quickly to new market opportunities.

AID FOR SMALL FIRMS

Small firms are less important in the UK than elsewhere. For example in Japan 66% of all employees work for small firms whilst in the UK the figure is 30%. Indeed until recently the small firm sector in the UK was declining.

> **Small firms are important.**

To the Committee of Enquiry on Small Firms (the Bolton Report) which was published in 1971, this was extremely worrying. It commented 'we can think of no substitute to the dynamic influence of these firms in preventing the ossification of the economy' and 'we should regard the decline of the small firm sector as so great an evil that energetic discrimination to avert it would be justified.'

The major problems facing small firms have already been mentioned above.

Government Aid

Since 1980, governments have introduced many measures designed to aid small firms. Thus owners of small firms can claim an Enterprise Allowance of £40 per week during their first year in business. The government has also sought to move finance into the sector through the Business Expansion Scheme. (Here investors of risk capital in a firm obtain tax relief on the investment at their highest rate of tax.) Under the Loan Guarantee Scheme, if a bank borrower pays a premium to the DTI, that Department will guarantee to repay the bank should the borrower default on the loan.

Small firms can now also obtain help on a whole range of business problems through the Enterprise Initiative. Assistance ranges from help on marketing or market research, design quality through to business planning and information technology. Firms planning to export will also receive advice and assistance.

> **Since 1980 there have been over 100 government measures to help small firms.**

The government has also tried to create a more favourable tax regime for small firms by:

- creating a reduced rate of corporation tax for small firms
- introducing thresholds below which firms do not have to register for VAT
- introducing changes to Capital Transfer Tax making it easier to pass a business on intact to the next generation.

Steps have also been taken to lift the burden of oppressive legislation. Small firms no longer have to provide much of the financial and statistical information that large firms do. They are also exempt from some employment legislation, e.g. that relating to maternity and unfair dismissal.

Venture Capital and Corporate Venturing

These are two ways in which the government has persuaded the private sector to aid small firms.

Venture Capital may be defined as the provision of finance to growing companies. Much of this money will be equity risk capital. Venture capitalists may demand as part of their agreement the appointment of directors, management changes, the distribution of profits and the right to realise their investment after a specified period. There are now over 150 firms providing venture finance in the UK. Probably the best known is *Investors in Industry* or 3i. Some investments are spectacular successes. For example a £½million investment in Oxford Instruments was valued at more than £100 million when the firm came to the stock exchange 16 years later in 1983. Not all investments are so successful, though it is only in about 20% of cases that the venture capitalist loses money.

> **Help from the private sector.**

There are now also some large industrial companies who pursue a policy of innovation and growth through investment in small firms. This is termed Corporate Venturing and is particularly advantageous where the two firms are operating in the same markets. Corporate venturing infers a situation where the larger firm offers money, management expertise and market knowledge. In return the small firm shares its new ideas and its ability to respond quickly to changed market conditions by giving its benefactor an equity share in the firm, a percentage of the profits or specified products or marketing rights.

For much of the post-war period the emphasis of government policy was to encourage growth in the size of the firm. Many economists argued that the level of efficiency needed to compete in international markets could only be achieved by large firms enjoying economies of scale. Thus during much of the 1960s and 1970s governments encouraged merger and takeover activity. However, the government's encouragement of the growth of larger industrial units merely accentuated a trend which had been evident since the turn of the century. Concentration ratios, which measure the sales of the five largest firms in each industry, have risen dramatically since 1900. In some industries the concentration ratio is 90% (cement, asbestos, motor vehicles, wines, tobacco) and the average for the whole of British industry is 47%.

We should also note that firms have not only been getting larger but also more complex. Many large firms produce a wide range of goods. Thus Hanson plc has subsidiaries operating in the following markets: tobacco, departmental stores, office equipment, domestic appliances, lesiure equipment, textiles, health products and restaurants.

ECONOMIES OF SCALE

These may be internal or external to the firm.

Internal economies of scale refer to the situation where unit costs of production fall as the scale of operations increases. They fall into five broad categories:

■ technical   ■ marketing   ■ financial   ■ managerial   ■ risk bearing

External economies are economies of scale enjoyed by an industry as it grows in size. All firms in the industry, large or small, benefit from these economies. The benefits of growth include the development of a skilled workforce and specialist courses to meet the needs of that industry. Trade Associations may be set up to represent industry interests. Magazines and technical journals will be produced and even research associations may be set up to investigate matters of common interest. Finally if an area gains a reputation for certain products, ancillary firms may move to the area providing specialist machinery or utilising (what would otherwise be wasted) by-products. These factors may exert a powerful influence when a firm is making a location decision.

Yet, despite the apparent advantages of large scale, the recent recession would seem to be encouraging a reverse of the trend in some cases. A number of large conglomerates have decided to return to the 'core' business, by selling off some subsidiaries which are in unrelated activities, and were possibly acquired as a result of one of the many 1980s mergers or takeovers. This process is sometimes called 'unbundling'.

The development of 'lean manufacturing' techniques on the Japanese model has encouraged a return to smaller production centres, often operated as separate profit centres. A good example is Spring Ram plc, a manufacturer of kitchens, bathrooms, and other furniture, and which is one of the most successful UK manufacturing firms. It has a policy of not creating production units with more than 200 employees. The objectives of this strategy are twofold:- to achieve the economies of scale available in batch production systems, combined with the flexibility of jobbing production; and secondly to ensure high levels of both management control, and employee motivation.

INTERNAL AND EXTERNAL GROWTH

Internal growth occurs when firms utilise retained profits and whatever other money they can raise to purchase fixed assets and expand their productive capacity. As a means of increasing size it is often slow.

External growth is a situation where two or more firms combine their assets and form a single organisation. This is by far the quickest and the most popular method of growth. (However, in the longer term note the potential organisational diseconomies which may occur, e.g. co-ordination, communication, conflict and motivation.) External growth may take the form of a merger or take-over bid. A merger occurs where there is an agreement on the part of two or more firms to combine their assets. A take-over bid is not the result of an agreement between two firms, but where one company offers to purchase the shares of another (normally reluctant) company and obtains a controlling interest through the open market.

THE DIRECTION OF GROWTH

Horizontal integration

This occurs where firms producing the same kind of product, selling the same kind of goods or providing a similar service come together. The more common motives for horizontal integration are:

Many motives are defensive.

- to obtain economies of scale
- to eliminate competition
- to gain market dominance
- to reduce capacity in a declining industry
- to fight off a bid from an unwelcome third party
- to offset weaknesses in one firm by amalgamating with a firm which has corresponding strengths. For example, merging with another firm may give you access to better technology, better locations, better products or a better R & D team than you yourself possess

Vertical integration

This involves bringing together under common ownership different stages in the production process. *Vertical backward integration* occurs where a firm amalgamates with its suppliers, for example a cement firm taking over a sand and gravel company. *Vertical forward integration* arises when a firm secures its production outlets, for example an oil refinery purchasing petrol stations. Motives for vertical integration include:

- strategic reasons; to safeguard supplies of raw materials or outlets for production
- economies of scale

Lateral integration

Technically this occurs where there is an underlying relationship between either the products or processes of the separate firms (e.g. technology which is used). The process of lateral integration is often termed 'diversification' and firms which have such a diversification of interests are called 'conglomerates'. Of course diversification could be undertaken by 'internal growth' but the costs of entry are often so high that it is cheaper to buy an established player in the market. (It also has the advantage of not increasing competition in that market.) Diversification is popular because:

- it enhances the firms chances of survival where:
    - i) some of its products are reaching the end of their life cycle
    - ii) the market is highly competitive
    - iii) product demand is highly variable

See chapter 5.

- it is a means of avoiding monopoly and merger legislation by expanding outside traditional markets.
- it is a means of making quick profits by breaking up the firm taken over into smaller lots and reselling them. This could happen where a firm's value on the stock exchange does not reflect the true value of the assets. Such a situation could arise if a firm's management was ineffective and not using the firm's assets properly. Alternatively a firm's shares may be undervalued because the firm is ploughing profits back into an expansion programme and consequently dividends are low.

MULTINATIONAL CORPORATIONS

A multinational corporation (MNC) is a business which undertakes production, R & D, finance and marketing on an international basis. Many MNCs are household names, for example Ford, Shell, Unilever, IBM, Sony or Nissan. MNCs are very powerful firms; some will have a sales turnover larger than the GNP of nations such as Belgium, Ireland, Malaysia or Hong Kong.

A definition.

Multinationals are not a particularly new form of organisation. They were first established in the 1700s as a means of trading with, and obtaining raw materials from, less developed countries. In the twentieth century though there has been a rapid growth in the number of MNCs. This has occurred in order:

- to avoid monopoly legislation in its home country preventing expansion of the firm in its 'core' activities
- to gain market dominance
- to obtain the benefits of cheap labour or materials
- to enter markets protected by tariffs

THE IMPACT OF MULTINATIONAL CORPORATIONS

Reaction to the growth of MNCs is mixed. Free enterprise supporters would argue that their activities are a rational use of the resources available to them and benefit everyone. Other people see MNCs as being socially irresponsible, using their great power to gain unfair advantage. The benefits and problems arising from MNC operations in 'host' countries are summarised below.

Benefits

- The development of new manufacturing capacity by the MNC will increase GNP and the general standard of living.
- Local firms will benefit from seeing the better production and management techniques used in MNCs.
- The balance of payments may benefit from the expert activities of MNCs.
- MNC profits are an important source of tax revenue to the 'developing' country.
- Competition within the 'host' country is stimulated, with beneficial effects on prices, efficiency and innovation.
- Workers benefit from greater employment opportunities, often with facilities for improving skills.
- There is a greater choice of goods and services available for the consumer.

Problems

> " Some multinationals are extremely large. "

We have already stated that many people believe MNCs are socially irresponsible, using their great power for their own advantage. Note that the turnover of Exxon or General Motors is greater than the GNP of all but 14 countries. Tensions between 'host' countries and multinationals centre around the following points:

- Multinationals are committed to furthering their own interests rather than those of the country within which they operate. For example, their ability to move vast sums of money between countries in order to protect the value of their reserves against currency fluctuations may contribute significantly to those very currency fluctuations they are so keen to avoid. They have also been criticised for adjusting costs between their subsidiaries so that profits are declared in those countries where the tax regime is most advantageous.
- Multinationals have the power to switch production between countries and allocate markets. For example in 1975 Chrysler announced the decision to close down its UK operation (this was later reversed) and switch production to the continent. Future UK demand for Chrysler cars would have been satisfied from continental production. As a result of this decision employment, economic growth and the balance of payments would have all been adversely affected.
- Multinationals are socially irresponsible. There are many accusations which are levelled against MNCs – particularly by third world countries. These include financing revolutions, accusations of bribery and corruption, the exploitation of natural resources or cheap labour, the repatriation of profits and the manipulation of governments.

The degree of concern amongst 'host' countries has led to the seizure of MNC assets in some countries and stringent controls upon their activities in many others.

MANAGEMENT BUY-OUTS (MBOs)

For many years the restructuring of business has arisen through large firms divesting themselves of operations which:

- do not fit logically with the main business of the organisation, and
- are often unprofitable because of the excessive amount of time devoted to them.

> " Not all mergers are successful. "

Many of the sales of subsidiaries which we see today are a result of the ill-considered mergers of previous years. In such circumstances the normal course of action was to find some other business to purchase the subsidiary or close down the operation. In recent years, the latter option has become unacceptable and a third option – that of selling to the management of the subsidiary has grown in importance.

 **A definition.**   We can say that a management buy-out occurs when the managers (perhaps with the employees) of a business operation purchase that business from their employers and exercise control over that business.

FINANCE FOR MBOs

Finance for the buy-out comes from two major sources. First the management will have to extend themselves financially – re-mortgaging houses and selling investments. This investment though vitally necessary (because it shows the commitment of the management) is normally only a small part of the total purchase price. The rest of the finance is obtained from city institutions such as banks, life assurance companies and pension funds. Most of the city investment is in the form of loans (rather than equity capital) which is secured on the assets of the company. This means that although managers will often only raise a small amount of the capital required to float the business they end up with a large equity holding. This is best illustrated by their *gearing ratio* (see Chapter 19). Typically British industry has a gearing ratio of 2:1; for buy-outs it is commonly 6:1 or higher.

REASONS FOR THE SUCCESS OF MBOs

Despite a high gearing ratio the mortality rate for MBOs has been low. There are several reasons for this:

- Many businesses are purchased at a discount on real asset values – making it easier to generate the cash flow necessary to make interest and loan repayments.
- Many buy-outs benefit from favourable loan agreements. For example, it is not unusual for repayments of capital to be delayed for up to three years and to be followed by a repayment period of up to fifteen years.
- City institutions undertake a rigorous screening process before lending funds, which tends to eliminate the majority of high risk situations.
- Many buy-outs, which were considered unprofitable by their previous owners, were only held back by the heavy overheads saddled on the business by those owners.
- The buy-out team comprises experienced managers knowing both the business and the industry. They were able to reduce costs by undertaking only essential activities.
- Managers (and workers) as owners are highly motivated. They make the decisions and are responsible for their own destiny. If successful they stand to make a lot of money, but failure could spell bankruptcy.

However, the problem with such high gearing ratios becomes apparent in a recession. For example, high interest rates associated with the UK commitment to the ERM between 1990 and 1992 put enormous pressure on the finances of such firms as sales revenues collapsed below expected values. The result has been a high mortality rate for such firms. This may prove to be a deterrent to some MBOs for the foreseeable future.

EXAMINATION QUESTIONS

1 Examine the particular problems posed for a country by the existence of multinational firms.
(AEB November 1987)

2 Before 1981 management buy-outs were unknown in the UK. In 1986 there were 281 with a total value of £1.2 billion. Analyse the reasons for this growth.
(AEB June 1989)

3 a) What is a small firm and why do such firms exist?   (5)
   b) From a human perspective what problems and opportunities might such firms present?   (*10*)
   c) What effect might an increase in the proportion of small firms have on the UK economy?   (*10*)
(Cambridge June 1985)

OUTLINE ANSWER

Question 1

You should begin your answer by explaining the term multinational (give some well known examples) and emphasise the importance of multinationals today by pointing to multinationals' domination of many industries or the fact that output from MNC subsidiaries overseas is now greater than the global value of exports.

The major thrust of your answer must be that the sheer size and power of MNCs poses a threat to many 'host' countries, particularly developing countries. To illustrate this point you should be able to draw a comparison between the GNP of some countries and the turnover of the largest MNCs.

'Host' countries believe that decisions taken in the interest of the MNC are not necessarily in the best interests of that country. Thus MNCs are able to transfer resources from one country to another so as to gain the benefit of cheap labour or low taxation. Moreover their very size enables them to negotiate benefits from the host government that are not available to other firms. They have been accused of perpetuating developing countries' dependence on western economies by producing goods for western rather than local markets, or merely producing parts of a product in one host country which are then transferred elsewhere for final production. It has also been suggested that MNC efforts to protect the value of their reserves has exacerbated monetary crises for countries such as the UK. MNC power within an industry may be so great that other firms will always follow their actions and real competition does not exist.

Finally the Green movement accuses one MNC of social irresponsibility in the way that it exploits natural resources, e.g. South American rain forests.

Your answer should conclude by emphasising that although tensions exist in the relationship between host country and MNC, there are also obvious benefits which the MNC confers on the host country.

STUDENT'S ANSWER

Question 2

> A management buy-out covers 3 different situations. There is the situation where the managers of a business purchase the business from their employers and become owner-managers of that business. Secondly share purchase may not be limited to senior managers but be open to all managers and employees. Thus when the Government privatised Victaulic, which was a subsidiary of British Steel, it sold shares to all employees. The third situation where an MBO may occur is when a company goes into liquidation. Here parts of the business may still be profitable. For example when a toy business went out of business, managers mounted a rescue bid for the 'Hornby' (model trains) part of the group.
>
> Many MBOs taking place today are a result of previous mergers. In the 1960's and 1970's governments encouraged mergers thinking that it was only large firms which would be able to compete in the international and world markets. Some of these mergers were not thought through enough and didn't satisfy the synergy concept. This states that the 2 parts when put together should be more efficient and profitable than the separate parts (2+2 = 5). This was particularly true in the case where the merger between the two (or more) firms was contested. Here the firm mounting the bid often had to pay more than the value of the other firms' assets so as to gain control. So it was always going to be difficult to make that firm more profitable than it was before, even if economies of scale were possible.
>
> Management buy-outs have grown in the UK over the past decade for a number of reasons. I've already pointed out that some mergers are not successful and eventually managers realise their mistake and sell the business on to its managers. Another reason

A good start, shows breadth of knowledge.

Good point!

for the growth of MBOs is that many firms now find it socially unacceptable to close down unwanted parts of their operations as they may have done in the past. Indeed it's in their interest to persuade the managers to take on the business because its sales value is greater as a going concern than its break up value.

> **Not always.**

The growth of MBOs has also been encouraged by both the government and the city. For most of the period 1981–89 the city institutions have had surplus funds to invest. Subject to the usual screening of each potential MBO the City has been keen to lend money this way. The government also encourages MBOs as part of its policy of wider share ownership, to ensure competition in all markets and to prevent further de-industrialisation within the UK.

Another reason for the growth of MBOs has been the trend for firms to distinguish between peripheral and core activities and to concentrate on the latter. This has resulted in the sale of many subsidiaries — some obviously as MBOs. The return to core activities has occurred because firms who diversified have found it increasingly difficult to co-ordinate and control all their separate activities. In some cases the difficulties and problems encountered by the subsidiary were totally different to those of the parent company, in which case senior managers of both firms had to spend great amounts of time discussing these problems. Moreover in some cases, such as Dunlop or Imperial Group, the problems of a few subsidiaries have affected the financial stability of the whole group and made it vulnerable to a takeover bid.

> **Try to give examples.**

The movement towards returning to core activities has also been encouraged by the last decade's recession and high interest rates. The recession has meant that, in many cases, sales turnover and therefore profitability hasn't been as high as anticipated while high interest rates have pushed up the cost of borrowing, reducing profitability further.

Yet many of these subsidiaries put up for sale during this period were not basically unprofitable. As we have seen, they were held back by a group management who couldn't understand their particular problems or afford to finance their development. Their profitability was also reduced by having to bear a share of the whole group's overheads. Managers within the subsidiary were, of course, in the best position to make this evaluation and faced with an otherwise uncertain future were prepared to take the risk and buy out the firm from its previous owners. They would also have been encouraged by the success of previous MBOs both here and in America.

> **This could be developed.**

Finally we can point to the financial arrangements as encouraging the growth of MBOs. The parent company has often been willing to sell the subsidiary's assets to the management at less than their market value, as well as deferring repayments of loan interest and capital for several years. Moreover city institutions have been willing to accept gearing ratios of over 500%. This has encouraged managers to risk and invest their own money in the business.

> **A summary is really required.**

Tutor's comment

This is an excellent answer covering the major points necessary to obtain a very high grade.

TUTOR'S ANSWER

Question 3

a) The Bolton report says a small firm is one which has a small market share, is owner managed and is independent of any other organisation.

   Small firms can exist for many reasons, for example the market might be limited or subject to sudden change. One example would be the fashion market (larger firms find it difficult to react so quickly). There are other industries like plumbing where an increase in size doesn't yield a fall in unit costs and there is no incentive to grow. In other industries, for example building, jobs of different sizes are available and the large firms will only find it profitable to undertake the bigger jobs. The smaller jobs, often containing an element of personal service, are left to the small firm.

b) From a human perspective the major opportunity small firms present is the chance for the owner to be his own boss. There are many people who find working for a large impersonal organisation unattractive. It may be they don't like doing the same job all day long or find that large firms stifle their creativity. Such people find the freedom and responsibility of working for themselves very attractive.

   For other people who had been made redundant, running a small firm meant that they could avoid unemployment. From a human perspective this was important because they could avoid the stigma of unemployment.

   Many small firms survive today because of the excellent relationships which they may have with their customers. Many people will, for example, continue to use their corner shop, not only because of its proximity and long opening hours but also because many get a personal service from the owner. He knows their name and generally provides a far more friendly service than the local impersonal superstore.

   Small firms owners don't only establish good relationships with customers; the same applies to employees. Again it's the fact that the boss knows them individually that is all important. Even more important is the fact that he talks to them and works alongside them. Generally people working within small firms establish close or strong informal relationships, each employee sees how his or her work is contributing to the good of the firm, feels wanted and important. This must be a powerful motivational force, for how else can we explain employee acceptance of low wages and poor working conditions?

   On the negative side the demands made by the business on the individual may be extremely high. Small business owners traditionally work long hours in the business and then come home to do whatever paperwork is necessary. Working such long hours must put a strain upon relationships within the family. An additional source of strain may arise where several members of the same family work in the same business. It's unlikely that each of them will have similar business aspirations to the others. Conflict is likely to occur and sour relationships within the business and the family.

   From an employee's viewpoint, working for a small firm, as we have already noted does have its drawbacks. Such employees often have poor working conditions and pay. Better employees may be attracted to the larger firm by reason not only of pay and conditions of work but also training and career opportunities.

   Finally, it is likely that the small business owner is under pressure through having to face a number of problems. These include a lack of managerial expertise and the inability to afford appropriate help, lack of financial support, high levels of competition and vulnerability to government fiscal and monetary policy. It is estimated that 130,000 small firms cease trading each year; many for the reasons mentioned above – it's not surprising therefore that small business owners may be worried about the future.

c) The Bolton Report on small firms in 1971 spoke very strongly about the good influence such firms have upon the economy. As we have already noted, they are an important source of jobs for those who have been made redundant or whose personality ill suits them for work in a large organisation. But small firms not only provide employment for their owners; some 30% of *all* employees work in this sector. An increase in small firms is therefore likely to have a positive impact upon the levels of unemployment.

   Small firms are also seen as the traditional breeding ground for new industries. Large firms are often slower to identify new market opportunities; moreover they may be unwilling to invest time and money in what is at that time, a small untried market. It is left for small firms to satisfy these new market needs. Some of these small firms will prosper, grow and eventually go on to challenge the established leaders of industry.

CHAPTER

THE ECONOMIC MICRO-ENVIRONMENT OF BUSINESS

ECONOMIC GROWTH

INFLATION

EMPLOYMENT

PUBLIC FINANCE

IMPLICATIONS FOR BUSINESS PEOPLE

GETTING STARTED

All companies and voluntary or public sector organisations operate in an economic environment over which they have no control. This environment is subject to both cyclical movements and random shocks. Governments seek to lessen these influences by use of fiscal policy, monetary policy, or legislation. The government is also impelled by political considerations to try and change the social structure. It may seek to redistribute income, either towards or away from the better off. It may seek to increase or reduce the number and type of economic activities which are undertaken in the public sector. It may seek to make the economy more open to international trade, or seek to protect it from international pressures.

Individual governments will face different structural constraints and weaknesses. For example, the UK has in recent years seen a dramatic decline of manufacturing, due to a lack of competitiveness and low labour productivity. This has produced an increased propensity to import, leading to a worsening deficit on the current account of the balance of payments. There have also been inadequate levels of investment in plant and in human resources.

The managers of the firm must seek to understand this economic process and be able to 'best guess' future developments. Failure to do so may lead to the demise of the firm. The economic variables which are most relevant to the businessman are:

- Economic growth
- Inflation
- Interest rates
- Unemployment
- Public spending
- Taxation

In this chapter we will explain briefly what these variables are, how they work and how a business might respond to the signal's which they offer. Other important economic influences on business planning are those relating to the international economy, which are dealt with in Chapter 5, and market forces, which are explained in Chapter 11.

ESSENTIAL PRINCIPLES

The Economy as a system.

Much of this chapter and the next are concerned with ways in which the government seeks to influence and manage the macro economy in order to achieve high levels of economic growth (in so far as that is consistent with low inflation and balance of payments equilibrium). Such government activities inevitably affect businesses. Before we look at the methods used, and their consequences for industry and business, we have to place them in context by using a familiar diagrammatic model. Economists see the economy as a *system* which generates a flow of goods and services produced by businesses, for the use of households and consumers. A counter flow of payments takes place to the factor inputs used in the production of those goods and services (land, labour, capital and enterprise). This is illustrated in simple form in Fig. 4.1.

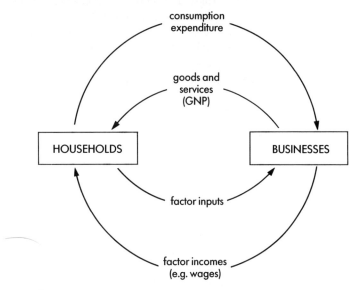

Fig. 4.1 Simple circular flow model of national income

This 'circular flow' is a basic model of the relationship between flows of physical goods and money flows. The model may be refined to show the existence of a range of *injections into*, and *leakages from*, this simple circular flow model (Fig. 4.2)

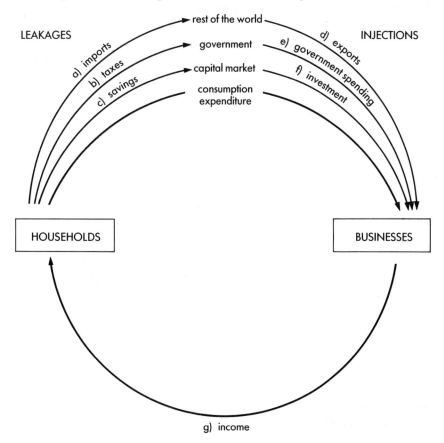

Fig. 4.2 Modified national income model

Some of the household incomes generated in producing goods and services in the domestic economy 'leak out' of the system. That is to say, the money is *not* passed on to domestic businesses. For example, spending on imports goes to foreign firms and individuals. Taxes go to the government and savings are held by financial institutions. Imports, taxes and savings are 'leakages' in that they are not directly received by domestic businesses. On the other hand, domestic businesses receive income from sources *other than* domestic households. We call these 'additions' to the circular flow of income 'injections'. For example, domestic businesses receive income from *overseas* households and businesses when they export. Some domestic businesses also receive income from the *government* (government contracts) or by way of investment when *other businesses* buy plant and equipment. Exports, government spending and investment are classed as 'injections' in that domestic businesses receive income from sources *other than* domestic households.

Any surplus of injections over leakages will increase the flow of income (create economic growth) whilst a surplus of leakages over injections will reduce the flow of income (cause negative economic growth). Since this flow of income passes through businesses, their activities will inevitably be affected and they will have to plan their activities with possible future changes in mind, if they are to survive and prosper.

Governments seek by various means to manipulate items (a), (b), (c), (d), (e) or (f) in Fig. 4.2 in order to maximise item (g), the flow of income in the system. It can be seen that government *management of the economy* in this way is channelled through businesses, hence the need for businesses to be aware of the threats and opportunities offered by changes in government economic policy.

ECONOMIC GROWTH

This is the most important of the economic indicators mentioned in the introduction. It is a measure of the rate at which the *real output* of the economy is growing over time. By 'real output' we mean the actual volume of goods and services produced by the economy (and the *incomes* which flow from this output). In other words we eliminate from our calculations of output (and income) the effects of inflation, which raises the 'value' measured by prices, but not the volume.

The Gross Domestic Product (GDP) is the concept often used to measure output. This refers to the output produced by individuals and businesses actually located within the boundaries of the domestic economy.

❝ UK and Japan: comparative growth rates. ❞

Economic growth is calculated as a *rate*, namely the percentage change in 'real' GDP (inflation eliminated). Historically the UK has generated growth of about 2% to 3% on average per annum. The range has been between − 1.5% in recessions and 4.5% (briefly) in boom periods (see Fig. 4.3). This compares with rates of 5% to 10% in Japan, which has been the strongest of the advanced economies for 20 years.

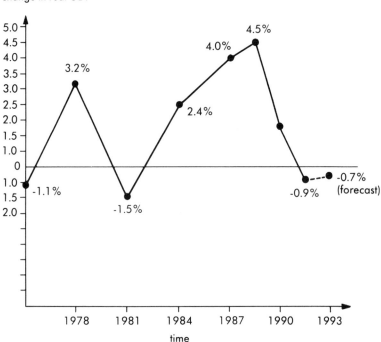

% change in real GDP

Fig. 4.3 Trends in economic growth in UK 1975–93

All modern economies are subject to cyclical variations in the rate of growth. Falling and even negative growth rates are, of course, associated with periods of recession. The 'high' growth rates in the mid-1980s in the UK are often called the 'Lawson boom years', after the then Chancellor of the Exchequer, Nigel Lawson.

WHY GROWTH IS IMPORTANT

The achievement of economic growth is important as a policy issue to all governments for a number of reasons:

Growth and the standard of living.

- The rate of growth of output in relation to the rate at which the population grows, will determine the rate of increase of *output per capita* and therefore the rate at which the *standard of living* improves over time.

- Strong economic growth means that the demand for goods and services will increase, offering opportunities for businesses to grow.

- Strong economic growth will also enable governments to increase public spending on the infrastructure without deflecting resources from wealth-creating activities.

- Strong economic growth will make full employment possible, but may cause 'overheating' and associated problems of high inflation and balance of payments deficits. These problems may make it necessary for government to use its fiscal and monetary policy instruments to slow down the growth of output.

Costs of economic growth.

- There are other costs of high economic growth levels. These stem from heavy and possible wasteful use of scarce resources, which may lead to 'externalities' such as pollution of the environment.

FACTORS LEADING TO GROWTH

Growth may be induced by the accidental coincidence of favourable resource conditions, or by government action on key economic indicators. The following factors may help to create growth.

- The discovery of a hitherto unexploited natural resource, such as oil, may generate a surge of growth. The value of the new output of oil and gas would obviously increase GDP in its own right. However there would also be enormous spin-offs in activity in all the necessary support industries, engineering, transport, etc. These 'spin-off' effects are referred to by economists as the 'multiplier effect'.

Factors leading to growth.

- An increase in population (especially in less advanced economies) may provide an increase in the available labour force, permitting a further growth in output. On the other hand a decline (or ageing) of the population in an advanced economy, as is occurring at present in Western Europe, may have the opposite effect of limiting growth possibilities.

- The development of human skills will increase the capacity of an economy to grow. Thus economies where a high proportion of school leavers proceed to further or higher education, especially in applied sciences, will tend to have higher growth rates than those where a lower proportion do so. Japan and Germany are good examples. Each has 80% of school leavers going on to do more education or training and these economies frequently generate growth rates for GDP of 5–10% per annum. In contrast the UK, where only 60% go on to further education and training, growth rates can rarely be sustained above about 3%. A highly educated and trained workforce is essential both for the generation of technical change and for its application to production.

- Capital accumulation is also critical to the generation of growth. This is often called *investment* and refers to the process of adding to the net stock of physical capital, machines, buildings and plant in the private business sector; it also includes additions or improvements to the infrastructure by public authorities.

- Rapid developments in technology, which bring about the possibility of productivity gains (more output from the same resources), may also induce a surge in growth. This can be observed in recent years in Japan.

A combination of rapid increases in capital accumulation, a highly trained workforce and modern technology, will generate very rapid growth as in Japan. Low levels of investment and an ageing capital stock will hinder growth, as in the UK

Once begun, a cycle of growth can be 'cumulative'. For example, the higher incomes which accompany economic growth may permit higher savings, which in turn may be channelled into the higher investment which promotes further growth.

GOVERNMENT POLICY AND GROWTH

The priority of any government in an advanced economy is to generate growth in the economy. In doing so it is constrained by the effects of growth on inflation, unemployment and the balance of payments. Thus it must act *counter cyclically*, dampening down periods of boom and stimulating the economy in periods of recession. In this way the government is seeking to level out fluctuations in economic activity. For instance, inflation must be kept to levels which do not cause long term damage, and unemployment must be kept within politically acceptable limits. Governments must also keep in mind the ultimate constraint of the balance of payments deficit level which can be financed in the long term. In seeking to reconcile the four key variables of growth, inflation, unemployment and the balance of payments, the government has various weapons at its disposal:

- The government may induce injections into, and leakages out of, the circular flow of income (see Fig. 4.2). For example, by adjustments in *public spending* it may manage the level of total (or aggregate) demand in the economy to make it consistent with sustainable growth.

- By adjusting the level and types of *taxation, social security benefits* and *subsidies*, it may also achieve the same effect.

Managing the key variables for growth.

- It may similarly use its powers of control over the *money supply* to manage aggregate demand. This may involve direct adjustments to the 'volume' of credit available from the banking system and/or adjustments in the 'price' of such credit, via interest rates.

- Any increased level of demand resulting from high levels of growth may cause inflationary pressures in the labour market, resulting in unacceptable rises in money incomes. An *incomes policy* may then be used to slow down temporarily the rise in wages and salaries, thus reducing aggregate demand and economic growth.

- Rapid economic growth may cause a surge in imports and a switch from export markets into the now easier domestic markets by businesses. A *protectionist policy* (see Chapter 5) may be used to return the balance of payments to equilibrium. The use of changes in the *exchange rate* to encourage exports and discourage imports has been illustrated by the departure of the UK from the Exchange Rate Mechanism in September 1992. The effective 10% devaluation of the £ reduced the relative price of UK goods in foreign markets and caused a surge in export business.

Problems of economic forecasting.

All of these measures are inclined to be subject to *time lags* and their overall effect cannot easily be forecast. For instance, if the government seeks to cut taxes in a time of recession, by the time the tax cuts work through to higher spending the economy may already be in recovery. There may then be the danger of over-stimulating the economy, so that the extra spending from the tax cuts causes excessive inflation and balance of payments problems rather than the intended boost at a time of recession.

INFLATION

A definition.

Inflation is best defined as 'the persistent increase in the general level of prices over time'. Fig. 4.4 shows the course of UK inflation since 1960.

The seriously high rates of inflation in the 1970s, produced by oil price increases combined with lax monetary policy, were followed by sharp reductions in the rate during the 1980s due to stringent monetary policies and the impacts of deindustrialisation. The return to high rates of inflation from 1987–1990, reflected the 'Lawson Boom' when credit restrictions were eased.

Inflation in the UK is measured by the *Retail Price Index* (RPI). It is calculated by selecting a representative sample of goods normally purchased by households. The items are weighted for relative importance and the cost of the basket of goods today is expressed as a percentage of the same basket of goods in some starting or 'base' year.

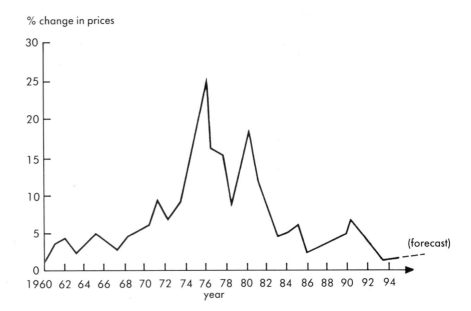

% change in prices

Fig. 4.4 UK inflation record
1960–94

This can be expressed thus:

Calculating the 'RPI'.

$$\text{Retail price index} = \frac{\text{cost of today's basket}}{\text{cost of basket in base year}} \times 100$$

The RPI takes no account of income tax payments, national insurance payments, or payments to pension funds and is distorted by the presence of mortgage interest and Community Charge payments. The RPI therefore may on some occasions over or under state the 'true' level of inflation. For this reason various other measures may be used.

CAUSES OF INFLATION

- *Demand pull influences*. These are factors which cause an increase in aggregate demand to levels beyond the ability of the economy to deliver the appropriate level of output. Such factors include increases in public spending, or sudden increases in credit creation and money supply by the banking system.

- *Cost push influences*. These are factors on the supply side of the economy which lead to increases in the costs of production which are then passed on in higher prices. Such pressure may be caused by the strong bargaining power of large labour unions (especially at times of full employment) or by increases in the cost of basic raw materials which force up industrial costs of production. A good example of the latter effect could be seen in the early 1970s when the price of oil increased fourfold, and again in 1979 when the price of oil doubled.

THE EFFECTS OF INFLATION

Inflation damages the economy.

Many economists see inflation as being the most damaging economic phenomenon which can affect an advanced nation. It may also have alarming political consequences. Some economists however take the view that some inflation is an acceptable 'price' for economic growth. There is no clear agreement as to when inflation becomes unacceptable, but rates in excess of perhaps 5% are generally thought to be threatening, whilst rates in excess of perhaps 15% (hyperinflation) may cause social and political breakdown. There are a number of reasons for arguing that inflation is damaging:

- When price rises surge ahead of rates of increase of money income, the *real income* of consumers will decrease. Consumers will then have to adjust their purchases and the demand for some products may decrease. High price consumer durables, for example cars, are likely to experience sharp falls in demand.

An extreme form of inflation.

- Hyperinflation may destroy confidence in money, leading to a return to barter and the collapse of normal trading.

- People who rely on incomes derived from past savings or who are in occupations where pay rates are slow to respond to changes in inflation, will be severely hit by inflation. In extreme cases the value of savings may be destroyed.

- Businesses are also affected adversely. The costs of inputs will rise, and the firm will need to raise prices if possible to maintain its profit margins. If it cannot do so, it may find itself in financial difficulties.

- Interest rates usually rise during periods of inflation. For instance the government may raise interest rates to discourage borrowing and spending, and thereby curb 'demand pull' inflation. Firms which rely heavily on borrowing will find that as interest rates rise, profit margins are squeezed.

- The attempts by workers and their unions to force up wages in response to inflation may cause widespread lay-offs where these cost increases cannot be passed on to consumers in higher prices.

- Firms which rely on export markets will find that their relative prices may rise, causing them to be priced out of world markets. If the exchange rate is allowed to fall in response to inflation, they may temporarily be able to hold onto markets, but the devaluation will produce further rises in the price of imported inputs, leading to a further twist to the inflationary spiral.

GOVERNMENT RESPONSES TO INFLATION

Broadly, governments will respond to inflationary pressures in one of two ways.

A *Keynesian* approach *would concentrate on attempts to reduce aggregate demand* through a combination of monetary and fiscal policies. A range of credit control measures would be used as part of monetary policy to increase the cost and reduce the availability of credit for consumer purchases, for example cars. Personal taxation may be increased and/or government spending cut as part of fiscal policy. Cost push inflationary pressures from higher taxes might be countered by the use of prices and incomes restraints. Foreign currency reserves would be used to support the value of the currency on the exchanges, thus reducing the inflationary effects which might otherwise follow from a forced devaluation.

Two responses to inflation.

A *Monetarist* approach would seek to reduce the growth of money supply by reducing government spending and hence the Public Sector Borrowing Requirement. Lower government spending would reduce aggregate demand. More important to the monetarist, it would also reduce the amount of bills and bonds issued by governments when borrowing, thereby cutting the money supply in the economy. The monetarist approach would also raise interest rates to deter borrowing in the private sector and to prevent a devaluation of the currency.

EMPLOYMENT

Difficulties in reducing unemployment.

The maintenance of full employment was a central policy aim of governments from 1944 to 1979 and was largely achieved through the use of policies of demand management. Since 1979 inflation has had a higher priority and it has been accepted that there is some level of unemployment below which it is not possible to go without the return of inflationary pressures. Inflexibility in the labour market has, it seems, fixed that figure at a rate of about 7% of the workforce. This rate is referred to as the 'natural' rate of unemployment. Any attempt to control the level of unemployment is further complicated by changes in the size of the labour force.

The measure of unemployment currently used is the number of persons 'registered as unemployed and claiming benefit'. It has been suggested that this figure understates the true number of persons wishing to be economically active, but unable to find a job. Fig. 4.5 shows the trend in UK unemployment since 1961.

The steadily rising trend in unemployment rates from 1961 to 1986, indicated the rapid rate of deindustrialisation (absolute loss of manufacturing jobs) taking place in the UK. The brief improvement from 1986 to 1989 reflected the 'Lawson Boom', which has been followed by deep recession and resumption of the trend.

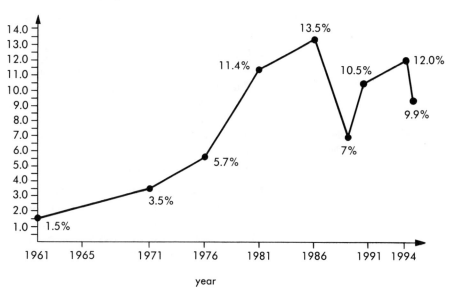

Fig. 4.5 General unemployment trends 1961–1994

CAUSES OF UNEMPLOYMENT

There are several *categories* of unemployment. It is important to distinguish between them as they will require different treatment.

- *Frictional unemployment (or search unemployment).* Persons who are made redundant will need time to search for and start a new job. The time involved in such searching may be increased by recession and the consequent fall in the demand for labour.

- *Seasonal unemployment.* Fluctuations in demand for labour in certain industries will be linked either to the seasonal nature of production, e.g. agriculture, or to seasonal patterns of demand, e.g. children's toys at Christmas, or summer holidays.

- *Technological unemployment.* This may result from new technology causing a change in the pattern of demand, e.g. where a new product replaces one of inferior quality. It may also occur where an established industrial process is replaced by new machinery, requiring less labour. Skills may then become obsolete, as in steel making, leading to sudden and often very localised increases in unemployment. This sort of change may also be referred to as 'structural unemployment'.

- *Cyclical or demand deficiency unemployment.* Fluctuations of demand, caused by the pattern of the business cycle, may compound some of the above effects to produce sudden increases in unemployment.

- *Unemployment due to obstructions to the labour market.* Monetarists believe that this is the major cause of long term unemployment. They see the excessive national bargaining power of trade unions as being especially important. They believe that workers are then priced out of work by excessive increases in real wages. They also see excessively high unemployment benefits as a cause of longer search times, thus increasing the number of workers unemployed at a given time.

> Unemployment has several causes.

Those economists who adopt a *supply side* approach are likely to emphasise the importance in creating unemployment of excessive increases in real wages, obstructions to the labour market and high levels of social benefits. Those who adopt a *Keynesian* approach are likely to emphasise the importance of inadequate levels of aggregate demand. Their prescriptions for reducing unemployment will reflect these views. On the one hand, those who support the supply side approach will emphasise the importance in reducing unemployment of curbing the power of the unions, reducing the real value of benefits, and improving the sources of information about available vacancies. Keynesians, on the other hand, argue for increases in government spending, encouragement for investment in the private sector and a relaxation of credit to encourage consumer demand and reduce unemployment.

RESPONSES TO UNEMPLOYMENT

Governments may respond in a number of ways to high or increasing levels of unemployment.

Government responses to unemployment.

- If it is believed that a deficiency in aggregate demand is the cause of unemployment, it is possible to increase demand by use of a package of measures, fiscal and monetary. Thus the government might lower taxation and/or increase public spending. It might increase effective demand by removing restrictions on credit creation by the banking system and/or by lowering interest rates to induce both individuals and businesses to borrow for consumption or investment purposes. In extreme cases it might even introduce protectionist measures to reduce imports and encourage domestic investment and production.

- If it is believed that imperfections in the labour market are the cause of unemployment, the government might seek to break the power of the unions by legislation. More modest wage increases might then help to 'price' people back into work. Alternatively, the government might reduce the real value of benefits in order to make jobs on low wages more attractive. It might also reduce the higher rates of tax on income and profits to encourage entrepreneurial activity and so encourage job creation.

- Where specific industries or regions are worst affected, it might use a policy of direct subsidy and regional aid measures in order to maintain existing jobs in the short term whilst encouraging the creation of new jobs.

PUBLIC FINANCE

You will have noticed that government spending and taxation, as part of *fiscal* policy, have been mentioned several times in this discussion. We must here briefly note the reasons why governments spend our money and the ways in which they raise that money.

REASONS FOR GOVERNMENT SPENDING

- *Defence and law and order.* The existence of a state requires that its boundaries be defended from incursions and that its citizens be protected.

- *Social security.* The principle has been accepted for many years that the state should support, wholly or partially, some citizens who are unwaged, or low paid. The various benefits are for the most part paid as a right, given various qualifications. The total amount of social security paid by government is therefore a result of prevailing economic conditions and is not completely in their control. In time of recession it may be the largest item of expenditure.

- *Local government spending.* Some 80% of such spending comes directly from the Treasury, much of this being spent on providing educational services.

- *National Health Service.* Virtually all such spending comes from the Treasury. The principle of a health service free at the point of use has been slightly eroded but remains central to the thinking of all political parties.

Public spending cuts concentrate on capital items.

These are the main items of government expenditure, but there are many others, including support for industry, contributions to the EC budget, infrastructure expenditure and other education spending. It is difficult to control current spending (on materials and wages and benefits); therefore cuts in public spending have often been concentrated on capital items, e.g. funding of road and railways construction, buildings, etc.

TAXATION

Government spending has to be financed either by taxation or by borrowing. Taxation is essential and unavoidable. It may be imposed on income, expenditure, capital gains or wealth. The main forms of taxation used in the UK are as follows:

- *Income tax.* Charged on all incomes from work or self employment *above* an amount dictated by a personal allowance plus allowances for certain other items such as mortgage interest, pension fund premiums, etc. Three rates are charged, a lower rate of

20% on the lowest levels of taxable income, a standard rate of 25%, and a rate of 40% on the highest incomes, above a set limit.

- *Corporation tax.* Charged on profits earned by companies. Small firms currently pay a lower rate than larger ones.

Harmonisation of tax may affect VAT.

- *VAT (Value Added Tax).* This is a charge on the value added at each stage of the production process. VAT paid by a firm on the cost of inputs is reclaimable. The result is a tax on expenditure by the end user. The current rate is 17½%, with a zero rate on certain items like food and children's clothes. Certain other goods are tax exempt which means that though they do not have to pay VAT on their sales they are not allowed to obtain refunds of taxes paid at previous stages of the 'production' process. VAT has been introduced recently on domestic fuel, as part of the government's response to escalating government debt.

- *Excise Duties.* Chargeable on certain products such as tobacco and wines and spirits. This may have to be reduced, again as a result of harmonisation of taxation in the Single Market.

- *Capital Gains Tax and Inheritance Tax.* There is no wealth tax as such in the UK, but tax is charged on the gains made from the sale of assets. Inheritance tax is charged on assets above a given amount which are inherited.

- *Local Taxation.* Originally in the form of a business rate and a domestic rate on houses. In recent years the Business Rate has been charged at a common rate throughout the UK and the domestic rate replaced by a Community Charge (or Poll Tax). The unsuccessful Poll Tax was replaced in April 1993 by a new Council Charge, based on property values. Domestic properties have been placed in bands on the basis of the price which was obtained for that type of house in that location, in mid 1991. The tax will be levied at increasing rates up the scale of value of property. There are likely to be many appeals against valuations, especially since the value of houses has fallen by up to a third since that date in certain areas. There is a strong possibility that the tax will be in practice as difficult to operate as the Poll Tax, and just as unpopular.

GOVERNMENT ECONOMIC MANAGEMENT

All governments must seek to manipulate the economic variables in such a way as to maintain stable and low inflation and unemployment levels, high levels of economic growth and equilibrium in the balance of payments on current account. This 'stability' is clearly difficult to achieve.

IMPLICATIONS FOR BUSINESS PEOPLE

Businessmen should forecast.

It is essential for any businessperson to be aware of the condition of the economic environment in which he or she is operating. The ability to be able to *predict* the likely movements of key economic indicators and the likely government responses to those movements may enable the businesspeople to 'place' their business in such a way as to maximise profits or growth or at least ensure survival. There is space here only to indicate some of the responses which they might make. You should use the sets of economic data given in Figs. 4.3 to 4.5, as basic information providing the context in which you examine any case study.

ECONOMIC GROWTH AND THE BUSINESS

- Recognition of a likely *downturn* in growth may allow the business to avoid being caught with excessive stock, too many employees and too much capacity. Reduction of inventory and overhead costs may enable it to survive as competitors fail and to emerge with increased market share when the upturn comes.

- Such recognition of a downturn in growth may enable the business to avoid being caught with excessive 'gearing' (borrowing) which may lead to cash flow difficulties and bankruptcy, especially if interest rates rise in the ensuing recession.

- Conversely, recognition of a likely *upturn* in growth may cause the businessperson to take other decisions. Greater production capacity and stock levels can be put in place *before* the expected upturn occurs, reducing the likelihood of bottlenecks and shortages impeding future increases in sales, etc.

INFLATION

- When inflation is ahead of the rate in competitor countries, the business may find itself 'priced out' of export markets and even of sections of its domestic market. Careful control of the purchasing of inputs and inventories might help the business to reduce its costs. So too might a greater use of more capital intensive production methods. In these ways the business may be able to gain market share by restricting its price increases relative to those of its competitors.

- A policy of 'natural wastage', together with the replacement of full-time by temporary workers, may enable the business to avoid the effects of wage-push inflation on its costs. Sometimes businesses seek to end long-standing industrial practices which are seen as 'restrictive' and as adding unnecessarily to costs.

- Since high inflation leads to high interest rates, the successful business will often be the one which reduces its borrowing requirement during inflationary times.

- In extreme cases it may be wise to shift all or some of the production process off-shore to a low wage economy.

> Business responses to movements in key indicators.

- Businesses operating in a high inflation climate will be wise to avoid competing with overseas producers in prices only, and instead to compete increasingly in terms of quality, delivery, service and value added.

HIGH INTEREST RATES

- A regime of high interest rates, such as that which has occurred in the UK in the early 1990s, will require the business to adopt an appropriate strategy. High levels of borrowing for expansion or acquisitions must be avoided. Growth must be 'evolutionary', so far as is possible, being financed from retained profits or from other internal sources of finance. This will be a slower route to growth but is less likely to endanger the firm's survival.

- Control of cash flow, trade credit and bad debts are essential in order to avoid high levels of working capital financed by an overdraft. This removes the risk of a sudden withdrawal of funds by a bank, which might bankrupt an otherwise profitable and viable firm.

- Any expansion of the firm which cannot be internally financed should be based on equity financing, rather than on loan finance.

UNEMPLOYMENT

- A rise in the level of unemployment will signal to the firm a possible fall in demand, requiring careful cutbacks of all costs and possibly a change in marketing strategy.

- Increased unemployment may mean that the firm can recruit key labour more easily and cheaply.

- Prolonged unemployment may weaken the unions and make it possible for the firm to restructure its labour force, introduce more flexible working practices and stabilise pay.

- A fall in unemployment may cause difficulties. Suitable skilled labour may then be hard to recruit and retain and wage levels may rise rapidly.

PUBLIC FINANCE

- Changes in public expenditure, especially on capital account, may improve or worsen the prospects of companies. This will be especially so in the construction industry. Firms which are heavily dependent on *public* procurement contracts will need to plan carefully to avoid these cyclical effects, avoiding if possible being caught with excessive stock (of land or materials) and a large permanent workforce.

- Major changes in the way in which public utilities are organised, such as privatisation programmes, or NHS reforms, may change the way in which supplier firms have to do business. A quite different marketing strategy may then have to be adopted.

■ Changes in the rules of company taxation must be constantly monitored, in order to minimise the corporation tax paid and to maximise the use of any grant or tax allowances available.

■ Changes in personal taxation and VAT will affect the demand for goods and services. Changes in marketing strategy and pricing policies may have to be used in order to avoid sudden loss of markets.

Lack of space makes a more detailed discussion impossible. However, the above illustrates why a business must continually monitor changes in the business environment. You could now look at some case studies used in past examinations. Consider the various influences coming from the economic environment on those aspects of strategic business planning raised in the Questions. If the business used in the case is operating in international markets, you should also look at the issues raised in Chapter 5.

EXAMINATION QUESTIONS

1   The Chancellor in his Budget proposes that tax thresholds should be lifted rather than reductions made in personal tax rates for higher income earners.
   a) What do the underlined terms mean?   *(5)*
   b) How might a personnel manager evaluate these changes?   *(10)*
   c) How would the marketing manager of a package holiday firm expect these changes to affect his business?   *(10)*
                                                                        (UCLES 1987)

2   Discuss how economic and other constraints might influence the exploration and development policy of an oil company.   *(25)*
                                                                        (UCLES 1989)

3   The Government is proposing to introduce further credit restrictions.
   a) How might this policy be implemented?   *(5)*
   b) What effect would you expect these measures to have on:
      i) The motor car industry   *(5)*
      ii) Builder's merchants supplying the DIY trade   *(5)*
      iii) The overall level of economic activity   *(10)*
                                                                        (UCLES 1986)

4   Examine how an enterprise might alter its plans if a prolonged period of heavy unemployment is predicted   *(25)*
                                                                        (AEB 1988)

TUTOR'S ANSWER

Question 1

a) In his Budget statement, made in March each year to the House of Commons, the Chancellor of the Exchequer sets out the Government's public spending and taxation proposals for the coming financial year.

Tax thresholds. A term used to describe the point at which income from employment begins to attract income tax at the current lowest rate. This is currently 25p per £ of taxable income (i.e. above the threshold) and the threshold in 1991 was £3,295. In fact most taxpayers are able to set some items against tax, thus raising their personal threshold by a considerable amount. The most common allowance is for mortgage interest payments.

The personal tax rate. This refers to the rate at which income from employment is taxed. Currently at 25p in the £ Basic Rate and 40p in the £ Higher Rate. The latter was charged in 1991 on taxable income in excess of £23,701 per annum, after the appropriate individual allowances have been taken into account.

b) These proposed changes would have considerable implications for the Personnel Manager, particularly in a firm which employs large numbers of lower paid (weekly wage) workers. The effect of lifting the threshold would be to increase the disposable income of an employee without any increase in the weekly wage paid. For example, a worker on £5000 per annum, where the tax threshold was previously £3000 (making no adjustment for any allowance other than the basic personal allowance, and assuming a lower band tax rate of 25p) would pay £500 in income tax (£2000 × 25%). If the allowance was raised to £5000 he would cease to pay income tax and would be £10 per week better off, with NO pay rise.

The personnel manager might find that this change would enable him or her to negotiate a wage freeze for one year, or at least a lower than expected rise. This would have a beneficial effect on costs of production, enabling the firm to be more competitive, especially in export markets. It would be particularly helpful if the firm is struggling to survive recession. On a wider front, such a change would help the government to counter wage inflation pressures in the economy (although it might see the resulting increase in consumer spending as having a counter effect). It would also diminish the 'poverty trap' where low incomes are insufficiently attractive to pull unemployed workers off benefits, which may give them a higher real income. If there are labour shortages, but nevertheless high unemployment figures, as in Northern England, the proposed change may free up the labour market and benefit all firms.

The proposal to NOT reduce personal tax rates in the higher band might also affect the personnel manager. All senior managers will not receive the increase in disposable income which they had anticipated and may be demotivated. As a consequence, if such high quality employees are scarce, the personnel manager will have to use ingenious ways of increasing managerial incomes by offering benefits in kind, e.g. bigger company car, free membership of BUPA, life insurance, car 'phone, company Barclaycard, etc.

c) The marketing manager of a package holiday company may have to adjust his marketing strategy to react to the changes in taxation. The increase in disposable income for all employees will possibly increase the demand for such holidays across the whole income range, with the lower band of wage earners pulled into the market for package holidays for the first time (*shifting* the D curve to the right, see Fig. 4.6). The result would be an increase in the price of such holidays, from OP to OP₁ in Fig. 4.6, and in the number of package holidays taken (from OQ to OQ₁).

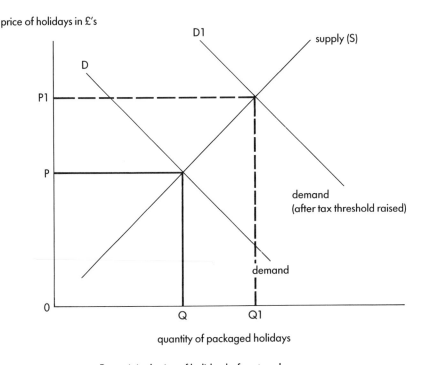

P = original price of holiday before tax changes
Q = quantity of holidays suggested before tax changes
P1 = price of holiday after tax threshold raised
Q1 = quantity of holidays supplied after tax threshold raised

Fig. 4.6 Effect of a rise in tax thresholds on package holidays

This would be so *unless* the holiday company was able to *increase the supply* of package holidays, as a result (perhaps) of the availability of spare capacity in both the airlines and hotels. In this case the supply curve may also shift to the right and more holidays would be supplied at any given price (see Fig. 4.7).

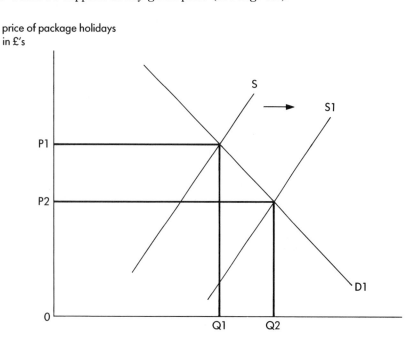

price of package holidays in £'s

quantity of package holidays

Fig. 4.7 Effect of an increase in supply of package holidays on price and quantity

The new price of package holidays is now lower than P_1 (namely P_2) and the quantity is higher than Q_1 (namely Q_2).

At the top end of the market, it may be that the anticipated growth in higher priced packaged holidays (had the government decided to lower the higher band tax rate rather than increasing the threshold) may not occur. The holiday provider might therefore switch some of his or her capacity to the lower priced range of holidays, giving the increase in supply shown in Fig. 4.7.

Whether or not the *final* price (OP_2) would be higher than the *original* price (OP), would depend on the magnitude of the respective demand/supply shifts. However both demand and supply shifts would work in the *same direction* for the quantity of package holidays, so that OQ_2 would be higher than the original quantity OQ.

STUDENT'S ANSWER

Question 2

An introduction indicating the broad nature of the constraints would be helpful.

What other factors?

Good use made of the diagrams.

The main factor which affects both exploration and development policy of an oil company is the price of oil. Certain oil fields are not profitable when the price of oil falls below a certain value. For example, it is only profitable for oil companies to develop oil fields in the North Sea when the price of oil is above $13 per barrel, because of both the high exploration and extraction costs of deep sea deposits.

The price of oil is determined by many different factors. One important factor is the stage of the trade cycle in the major industrial nations, which are the largest users of oil. If these countries are moving into a recession, then the demand for oil-based products such as petrol, diesel fuel and chemical by-products will fall. Conversely, if the economies are moving into a boom, demand will increase. This may be demonstrated in a diagram.

A shift of the demand schedule will occur, to the left in Fig. 4.8a) and to the right in Fig. 4.8b). Assuming there is no change

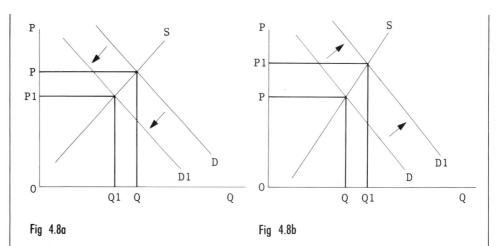

Fig 4.8a   Fig 4.8b

in the supply of oil, the price of oil products will fall in the
first example and rise in the second. This will affect the
viability of more marginal oil developments.

In recession, the shift of the Demand curve to the left, causes a
fall in price from P to P_1 and output from Q to Q_1. In a boom, the
opposite occurs.

> The need for long term
> planning of development and
> investment should be pointed
> out.

If the demand for oil is stable or rising from year to year,
various factors influencing the supply side may cause a change in
the price of oil, thus affecting the viability and profitability
of specific development projects planned by oil companies.

For example political relationships between member countries of
the OPEC cartel may change. In the 1970s the cartel was strong
enough to raise the oil price fourfold in 1974 and double in 1978,
until it reached over $30 per barrel. These actions caused
recession in the major oil-using countries and led directly to a
search for more efficient ways of using oil. Oil companies were
very profitable and the price rise lead directly to the
exploration and development programmes which opened up the North
Sea deposits and others in deep sea locations. In more recent years
the weakness of OPEC and the development of deposits in non OPEC
countries such as UK, produced a flood of surplus oil and a fall in
the price to the point where these deposits were less profitable
than expected, leading to a slowdown in development.

> The impact of recent
> events in the USSR might be
> mentioned.

Other international political factors will influence decisions
about oil development. For example, the known large deposits in
Antarctica may not be developed because of the recent
international treaty banning all such activities in that area. The
outbreak of war in the Middle East has put both the Kuwait and Iraq
fields out of action for the time being and only the depth of
recession and the increased production in Saudia Arabia has
prevented huge increases in the oil price. Such political
instability will be a deterrent to development and exploration in
such politically volatile areas.

> These points should be
> developed further.

Just as developments in technology made the exploitation of the
North Sea deposits viable, so the search for improved technology
to reduce fuel consumption and for alternative, more
environmentally friendly energy sources, will affect the plans of
oil companies.

There are thus many constraints which affect the strategy of the
oil companies, but the price of oil, which is determined by demand
side factors, combined with the OPEC cartel and the oligopolistic
nature of the industry, is probably the most important. Any of the
constraints mentioned here could be shown on a price mechanism
diagram.

Tutor's comments

This student has shown a general awareness that both economic and political facts influence the strategies of oil companies. He might have pointed out that such strategies must not be solely reactive to events. They must take a long term view about fuel needs and by-product needs from oil on a global level, over long periods of years. The rate at which they pursue development of new oil sources may be slowed down by recession but exploration must be ongoing.

It was sensible to use simple supply and demand diagrams to illustrate the points made, but he might have illustrated supply side effects on the diagram as well as demand side effects.

He has raised the main points, without developing them as far as he might. He could for instance have said more about the effects of random shocks such as regional wars (e.g. Gulf War) or the impact of environmental pressure groups. Other political influences might be raised, e.g. the attitudes of Third World countries to oil multinationals.

This is a slightly simplistic answer, but would probably be worth a 'C' grade.

OUTLINE ANSWER

Question 3

a) The removal of exchange controls in 1979 and the 'corset' on bank lending in 1980, left government with few options in managing credit creation other than the combination of high interest rates and high exchange rates. The excessive growth of lending in the mid 1980s, based on the 'wealth effect' of economic recovery and the booming house market, brought renewed inflation and balance of payments deficit, leading to a regime of very high interest rates. This has produced a sharp squeeze on credit.

b) i) The car industry is faced by a sharp fall in demand (in the domestic market) caused by:
   a) the cost and unavailability of credit to private buyers, who are faced by a squeeze of disposable income as mortgage rates rise, and
   b) the retrenchment of spending on company car purchases, as the cost of borrowing for all firms rises and revenues decrease. The loss of sales revenue for car companies, in an industry where economies of large scale production are critical, causes a steep decline in profits, unless home sales can be replaced by exports.

   ii) The slow down in the housing market, as people abandon plans to trade up, might lead to an increase in DIY activity as householders pursue the alternative of improving their existing property. Thus a builders' merchant who primarily supplies DIY customers, trade or private, may find that demand increases, causing higher sales and profits. He may also be able to obtain better discounts from his suppliers as a result of a sharp fall in demand for building-related products from builders and property developers. Thus his margins and so net profit may improve. However, these effects may be offset by the squeeze on personal disposable income of householders, should the recession induced by the credit squeeze prove to be deep and prolonged. Since most builders' merchants supply both markets, it is difficult to generalise about the net effects.

   iii) An increase of credit restrictions, whether introduced by direct controls, or by increased interest rates (as the present government did between 1989–1991), will reduce the level of aggregate demand in the economy. Consumer spending will fall and this will hit the sales and profits of producers of consumer goods. They, in turn, will reduce their stocks of products and will reduce purchases of inputs, thus affecting sales of suppliers of components and other inputs. Investment plans will be revised downwards by all firms and thus sales of machine tools and other capital plant will fall. High interest rates will make mortgages more expensive and the general loss of confidence will reduce house sales. The construction industry will reduce housing starts and orders for office and factory accommodation will dry up. Related service sector industries, from architecture to accountants will record a fall in business. This overall decline in activity will have a more than proportionate effect through the 'multiplier effect' and unemployment will rise sharply, whilst inflation will fall and the trade balance will improve as imports are cut. The result may be a brief halt to growth, or a major recession depending on the severity of the measures taken.

OUTLINE ANSWER

Question 4

Once a company becomes aware that a period of prolonged (perhaps two years plus) unemployment (heavy implying perhaps in excess of 2m in the UK), it will need to review its plans. How sharp the change of direction will need to be depends on its degree of over-reaction to the preceding boom. If it has been cautious in its expansion plans and has accumulated a 'cash mountain', it may not only not be thrown off course, but have opportunities to profit from the distress of others in its industry sector. Similarly, if it is engaged largely in exporting to countries which are not hit by recession, as against domestic markets, it may have less need to change its plans. Any company will however need to review most aspects of its business.

Rising and high unemployment will inevitably be accompanied by a fall in demand within the economy, especially for consumer goods and leisure services. Potential falls in sales may require heavy discounting of existing prices to maintain sales. A review of marketing strategies may be required, e.g. targeting new and less affected markets, especially exports. Expenditure on new product development may have to be curtailed, products which' produce little revenue may have to be abandoned, as will activities peripheral to the core business.

The fall in sales revenue may cause a cash flow crisis, especially if the company is highly geared, or requires large amounts of overdraft finance for working capital. Default by customers and pressure to reduce trade credit from suppliers, may also adversely affect cash flow. In some cases this situation may lead to withdrawal of bank support and so bankruptcy may ensue. This may be avoided by the disposal of assets, e.g. non-core businesses, satellite plants, etc.

This latter response will probably require a review of staffing needs, leading to voluntary or compulsory redundancies at all levels in the company. Industrial relations problems may then ensue. However, should the company have anticipated the recession and responded appropriately in order to turn the threat into an opportunity, e.g. by successfully targeting export markets, it will be well placed to recruit labour at advantageous rates of pay. It may also be able to acquire assets (whether plant or other businesses) at a discounted price. This latter possibility of taking advantage of recession is clearly exemplified by the activities of companies such as Hanson plc.

FURTHER READING

Beardshaw, *Economics*, 2nd Edition, Pitman, 1989:
    Chapter 41, Direction of the economy and public finance;
    Chapter 42, The control of inflation;
    Chapter 43, The attainment of full employment;
    Chapter 45, Economic growth.
Buckley, *Structure of Business*, 2nd Edition, Pitman, 1990:
    Chapter 5, Economic Growth;
    Chapter 6, Inflation;
    Chapter 9, The problem of unemployment;
    Chapter 9, Public finance.

THE INTERNATIONAL ECONOMY AND BUSINESS

THE IMPORTANCE OF TRADE

THE BALANCE OF PAYMENTS

EXCHANGE RATES

GETTING STARTED

Since the 1970s the global business environment has become increasingly unstable. In the 1960s a business could assume stable inflation, fixed exchange rates and stable oil prices. It could also be assumed that the governments of the major industrial economies would successfully pursue counter-cyclical (Keynesian) macro economic policies, in the search for full and stable employment. Even technology was relatively stable, with the main technical changes involving the development of concepts discovered pre 1939. These comfortable conditions no longer exist, and business must be prepared to respond to constant changes and fluctuations in all these variables, as well as fast changing consumer tastes.

National economies can no longer be insulated from change elsewhere, and in this sense every business, however small, is operating in a global environment. It must be prepared for the sudden appearance of a new competing product or service, probably from another country, at any time. Even small firms are often thinking in terms of exporting their products.

It follows that business planning must take *international* factors into account. Thus senior managers must be aware of changes in the following variables:

- UK performance in the world economy, relative to that of other major trading nations.
- Major changes occurring in world markets.
- Major changes in key world economic variables, e.g. oil prices, exchange rates, etc.
- Nature and role of multinational firms, and their current strategies.
- Reasons for the success of some economies, e.g. Germany and Japan.
- Government economic policy on exchange rate and Balance of Payments issues.
- Developments in the European Community.

Any exam question which requires consideration of strategic issues for a firm must demonstrate an awareness of these issues.

ESSENTIAL PRINCIPLES

THE IMPORTANCE OF TRADE

❝National economies depend on trade.❞

The basic economic process is the allocation of scarce resources to different uses in order to satisfy wants and needs. Advances in technology and transport have made possible the use of more kinds of resources, from all parts of the world. It is no longer possible for an advanced economy to satisfy all its needs solely from the resources present within its own boundaries. The growth of advanced economies in this century has therefore been based on the exploitation of resources on a *global* scale, in other words on the process of international trade. All national economies are now dependent to a greater or lesser degree on trade.

FREE TRADE

This is a situation where the flow of exports and imports between countries is unhindered by any protectionist devices such as tariffs or quotas.

Free trade theory

International trade is based upon either absolute or comparative cost advantages in the production of a commodity, i.e. situations where a country is more efficient at producing a commodity than other countries (given the same amount of resources).

❝Absolute advantages.❞

If two countries are trading and each has an *absolute advantage* in different commodities, then total world output can be increased where each country *specialises* in the production of those commodities in which it has an absolute advantage. For example, suppose France and the UK, using the same resources, can produce the following units of each commodity:

	FRANCE	UK
Food	6	4
Machinery	4	8

❝Self-sufficient solution.❞

Without trade and specialisation, and assuming each country devotes half its resources to each product, total production is as follows. We can call this the 'self-sufficient' solution.

	FRANCE	UK	TOTAL PRODUCTION (UNITS)
Food	3	2	5
Machinery	2	4	6

Conversely if trade takes place with each country *specialising* on that product in which it has an absolute advantage, total production is:

	FRANCE	UK	TOTAL PRODUCTION (UNITS)
Food	6	-	6
Machinery	-	8	8

❝Benefits from specialisation and trade.❞

Through trade, each country can benefit from such specialisation. For example, if we assume a trading ratio of 1:1 then the final position could be as follows:

	FRANCE	UK	TOTAL PRODUCTION (UNITS)
Food	3 (6–3)	3	6
Machinery	3	5 (8–3)	8

❝Comparative advantage.❞

Clearly, each country is in an improved position as compared to the 'self-sufficient' solution presented previously.

Where a country has an absolute advantage in the production of *both* products, trade can still be beneficial as long as each country has a *comparative* advantage – that is a lower domestic opportunity cost ratio than its competitor.

Take the following example, again assuming that each country uses the same resources and devotes them entirely to each respective product:

	FRANCE	UK
Food	6	4
Machinery	8	4

France has an *absolute advantage* in *both* goods, in that it can produce more food *and* machinery than the UK using the same resources. Yet it has a *comparative advantage* in machinery, in that its absolute cost advantage is *greatest* in that particular good. Similarly the UK has a *comparative advantage* in food production, in that its absolute cost disadvantage is *least* in that particular good.

We can use the idea of 'opportunity cost' (what is given up) in order to identify comparative cost advantages. A country is said to have a comparative advantage in the good for which it has a *lower opportunity cost ratio* than its competitor.

In our example, the opportunity cost of 1 unit of *food* for France is $1\frac{1}{3}$ ($\frac{8}{6}$) units of machinery; whereas for the UK the opportunity cost of 1 unit of food is lower, namely 1 unit ($\frac{1}{1}$) of machinery. The UK has the lower opportunity cost, and therefore the *comparative advantage*, in food production. Conversely, you should be able to work out that France has the lower opportunity cost (and therefore comparative advantage) in the production of machinery ($\frac{6}{8}$ units food $< \frac{4}{4}$ units food).

We now need to show that specialisation according to comparative advantages can benefit both countries. Let us draw up an opportunity cost table.

	FRANCE	UK
opportunity cost of 1 extra food	$\frac{8}{6}$ machine	1 machine
opportunity cost of 1 extra machine	$\frac{6}{8}$ food	1 food

Specialisation according to comparative advantages could give the following, with France producing more machinery (less food) and the UK less machinery (more food):

FRANCE   1 extra machine   LOSS $\frac{6}{8}$ food
UK   1 less machine   GAIN 1 food

So machinery production is unchanged, food production is higher as a result of specialising according to comparative advantages.

By specialisation and trade each country does better than if it were self sufficient. Total production in the system is also greater than if each country sought to be self-sufficient.

The lesson here is a very important one. Even if a country is *absolutely* more efficient (or inefficient) in every commodity than another country, both countries can still benefit from specialisation according to comparative advantages and trade with each other.

In other words, provided opportunity costs differ between trading partners, there are potential benefits from specialisation and trade. Even in the unlikely event of two countries having the same opportunity cost structure, trade may still be advantageous where specialisation leads to economies of scale and falling prices.

Comparative advantages as the basis for trade.

Benefits of trade

International trade has the effect of enabling countries to consume some goods and services more cheaply by importing them, as well as gaining access to some products which would otherwise be unavailable. It also has the effect of encouraging the reallocation of resources away from activities best served by imports into activities where the country has itself achieved a comparative cost advantage.

The idea of comparative and absolute advantages as a basis for trade is a dynamic concept and one which may change over time in response to a number of influences:

- Government-induced programmes of structural change, leading to redeployment of resources away from, say, primary production (of perhaps a single crop such as coffee) and towards industrialisation (perhaps car assembly). Such a change of emphasis can help to generate faster growth in developing countries, greater employment and higher standards of living. However, it can also distort existing absolute and comparative advantages between countries.

- International flows of capital and transfers of technology take place, often as a result of the activities of multinational companies. Growth has been induced by such activities in countries as diverse as Malaysia, a developing economy, and Spain, a developed industrial economy. Again, these flows of capital and transfers of technology can change the existing patterns of absolute and comparative advantages between countries and thereby affect the basis for specialisation and trade.

> Patterns of trade vary over time.

The benefits of world trade are optimised in conditions of Free Trade, where no artificial barriers to the flow of goods, services, labour or capital occur. Completely free trade conditions have never existed, but since 1945, as a result of the work of the General Agreement on Tariffs and Trade (GATT), relatively free conditions have existed, resulting in the rapid growth of trade and of world GDP. The pattern of trade flows between nations in terms of geographical direction, and types of product traded, change over time, as does the degree to which obstructions to free trade are imposed. Thus the UK throughout the 19th century and up to about 1950, exported basic industrial products (steel, machinery, coal, etc.) to, for the most part, countries within the Empire, whilst our imports were largely of food and raw materials. Since 1950 we have moved to a position where over 50% of our trade is now with Europe. The emphasis has also swung away from manufactured exports to oil and service sector products such as financial services. These changes are vital to the understanding of our current economic and political relationships and the environment in which businesses in the UK must operate.

> Changes in the pattern of UK trade.

General Agreement on Tariffs and Trade (GATT)

The General Agreement on Tariffs and Trade was a system set up in 1948 to promote international trade by the systematic removal over time of tariff barriers. Since 1947, eleven rounds of negotiations have taken place and have greatly reduced tariffs, especially on manufactured goods. The current 'Uruguay Round' of talks is especially concerned with the liberalisation of trade in services and with reductions in systems of agricultural subsidy and tariffs (e.g. Common Agricultural Policy (CAP)). Recent difficulties in the final stages of negotiation of the 'Uruguay Round' of GATT, have been resolved. The problem has been the incorporation of trade in agricultural products, which has led to serious disagreement between USA and EC over the subsidisation of agriculture in EC through CAP.

> Freeing trade.

Together with the work of the International Monetary Fund (which enables short term trade deficits to be financed) and the establishment of various free trade 'blocs' such as the EC, GATT has played an important part in the record expansion in world trade over the post-war period.

PROTECTIONISM

This idea refers to the measures taken by a country to protect key industries from competition by imports from countries with a cost advantage. It is undertaken particularly when such industries are seen as having key strategic or political significance. Such significance may be military or in terms of employment. It will also be undertaken when a country feels that its competitors are penetrating its markets by 'unfair' means. One example is 'dumping' products at below cost in order to earn hard currency. It is also often undertaken in order to protect 'infant' industries. These are industries which are perhaps newly developed and unable to compete on equal terms in world trade due to a lack of economies of scale. Third world countries are particularly prone to this in the process of seeking to induce growth by industrialisation. India has been a case in point. Conversely mature economies may seek to protect old and inefficient industries either for strategic reasons, or to lessen the pains of structural change involved in running them down; European textile industries are a case in point.

> Why protect industry?

Types of protectionist measures

Protection takes a number of forms. The most obvious, or 'overt', is the use of *tariffs* on imports (taxes imposed either generally, or on particular industries) and *quotas* (quantity restrictions imposed on specific products). In manufacturing industries these are less easy to use as a result of GATT agreements and they have been largely replaced by 'covert' measures which are not covered by GATT. Such measures include the use of direct government subsidies to industries (favoured by France), government procurement

> Covert protection is practiced widely.

policies favouring domestic suppliers (often used in the case of military equipment), and voluntary export restraint agreements (VERs). The latter is an agreement between two countries to limit the import of a specific product to an agreed percentage of the market. Japan has made a number of such agreements with advanced economies on the import of cars. Thus Japanese car imports to the UK are at present limited to 11% of the previous year's total UK car sales.

Protectionism is motivated by self interest, and is damaging to trading partners, leading to successive retaliatory measures. If continued, these could stifle world trade and economic growth. Protectionism can have the effect of reducing economic welfare by denying access to cheaper and more varied products. The current recession and the possible failure of the GATT round, threaten the acceleration of a return to large hostile trading blocs (based on USA, EC and Japan) on the lines of those which were so damaging in the 1930s. The protection of inefficient industries and the resulting hinderance to dynamic structural changes in economies, can damage the consumer and penalise the successful entrepreneur.

THE EUROPEAN COMMUNITY (EC)

> Since the Treaty of Maastricht (1993), the European Community has been renamed the European Union.

Formerly known as the European Economic Community, it was established by the Treaty of Rome in 1958 with six member states. It has since expanded to 16, with the UK joining in 1973. Current membership is: Norway, Sweden, Finland, Austria (most recently joined), Greece, Spain Portugal, France, Italy, Germany, Netherlands, Belgium, Luxembourg, UK, Denmark, Eire.

> An expanding European market place.

The purpose of the EC is to form a common market between members that is unrestricted by tariff barriers. A common external tariff against non-members was imposed, which is now much resented by them, although it has been systematically reduced under GATT. The European Free Trade Association states have tariff-free access to the market.

The activities of the EC

> CAP is a form of protectionism.

Through its political and administrative institutions, the EC carries out a number of important economic activities which affect business. The two most important are the Common Agricultural Policy (CAP) and the Regional Fund. The price support system used by CAP has resulted in the generation of vast surpluses of food products, especially grain and dairy produce. This is a maldistribution of resources, and costs the average householder some £14 per week in higher food prices than those which world prices dictate. The practice of periodically dumping these products on world markets at less than world prices is very damaging for other primary producers, especially in the Third World. CAP is the main reason for the problems encountered in the Uruguay Round of GATT talks and could potentially accelerate a return to protectionism on a world scale. However, the reform of CAP, if undertaken rapidly, would have a major impact upon agriculture and agri-business in Europe.

The Regional Fund, also recently under reform, is intended to ease the regional unemployment and development problems of peripheral areas of Europe. Knowledge of its provisions would be useful to a businessman seeking to relocate his activities to take advantage of other changes going on currently in Europe. This is because the Regional Fund makes available a variety of financial inducements for relocating in peripheral regions,

The Single Market 1992

> Removing further barriers.

This is perhaps the most important single development in recent years for UK-based businesses. The Single Market Act of 1986 provided for the removal by 1992 of the remaining barriers to trade between members. In particular it sought to:

- remove administrative barriers to trade (border crossing formalities etc)
- establish common technical standards
- ensure free movement of labour
- remove remaining exchange controls restricting the flow of capital

- recognise professional qualifications gained in one country in all member countries
- eliminate price fixing, market sharing cartels and abuse of market position.

These measures will have major implications for all UK businesses. There is also a possibility that a Social Charter will be imposed on members. This seems likely to contain provisions on safety at work, working hours, overtime and a minimum wage, all of which would also have major implications for UK businesses. The key questions which a firm must answer are set out in Table 5.1.

MARKETING	Different customer requirements in EC countries.
	Market research essential.
	Re-examine product life cycle and product mix.
	Use agents, or establish a European base?
TECHNICAL STANDARDS	Ensure product meets EC standards.
	Re-design if necessary.
	Make sure you have IS 9000 Quality standard.
LOCATION	Is your current location logical for EC delivery?
	Examine your distribution arrangements and costs.
	Needs an EC distribution depot?
	Need to locate all/part of production facility in EC?
	If so, what funds available from Regional Development Fund?
TRAINING	Is your workforce sufficiently skilled?
	Have you enough linguists on board?
	Will you lose skilled or graduate workers to EC?
	If so, what inducements needed to keep them?
	Should you recruit workers in EC?
COMPETITION	Who are your competitors in/from EC?
	What are they doing differently from you, or better?
	What is their market place in relation to yours?
LABOUR SUPPLY	How will the 'demographic time bomb' affect you?
	Can you get the people you need?
	If so where, and how?
	Can you keep them on realistic wages?
	How would the Social Charter affect you?

Table 5.1 The Single Market 1992 and the Firm

THE BALANCE OF PAYMENTS

 A definition.

This is the financial record of trade and capital flows between the UK and the rest of the world over a period of time. It is divided into Current and Capital Accounts. The *Current Account* is a summary of trade transactions with other countries in goods (visibles) and services (invisibles). The *Capital Account* records all transactions in assets, real or financial. Movements of official reserves and other official currency flows are the total of *Official Financing*, which is required after the summation of the current and capital accounts. The *Balancing Item*, which is now often very large indeed, reflects unrecorded transactions. Since this may amount to a sum close to the final residual deficit or surplus, it throws some suspicion on the account as a true record of trading activities. This causes problems for governments which have in the past been bound to regard equilibrium on the current account as a major priority of economic policy.

Surpluses may cause problems.

A balance of payments *surplus* is effectively an injection of money into the economy. At low levels of economic activity it leads to an increase in economic activity and employment. This is sometimes termed 'export-led growth'. Nearer full employment, a balance of payments surplus can, however, lead to demand pull inflation.

A balance of payments *deficit* is a withdrawal of money from the economy. It leads to a reduction in economic activity and employment and also the weakening of the currency,

A balance of payments deficit cannot be sustained indefinitely. In the short term it will be financed by running down reserves or borrowing from abroad. But persistent deficits will soon exhaust these resources and other measures will have to be considered.

REMEDIES FOR BALANCE OF PAYMENTS PROBLEMS

The ultimate constraint on any government is the need to manage the current account in such a way as to achieve equilibrium over the long term. To do so countries have traditionally used a number of measures (though some may now be ruled out as a result of trading agreements).

Deflation

This is a term given to those monetary and fiscal measures designed to reduce the level of demand within the economy. Monetary measures would include the restriction of bank credit, the control of government borrowing and the raising of interest rates. Higher taxes and lower government spending are examples of fiscal measures. These measures not only have the impact of reducing a current account deficit on the balance of payments, but also of reducing investment and economic growth and increasing unemployment in the domestic economy.

Devaluation or depreciation

Devaluation is a measure where the fixed price value of the domestic currency is reduced against other currencies. For example in 1967 the UK devalued its currency, reducing the sterling–dollar exchange rate from £1 = $2.80 to £1 = $2.40. The aim of devaluation is to:

- discourage imports by making them more expensive;
- encourage exports by making them cheaper.

Of course today the UK is a member of the Exchange Rate Mechanism (ERM), where the pound 'floats' within specified limits. It is important to remember that a fall in the exchange rate under this system is called a *depreciation*, if the fall occurs *within* the specified limits. However, if the government formally applies to *lower* the whole exchange rate band within which sterling operates, then the term *devaluation* is often applied. Of course the effects on export and import prices of a fall in the exchange rate are the same, whether via depreciation or devaluation, as we can see from Table 5.2

	EXCHANGE RATE	PRICE
EXPORTS £500	£1 = $2	$1000
	£1 = $1	$500
IMPORTS $500	£1 = $2	£250
	£1 = $1	£500

Table 5.2 The impact of a fall in the exchange rate from £1 = $2 to £1 = $1

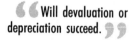

"Will devaluation or depreciation succeed."

Devaluation or depreciation is not always successful though. For example, imports may include items we cannot do without, in which case depreciation merely forces us to pay a higher price for these essential items. Conversely, although exports are now cheaper we will have to sell a lot more in order to obtain the same amount of revenue. Whether or not that will happen depends upon the price elasticity of demand for products entering international trade.

Other measures

We have already noted certain other protectionist measures which may be used to reduce a current account deficit, e.g. tariffs, quotas, VERs (see page 57). Governments have also tried to make it more difficult for capital to leave the country or have encouraged exports by generous credit facilities.

EXCHANGE RATES

This is the rate at which one country's currency is exchanged for another. It is clearly of great practical importance to all businesses, but especially to those dependent upon exports or using imported inputs. Movements in the exchange rate may wipe out profit margins, even where a firm has sought to anticipate or limit such fluctuations by using the forward markets.

There are several kinds of exchange rate systems but we will consider two broad types, floating exchange rates and fixed exchange rates.

FLOATING EXCHANGE RATES

> *The price mechanism at work.*

Since 1973 many countries have experimented with *floating exchange rates*. Under this system it is the interaction of supply and demand for currencies which determines the exchange rate. Thus demand for sterling arises from people and organisations in other countries wishing to purchase UK goods. The supply of sterling on the foreign exchange market reflects the desire of UK nationals and organisations to exchange sterling in order to purchase overseas goods.

Figure 5.1 shows how the rate of exchange is determined in a free market.

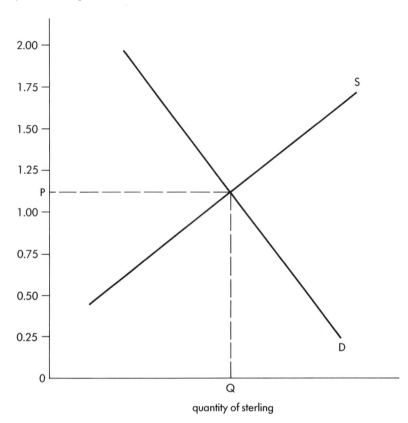

Fig. 5.1 Supply and demand determine the free market rate of exchange

Factors influencing floating exchange rates

The price of any currency is determined primarily by the volume and value of goods entering international trade. Government action may also influence the level of the exchange rate. For example the government may utilise foreign reserves to prop up or reduce the exchange rate. (Selling foreign currencies and demanding sterling will shift the demand curve for sterling to the right and therefore increase the 'price', i.e. the sterling exchange rate. Conversely selling sterling will shift the supply curve to the right and lower the sterling exchange rate.) This action might be taken to counter fluctuations in the market rate caused by unusual trading transactions of a very large value. Such intervention is more likely when the exchange rate is moving in a direction *opposite* to that desired by the government.

Government changes in interest rates are also important because they affect short term capital movements and therefore the supply and demand schedules. Market sentiment and rumours may also influence capital flows. For example, if the market believes the present sterling exchange rate is unsustainable in the long term or that a devaluation within the ERM is imminent, traders will sell sterling in order to limit their potential losses. This would shift the supply curve of sterling (S) to the right in Fig. 5.1, causing a fall in the exchange rate below OP.

An assessment of floating exchange rates

Benefits

■ With floating exchange rates, currency fluctuations take the place of balance of payment problems. In Fig. 5.2 below, we start by assuming that relative inflation rates are higher in the UK. As a result the UK is less competitive than before and suffers a balance of payments *deficit*. As imports increase and exports decrease, the supply of sterling increases (shifts to the right) and the demand for sterling decreases (shifts to the left). Thus the value of sterling falls, raising the price of imports and reducing the price of exports. The fall will continue until the value of imports and exports is once again the same.

■ Because balance of payment problems are corrected *automatically* in this way, this allows a government to pursue those domestic policies which they believe are most appropriate for employment and economic growth. Remember, with a fixed exchange rate a balance of payments deficit would force a government to adopt deflationary policies to cut imports. This would raise unemployment and reduce economic growth.

■ Floating exchange rates allow for a *gradual* reduction in the value of a currency, thus avoiding the massive speculation against an imminent change which may occur under fixed rates. Governments under fixed rate systems have sometimes been forced to devalue as a result of large scale speculation, even where there was little underlying weakness in the currency.

> **An automatic adjustment to balance of payments problems.**

> **Domestic policy unhampered.**

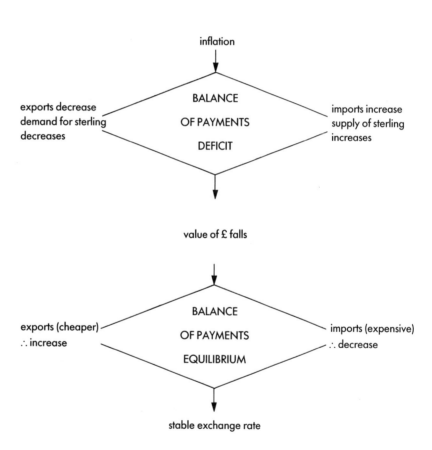

Fig. 5.2 The process of balance of payments adjustment under floating exchange rates

Problems

■ The development of international trade may be retarded by fluctuations in exchange rates. Even small changes may turn a profit on export into a loss.

■ Long term international capital investments may also be deterred by uncertainties over the future levels of exchange rates.

■ Speculation on exchange rate movements may rise, not fall, due to the volatility of currencies. Although speculators may now 'lose' if they guess a future change in the exchange rate wrongly, there will also be more changes and so more opportunities for 'gains' should they guess correctly. For instance, opportunities will occur for a speculator to buy a currency when it is lowly priced and sell it later at a higher rate. [NB. The activities of such speculators can actually help to stabilise the market.]

■ Fluctuations in exchange rates may occur for reasons other than the flow of goods in international trade; for example, due to large capital movements.

> **Speculation may stabilise exchange rates.**

FIXED EXCHANGE RATES

From 1944 to 1972 exchange rates between major currencies were *fixed* under the Bretton Woods agreement. Under this system governments stipulated the rates at which they would exchange currencies. For example, the rate between sterling and the dollar was set at £1 = $2.40, although this rate was allowed to fluctuate within narrow bands (see Fig. 5.3).

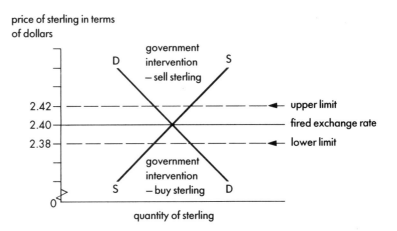

Fig. 5.3 Stabilisation of fixed exchange rates through government intervention

Should the UK demand for imports increase, causing fluctuations *outside* the permissable band, the authorities would be forced to purchase the excess supply of sterling (using their reserves of dollars) in order to maintain the fixed rate. In terms of Fig. 5.3, a shift to the right of the supply curve of sterling, S, may need to be offset by a shift to the right of the demand curve for sterling, D, in order to preserve the lower limit. Indeed, it does not matter what causes the fluctuation in the fixed exchange rate, the authorities are committed to action which offsets that fluctuation should the upper or lower limits to the exchange rate be under threat.

> Constant intervention required.

Fixed exchange rates produced a stable environment for trade which was seen as advantageous by many businesses, and produced a long period of rapid trade growth.

THE RETURN TO FIXED RATES

> EMS – back to fixed rates!

In 1979 the EC member countries agreed to establish a European Monetary System, which was to be the vehicle for the achievement of eventual monetary union and a single currency. Such a union would only be possible if inflation rates and levels of economic activity across Europe could be made to converge. The key to this convergence was thought to be the creation of an *Exchange Rate Mechanism*, within which exchange rates between member countries would be fixed, and able to fluctuate only within a range of 2½% of the agreed position. Structural divergence of a member from the wider development in Europe would mean that that government would have to take whatever inflationary or deflationary measures were required (with attendant levels of unemployment) to keep the currency within its bands. This meant, in effect, tying all European economies to the lowest inflation, most efficient, economy (viz Germany) whatever the costs in domestic terms. Eventually, the UK joined in October 1990. The rate was fixed to DM 2.95, but with a wider 6% band. Proponents argued that joining would:

- provide a more stable exchange rate and thus encourage international trade. Remember – a sudden rise in the previously floating sterling exchange rate would have made UK exporters uncompetitive.

- allow the UK to reduce interest rates. It was argued that relative UK interest rates were higher because of the need to compensate holders of sterling for taking the risk of currency depreciation due to a poor current account position.

- prevent inflation as a result of a rapid fall in the sterling exchange rate. It was also argued that the discipline of fixed exchange rates would force the UK authorities to take whatever measures were necessary to reduce inflation to that of our major competitors. The alternative would be to devalue.

The major argument put forward for not joining was that it limited the Government's freedom of action in deciding what was best for the economy. Thus the Government would not be able to use interest rates or money supply instruments insofar as these measures were incompatible with maintaining a fixed exchange rate; nor could the exchange rate itself be used as an instrument of economic policy.

...And back to Floating rates again.

The global recession, combined with the impact on Germany's inflation rate and the reabsorption of East Germany, produced enormous strains on the ERM mechanism. German interest rates remained very high, making the DM too strong. This led to continued high interest rates in the UK and an intensification of the recession. The pressures on the £ downward were very great, leading to the need for central bank intervention in support of the £. By early September 1992, the £ was a one way bet downward, and vast speculative pressures developed. After both Italy and Spain were forced into devaluation within the ERM, the strains on the £ became too much, and the Government was obliged on September 16th to withdraw from the ERM, causing over the next few days a 15% devaluation of the £. This enabled the Bank of England to reduce Base Rates over the next few weeks to 7%. The combined effect of the devaluation and the drop in interest rates was the equivalent to a fall of 6% in interest rates. This should provide the conditions for a recovery of export-led growth provided that the recession in Europe does not deepen further. Unfortunately domestic confidence is low as unemployment continues to rise. Export-led growth was better than expected at 2.5% in 1993. However, prospects for 1994 are of restricted growth due to the effect on fragile consumer confidence of major taxation increases.

EXAMINATION QUESTIONS

1   Read the article and answer the questions which follow.

TOURISM PERFORMANCE IN 1986

%
20 OVERSEAS VISITS 1986
% change over same month previous year

The United Kingdom attracts visitors from all over the world. Last year 13.8 million came, 60% from Western Europe, 21% from North America and the rest mainly from the Far East and Australia. Visits from Western Europe increased by 5% over 1985 whilst due to well published but essentially short-term fears those from North America fell by 24%, with the drop largely
5   concentrated during the summer months. But our broad market base meant that overall, visits fell by only 4%, and the picture on spending was even more encouraging. Many of our European competitors fared worse. Recent trends indicate continued long-term growth.
   After the sharp fall in numbers of overseas visitors early in the year, there was a strong recovery in the last quarter making 1986 the second highest year on record. December visits from North
10   America were 10% above 1985 – which, together with the high level of forward bookings, promises well for 1987.

Source: "A Bumper Year for Tourism", *Action for Jobs*, Department of Employment, 1987

   a) Explain why the data in the diagram on "Overseas Visits 1986" is presented in two different ways.   *(2)*

   b) Explain why a "high level of forward bookings" (lines 10–11) would benefit businesses involved in tourism.   *(2)*

   c) Within which category would earnings from foreign tourism appear in the Balance of Payments Current Account?   *(2)*

   d) State and explain **three** positive effects that "continued long-term growth" (line 7) in overseas visitors is likely to have on United Kingdom industry.   *(9)*

   e) Explain how a rise in the value of the £, via its effects on foreign tourists in the United Kingdom and United Kingdom tourists abroad, would affect the tourist industry in the United Kingdom.   *(10)*

(AEB 1989)

2   One consequence of Britain and America's international trade problem has been renewed calls for a degree of protection. Assess the arguments for and against protection.
   (London Overseas 1991)

3 'Most internationally traded products compete more on quality than price.'

'Exchange rates fluctuations are relevant only in that they alter individual importer's and exporter's profit margins.'

Comment on these statements and explain the relationship between exchange rates and profit margins. (*25*)

(AEB 1987)

4 a) A UK-based manufacturer of paper tissue has launched a new range of paper towels.

What factors might influence the company's choice of distribution channel? (*10*)

b) Discuss the likely implications for such a firm of a fall in the effective exchange rate of the £ sterling. (*15*)

(Cambridge 1989)

TUTOR'S ANSWER

Question 1

a) The data is presented in two ways, a *bar chart*, indicating the % change in the number of overseas visits in each month against the same month in the previous year. This may allow factors specific to the same month in each year to be picked out for comment. The *linegraph* is intended to demonstrate a broad trend in more general terms.

b) A high level of forward bookings is helpful for the hotel industry, in order to permit forward planning. A hotel knows that it must achieve 66% occupancy in order to break even. If there is doubt that this can be achieved on the basis of known forward bookings, it can at least adjust its staffing, much of which is of a casual and part-time nature. It may also be able to adjust its forward ordering of stocks of drink, etc. High levels of forward bookings, together with the trend to increasing numbers of visits from overseas, suggest that in 1987 hotels may be able to anticipate occupancy rates well in excess of 66% and thus may expect improved profitability in 1987.

c) Earnings from foreign tourism would appear in the Invisibles sector of the Current Account of the Balance of Payments as an invisible export, i.e. a positive item.

d) Three positive effects on UK industry of 'continued long term growth' of overseas visits might be:

1 Higher levels of occupancy in the hotel industry, leading to higher profitability.

2 This profitability in the hotel business will probably lead to higher levels of development of new capacity in the industry, leading to greater activity and profitability in the construction industry.

3 Industries which supply the tourist trade will experience high levels of activity, and profitability. For example, stately homes, coach companies, air lines, manufacturers of souvenirs etc, brewers, food suppliers and processors. There will be a general positive multiplier effect on activity in the UK leading to higher levels of employment and output, and increased economic growth.

e) If the £ rises in value on the foreign exchanges, the tourist industry will be affected in various ways. Incoming tourists will need to spend more of their own currency in order to purchase £s to spend in the UK. Thus the price of accommodation, travel, etc will rise. The consequence might be either less foreign tourists, or the same number of foreign tourists, each spending less. Either way there would probably be a fall in revenue from tourism, which would have adverse effects on the current account balance.

UK citizens taking holidays abroad, or considering doing so, would find that the £ would buy more foreign currency, enabling either more people to afford foreign holidays, or the same number purchase more upmarket or longer foreign holidays. This response would again have an adverse impact on the current account, since expenditure on tourism will probably increase.

The degree of these responses will depend on the price elasticity of demand of foreign citizens for holidays here, and for the demand of UK citizens for holidays abroad.

STUDENT'S ANSWER

Question 2

> Some good examples here, but under-plays the importance of covert measures.

> You should also discuss the nature of the UK/USA balance of payments problems.

> Is this of major importance.

> For maximum impact it is better to have one point to a paragraph.

> Explain!

> This should be developed.

Protectionism is where the individual governments set import restrictions and barriers for imports from other countries in order to protect local industry, consumers etc. These protectionist measures could take the form of import duties and taxes where a certain proportion of the value of the product is paid to the government as taxes. In addition they could include quotas, where the amount which could be imported is restricted, or a total ban of importation of those products. Protectionist measures could also include lengthy import documentation and regulation or exchange controls where foreign currency trading is controlled. There could be several advantages and disadvantages of Protectionism as a policy.

There are several arguments in favour of the policy. Firstly it will reduce imports, thus promoting local industry who are producing the same product. This will ensure and create job employment for the population who will then be better off. If price controls are used, it will increase the price of imports, therefore reducing their competitiveness with local products. By creating jobs it will increase the standard of living for the general population. Secondly, by having import duties and taxes, it will provide revenue for the Treasury and the government. This money can be used for development purposes and improving the economy and the welfare of its citizens. Thirdly, it would reduce foreign exchange spending therefore increasing foreign exchange reserves and making the currency more stable and stronger. Fourthly, it may protect infant industries who would otherwise be unable to survive. A greater demand for local products would also help local industries achieve economies of scale and therefore extra benefits.

On the other hand a protectionist policy may have its disadvantages. Since local companies are protected, they may become inefficient. This is because it would be alright if their costs increased as they are still protected. Secondly, the local company may start to exploit the consumers by raising prices since the prices of imported goods may be much higher because of import duties and taxes. This would cause an inflation spiral in the economy. Thirdly, the country who was previously exporting to the country in concern may take retaliatory measures by also being protectionist. This will mean, the exports of the country who first introduced protectionist measures may end up losing demand and therefore causing unemployment etc in its own country. Lastly the reduction in imported goods would deprive the local residents of the right to enjoy a possible better standard of living or variety of goods to purchase since they can no longer buy the imported ones.

Thus protectionist measures may have their advantages but may also cause severe harm to the economy and country.

Tutor's comments

He has indicated in the introduction some of the principal methods of protection, but ought also to have mentioned 'covert' protection through government procurement policies, Voluntary Export Restraint Agreements etc. He might also have indicated that there exist some protectionist regimes instituted by international agreement, such as the European Community's Common Agricultural Policy, and the Multi-national Fibre Agreement.

He has not at any point referred to the comment in the question about UK and USA trade problems. He should have indicated briefly in para 2 what they are (unsustainable balance of payments deficit, due to inability to compete with imports from Europe and Japan). Examples from these two countries could then have been used to develop the argument in his essay.

His argument is quite well organised, and raises the key points for and against protection. He does not however complete his analysis by demonstrating the general arguments based on maximisation of economic welfare globally, through free trade. This would have enabled him to point to the possibility that the trade difficulties of UK and USA might lead to further consolidation of trade blocs, in Europe around Germany, in the Far East around Japan, and in the Americas around USA. This would diminish world economic growth and be disastrous for the Third World.

Overall not a bad answer under exam conditions, and worth perhaps a high C grade.

OUTLINE ANSWER

Question 3

Internationally traded products fall into three categories, primary (raw materials), semi manufactures and finished goods. It must be always true to some extent that competition is by price, but this is likely to be so most in the case of raw materials, e.g. wheat, where markets are nearer to the perfect competition (price taker) market form. In most other markets and some primary markets, quality is likely to play an increasingly important role. This is so for a number of reasons:

- as real income rises, consumers become more choosey
- as technology advances a greater variety of products and varieties within product ranges, is possible, and is required
- as markets become more global, customers have greater choice and knowledge of what is available
- improved production technology makes it economic to produce ever shorter runs of different forms of a basic product.

In this environment, firms must seek to add value through quality and variety if they are to survive. In order to do so they must demand from suppliers guaranteed quality, first time, every time. This is so as to implement Just in Time inventory management, which is essential to the new flexible and responsive production methods. The days of the Ford Model T – available in any colour you like so long as it is black – are over. In an unstable global economic environment, flexibility and quality are everything. The problem in the UK (until recently) has been that we produce too many simple products which still seek to compete largely on price, despite the disadvantage of much higher wage levels than Far Eastern industrial nations.

Where exchange rates between currencies are free to fluctuate according to market forces, or even where they are fixed, as in ERM, the rate may be more reflective of capital flows than trade flows, and of world perceptions of the condition of a national economy than the reality of relative prices. Thus at any given time a producer in the UK may be faced with an exchange rate for sterling which renders him uncompetitive on price in export markets (exchange rate too high), or in home markets (exchange rate too low). He may be able to eliminate this problem to some extent by using the forward exchange market, but he cannot altogether avoid its effects.

If he seeks to compete on price in a basic product market (e.g. cream cracker biscuits), even a slight adverse movement of the exchange rate may wipe out his profit margin, whereas if he is competing in a specialist market (e.g. speciality biscuits, packed in a tin decorated with pictures of UK castles), his margin may be sufficiently high for him to remain profitable. An economist would suggest that he should be more concerned with income elasticity of demand for his product than price elasticity. Even so, whilst quality and value added is the best strategy, a very sharp adverse exchange rate movement may endanger his existence if he is very dependent on that market, as Jaguar discovered in the USA in 1989.

OUTLINE ANSWER

Question 4

a) A distribution channel may be defined as 'a route used in the physical distribution of a product from the manufacturer/supplier to the ultimate buyer of the product'. The complete channel involves three functions in line: manufacturing > wholesalers > retailers > buyers (MWR). The three functions may be carried out by separate firms/organisations, or two or three may be carried out by one firm, as integrated functions. In the latter case transaction costs are reduced, better control and co-ordination of movement and more effective marketing might result. For example, a firm manufacturing cosmetics will improve cash flow margins by concentrating on direct mail order marketing rather than using a chain of wholesalers and retailers. Firms may additionally or alternatively use sales agents at some stage in the sequence to obtain business on commission-only basis. This is common amongst small firms and for export business.

The manufacture of paper tissues is a process where large economies of scale are involved, since it is a mass produced, low value added product. The retail outlets most appropriate for such a product are: (a) supermarket chains (b) stationery chains (c) small independent retailers. If the company has an established brand name e.g. 'Kleenex' for a higher quality product, it probably supplies (a) and (b) in bulk at discounted prices and (c) via wholesalers. Alternatively, if it has no strong brand name it may supply (a) and (b) on the basis of 'own brand' products and (c) via wholesalers specialising in supplying 'member' independents e.g. NISA (National Independent Supermarket Association.

b) The term 'effective exchange rate' is used to describe the value of a given currency against a 'basket' of other currencies on the basis of a weighted average. If the effective exchange rate falls, this implies an improvement in the price competitiveness of the country's goods and services in the other countries whose currencies are included in the basket. This statement may however be distorted by the effects of membership of ERM, where the £ is at a fixed rate against currencies of EC members, arguably at present at too high a rate. The fact that the dollar is free floating against the £, means that movements of the dollar up or down may counteract or reinforce the effects of the rate of the £ as an effective exchange rate. The consequent impact on the UK business will depend on whether its export business is primarily with the EC or with countries whose trade is priced in dollars. The reverse effect would be true with regard to the relative price competitiveness of imports into the UK.

If we assume that the manufacturer of paper towels sells largely in UK markets, then the effects would be as follows. Imported competing products would be relatively more expensive and our manufacturer would be able to increase market share by simple price competition rather than by adding value and creating a brand image. Perhaps more important would be the effects on the price of inputs of raw material – timber to make paper pulp. Much is probably imported. If it comes from North America, it will be cheaper. If it has to be imported from Europe, it will be dearer. The company may be able to change its sources in response to effective exchange rate changes, and so gain in either case.

FURTHER READING

Beardshaw, *Economics* 2nd Edition, Pitman, 1989:
   Chapter 37, The growth of international trade;
   Chapter 38, The balance of payments;
   Chapter 39, Exchange rates.
Buckley, *Structure of Business* 2nd Edition, Pitman, 1989:
   Chapter 8, International Trade
Begg Fisher Dornbusch, *Economics* 3rd Edition, McGraw Hill, 1991:
   Chapter 29, Open Economy Macroeconomics;
   Chapter 32, International Trade and Commercial Policy

THE POLITICAL, SOCIAL AND TECHNOLOGICAL ENVIRONMENT

THE POLITICAL ENVIRONMENT

CONSUMER PROTECTION

COMPETITION POLICY

REGIONAL POLICY

THE SOCIAL ENVIRONMENT

TECHNOLOGY

GETTING STARTED

We have already seen that organisations do not exist in a vacuum. Various aspects of the national and international economy impinge upon the activities of the firm, providing new market opportunities and also limitations upon their activities. The environment of business though is very much more complex than has been indicated so far. Quite apart from the *economic* influences on the activities of the business, we should also consider political, social and technological factors. This is the subject matter of this chapter.

An understanding of the environment of business is of practical importance to any business. History is full of examples of firms which failed to survey their environment and which, consequently, did not identify developing opportunities or constraints upon their action. The traditional Swiss watch industry is just one example. However, being *aware* of one's environment is insufficient; the successful business must *respond* to these changes by:

■ adjusting to the new environment, e.g. producing a new product or reducing pollution; or

■ changing the environment in favour of business. Thus falling sales may be reversed by advertising, or trade associations may press for a change in government policy.

ESSENTIAL PRINCIPLES

❝The level of government
intervention.❞

Attitudes of the government toward business have a direct impact upon business. In Britain, these attitudes have varied from antipathy to enthusiastic support. The UK as a *mixed* economy has seen marked variations in the level of government intervention into the affairs of business during the twentieth century. During the second world war the UK was one of the most highly planned economies the world had ever seen. Although the level of central planning was markedly reduced in post-war Britain, the period 1914–1979 was generally one of increasing government involvement in the affairs of business. Between 1979 and 1992 the Conservative government attempted to reverse the trend of 'creeping state socialism' by reductions in the number of quango's (quasi autonomous non-governmental organisations), privatisation and deregulation. Even so, the state still affects many aspects of business activity (see Fig. 6.1).

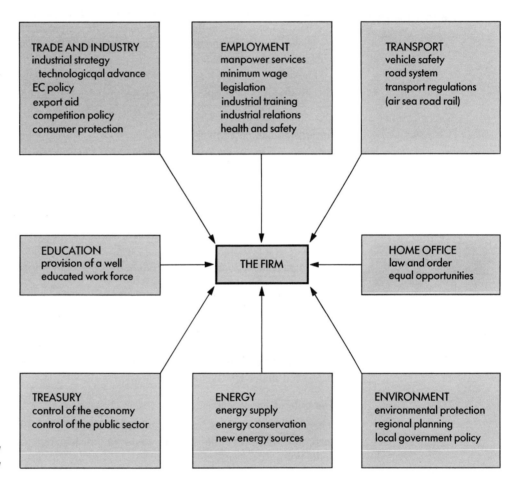

Fig. 6.1 How the firm is affected by
state activity

REASONS FOR STATE INTERVENTION

- Private industry is *unable to provide* certain essential community (or public) goods, e.g. defence, law and order

- It is not certain that *sufficient* of certain goods will be provided if left to the market, e.g. health service, education and training

- To control the level of economic activity

❝Why the state might
intervene?❞

- To ensure groups with little bargaining power are not exploited by organisations or other individuals

- The private profit motive does not always ensure the 'best' allocation of resources, e.g. text books vs pornographic magazines

- To control social costs arising from business activities; e.g. the costs of pollution, although largely caused by private industry, are borne by the public.

It is impossible to consider in detail all the different ways in which the state intervenes into business affairs. We will look at just three areas of government intervention which illustrate some of the points made above.

CONSUMER PROTECTION

Consumer unprotected.

Trading at the beginning of the century in the UK was best summarised by the legal maxim *caveat emptor* or 'let the buyer beware'. This indicated that buyers and sellers were of equal bargaining strength and entered into a purchase contract with full knowledge of the goods and conditions attached. The onus was on the *buyer* to ensure everything was satisfactory and functioning as claimed. This view left the consumer wide open to abuse, especially when products became more complicated and sophisticated and their operation extended well beyond the knowledge of the average buyer. The manufacturer or the retailer was therefore in a much stronger position to resist consumer complaints and possessed greater financial resources to fight any legal action brought by individual consumers.

The impact of pressure groups.

Today the consumer is in a much stronger position through the actions of *pressure* groups which have persuaded a succession of governments to enact legislation to redress the balance of power in the market place. The responsibility for the quality of the product or service is now placed firmly on the shoulders of the *supplier*, so much so that the maxim could be changed to *caveat vendor*.

The consumer is now protected in a series of ways, ranging from the initial advertising of the product, its description, the quality of the item and its purchase on credit. The major areas of protection and the appropriate legislation are as follows:

Advertising and description

The *Trades Descriptions Acts* of 1968 and 1972 make it a criminal offence for a trader to give a false or misleading description of the goods or services on offer. This includes claims about composition and performance of goods as well as the manner and timing of services. It also prohibits false statements about prices, particularly those claiming price reductions.

The Advertising Standards Authority seeks to enforce a code of advertising practice. It receives and investigates complaints from the general public and then negotiates with the firms concerned to alter or stop offensive or misleading adverts.

Quality and quantity of the item or service

Consumer protection.

The *Sale of Goods Act* 1979 protects the consumer by insisting that products are of 'merchantable quality' and fit for the purpose intended. Safety standards are further reinforced by the *Consumer Safety Act* of 1978 which governs the safety requirements of electrical items, toys and inflammable clothing. The quantity provided of a good is protected under the *Weights and Measures Act* of 1985.

The price of the product

The *Trade Descriptions Act* 1972 and the *Prices Act* 1974/1975 govern the display of prices, ensuring there are no hidden costs or misleading claims, particularly about price reductions.

Consumer credit

The *Consumer Credit Act* 1974 protects the consumer involved in credit agreements up to £15,000 in value. It ensures that credit can be provided only by licensed credit brokers and that the true cost of borrowing is displayed by publishing the Annual Percentage Rate (APR).

The consumer is further supported by the work of pressure groups and independent bodies such as the Consumers Association (publishers of the Which? magazine), Consumers Advice Centres and the Citizens Advice Bureaux. For claims under £500, the consumer can follow a simple small claims procedure through the County Court and avoid expensive legal costs.

COMPETITION POLICY

In the 18th century the renowned economist, Adam Smith, observed that:

> 'people of the same trade seldom meet together for fun and merriment, but the conversation ends in a conspiracy against the public, or in some contrivance to raise prices.' (The Wealth of Nations, 1776)

Adam Smith's concern that businesses would form agreements or associations that would be detrimental to consumers is still valid today. Since 1948 several pieces of legislation have been enacted by government in an attempt to keep the markets *competitive* and to prevent price-fixing or anti-competitive, practices. The main acts are detailed below:

1948 Monopolies and Restrictive Practices Act

- This established the Monopolies Commission with powers to investigate any accusations of unfair dealing, e.g. price or quota fixing.
- The Commission's report, if considered against the 'public interest', could be submitted to the government for action
- A monopoly was defined as a business or association which controlled a third or more of the market.
- The Commission worked slowly and only 17 reports were issued up to 1956. However, the Commission did highlight the extent of collective agreements and restrictive practices and the need for much tougher legislation.

1956 Restrictive Trade Practices Act

- This ensured that agreements concerning prices, output or conditions of sale had to be registered with the Director General of Fair Trading
- The onus was now on the business to prove that the restrictive practice was justified. The companies had to show that the agreement had one or more beneficial effects in the areas of employment, research, exports, physical injury, existing agreements in the public interest, or to counteract other restrictive groups or monopolies.
- Collective resale price maintenance was abolished, thus preventing the withholding of supplies by a group of manufacturers in an attempt to force retailers to maintain list prices.
- Many companies abandoned existing agreements rather than submit them to the Restrictive Practices Court and prove their acceptability.

1965 Monopolies and Mergers Act

Competition policy.

- This act expanded the powers of the Monopolies Commission to include the investigation of proposed mergers. As collusion between businesses had been made illegal by the 1948 Act, many companies began to undertake mergers in order to protect their retail outlets, sources of supply or to control their competitors. The proposed takeover by ICI of Courtaulds prompted the government to act.
- Any proposed merger which would result in control of a third of the market or involving assets taken over in excess of £5m could be referred to the Commission.
- The merger could be prevented, broken up or allowed to proceed but under imposed guidelines.

1973 Fair Trading Act

- In this Act, the definition of a monopoly for referral purposes was reduced from a third of the market to a quarter of the market.
- The Act established the role of the Director General of Fair Trading with the power to investigate commercial activities and refer suspect cases to the Monopolies and Mergers Commission (MMC).
- The Act made it possible to refer monopolies of a local nature, as well as those operating at the national level.
- National corporations and statutory bodies could also be referred for unfair trading practices.
- The 1973 Act represented a more open commitment by government in the virtues of competition.

1980 Competition Act

- This Act extended the powers of the Office of Fair Trading to include local authorities within the scope of their investigations as well as any trading activity which was felt to be unfair to the consumer.

- Anti-competitive practices with regard to prices of goods and the distribution of goods were also to be investigated. This included such practices as price discrimination, predatory pricing (selling below cost), tie-in sales, rental-only contracts and full-line forcing.

These five Acts have attempted to redress the balance of power between the consumer and the ever-more powerful supplier, in order to ensure that trading activities are carried out in the 'public's interests'.

REGIONAL POLICY

The regional problem.

In the early part of the 20th century, the UK economy had many localised industries, i.e. industries which dominated specific geographical areas. A decline in an industry would have adverse effects on the entire *region* and create structural unemployment, particularly if the decline was extensive and rapid. From the 1920s, staple industries such as ship-building, coal-mining, heavy engineering and textiles went into such a decline with dire effects for the respective regions. The 1934 *Special Areas Act* was the first of many legislative attempts to help alleviate the effects of industrial decline by offering incentives for new firms to establish themselves in the areas of high unemployment. From that date the government has tried a succession of measures to take 'work to the workers' or to take 'workers to the work'. However, the latter has proved particularly difficult as labour tends to be geographically immobile.

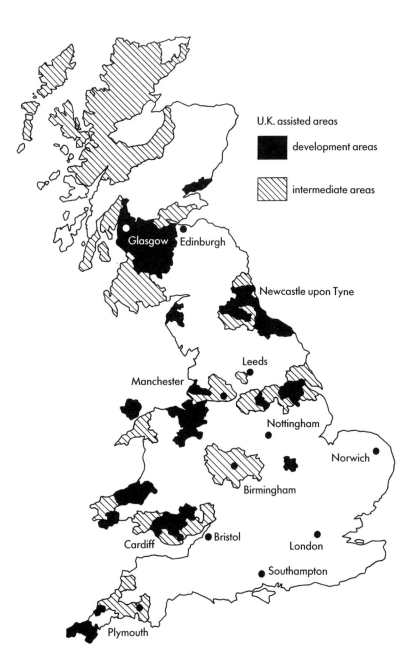

Fig. 6.2 The development and intermediate areas in the UK

In the 1970s, areas of unemployment and industrial decline were designated Special Development Areas (SDAs), Development Areas (DAs) or Intermediate Areas and were eligible for a variety of incentives such as:

- subsidies on employment
- tax relief on investment
- grants for new investment
- subsidised rent
- making development permission easier to obtain in the designated areas (Industrial Development Certificates)

The 'broad-brush' approach was significantly altered in 1984 when the current regional policy was introduced. The new system is based on more selective regional assistance. The areas eligible for help under the new scheme were substantially reduced and demarcated as either *Development Areas* or *Intermediate Areas* (see Fig. 6.2).

A range of incentives was made available which included:

- £3,000 for each new job created
- 15% of new investment expenditure
- Training grants
- Grants for projects which created or protected employment

The incentives were awarded on a selective and discretionary basis as the Department of Industry attempted to provide only the minimum of financial support in order to create employment.

Alongside this reduced and selectively targeted policy the government also created *Enterprise Zones*, particularly in the inner cities and areas containing derelict land and buildings. The Enterprise Zones encourage industrial development by offering tax incentives, reducing official 'red-tape' such as planning permission and the offer, in some cases, of subsidised premises. In addition to assistance from the UK government, areas may also be eligible for grants from the European Community, particularly for projects which aim to improve the infrastructure of the region.

Regional policy impact.

It is debatable whether regional policy has ever been a fully effective tool for curing structural unemployment, as the regions in decline in the 1930s still have the highest unemployment levels today. It is certain, however, that it was very costly, with over £20 billion being spent between 1963 and 1983 at a cost of £35,000 for each new job created. From the firm's point of view, government regional policy is one of the factors which it must consider when deciding on the location of its business.

THE SOCIAL ENVIRONMENT

Social attitudes provide a framework within which business operates. These attitudes may be reflected in law, e.g. consumer protection or in the customs of society, e.g. the role of women in society. These attitudes are not constant but will vary over time. Such changes in attitudes are important to the firm – they must 'move with the times' and may provide opportunities or constraints upon their activities. For example, attitudes to 'dirty work' in factories and engineering have caused firms to review their labour policy, attitudes towards smoking have forced tobacco companies to diversify, whilst attitudes towards the working class image of many public houses has forced breweries to change the traditional image of the 'pub'. Equally the decline in church membership and attitudes towards Sunday trading provide opportunities for retailers, whilst working wives provided a ready market for convenience foods and labour-saving gadgets.

PRESSURE GROUPS

A definition.

We are interested in *pressure groups* because they are one way in which individuals can make their feelings known to organisations and cause those organisations to change their behaviour. A pressure group may be defined as any group which seeks to influence government rather than taking over the formal powers of government themselves. Such groups, e.g. BMA, NFU, NUT, RAC, CBI, ASH are not *necessarily* organised in order to influence government, but as part of their activities may wish to bring certain matters to the attention of government. Pressure groups can be divided into two types.

Spokesman groups

These represent a recognisable section of society or interest in the community. For example:

Chambers of Commerce:	business
Automobile Association:	car users
Trades Union Congress:	unions
British Medical Association:	doctors

These groups are easily defined and located. Their potential membership can be calculated and they will be affected by socio-economic policy in the same way.

Cause groups

Such groups aim to promote a particular cause. Examples include Child Poverty Action Group, Age Concern, Campaign for Nuclear Disarmament, or the RSPCA. These groups have no clearly defined membership as compared to a spokesman group. Instead they attract their membership by agreement on a particular issue, e.g. war, abortion, smoking, pollution, censorship. Such groups are often short term coalitions of very diverse interests. Thus the anti-abortion movement receives support from Catholics, doctors, and women's rights groups. Once these groups have achieved their objective they will disband because they have little in common other than that specific issue.

The impact of pressure groups on business

Pressure groups may have an impact on business in several ways:

■ their aims may be adopted by a political party and eventually the law will be changed (probably constraining some business activity).

■ activities of the pressure group may unintentionally affect business activity. For example, demonstrations in a town centre may delay the delivery of supplies or reduce retail sales.

■ the activities of the pressure group may be directed specifically against a firm or industry. Thus student unions in many higher education establishments– in order to promote their anti-apartheid policy– took action against banks who maintained links with South Africa.

As a result of the activities of the pressure group, the firm or industry will have to:

■ change its actions, e.g. introduce more environmentally friendly production processes or improves product safety features.

■ incur costs in order to offset the impact of the pressure group's campaign. Such costs might include legal action or an advertising campaign to bolster the company image.

Factors affecting the success of pressure groups

Pressure group success may be affected in several ways:

> *It is interesting to compare public sympathy for coal miners when widescale pit closures were announced in 1992, with that at the time of the miners' strike in 1984/5.*

■ In trying to change the law, the relationship which a pressure group has with the government of the day is critical. You will find that some groups are very well integrated with the decision-making process. For example, the National Farmers Union (which is an employer's association) has, by law, to be consulted on agricultural price reviews. A lack of access through constitutional channels may cause a violent reaction on the part of the group.

■ In trying to influence public opinion resources – financial and personnel aspects are important. Money will be needed for advertisements and the printing of leaflets. Members will need to be mobilised for demonstrations. For pressure to be exerted effectively, 'organisation' will also be needed and some members will need to take on 'managerial' roles leading and motivating the membership.

■ The pressure group must be able to mobilise public sympathy. Thus, where a pressure group is seen as being at odds with mainstream societal attitudes its activities will gain little support. For example, in an area of high unemployment, pressure group action to close a local firm down for breach of pollution regulations will gain little public sympathy.

SOCIAL RESPONSIBILITY

There are two broad views of the position of a business in society. The *shareholder* view of business is that a firm is responsible to its shareholders: the primary purpose of business is to make profits for the shareholder. A more recent view, the *stakeholder* view says that not just shareholders but, for example, customers, employees, managers and the local community *all* have an interest in the firm and the firm owes a (social) responsibility to *all* the stakeholders.

Holders of the *shareholder view* argue that it is not the responsibility of business to be concerned about social issues. To do so would be to detract from their primary duty to society – that is the provision of goods and services in an economically efficient way. This primary duty to society is seen as entirely consistent with seeking to make profits for shareholders. Social responsibility is the domain of government and it is the government (through legislation) which should set the parameters within which business operates (paradoxically many holders of this view resent 'government interference' in the affairs of business).

Holders of the *stakeholder view* argue that firms should be more socially responsible because of the large amount of economic power they hold. Their decisions may have an impact upon jobs, consumer safety, pollution and even the propping up of unacceptable political regimes. In this situation it is felt that economic power brings with it an economic and social responsibility.

Two views.

Power brings responsibilities.

Areas of concern

Many firms now recognise the stakeholder view that business is not just about obtaining a return on capital for the shareholders. It is also a means of delivering satisfactory products and achieving social acceptance in the community. This would suggest that management has to devise policies for research, production, marketing, etc. which are compatible with each other and which satisfy the requirements of the stakeholders. Fig. 6.3 shows the areas of concern for a socially responsible organisation.

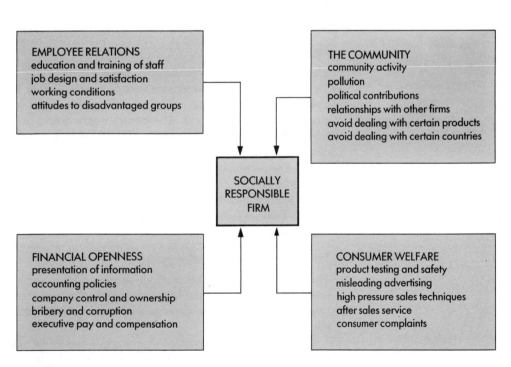

Fig. 6.3 Areas of concern to the socially responsible organisation

However, even where a firm accepts social responsibility as an objective, it may still be criticised. This is because different groups in society will judge a firm's actions in different ways. For example, a firm in a high unemployment area may be polluting a river badly, but the costs of altering the production process to avoid pollution might make production uneconomic. Should the firm (and the local authority) allow the pollution to continue, or should the firm be closed down – with the consequent loss of jobs? Different groups would answer this question in different ways.

So what is social responsibility?

Barriers to social responsibility

Most organisations would accept that they have a social responsibility to the community. Unfortunately it is often *not* translated into action as fully as we would like. Here are some of the 'barriers' to social responsibility for firms:

Barriers to the social responsibility of firms.

- There is often a conflict between social responsibility and profitability. Spending money on socially responsible activities limits the profits available for dividend and future investments.

- Social responsibility may need to be exercised in a carefully selected way and justified in terms of economic common sense – business should be socially responsible only where it *pays* to be so.

- Both firms and managers are evaluated strictly upon economic performance. Shareholders are more likely to invest in the firm with the higher profits, despite the fact that it is less socially responsible. Equally, managers who keep costs down most successfully (and that includes social responsibility costs) are the ones who will be rewarded and promoted.

- Many managers find that being socially responsible makes their jobs far more difficult. Instead of just having to consider the needs of the shareholders they are now required to assess the impact of their actions on other interest groups. Often they feel they will be criticised whatever they do.

- It is difficult to measure social responsibility in the way that you measure costs, revenue and profits. *Social audits* can be undertaken to identify those elements of the firms activities which harm, or are beneficial to, the environment. However, any final judgement on the firm as regards its social responsibility is essentially qualitative, rather than quantitative.

TECHNOLOGY

The last twenty years has seen the world go through a second Industrial Revolution, based on electronics and the microchip. This revolution has had a major impact on all aspects of business activity and has produced rapid and 'chaotic' change to which all organisations have had to respond in order to survive. It is only possible here to summarise briefly some of these changes.

Technology and design

The development of powerful micro computers had led to the transformation of the *design process* at all levels. Programmes for Computer Aided Design are now available, with colour graphics, which have eliminated the need for the draughtsman laboriously drawing working drawings by hand. The designer now works with a keyboard, VDU, graphics tablet, light pen and laser printer. He is able to interact with the computer system to develop a detailed product design and to modify it and refine it without putting pen to paper. Any section of the drawing may be enlarged, rotated or sectioned. Dimensions and tolerances may be calculated and the finished drawing retained on computer file and pulled out as a drawing of the detailed product design. The design process is greatly speeded up and so increases productivity in the design department, but often at the expense of employment.

Technology and the production process

The greater flexibility now available at the design stage makes possible faster and more precise responses to customer requirements. It has encouraged a shift from production of standardised products on an 'economic order quantity' basis, to job and batch production, even in the car industry.

The use of computer-controlled production and robotic machines has also facilitated this development. The Japanese 'Kanban' system and 'Just in Time' inventory management methods have stemmed from this development. Productivity and quality have been greatly increased, again at the expense of employment amongst unskilled and semi-skilled workers.

Technology and the product

The power of electronics and the microchip have not only greatly increased the quality and sophistication of existing products, from cars to washing machines, to textiles, but has also generated a whole family of new consumer products which were previously impossible, or much too expensive, to mass produce. Typical of these new products are the pocket calculator, the personal computer, the personal stereo and many others. Electronics and miniaturisation are likely to continue to generate new products and markets. Similar effects may be observed in the service sector industries. The electronic transfer of money has transformed the banking system and the world security markets. Storage and retrieval of information has transformed the process of research, library management and direct marketing, for example.

Technology and location of businesses

The ability to transfer and transmit information rapidly has aided the development of large multinational companies, since distant subsidiaries are now much easier to control. The location of plant may now be undertaken on the basis of the cheapest relative factor costs across the globe. This has led to an increasing trend for the manufacturing function of western or Japanese companies to be located near to markets, in low wage cost countries. Meanwhile the 'old' industrial economies with high labour costs, must concentrate on high value added activities in either manufacturing or service industries.

The same pattern may be observed at a national level. Large scale administrative units, for example in the insurance industry, may be located not in London as before, but in suburban, or more distant locations, where the costs of buildings and labour are lower. The same is true of government and local government activities of an administrative nature, which may again be located in distant parts of the country without any loss of efficiency.

Technology and the business organisation

Modern technology has the power to totally transform the structure of the business organisation and the management process. This is largely the result of computerisation. The computer is a powerful management tool which can:

- perform operations (such as calculations) very quickly
- store data in large quantities, very compactly

It is, therefore, possible to computerise many routine tasks which involve data processing and retrieval, for example wages, stock control, invoicing, production planning (using linear programming) and control of machines. It also facilitates all communication functions, such as standard letters, financial statements, sales material etc. It also permits rapid access to vital management information, over large distances and from many production units. A good example is where a large brewing chain might install a system which can instantly process and produce information on takings, stock levels, wages, etc. in a very large chain of hotels and public houses.

The impact on the structure of the organisation may be very considerable:

- Decentralisation of management may be possible to a much greater extent, which reduces the size and cost of the headquarter's functions of a large company.
- The hierarchy may be 'flattened' as a result of the elimination of many routine middle management processes.
- The workplace may be reorganised on the basis of workstations and teams, rather than continuous flow production on a 'line'. This may facilitate greater worker participation in the business through quality circles or quality improvement teams.

Technology and the worker

The impact here may also be very great in a number of ways:

- A reduction in the number of semi-skilled and unskilled jobs in both production and service areas of a business.
- A corresponding increase in the need for higher skill levels amongst the remaining workforce, leading to the need for better recruitment and training activities.
- A reduction in the number of middle management and supervisory posts and a change in the role of middle manager and supervisor from controller to facilitator.
- The deskilling of formerly high skill jobs, e.g. in printing trades.

New technology and the workforce.

- A weakening of the power of trade unions and a change in their activities and strategies.
- The transfer of routine or professional tasks either to sub contractors, or to homeworkers.

- The development of a new range of industrial sicknesses, resulting from the use of VDUs, ranging from back troubles to eyesight problems.
- Stress caused by the need to be able to be flexible between a range of operations and the resulting need to constantly retrain.
- Stress caused by the faster pace of work and the need for concentration to achieve demanding quality standards.
- Stress caused by loss of status and reduced job security.

The overall result is likely to be an increase in the total amount of unemployment, particularly long term unemployment of people with low skill levels.

EXAMINATION QUESTIONS

1   There are a number of groups with an interest in the activities of businesses. What are these groups, what are their objectives and how might a business respond to them?
(AEB 1990)

2   'Legislation such as that concerned with employee and consumer protection and the regulation of potential monopolies causes the loss of international competitiveness. This is too high a price to pay.' To what extent do you agree?   (AEB 1989)

3   Why might an organisation experience a reduction in profitability following the introduction of information technology?   (AEB 1988)

TUTOR'S ANSWER

Question 1

Businesses do not exist in a vacuum – they are part of society. This society provides the inputs for the organisation and accepts its output. Society provides the opportunities for that organisation and also puts constraints upon its actions. For the business to be successful it has to turn the inputs it receives from society into outputs that are acceptable to society. The diagram below (Fig. 6.4) illustrates this process.

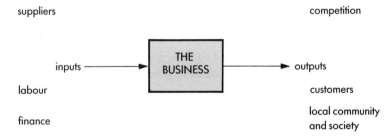

Fig. 6.4 The micro environment of business

To carry on its business the firm needs certain inputs. Labour, capital and raw materials are obvious, but there may be others such as licenses granted by government for it to carry on in business. The outputs from business are primarily the goods and services it produces, but we might also consider by-products of the production process (e.g. pollution) or the impact that it has on other firms with whom it is in competition. Of course, there may be other inputs and outputs.

Until fairly recently business would only admit to one group with a legitimate interest in business – that was the shareholders. As the owners and financiers of the business their interest is fairly obvious. They are interested in the survival, profitability and growth of the business. Their objective is to ensure the safety of their investment.

Of course, the shareholders are not necessarily the only financiers of the business – particularly in the case of a large firm. Other financiers could include preference shareholders, mortgage and debenture holders, hire purchase companies and banks. In all of these cases the objective of the lender is to ensure the safety of their investment (i.e.

the repayment of interest and capital or adequate security in lieu of payment).

Other major providers of inputs include labour and suppliers of parts and raw materials. The objectives of labour are complex, but would probably include, adequate remuneration, security of employment, good working conditions, promotion paths and challenging work. As far as suppliers of parts and raw materials are concerned, their objectives would be to ensure that the firm is capable of paying their bills as and when they become due and to maintain satisfactory trading relationships with the business.

Turning now to the 'outputs' side of the diagram, competitors are interested in our business because it is a potential threat to them. Their objective would, in normal circumstances, be to contain this threat through their marketing strategies. Consumers, like labour, also have complex objectives. They would certainly expect safe products, a good after sales service and an effective complaints service. They may also in specific cases wish to curtail activities such as misleading advertising or high pressure sales techniques.

Finally, the community. In the first place, the community would have as an objective ensuring that the business dealt fairly with all the groups mentioned above. It would also be concerned to see that the firm acted as a good member of society, perhaps supporting worthwhile charitable or sporting events, but certainly in relation to the physical environment.

It is difficult to predict how a firm will react to the demands of these groups. At one extreme would be an organisation which conforms to Friedman's maxim 'the only social responsibility of business is to increase its profits'. The managers and directors of such firms believe that should society wish business to act in a certain way (which would constrain its activities) it should introduce legislation. The only obligation which such a firm would recognise would be to its owners – the shareholders.

A second approach can best be described as enlightened self interest. Such firms believe that being seen to recognise social responsibilities could be in the long term interest of the business. The catch is that the firm's commitment to social responsibility is limited in what can be justified – in terms of economic commonsense, business should be socially responsible – as long as it pays! Thus sponsorship would be justified in terms of the improved profit it gives the business, and in the employee welfare provided in terms of retention and motivation of employees.

The third approach is that which would be adopted by 'progressive' organisations. Such organisations would acknowledge the powerful influence of social responsibility upon decision making. Such organisations would recognise their responsibilities towards their interest groups or stakeholders. For example, such a firm might retain uneconomic units to preserve jobs, or if a decision was made to close a site down, offer workers a transfer to other company sites. The company might also offer enhanced redundancy payments and grants for retraining purposes. However, even for the progressive firm conflicts still occur. It would for example be unrealistic, given a choice between social responsibility and survival, to expect the firm to choose social responsibility. It is also very questionable how the firm's managers would act in a conflict between social responsibility and the shareholders. It is precisely for reasons such as this that many people feel that social responsibility is too important an issue to be left to the whims of the individual firm, or vague and unenforceable industry-wide codes of conduct. In short, to ensure firms will act in a socially responsible manner, we must legislate.

A STUDENT'S ANSWER

Question 2

> In the last forty years each government has been concerned with introducing and tightening legislation concerned with the protection of both the employee and the consumer as well as restricting the growth of mega-companies. The employee is protected from discrimination, unfair dismissal, redundancy and poor working conditions. The consumer is protected by various Acts from faulty goods, poor quality, unhealthy food, short measure, misleading advertising and unfair credit terms. The Office of Fair Trading and the Monopolies and Mergers Commission

❝❝The candidate has realised that the question is about the impact rather than the detail of legislation.❞❞

investigate monopolies, proposed mergers and uncompetitive practices. To the general public this appears as sound practice aimed at redressing the imbalance in power between the individual and the far stronger business concern. To the businessman, however, this legislation may appear to be unnecessary central government interference which only results in increased costs. The two viewpoints are examined below.

The main disadvantage of all this legislation to the average company is the added cost. The safety at work regulations results in a more complicated and costly production system. The regular oversight of the regulations and their maintenance means that more non-productive personnel must be employed. The extra dimensions which must be considered (e.g. legal requirements of new work practices) for each proposed change means that the decision-making process becomes larger and less responsive to market shifts. Some managerial staff feel their efforts to improve productivity, distribution or the product itself are being frustrated by the bureaucratic regulations which must be adhered to at each stage. They see the domestic regulations as an unnecessary cost imposition which foreign competitors do not, in the main, have to follow. This places the UK firm at a distinct disadvantage.

With regard to monopoly and merger legislation, UK firms may feel that they are being kept too small by international standards. A monopoly is now defined as an organisation which controls one quarter of the UK market, which in the context of European and world trade is relatively small. The firms also argue that restricting home monopolies does not prevent monopolies from other countries from invading and securing the domestic market, e.g. the recent Japanese invasion into the UK car market. A final argument put forward is that the companies would move towards the goals of much of the present legislation for sound, commercial reasons without being told to by government, e.g. better quality control in order to win a larger market share. For all of these reasons firms may resent the myriad of legislation especially as the cost is nearly always passed onto the consumer thus making the products even less competitive internationally.

The alternative argument points to the advantages of the legislation. A healthy, safe workforce should be more productive and more responsive to change if they have been well treated by the employers. The added cost of safety or health legislation is often small compared to the cost of litigation and settlement in the case of accidents and prosecution. The legislation aims to protect the employer as much as the employee. Legislation concerning quality will ensure that shoddy goods do not give the country a bad name, e.g. Hong Kong took many years to rid itself of its 'cheap and nasty' image. Also the legislation aims to provide only a framework or minimum standard which it is hoped would be exceeded by all major efficient concerns. It is also spurious to assume that all foreign competitors operate under less strict regimes. Most of the UK's trade is with other developed economies such as Germany, USA, Japan and France. These countries have similar legislation to our own.

The monopoly argument is also spurious as domestic monopolies are more likely to exploit their home advantage, become inefficient and fail to compete internationally anyway.

In the final analysis international competitiveness depends on many more factors than just protective legislation. All businesses are an integral part of society and as such have no more right to complete freedom of action than any individual has.

Margin notes:

" One of two points could have been expanded to show the full impact on the firm. "

" Give an example, eg. Vauxhall as against Ford. "

" A good point. "

" Give examples, eg. exchange rates, government subsidies, etc. "

> The growth of international pressure groups such as Greenpeace should ensure the adoption of internationally agreed standards of conduct to which all firms must comply. The lack of legislation elsewhere in the world is a poor excuse for a lowering of our own standards.

Tutor's comment

This is a good, well argued essay which considers many of the issues without getting too involved in unnecessary legislative detail.

OUTLINE ANSWER

Question 3

An organisation would introduce information technology (IT) in the anticipation that it will increase profitability. This may in fact not be so, especially in the short run for a number of reasons. In general terms the introduction of IT may take place in design, production, marketing and administration functions, but not necessarily all at one time. Its introduction into any of these will have the effect of increasing overhead costs in the short term, thus the 'contribution' made by sales revenue (difference between sales revenue and variable costs) will have to increase, through either increases in sales, reductions in variable costs, price increases, or some combination of these factors.

The increase in overheads in the short term would be caused by the following factors in some combination:

- Consultancy costs incurred in the process of deciding which system to purchase.
- The costs of installation of the system.
- The costs incurred in installing and activating the system by converting from manual storage and processing of data to computerised systems.
- The costs of training existing staff to operate the system, or of employing more highly skilled staff to do so.
- The costs of maintenance of the system and its constant updating (both hardware and software).
- An increase in the 'costs of quality', i.e. the increase in errors and mistakes resulting from inexperience in the use of the system.
- The resulting cost of maintaining a manual system in the short term as back up in case of such mistakes.
- The costs of redundancy amongst administrative and other staff who are no longer required.
- The costs of installing new machine tools in the production department which can take advantage of computer controls.
- The cost of employing a highly qualified data processing manager.

In the longer term, hopefully the advantages accruing from the installation of IT would greatly offset some of these costs, and the transitional costs should be out of the system within a year or so. The benefits of more efficient data processing, communication systems, sales and marketing procedures, computer aided design and computer-controlled production and Just in Time inventory management, should both increase sales revenue and reduce overheads in terms of storage and administrative buildings and staff. At this stage, hopefully the company would benefit from higher profitability as a result of the introduction of IT.

MANAGEMENT AND THE ORGANISATION

GETTING STARTED

All human activities take place within a structured social system or 'organisation'. This is true whether it be a family, a city, a business or a church. Many of these organisations have a formal structure, the purpose of which is to make it possible to achieve the objectives of that organisation. Within that formal structure there is a group of people who plan, organise, direct and control the day-to-day operations of the organisation – the managers.

Management is that group of activities undertaken by managers. It has been defined by E.F.L. Breech as:

> ". . . a social process entailing responsibility for the effective and economical planning and regulation of the operations of an enterprise in the fulfilment of a given task or purpose."

In this chapter, we will look at some of the ideas that have shaped how managers act today, before considering some organisational characteristics which are present in every organisation.

ESSENTIAL PRINCIPLES

THE DEVELOPMENT OF MANAGEMENT THOUGHT

❝The definition.❞

❝Some models of management.❞

Management theory is the attempt to discover and develop models which may be used in order to analyse and understand the process of management within organisations. Contributions to its development have come from a number of disciplines, for example statistics (management of production, marketing, and quality), sociology (behaviour within organisational systems), social psychology (motivation and leadership), and behavioural psychology (motivation and control). These theories are useful in explaining the management style which is most common at a particular time but may themselves cause changes in management style as a result of the influence of management education. It is possible to classify such models into groups or theories.

CLASSICAL THEORY

This was the earliest attempt to identify the important elements in management, and the best form of organisational structure. It is best exemplified by Fayol (1841–1925). This approach recognised the advantages of division of labour and sought ways in which to make it most effective. It stressed the importance of a formal hierarchical organisational structure and the concept of 'span of control'. The emphasis was on the exact definition of tasks and the relationship between them. Control would be achieved through an authoritarian style and the use of authority. The greatest contribution made by this school of thought was to suggest that management is a set of skills which may be taught. Their stress on the importance of the organisational structure has led in recent time to a recognition of the importance of further study of the impact of structure and hierarchies. Despite the emphasis on control, this school recognised the importance of job satisfaction and the need for equity in industrial relations. These latter ideas were lost sight of in the middle years of this century but have more recently re-assumed importance.

SCIENTIFIC MANAGEMENT

This approach to the process of management stemmed from the work of F.W. Taylor (1856–1915). He was concerned about the inefficiency which he had observed in industry and developed the view that it was the result of managerial failure. It was not clearly understood what amounts of work could be expected of a worker and as a result, because of human nature, workers would underperform. Low motivation and bad industrial relations were the result. Taylor stressed the importance of the planning, organisation and supervision of work by managers. In common with his times, Taylor had an exaggerated respect for the possibilities of a scientific approach. His view of motivation was that workers needed only high wages and the possibility of advancement as motivators. In consequence he developed a system of work and method study in order to establish exactly what the attainable performance level was in any task. This was done by systematic observation and measurement of the way the task was best done and the speed at which it could be done. Once done, this allowed managers to organise and control what was done and how it was done, dealing with workers as individuals and relieving workers of responsibilities which they were unfit to undertake. This approach spread rapidly in both capitalist and centrally-planned economies and is still very influential. Its most positive contribution was to stress the importance of the collection and analysis of data in the decision-making process. Its mechanical view of human motivation, stressing monetary reward for achievement of targets, is much too naive.

THE HUMAN RELATIONS APPROACH

This approach stresses the importance of morale and informal social relationships as determinants of organisational effectiveness. Much of the work done in this field stemmed from the Hawthorne Investigations. These were the work of E. Mayo between 1927–32. The experiments were undertaken for the Western Electric Co., whose earlier attempts to scientifically analyse the relationship between working conditions and output by workers, had been inconclusive. Over a period of time Mayo carried out a study on a group of six female workers, and sought to establish the link between different working conditions, especially lighting and output. The variables tested proved to have no measurable influence; even a worsening of conditions produced improved output. It became apparent that the improvements were due to social relations amongst the six workers, their freedom from supervision and their feeling of enhanced self esteem resulting from their apparent importance. Further studies confirmed that worker attitudes stemmed from the social context and were more important in motivation than financial or other incentives. There were clearly important issues also raised in the area of supervision and management style.

This important study led to the development of a school of thought which was profoundly opposed to scientific management. The adherents of the classical theory found no difficulty in reconciling the two approaches. The human relations view is however now seen as being too simplistic, and based on too narrow a range of variables. It has now been largely superceded, but did establish the importance of social factors in the organisational context.

NEO HUMAN RELATIONS SCHOOL

The Hawthorne experiments led to the development of further models which sought a new approach to organisational design in order to increase management effectiveness. It was becoming clear that attempts had failed to modify work practices and organisation structure on the basis that worker satisfaction would produce greater productivity. Mayo's work was modified by McGregor, Argyris and Maslow, who all suggested that the links between organisation design, motivation and productivity were more complex than had been thought.

Maslow

Maslow stressed the importance of 'intrinsic needs' which the individual will seek to satisfy. These needs are set out in a hierarchy, with physical needs at the bottom, then security needs (both of which need to be satisfied first), social needs, then self esteem and finally self actualisation (realisation of potential). These latter two are very important and most likely to be met at work. This idea was developed by Herzberg.

“Motivation through needs.”

Herzberg

Herzberg developed this idea and suggested that there are two kinds of needs which are important. 'Hygiene needs' (equivalent to Maslow's physical and security needs) are those needs which should be satisfied in order to avoid job dissatisfaction. 'Motivators' are those needs which when satisfied lead to job satisfaction (equivalent to Maslow's self esteem and self actualisation). This modification leads to the view that employers must satisfy both hygiene needs, through good working conditions, and 'motivator needs' through the possibility of personal fulfilment.

McGregor

McGregor applied the concepts above to the assumptions underlying formal organisational structures as he observed them. He suggested that basically two sets of assumptions are available, which he labelled *Theory X* and *Theory Y*. This model is very useful to a student who is observing an organisation in action.

Theory X is based on negative assumptions about workers:

“Work – unavoidable necessity, or enjoyable experience?”

- Man dislikes work and will avoid it if at all possible.
- Man wishes to avoid responsibility and prefers to be directed.
- Above all, man demands security.

This view suggests that the role of manager is to *direct* and *control*, using fear of punishment as the motivator.

Theory Y is based on positive assumptions about workers:

- Man enjoys and finds satisfaction in work.
- Man accepts and seeks responsibility.

- Man can be committed to, and strive for, organisational objectives without the threat of punishment.
- Modern industry only uses a small part of human potential.

The role of the manager in this case is to provide an environment in which employees can best achieve their own goals whilst striving for organisational objectives. The organisation would be structured to allow more self management, more upward communication and more participation in decision making. If this view is correct, the use of Theory X is likely to produce apathy, low productivity, poor morale, high absenteeism and poor organisational performance. The modern Japanese approach – known as 'Total Quality Management' – and now rapidly being introduced in the UK is essentially based on Theory Y.

THE SYSTEMS APPROACH

In this case the organisation is seen as a particular type of social system. That is, it is a network of persons, performing interrelated roles. The approach recognises the interdependence of technical and social factors in an organisation. Such a socio-technical system is seen as having three elements; *technical factors* (physical environment, equipment and technical processes), *social factors* (social relations and attitudes within the group) and *economic factors* (measure of the efficiency of the technical and social mix). This view recognises the interdependence of groups undertaking overlapping tasks, but also their tendency to develop group identities, rivalries, hostility and conflict. This situation leads to low productivity. There is a need to break down and replace existing work groups in such a way as to encourage cooperation in pursuit of a common objective. This concept was developed by the Tavistock Institute of Human Relations in a study of coal mining.

THE CONTINGENCY APPROACH

This approach was developed by the 1960s, primarily by J. Woodward (1916–71). It emphasises that there exists no single approach to organisational structure which will suit all conditions. Rather, the approach in any particular case will depend on the circumstances. It will draw on any of the earlier theories as seems appropriate and would stress three factors;

- the strengths and weaknesses of the organisation
- the objective of the organisation
- the external environment of the organisation

This view stresses also a link between technology and organisational structure, suggesting that the more advanced the technology, the longer the chain of command. This view would not be acceptable to advocates of 'Japanisation'. The approach leads to the rather common sense conclusion that there is an appropriate organisational structure for any type of environment. The problem for managers is to identify accurately which it is. More recent workers in this area have suggested that the correlation is not with technology, but with the size of the organisation.

THE ROLE OF THE MANAGER

Management – a unifying resource.

Any organisation has a role or objective. In private business that would be to produce and offer for sale a product or service, in order to maximise profit and the wealth of the shareholders or owners. In order to do so the organisation must have a structure. That is to say an interconnected system of departments and units, together with a set of operational rules and regulations governing their work. To operate these departments will need the appropriate plant and equipment and above all the personnel to operate the system. The decisions as to how this system be structured and operated, and for what purposes, are decided by managers. Management is, therefore, best seen as a unifying resource, bringing together resources in order to achieve the objectives of the organisation. As may be seen from Fig. 7.1, the resources which management brings together for an organisational objective are; people, materials, machines and money.

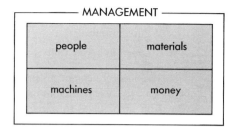

Fig. 7.1 Management – a unifying
resource

THE FUNCTIONS OF MANAGEMENT

Four management functions can be identified. These were first formally set out by Fayol and are Planning, Organising, Directing and Controlling (see Table 7.1).

Planning

This is the starting point for all management activity. It involves:

- setting clear objectives
- devising strategies to achieve those objectives

Organising

This is essential in order to achieve organisational goals. It involves:

- developing an organisation structure
- creating departments within that structure
- establishing communication networks

> " What managers do. "

Directing

This may also be referred to as coordinating or motivating. It involves:

- finding and training staff for specific tasks
- ensuring they are motivated to perform those tasks

Table 7.1 Functions of
management

	PLANNING	ORGANISING	DIRECTING	CONTROLLING
SENIOR MANAGEMENT	long term planning and policy decisions. Time horizon 5–10 years. Determining profit targets	determining the basic structure of the organisation e.g. division, departments. Whether to organise by product or territory	provide leadership and motivation through praise, promotion, criticism and dismissal. Acting as a figure head for line organisation. Span of control small.	measurement of long term planned against actual performance. Reviewing plans and organisational structure
MIDDLE MANAGEMENT	development of detailed operational plans and procedures to attain organisational goals. Time horizon normally 1 year	delegation of work to subordinates and coordination of their work. Development of horizontal relationships	creating situations where subordinates are motivated to achieve organisational goals e.g. monetary incentives job rotation enlargement and enrichment. Span of control 4–9	comparison of actual with budgeting results action to prevent deviation re-occurring
SUPERVISORY MANAGEMENT	development and implementation of short range plans e.g. detailed schedules of work. Time horizon 1 week – 1 month	implementation of work schedules	application of motivation and discipline to overcome resistance. In many firms the supervisor will depend on discipline to ensure compliance with organisational requirements. In more enlightened firms the supervisor is more of a sports coach encouraging employees to do the job as well as possible.	ensuring that work completed is of the correct quality and on schedule

Controlling

This is essential to ensure that organisational goals are achieved. It involves:

- collecting, collating and analysing key management information
- comparing actual with planned performance
- critically reviewing plans and organisational structure

According to Fayol these functions are common to managers at all levels within the organisation, though the emphasis which is placed on each activity will vary according to their position in the hierarchy.

In carrying out these functions of management, managers use three broad groups of skills:

1 *Technical skills*. These embody the ability to use the tools and techniques of a particular profession. For an accountant this would imply an understanding of, and an ability to use, accounting information in order to control the financial side of the organisation. Technical skills are of particular importance to supervisors.

2 *Human skills*. It is difficult to underestimate the importance of the human resource within the organisation. Managers have to work through and rely on their subordinates. They therefore need high levels of inter-personal skills. Human skills are important to all managers.

3 *Conceptual skills*. This is the intellectual ability to see and understand the whole problem. A manager needs to be able to see first, how factors in a situation are inter-related, and second, how a change in one part will affect the whole. Conceptual skills are particularly important amongst senior managers.

> " What managers need. "

> " Organisation – formalising group activities. "

THE FORMAL ORGANISATION

This term refers to the structure which is developed to enable the organisation to achieve its objectives. This begins to develop at an early stage in the life of an organisation as a result of the need to group activities. As a result of the formal organisation you will find that:

- Activities are separated into departments such as production, marketing, finance, and personnel. Further sub-departments will develop as the organisation grows in size.
- Tasks are divided in such a way as to make use of specialist technical and management skills.
- Relationships between employees are defined.
- Rules and procedures to be followed are established.
- It is established where decisions are to be made.
- Channels of communication are created through which information and decisions may pass.

THE ORGANISATION CHART

The formal organisation structure may be best represented by an organisation chart, as in Fig. 7.2, which represents the structure of a typical manufacturing company.

This diagram indicates a number of features of organisational structures:

- The grouping of activities, on the basis of function.
- The division of labour. The degree of specialisation by function and technical skills is indicated, both between and within departments.,
- The chain of command. The lines of control and responsibility are clearly shown. The broken lines show where a department has specialist functional responsibility throughout the organisation.
- The communications channels. Unbroken lines show formal lines of communication within the organisation. Not shown are the horizontal and diagonal communications channels which will develop either formally or informally within the organisation.

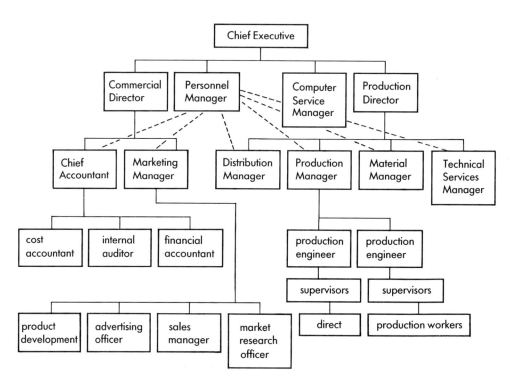

Fig. 7.2 Organisational chart of a typical manufacturing firm

Advantages of organisation charts

■ They provide information on the formal structure of the organisation in a form that is easily understood by all. It may be displayed on staff notice-boards, thus providing a focal point for information on changes in organisation structure or personnel.

■ The preparation of the chart draws attention to organisational defects, for example areas of conflict, areas of duplication, an excessive span of control or an excessively long line of authority.

■ The organisation chart is also the basis from which any proposed changes to the organisation are made.

Disadvantages of organisation charts

■ The chart is a picture of the organisation at a certain time and is rapidly outdated by changes in structure or personnel.

■ The designer faces the difficulty of showing the organisation structure in full, in which case the chart is complex and confusing, or simplifying the structure and thereby presenting an inaccurate picture.

■ The organisation chart may cause employee discontent. Employees often believe status within an organisation is implied by their proximity to the Chief Executive, or the size of their box!

■ Organisation charts do not reveal the different degrees of responsibility borne by executives.

■ Charts do not show the unofficial relationships and chains of communication without which the organisation would not function properly.

There are alternative ways of representing structure in diagrammatic form, but the vertical arrangement remains the most commonly used. In the chart an important distinction may be made between 'line' and 'staff' departments within the firm.

LINE DEPARTMENTS

These are the activities which are essential to survival, since they are directly concerned with the production and distribution of the product or service. Where the formal structure of the organisation is based on line activities, it is referred to as 'line organisation'. In the case of a manufacturer, the key activities are production, sales and product development. All other activities are grouped around these key areas. A retail organisation adopting a line organisation would group its activities around purchasing, finance and sales.

A line organisation has some advantages:

- It is easy to understand.
- Responsibilities are well defined.
- Few communication problems arise since it is a relatively simple organisational structure.
- It develops all-round managers rather than specialists.
- It is particularly suitable to a small firm.
- It can respond quickly to new situations.

The disadvantages of a line organisation are:

- It neglects the benefits of specialists.
- It relies too heavily on key staff.

LINE AND STAFF ORGANISATION

As an organisation grows in size, the line manager needs to divest himself of peripheral activities. Thus specialist departments are created, and managers are appointed, who do not have line responsibilities. A further development as the firm expands again, may be the appointment of general staff, who are used to relieve senior managers of specific onerous tasks. Specialist staff, such as personnel managers are appointed to provide particular support functions, such as training, recruitment and industrial relations. Or in very large companies what might be called specialist all-rounders may be used in a unit which concentrates solely on forward strategic planning.

Although this form of structure allows the organisation to grow in size it does have a number of disadvantages:

Allies or enemies – line and staff.

- Line managers find that the appointment of specialists limits their authority and responsibility. They may feel their status is threatened.
- Line managers may feel specialists are used by senior management to spy upon their activities.
- Specialists may have a narrow outlook and be unable to understand the problem of the line manager.
- Specialists may suggest change as a means of justifying their existence.
- Specialists often have a technical language (jargon) and use techniques which are not understood by the line manager.
- The complexity of the organisational structure may cause problems of communication, coordination and control.

MATRIX ORGANISATION

This structure was developed first in the USA aerospace industry in order to overcome the problems outlined above. It is now widely used in the construction industry and in other industries where a high degree of cross functional coordination and cooperation is required. The departmental structure still exists, but project teams, cutting across functional boundaries, are formed as necessary. Members of such teams are drawn from all the appropriate departments and the team exists only for the duration of the project. The method has three major advantages:

- Interdepartmental barriers and defensive behaviour patterns are broken down by the team approach.
- Coordination by a team or project leader provides the company with greater control over the project.
- The client has a point of contact close to his immediate interests, thus ensuring that customer requirements are met.

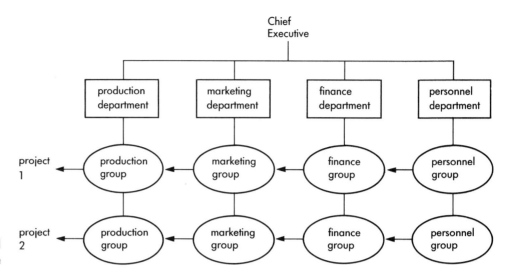

Fig. 7.3 A 'matrix' organisational structure

The problems which emerge are that it is a complex and fluid format, which may result in less efficient use of resources. Fig. 7.3 shows such an organisation in the form of an organisational chart.

DELEGATION

At any level in the organisation it is unlikely that managers will be able to cope adequately with all aspects of their jobs on their own. To function efficiently they must *delegate*. Provided that they have chosen and trained the right people, they should be able to allocate important aspects of their jobs to subordinates. This will have the advantage of furthering the development of the next generation of managers. There are three important aspects to delegation:

1   *Responsibility.* An obligation is placed on the subordinate to ensure that the delegated tasks are carried out efficiently on time. The responsibility therefore must be clearly defined, and should be set out in the job description.

2   *Authority.* If delegation is to work, the subordinates must in turn be authorised to carry out their responsibilities. They must have access to the necessary information and the power to make things happen by requiring action from others. They must have an adequate budget and time within their day to undertake the task effectively.

3   *Accountability.* Standards of performance in the task must be set out beforehand in order that the subordinates may be held accountable to the manager for their efforts. The managers are also accountable to their superiors for the actions of their subordinates. There are, however, some limits to delegation:

■ Highly specialised or confidential work cannot be delegated in many cases.

■ Very important decisions with high resource implications may have to be taken at senior level.

■ Some senior managers find delegation very difficult. Psychologically they may not feel totally in control, either in terms of their ability to lead and direct subordinates or in terms of their own technical competence.

■ There may be doubts about the ability of the subordinates to carry out a task, even though it may be within their job description, perhaps because they were a bad choice, or have had insufficient training.

■ Due to their own lack of confidence, or experience, subordinates may be unwilling to accept the delegation of a difficult task. Their constant need for help and reassurance may be wasteful and time consuming so the manager does the job himself.

SPAN OF CONTROL

The problems of delegation outlined above will influence the way in which delegation is structured. Management has ·to decide what is the appropriate span of control for managers and supervisors at different levels in the company. How many workers or subordinates can one person supervise without losing control? The concept of 'span of control' was first set out in 1933 by V.A. Graicunas. He argued that the limiting number was six subordinates. This is not necessarily so and inefficiency should not be inferred from an organisation chart which shows wider or narrower spans of control than this. The main factors affecting the span of control are shown in Table 7.2.

■ Similarity of work:	the greater the degree of similarity, the wider the span.
■ Geographic proximity:	where a 'work group' is located in the same place, a wider span is possible.
■ Level of supervision:	the less supervision required, the wider the span.
■ Level of coordination:	where less coordination is necessary the wider the span.
■ Complexity of work:	more repetitive work by subordinates requires less supervision and allows for wider span.
■ Planning:	the less planning required of the manager, the wider the span.

Table 7.2 Factors affecting the span of control

COMMITTEES

A committee is a group of people who have been appointed to undertake a specific task. It is a form of delegation often used in large organisations. The members are charged with a responsibility for a task, given the necessary responsibility and are accountable for their performance. A summary of the advantages and disadvantages of committees is given in Table 7.3.

ADVANTAGES	DISADVANTAGES
■ *Coordination*: enables the exchange of information and the systematic coordination of activities	■ *Cost*: very costly in terms of executive time (and therefore money)
■ *Decision making*: far greater variety of expertise can be drawn on in making a decision	■ *Quality*: decisions are often a compromise, not dealing with the problem properly
■ *Creativity*: working in a group can stimulate creativity	■ *Indecision*: difficulties in reaching a decision caused by inability to agree or arrange meeting date
■ *Acceptance*: participation tends to increase acceptance of the decision	■ *Accountability*: decisions often more risky because participants now avoid individual responsibility
■ *Abuse of power*: dispersion of power prevents one person abusing his or her position for their own ends	■ *Ineffectiveness*: caused by inability of chairperson or incorrect size/structure of committee

Table 7.3 Advantages and disadvantages of committees

DECENTRALISATION

This refers to the extent to which a company pushes down authority for major decisions to lower levels. In some organisations power is highly centralised and concentrated in few hands, whereas in others a more fragmented company structure with a very small HQ and a largely coordinating role is used. The degree of decentralisation used depends on a number of factors:

- the history and philosophy of the organisation.
- the method of growth; firms which grew in an evolutionary way are likely to be centralised; those which grew by acquisition are more likely to be decentralised. The Hanson Corporation is a good example of the latter type.
- an unstable environment makes decentralisation and its accompanying flexibility of response highly desirable. This is increasingly the situation of companies in all industries; the greater the number of markets and products in which the firm is involved, the greater the degree of decentralisation (Table 7.4).

    However, whatever approach is used to the structuring of an organisation it will both reflect and take place within a prevailing organisational culture.

CENTRALISED ORGANISATIONS	DECENTRALISED ORGANISATIONS
Benefits:	Benefits:
■ Uniformity of decision making ■ Duplication of effort eliminated ■ Highly skilled personnel available to whole organisation, not just one unit	■ Reduces workload on senior managers ■ More managers involved in decision-making process ■ Decisions made by managers who 'know the situation' ■ Power is dispersed
Problems:	Problems:
■ Heavy strain put on a few managers ■ Communication difficult with senior management (lack of time) ■ Demotivating influence for all but senior managers ■ Too much power given to a few individuals	■ Lack of uniformity in decision making ■ Uncoordinated effort between separate units ■ Inter-unit conflict may arise ■ Managers may not be willing to accept responsibility

Table 7.4 Benefits of centralised and decentralised organisations

ORGANISATIONAL CULTURE

> ❝ Organisational culture – a constraint on performance. ❞

Just as wider society has a set of characteristics and values which define people's understanding of their circumstances and conditions their behaviour, so any subculture within the wider culture will also have such characteristics. An organisation is such a subculture. The norms, values and shared attitudes which pervade the organisation are often long standing and derived from both the wider culture and the particular values of the founders of the organisation. This culture may be expressed in symbols, ritual and language. It is increasingly recognised that the culture of the organisation may be a major constraint on its performance. A number of types of culture have been identified:

■ Power culture. Characterised by emphasis on charisma, risk taking, low respect for established procedures. This form is associated with entrepreneurial attitudes and small firms.

■ Role culture. Characterised by well defined procedures, conformity and emphasis on rule-bound behaviour. This form is bureaucratic in nature and found in public sector authorities.

■ Task culture. Characterised by team work and problem-solving behaviour in groups. The emphasis is on creativity and flexibility, as in scientific research organisations.

■ Personal orientated culture. Characterised by emphasis on meeting the needs of clients and members of the organisation. Commonly found in professional partnerships and small consultancy type firms.

An inappropriate culture may inhibit the development of a firm in a rapidly changing economic environment. For example, much more creativity may now be needed in public authorities with a rapidly changing role, especially where they have been privatised. The prevailing culture (e.g. in British Telecom) may make adaptation very difficult. Thus the first step in changing BT into a successful private sector company, was to set out to change the culture from 'role' to 'task'. This change may take years in some large organisations.

Peters and Waterman in their book on successful companies, *In Search of Excellence*, identified eight elements within these organisations' culture which contributed to their success. They were:

■ Bias for action: define objectives and let managers act.

■ Closeness to the customer: the customer is the most important person in the organisation. Know his needs.

■ Risk taking: an accepted feature of the organisation is that managers will innovate and try things out. 'Mistakes' do not necessarily result in punishment.

■ Productivity through people: employee involvement improves motivation.

■ Hands on, value driven: senior managers should not remain aloof from the rest of the organisation.

■ Cling to the core:
the business should concentrate on what it knows/does best rather than diversifying into unknown activities.

■ Simple form, lean staff:
complex structures are inefficient

■ Simultaneous loose-tight properties:
whilst decentralisation is essential for motivation and efficiency, Head Office should keep control on key decisions.

INFORMAL ORGANISATION

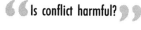
Unofficial subcultures!

A major problem in bringing about cultural change within an organisation lies in the existence of an underlying subculture beneath the official culture. This may be reflected in an unofficial hierarchy of control and influence. In an organisation like Britain Rail, this sub-organisation and culture may be a powerful combination of unionisation and long standing family connection with the railways going back several generations. In this climate management is seen as a group of temporary outsiders who know nothing of railways. Such an organisation is even more impervious to change.

CONFLICT

Conflict is inevitable!

Employees enter an organisation with very great differences in education, experiences, attitudes and motivation. It is not surprising, therefore, that conflict is inevitable within any organisation.

Conflict exists where one person believes his interests to be frustrated by another person. It may arise as a result of:

■ Poor communication, including incomplete information, unfamiliar language and misunderstandings.

■ Organisational structure: including conflicting objectives between departments, interdependence of groups and competition for scarce resources.

■ Personal factors: including management style, dogmatism and incompatibility of personal goals with organisational goals.

Is conflict harmful?

In some organisations the prevailing culture is that conflict is harmful. It can, after all, lead to low morale, low productivity and poor industrial relations. Senior management's expectations are that all employees have the same objectives, will work towards these objectives as a team and recognise hierarchical authority. Any challenge to their views is seen as bad and will be dealt with through rules and procedures existing in that organisation.

However, in other organisations, conflict is seen as inevitable due to the existence of many different interest groups. This conflict is seen as healthy and desirable. It may increase motivation, encourage creativity and encourage better management decisions. It enables the organisation to progress. In such a culture the role of management is to channel conflict so that its effects are positive rather than negative and to provide a means by which the conflict may be resolved.

EXAMINATION QUESTIONS

1 a) Distinguish between autocratic and democratic management styles.   (5)

b) Why is the 'span of control' relevant in any discussion of management style?   (8)

c) Compare and contrast the advantages and disadvantages of the following methods of communication and say to which management style they may be appropriate:

1 letters	3 telephones	(12)
2 notice boards	4 meetings	(Cambridge 1989)

2 Why is delegation so necessary to the success of a business and why is it so difficult to carry out? *(25)*

(AEB 1989)

3 a) Compare and contrast what is meant by 'line' and 'staff' relationships within an organisation. *(10)*

   b) Distinguish between 'cost centres' and 'profit centres'. How do these help organisations in planning and controlling their operations? *(15)*

(Cambridge 1988)

4 Change is a critical element in an organisation's ability to survive and grow. Why then is change often resisted and how might the process of change be eased?   (AEB 1988)

TUTOR'S ANSWER

Question 1

a) Management style may be said to reflect the culture of the organisation. The characteristics of an autocratic style are: top down communication; decision making centralised in the hands of senior management; an overriding concern for production. The approach is likely to be task-centred and based on the philosophy of 'scientific management', using the reward/punishment approach of work study. Employee compliance could be said to be achieved through coercion. Industrial relations are likely to be conflictual. This style has been called by McGregor the 'Theory X' approach.

   Democratic management style referred to by McGregor as 'Theory Y' is more commonly found in smaller firms, but may be present in some large firms, where the corporate culture is based on a philosophy of concern for human relations. Its characteristics are likely to be: a flatter hierarchy; open communication systems (vertical, horizontal and diagonal); delegation of authority; trust; responsibility given to workers at all levels. The industrial relations are likely to be less conflictual and employee motivation greater without fear or monetary reward.

b) The assumed span of control will influence the organisational structure and hierarchy of the organisation. It is commonly assumed that the greatest 'span of control' is likely to be 1 to 6 at any level of an organisation. Thus in a firm where this view is part of the corporate culture and where there are more than say 100 employees, there will need to be several layers to the hierarchy. For example, the Managing Director leads five directors, each of them is responsible for (say) five departments. Each department head has up to six supervisors under his control and each supervisor has up to six workers to direct. Such a firm would have therefore approximately 300 employees. Thus the span of control is inversely related to the number of levels in the organisation. Modern business organisations (based on the 'Human Relations' school of thought) with a shallow hierarchy and a much wider span of control are based on greater delegation of authority, and commitment in the workforce. Old fashioned organisations based on the assumption of a narrow possible span, are likely to have deep hierarchies and an autocratic management.

c) All the methods of communication given are likely to be used in any organisation to some extent. The degree to which each is used is likely to reflect the management style and corporate culture. It is vital in any organisation that information be communicated to those who need it to do their job properly. Communication methods must also be used to motivate workers to achieve at high levels of success. Communication failures may occur for a number of reasons: use of inappropriate vocabulary which may obscure meanings; excessive information overload which reduces understanding through lack of attention; deliberate manipulation or distortion of information. Geographical and hierarchical distance may reduce communication delivery. Use of the inappropriate format which offers a message which conflicts with the message being (ostensibly) delivered, will destroy the impact of the message. Thus the methods given must be used in the appropriate situations and proportions so as to convey accurately and efficiently both the message substance and also the 'hidden agenda' in relation to the corporate culture. Therefore, the following comments might be made on the methods given in the question.

1 *Letters*. Appropriate for communicating with customers or suppliers outside the firm, but inappropriate for instance for a senior manager to communicate with his immediate subordinate. Where the latter situation occurs, the management style is likely to be autocratic and the climate one of fear, in which everyone wants to 'cover his back' against any later suggestion of incompetence.

2 *Notice boards*. Appropriate for communicating forthcoming events, social occasions, successes recorded in any part of the organisation and immediate diary information of a routine nature. Where attempts are made to use notice boards for motivational purposes, by displaying exhortive posters and slogans related, say, to achieving better quality, they are certain to fail. This is because they imply distance between management and workers and a lack of total commitment by senior management to the proposition contained in the slogan.

3 *Telephones*. Appropriate in informal and urgent dealings with internal or external 'customers', for arranging meetings which are to be confirmed later, or for obtaining urgent information which is not so exact in nature as to be capable of later misinterpretation. It is inappropriate where a record must be kept of detailed matters. Excessive use of telephone communication may imply a loose and possibly inefficient management style or possibly an environment where informal networks are important and inter-departmental cooperation is normal,

4 *Meetings*. Large scale use of meetings (between managers) may suggest an informal and relaxed, but efficient organisation where cross departmental boundary cooperation is normal and where the hierarchy is flat. But it may equally imply a rigid management structure, deep hierarchy and autocratic management style. This would be because meetings are an excuse for inaction, a means of 'passing the buck' and a forum in which the power struggle for resources is undertaken.

STUDENT'S ANSWER

Question 2

> Comments on span of control should be included.

> How are priorities decided?

> What happens if things go wrong?

> Some mention of motivation theory (eg. Maslow) might help.

> Lots of good points here, but presentation lets you down badly.

> It is difficult to make sense of this – use short, sharp sentences – there are at least three different ideas here!

> How might organisation structure affect delegation?

Delegation is a means of getting greater results through people. It is the passing on by one person to another of responsibility for a given task.

A manager by conferring authority on a subordinate to act on his behalf, having decided his priorities, can concentrate on the work of most importance, leaving the work of lesser importance to be done by others. Therefore; delegation allows the manager more time for thinking and planning; the person closest to the activity delegated should be better able to make decisions than a distant superior; by delegating, the manager encourages initiative in his subordinates who are able to develop and make effective use of their skills, this aid to employee growth improving morale and thus perhaps productivity; decision-times are reduced as the need for recommendations going upwards to a superior and a reply returning downwards with an associated time delay are eliminated.

A manager's time is limited 'there is never enough time to complete all necessary and expected tasks' – the workload and schedules of managers hectic; delegation in other words effective time-management by managers is, 'so necessary to the success of a business' because it:

1 increases the likelihood of the organisation meeting its objectives efficiently;

2 creates greater devotion to and focus upon important long run managerial activities rather than to short run issues drawing the organisation away from a 'crisis-management' and a reactive stance to a pro-active one;

3 the organisation will have better developed managers as a result of delegation because it opens up channels of communications with subordinates allowing management to improve their interpersonal skills.

I am sure most managers recognise the advantages of delegation yet there are a number of barriers, even constraints to effective delegation, which make unbridled success very difficult to achieve and carry out in business. Paradoxically delegation may initially be time-consuming! Careful thought and planning about the content of subordinates' work (what the delegator can pass onto them), what training they may require to complete the tasks set them and the establishment of a suitable control network is necessary. If a manager does not think carefully about implementing a delegation policy, utopian visions he may hold will quickly dissolve and become a dystopian disaster, discouraging him from further attempts. Factors outside the manager's control may also impinge on his ability to delegate successfully; he may have little authority assigned to him leaving him very little to pass on. A manager may also not have sufficient subordinates or subordinates of sufficient competence for delegation to be effective. Also, political factors may make it prudent for a manager not to delegate — if there is excessive rivalry between subordinates for example.

In business, much depends on the ability of the person running or managing the operation to identify and concentrate on key tasks, leaving the less critical (even sometimes more enjoyable) tasks to others. Delegation allows the manager to achieve this but the difficulties associated with its implementation also lie at his door.

Tutor's comments

A thoughtful answer which raises important issues. Some discussion of the 'span of control' and perhaps motivational and leadership theory, plus perhaps some examples, would have raised this from C to B grade. The candidate *must* learn to present work more clearly.

OUTLINE ANSWER

Question 3

a) All organisations are hierarchical, some flatter, some deeper. The nature of the hierarchy depends on management style and size of the organisation. In any large organisation divisions are likely to develop between 'line' and 'staff' personnel and functions. 'Line' managers are often said to be those with direct responsibility for production functions and related functions. The employees who they supervise and manage are directly involved with the manufacture or delivery of the product or service and are often mostly rewarded on a weekly wage basis, on a weekly or daily notice basis. They have little security of tenure and worse conditions of work. 'Staff' functions are those which service the production facility, e.g. research department, or typing pool. They are mostly on monthly notice and salary and have more congenial conditions of work plus greater security. The managers in these areas are often concerned with activities which are apparently detached from production. They may be seen as 'enemies' by line management, obstructing rather than assisting.

b) A 'cost centre' could be said to be a group of related machines producing a single product; or a sub-unit of a firm, for example the leisure centre, associated bar and restaurant facilities within a five star hotel. The common characteristic is that costs and sales can be separately monitored by the immediate manager and/or his superior. A 'profit centre' is a similar sub-unit of a firm, but where the line manager is given total responsibility for not just sales and costs, but for achieving given levels of profit or performance. An example might be a managed public house within a group of similar hotels. It is, therefore, effectively a separate business entity, but financed by the 'holding' company.

Whereas cost centres may be identified within most businesses, it would be inappropriate in say a factory manufacturing four brands of biscuit on separate lines, to make each line a profit centre, but it would be useful to senior management to regard each as a cost centre. This will help to identify for example the stage in the product life cycle each has reached in order to plan future marketing strategy. In some businesses, where it is easy to identify free standing units, in for example a group of supermarket outlets, it will be helpful to make them profit centres. This will aid strategic planning, marketing etc and will also make it easier to measure the performance of both management and workforce.

OUTLINE ANSWER

Question 4

Organisations exist in an environment, both social, economic and political. They will have developed to provide some desired product or service in the context of a particular moment in history. Changes in any of these environmental areas will require these organisations to respond. The pace of such change and their degree will vary from time to time in different business areas and industries.

For many years, from 1945, the economic environment in advanced countries was relatively stable. Forward planning could be based on reasonable and potentially accurate extrapolations of past trends in important variables; viz. population change, technological change, input prices, market prices, exchange rates, etc. Growth of world trade was rapid and consistent. Since the early 1970s this stability has been eroded. This is particularly so in terms of technological change, disposable incomes, input prices and consumer tastes. All firms and organisations have to respond and do so without being able to forecast accurately the coming changes. They must, therefore, be even more responsive to change and flexible in response. Failure to respond may hazard the survival of the organisation.

Change is however resisted within organisations. It is therefore difficult for senior management to propel the organisation in new directions. They may be hindered by a static corporate culture; rigid organisational hierarchy and by divisions between 'line' and 'staff' functions. Narrow departmentalism tends to produce a situation where much energy is expended defending departmental boundaries and functions. This stems from increasing insecurity and fear.

A more responsive climate for change and flexibility may involve a radical restructuring of the organisation in order to flatten the hierarchy, motivate employees, cut across departmental boundaries and introduce a team drive approach. This will be painful unless management is able to defuse anxiety and fear in employees. The introduction of a Total Quality Management approach (or Japanisation) in say a car firm may be essential, but will take years rather than months to implement.

FURTHER READING

Torrington and Weightman, *The Business of Management*, Prentice Hall International 1985:
  Chapter 2, The development of management;
  Chapter 3, Types of organisation structure;
  Chapter 4, Types of management jobs;
  Chapter 5, Managerial work.
Appleby, *Modern Business Administration*, 5th Edition, Pitman 1991:
  Chapter 2, Management principles;
  Chapter 4, Organising.
Jewell, *An Integrated Approach to Business Studies*, Pitman 1990:
  Chapter 12, Management and Organisation Theory.
Buckley, *Structure of Business*, 2nd Edition, Pitman 1990:
  Chapter 12, Organising.

MANAGEMENT STYLE: MOTIVATION AND LEADERSHIP

MOTIVATION

MOTIVATION IN PRACTICE

LEADERSHIP

GETTING STARTED

We have now seen something of what managers in organisations do, how they do it, and the skills which they require. We have also seen that the structure of the organisation in which they work will both assist and constrain them in their efforts to achieve the objectives of the organisation. We have noticed that all organisations are subcultures, with their own values, rules and symbols which influence and constrain what is possible for managers and what they are likely to find acceptable. The outcome of all these factors is a distinct management or leadership *style*, which will be reflected throughout the structure, communications channels and decision-making machinery of the organisation.

There is no doubt that the most valuable resource within an organisation is its personnel. Whatever approach is adopted to the management of personnel will have the effect of motivating (or failing to motivate) the workforce at all levels – with obvious implications for the achievement of organisational objectives.

In this chapter we look at some of the theories that have been developed which may help managers in their 'directing' role.

ESSENTIAL PRINCIPLES

MOTIVATION

66 A definition. 99

Motivation may be defined as 'the force of process which impels people to behave in the way they do'. In the context of an organisation this means the extent to which they behave in a way which is consistent with the achievement of the objectives of the organisation. Psychologists have been interested in identifying these forces and processes which motivate workers for some 80 years. The models of motivation which they have developed have greatly influenced management practice and style. We have summarised below the key propositions and applications set out by some of the more important theorists.

66 Employee performance is not always related to motivation. 99

However, first of all, the point must be made that differences in employee performance are not necessarily due to differences in motivation. Performance in a job is also a function of an employee's *ability level*. A manager, before criticising an employee's work effort, should first find out if that employee has the ability to do the job. Normally this would have been determined at the recruitment interview or ensured through training courses after recruitment.

MASLOW'S HIERARCHY OF NEEDS

Maslow believed that an individual had certain *needs* which he or she strived to satisfy. These could be arranged in a *hierarchy* (see Fig. 8.1).

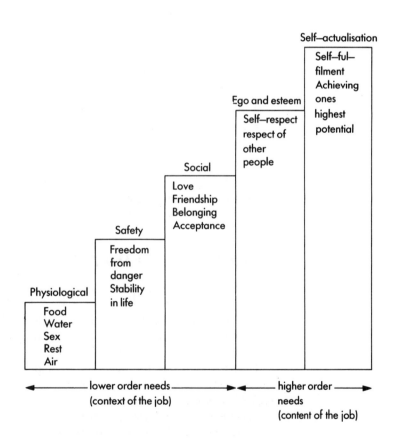

Fig. 8.1 Maslow's hierarchy of needs

66 A satisfied need is *not* a motivator. 99

At any one time one need is dominant – i.e. it needs to be satisfied. The need is a *motivator*. However, once satisfied it is no longer a motivator, but is replaced by a higher order need which is yet to be satisfied. Thus, an individual whose *physiological* needs have been satisfied would now want to satisfy his *safety* needs.

If managers agree with Maslow's analysis of motivation they must provide the means of satisfying these needs in the organisational context. Within each 'area' of need there are various ways this can be done (see Table 8.1).

NEED	EXAMPLE
Physiological	Pay, holidays, rest periods, canteens
Safety	Security of employment, health and safety measures, pensions
Social	Formal work groups, sports and leisure facilities, organised social events
Ego and Esteem	Power, titles, status symbols, merit awards, promotion
Self-actualisation	Challenging work, developing new skills

Table 8.1 Methods of satisfying employee needs

Comments on Maslow's hierarchy of needs

"Maslow's work has been criticised."

1 Satisfaction of needs is not the *only* motivator at work. Group allegiances or attitudes towards management may be more important than organisational motivators.
2 Some people may have very low levels of aspiration, in which case motivators aimed at ego/esteem and self actualisation will have no impact on the level of performance.
3 Needs, particularly higher order needs, may be satisfied *outside* work. For example, an employee may satisfy ego/esteem needs through being a Scout leader, a member of a dramatic society, or the treasurer of a club or charity.
4 Creative people may be motivated by higher order needs, even though lower order ones have *not* been satisfied.

McCLELLAND'S ACHIEVEMENT MOTIVATION

McClelland took Maslow's higher order needs and, using *personality tests*, studied the characteristics of people who he had identified as being 'achievement orientated'. He found that they had a number of common characteristics, including:

- taking sole responsibility for a task in order to identify themselves more closely with its (successful) outcome

- setting themselves moderate goals, thus maximising their chances of success

- needing the stimulus of continual feedback (thereby gaining the satisfaction they rely on)

McClelland also looked at why certain people were low achievers. His research suggested that education, parental influences, cultural background and societal values were important. More importantly though, he believed such people could develop (through training) a higher urge to achieve.

McGREGOR: THEORY X AND THEORY Y

This has been mentioned already in Chapter 7. McGregor's set of assumptions labelled Theory X, is based very much on F.W. Taylor's ideas of economic man and scientific management. It is easy to criticise the assumptions behind scientific management (as outlined in Theory X) but *money* does remain an important motivator for most people, and in some industries (e.g. engineering) incentive pay schemes are still widely used.

Theory Y embodies the views (or assumptions) of the human relations and neo human relations schools of thought. In contrast to Theory X, it emphasises the importance of *higher level needs* which workers may try to satisfy through the work situation. The role of management in these circumstances is to create a work environment which enables workers to satisfy these needs. However, it is difficult to structure an organisation so that all jobs are challenging and rewarding and yet achieve the necessarily high level of efficiency. The result is that those workers who can best be described as Theory Y employees, but who are managed according to Theory X assumptions, will rapidly become disenchanted with the situation. Poor morale, poor productivity, absenteeism, high labour turnover rates and difficult industrial relations will ensue. All these will confirm the manager in his belief that he was right to treat these workers according to Theory X assumptions.

In short, the assumptions which managers make about their workers tend to become a 'self-fulfilling prophecy'.

HERZBERG'S TWO FACTOR THEORY

Hygiene factors are not motivators.

As a result of his research Herzberg identified two sets of factors. The first group he called 'hygiene' or 'maintenance' factors. This group included factors such as working conditions, job security, salary, quality of supervision and interpersonal relationships. These factors, if not present in the job, caused job dissatisfaction. However, their presence does not positively motivate employees.

Herzberg called his second group of factors 'motivators'. This group included recognition, achievement, responsibility, advancement and challenging work. These factors, if present in a work situation, give rise to satisfaction. (N.B. 'Hygiene factors' relate primarily to the *context* of the job – they are Maslow's lower order needs, whilst 'motivators' relate to the *content* of the job – Maslow's higher order needs.)

For managers, the implications of Herzberg's work is that it is necessary to provide strong 'motivational' factors whilst at the same time ensuring that negative 'hygiene factors' are not present. Herzberg's work has been criticised as lacking scientific method. The findings of later research studies have been less conclusive. Many writers have also questioned the placing of money as a 'hygiene factor'. However, the implications of Herzberg's work are very much the same as Maslow's. Managers should concentrate their efforts on designing jobs which give the employee the opportunity for greater autonomy and responsibility. The job enrichment programmes of many companies were strongly influenced by Herzberg's two factor theory.

So far the theories we have looked at are termed 'content' theories. They answer the question 'what causes behaviour?'. In short, the answer is unsatisfied needs. But *content* theories have been criticised for simplifying the subject of motivation. In the first place people's needs differ from one to another. Secondly, motivation is partly determined by personal circumstances (this implies that subordinates will not act consistently over time – today's motivating factor may fail tomorrow!). Finally, from the organisation's point of view the link between job satisfaction and productivity is not as strong as these theories would have us believe.

PROCESS THEORIES

Expectations may affect motivation.

'Process' theories of motivation look at *how* people are motivated. They consider the *process* by which people reach a decision to act in a particular way. Process theorists believe that an individual's expectation of the outcome of a particular course of action will considerably influence that person's actions. We will consider two such theories.

Vroom's value–expectancy theory

Motivation depends on two factors. First, the *value* that an individual places on a certain outcome (i.e. the satisfaction he or she obtains). Second, the *level of expectation* as regards the idea that increased effort will lead to the desired outcome. Thus, an individual will be highly motivated if they value the reward (e.g. promotion) and firmly believe that they can obtain that reward through increased work effort. However, if they do not value the goal, or believe it to be unattainable, then the motivational force will be low. Value – expectancy theory has been criticised for suggesting that individuals will always act in a rational way.

Skinner's operant conditioning

Skinner suggests than an individual's behaviour can be modified by forces in the environment. If a particular pattern of behaviour consistently results in unpleasant outcomes, then the individual will soon *learn* to avoid that behaviour pattern. Behaviour yielding pleasant results will, on the other hand, be repeated.

In organisational terms the implications are clear; managers can modify the behaviour of subordinates by punishing behaviour which is not acceptable and praising behaviour which they wish to encourage.

MOTIVATION IN PRACTICE

It is essential that managers are able to motivate people. They are unable to deal with all aspects of their job without the supporting activities of subordinates. Not only will a failure to motivate his or her subordinates reflect badly upon the manager concerned, it will also have implications for the organisation in terms of loss of orders, and also high costs and low profits due to waste and inefficiency.

This state of affairs cannot be allowed to continue if the organisation is to survive. Managers must be able to *recognise* the causes and symptoms of poor motivation and attempt to *remedy* the situation.

SYMPTOMS AND CAUSES OF POOR MOTIVATION

You must be able to distinguish between the *symptoms* and *causes* of poor motivation. The 'symptoms' are the outward manifestation of a deeper problem. Thus a student may miss college on Fridays so as to avoid lessons he or she dislikes. In this case the symptom is missing college; the 'cause' of this action is to avoid the lessons disliked. Of course in practice whilst it is easy for a manager to identify symptoms of poor motivation, it is very much harder to establish the causes. However, in a case study situation you may find the following pointers useful.

Symptoms of poor motivation

- sub standard performance, e.g. many mistakes, failure to meet deadlines
- high levels of absenteeism, sickness or labour turnover
- poor timekeeping
- sullen acquiescence rather than positive response to orders and requests from supervisor or customer
- untidy and dirty work station
- disciplinary problems
- industrial relations disputes

Causes of poor motivation

The underlying causes for such action may be:

- fear of redundancy or short time working
- unsatisfactory pay levels (absolute or comparative)
- unsatisfactory working conditions
- unsatisfactory social relationships
- uninteresting or undemanding jobs
- changes in work, work groups or working conditions
- poor communication between management and workers (n.b. rumours resulting from informal networks)
- ignorance of organisational objectives

STEPS TO MOTIVATE EMPLOYEES

Successful managers will quickly realise that there is no single management style which will motivate all employees or which will be successful in all situations. However, whatever system of motivation is established, the manager must ensure that:

- it is seen as fair by all employees
- it is flexible
- it covers all employees
- it is in tune with the political and economic climate

Where poor motivation exists within an organisation a manager should:

- ensure that pay levels within the organisation and with comparable organisations are fair
- consider establishing incentive pay schemes (which are not divisive)
- ensure working conditions are adequate, train the subordinate to do his job and provide opportunities for promotion
- develop team spirit – a situation where group members are mutually supportive
- provide the employee with the means to measure his progress in the job

- improve worker's feelings about their job; for example, recognise and celebrate achievement, involve in decision making, introduce quality circles, etc.
- make sure the job is challenging, even in mundane occupations, through job rotation, enlargement and enrichment, etc.
- make sure the worker is well informed on all matters within the organisation which might affect him or her.

LEADERSHIP

❝A definition.❞

This is a key element in any manager's job. *Leadership* has been defined in many different ways, but central to most definitions is that it is a process by which individual and group activities are influenced toward organisational goals. The central problem facing researchers is why some people are more successful in getting others to follow them. We will, shortly, look at three approaches to the study of leadership: trait, behaviour and contingency.

CLASSIFYING LEADERS

In a discussion of leadership the following terms are often used. They represent basic approaches used by leaders.

- *Autocratic leaders*. These make most of the decisions, expect others to carry out decisions without discussion. It is a form of leadership often used in the armed forces or, in times of crisis, within other organisations.
- *Democratic leaders*. Their followers are heavily involved in the decision-making process. The group is involved in defining objectives, devising strategies and allocating work assignments. It can produce a high level of commitment to achieve objectives.
- *Laissez faire leaders*. These give little direction. Responsibility lies in the hands of subordinates.

❝Common terms for leadership.❞

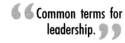

Leaders may also be categorised according to their emphasis in getting the job done.

- *Task orientated leaders* focus on the 'work' aspects of the task. They are primarily concerned with planning, scheduling quality and output of work.
- *People orientated leaders* are more concerned about the welfare and feelings of their subordinates. They often have a strong need to be accepted by their team members.

Trait theory

This starts from the assumption that 'leaders are born, not made'. If this is so, it follows that there must be some *personality traits* which are found in good leaders. The findings were inconclusive. Individuals, who were regarded as leaders, exhibited remarkably different characteristics.

Other researchers tried to identify the characteristics which were necessary for good leadership. They were more successful. These seem to be:

- intellectual skills
- interpersonal skills
- task-based knowledge
- task motivation
- dominance

However, no *one* characteristic has been identified as being essential for a leader. The trait approach may also be criticised for ignoring the environment within which leadership operates, or the followers needs.

Behavioural theory

The failure of the 'traitist approach' to leadership shifted attention to studying leadership *behaviour*. The change of approach is significant – behaviour can be learnt or modified! Thus leaders *can* be made. Individuals, through training and experience, may be capable of undertaking a leadership role.

Lewin's research in the 1930s concentrated on small group behaviour under autocratic, democratic and laissez faire styles of leadership. The results are summarised below:

STYLE	RESULTS
AUTOCRATIC:	Group didn't plan at all; considerable aggression amongst members; output high in leader's presence but far lower in their absence; quality levels were low.
DEMOCRATIC:	Level of motivation high; group worked well together; work output was high in all situations; quality levels were high.
LAISSEZ FAIRE:	High degree of frustration amongst members; group did not work together; work output very low; quality levels low.

Lewin concluded that, in this situation, the *democratic* leadership style produced the best results. One interesting factor of these studies was that when the leaders switched groups, but maintained their leadership style, the group's behaviour quickly changed. Thus when the democratic leader was moved to the group formerly organised along autocratic lines, the group quickly developed the characteristics associated with democratic leadership. Further studies by other researchers (e.g. Likert) have also concluded that a democratic style of leadership is most preferred.

Democratic style is not always best.

However, the democratic style of leadership is not suitable in all situations. For example, if a manager believes his workers fall into McGregor's 'Theory X' category he would *not* use a democratic style. (But beware! The use of an autocratic management style may force workers to adopt Theory X type behaviour as the only way of showing their frustration with the situation.) Equally, where the manager alone has the information needed to make a decision or where he or she is involved in an emergency situation, the use of a democratic leadership style may also be inappropriate.

Contingency theory

This theory stems from the apparent failure of trait and behavioural theories of leadership to arrive at a satisfactory explanation of leadership. An alternative approach is to see leadership as being related directly to the *circumstances* in which it is being exercised. That is to say, a style of leadership which works in one situation may be inappropriate in another. A good leader then is not one who possesses certain characteristics or traits, nor one who has one ideal behaviour pattern, but rather one who adopts the right leadership style in particular circumstances, and is able to adopt a different style as circumstances change. Tannenbaum and Schmidt have set out a simple model to illustrate this view, which is set out in Figure 8.2.

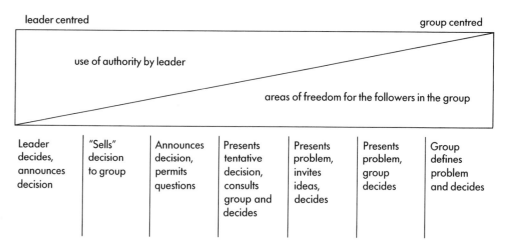

Fig. 8.2 Tannenbaum & Schmidts continuum of leadership

From Figure 8.2 you may be able to recognise the leadership style which is used in organisations of which you are a member, be it a school, firm, cricket team or church. If you are cynical, you may conclude that good leadership is not just a matter of adopting the style of leadership which is appropriate for the circumstances, and being able to change to a different style as circumstances change. Perhaps it is also a case of being able to convince your followers that you are using one style, when in fact you are using a quite different one which the followers might not accept if they knew!

EXAMINATION QUESTIONS

1   'The job of a manager is to make decisions, not motivate others'. Discuss this
    statement with reference to the production manager of a soft drinks factory.   *(25)*
                                                                        (Cambridge 1986)

2   What does the work of the major authorities tell us about employee motivation? Why in
    practice is there a failure to meet such expectations?   *(20)*
                                                                        (AEB 1987)

3   Should production line managers wear suits to work or dress in overalls as their
    shopfloor personnel do?   *(20)*
                                                                        (AEB 1987)

4   a) Why is 'job enrichment' considered to be an important part of motivation?   *(15)*
    b) How can the concept of job enrichment be effectively applied to workers on the
        production line?   *(10)*
                                                                        (Cambridge 1990)

TUTOR ANSWER

Question 1

The job of all managers contains four vital elements, planning, organising, controlling and
directing. The proportions of a manager's time spent on these activities will depend on his
role in the organisational structure. Thus the senior manager will spend proportionately
more time on *planning*, in other words on setting the objectives of the organisation and
deciding on strategies for their achievement. The production manager in a soft drinks
factory, for example, will spend less time on these activities, and then only in connection
with his function's part in achieving the overall objective. He will spend correspondingly
more time than the senior manager in controlling and directing his team of workers.
However, the one common feature of management at both levels is 'people management'.
Both managers would need to delegate in order to use their time effectively, and this
involves placing some degree of responsibility on lower level workers, within an agreed
span of control. Delegation involves the motivation of the workers or other subordinates.
Motivation is therefore the common factor in all management activities.

   Motivation is best described as 'the force or process which impels people to behave in
the way they do'. To motivate people in an organisation is to induce them to act in a manner
consistent with the achievement of the organisation's objectives. A manager is required to
make decisions about the operation of his part of the organisation in the light of given
objectives. Once made, these decisions must be carried out by the workers. Whether or
not they do so effectively depends on the degree to which they are motivated by the
manager. He in turn will seek to motivate them within the style and culture of the
organisation as it is expressed in policies about the following items; organisation of work,
pay and non-financial rewards including recognition and status symbols.

   A soft drinks factory is a highly automated production system, within which most jobs
are semi-skilled or unskilled, and by their nature are more likely to be monotonous and
boring. Also such a factory is likely to be part of a corporate culture which is based on
McGregor's Theory X, which contains the assumption that motivation is purely monetary,
and that workers dislike work, and will avoid it where possible. Thus this approach also
implies a high level of control by the manager, a constant end-of-line inspection process to
check quality, along with a work study/methods study approach to job design and payment
by results. This approach originated with F. W. Taylor's model of scientific management
developed in the early years of this century. If this *is* the situation, then the role of the
production manager will be centred around maintaining control by punishing any dereliction
of duty, such as absenteeism or excessively high levels of waste. This will have to be
combined with a careful monitoring of the piece rate scheme based on work study. Thus in
this climate the manager's role will be based on minimising demotivation rather than on
maximising motivation. If the corporate culture of the company is more enlightened and
based on McGregor's Theory Y, which suggests that workers work for intrinsic
satisfaction from a job well done rather than purely instrumental rewards in money form,
then the production manager's role would be very different.

Such a company would then benefit by being aware of the theory set out in Maslow's 'hierarchy of needs', which suggests that once lower order needs (physiological needs such as food, safety needs and job security) are satisfied, then the motivation of workers lies in satisfying higher order needs (ego, self esteem, and self actualisation – the achievement of fulfilment of potential). It will also be helpful if the company is aware of Herzberg's view that 'hygiene factors', in the form of excellent working conditions, are the first priority, after which various 'motivators' may come into play. These would include the recognition of achievement, and the setting of work which is stimulating and challenging.

The production manager of a soft drinks factory run on these, more enlightened, lines would be seeking to achieve the various 'higher order' motivators in a number of ways within the limitations imposed by an automated line. Thus 'job rotation' could be used to alleviate boredom. This might involve further training, which in turn might lead to 'job enrichment' by giving groups of workers at 'stations' on the line additional responsibility for gathering information on costs or on quality. They could be encouraged to feel that they had some participation in decision making by the use of 'quality circles' or 'quality improvement teams', which would meet in official work time in order to develop methods of improving performance in their work group (or in the factory as a whole). Their suggestions would be listened to by senior management and implemented where feasible. Successes of this kind would be celebrated and recognised publicly, perhaps in the company newspaper. Payment by individual results, which is divisive, could be replaced by performance-related pay based on the performance of the plant.

The benefits of such a system for motivation might then be: lower levels of absenteeism, better punctuality, more consistent performance, continuous productivity improvement, and a better quality product, leading to better industrial relations and higher profits.

STUDENT ANSWER

Question 2

> Careful, the question is on motivation, not leadership!

The most important asset of any organisation is its people. They have to be led and motivated by management. The manner in which this is due will depend on the organisational culture which operates within an organisational structure. This structure will reflect the style of leadership adopted by the top management or owners.

Tannenbaum and Schmidt set out a continuum model of leadership styles, ranging from authoritarian and exploitive at one extreme to democratic and participative at the other. Across this continuum the degree to which management hands over 'control' to the workers in the context of his particular job, will increase. The more authoritarian styles would correspond to McGregor's Theory X model. Theory X suggests that workers dislike work, will avoid it where possible, and will only respond to a regime which includes both rewards and punishment. Theory Y takes the opposite view, that work is enjoyed by workers, and is done well provided that effort and commitment are recognised.

Whichever style is dominant in an organisation, there is a need to motivate employees. That is, they have to be made to behave in a way which is consistent with the achievement of the organisation's objectives. Assuming that they have been carefully selected through a process which accurately identifies their ability to perform to the required standard, motivation then becomes a matter of creating positive attitudes, leading to suitable performance. Numerous psychologists have developed theories of motivation which may be applied in the context of motivating workers. Which ones underpin company policy on pay, reward and recognition, training, etc, will be closely related to the values of the organisation as expressed in their management style.

Thus for example Maslow's hierarchy of needs model, suggests

> This theory needs to be explained further.

that once the lower order needs have been satisfied
(physiological, safety, social) by the provision of good basic
pay and working conditions, the worker wants to satisfy higher
order needs (self esteem and actualisation). This he may do
outside the context of work if he cannot do so within the
organisation. McClelland identifies ways in which these needs may
be met at work, by giving the worker greater responsibility, and
goals which are achievable, and recognised when achieved. Various
methods may be used, e.g. job enlargement, job enrichment,
quality circles. Herzberg also stressed the importance of
'hygiene needs', i.e. good working conditions, as well as the
need for 'motivators', such as recognition, good interpersonal
relations, and responsibility. Vroom suggests that it is
necessary for the worker to value the outcome expected of him,
and must have an expectation that increased effort will lead to
that outcome. Skinner suggests that it is not necessary for the
worker to place meanings on what he does. It is enough that the
actions desired by the organisation be positively reinforced when
carried out, and undesired actions not be reinforced by this
action. This approach is called 'Behaviour Modification'.

   In practice, attempts at motivating workers will fail if they
are based on the above theories, but inconsistently and
insincerely carried out. A more likely reason for motivation
efforts to fail is that they are based on Taylor's theory of
scientific management. This fits in with McGregor's Theory X
approach, and suggests that workers will only respond to monetary
reward, simplified jobs, and punishment. This approach is usually
based on work and method study which dehumanises and alienates
the worker from product, job, employer and colleagues. It also
generates a great deal of waste, scrap, and rework, which is
costly for the company. Many companies, especially in
manufacturing industries, but also in the service sector, use
this approach. When combined with an authoritarian/exploitive
management style, the result is likely to be persistent
industrial relations problems.

> **You should distinguish between content and process theories.**

> **Theory X motivational techniques may work with some employees.**

Tutor's comments

This answer covers some of the material required but in a haphazard and disorganised fashion. A little time spent on planning would have paid dividends. In particular, the contribution of F.W. Taylor has been underplayed and the contribution of E. Mayo totally unrecognised. The second part of the question goes largely unconsidered. The answer should have looked at whether workers always act rationally, how needs may vary between workers and over a period of time, and how expectations may affect motivation. In view of the fact that much of the obvious knowledge is badly organised or unrelated to the question this is, at best, a marginal fail.

OUTLINE ANSWERS

Question 3

This question invites a subjective argument as to the relative merits of the industrial culture prevalent in most Western advanced economies, in contrast to that operating in large private sector companies in Japan. It is often supposed that 'Japanisation' of a western firm is not possible because of key cultural differences. That is to say, it is assumed that Japanese culture (because of its Confucian origins) is based on conciliation and co-operation rather than on confrontation, and on decision taking on the basis of teamwork. It is also said that the absence of a rigid class system in Japan makes this style possible. It is believed by many Western managers that this style is not transferable to the west. Recent advances in major western companies which *have* adopted the Japanese approach, in particular Total

Quality, have demonstrated that this assumption is untrue. For example, Ford in both USA and Europe, and British Steel have gone some way down this road.

The establishment of 'single status' in a factory is arguably more difficult. The practice in Japanese firms of having all workers dress in the same company 'uniform', the use of one canteen for all, the elimination of other status symbols, such as executive cloakrooms, car parks, etc. is the outward and visible sign of the 'family' approach to employees. It is accompanied by life time employment, and company provision of welfare facilities. Some movement in this direction may help to induce greater team spirit, co-operation and emphasis on quality, particularly on the production line, where traditionally workers have been seen as 'hands', not brains. That it can be done in the UK, even in a very traditional industrial environment, has been demonstrated by the success of Nissan in operating a car plant in this way in Durham.

However, it can be argued that the differences in the way production managers dress, together with the other status symbols associated with their position, are a powerful motivational force. Maslow, for example, suggests that power, titles and status symbols satisfy important ego and esteem needs. Employees will strive to achieve organisational objectives (and promotion) so as to obtain these benefits.

At the crux of this question lies the problem of what really motivates workers. There is no easy answer to this question. What motivates one worker will fail to motivate another. Moreover what motivates one worker today may fail tomorrow. The team approach implied by single standard dress may appeal to some workers but not to all. Finally it could be argued that a team approach could be, and has been, adopted in many factories without the imposition of uniform dress.

Question 4

a) Motivation may be defined as 'that force or process which impels people to behave in the way they do'. In any business organisation human resources are a key input, the productivity of which must be maximised. Within the concept of scientific management as developed in early 20th century factories, the emphasis is on division of labour (that is the breakdown of the production process into simple, specialised tasks, which may be carried out rapidly, with minimum skill). This is combined with maximum mechanisation of the task. The result is a system of flow production, to produce economic order quantities, taking advantage of the economies of scale and standardised products. The same principle is applied to some clerical and administrative tasks. Motivation of workers is thought to be possible only through fear of punishment, combined with extra financial reward for above standard performances as measured by work study methods. Workers are seen as an adjunct of the technology, and are not expected to demonstrate initiative or responsibility. Managers are there to control the process.

Modern technology has reduced the advantages of scale, and the emphasis in a modern factory is often now on flexibility of response. This involves the need to have better trained and more flexible workers, capable of controlling their own pattern of work. As this change began to be recognised, the emphasis in the motivation of workers shifted towards the views of the Human Relations school of thought.

As a result, attempts were made to re-design jobs in order to increase job satisfaction. This is intended to reduce the 'time span of discretion', i.e. the intervals between checks by supervisors. The recent innovation of Total Quality approaches to management has intensified this trend. The re-design of jobs may involve enlargement (range and type of jobs), rotation of jobs (increased variety and flexibility), and job enrichment. This goes one step further and gives more discretion to workers as to how tasks should be performed. It is often undertaken in conjunction with a shift from flow to batch production on a kanban/JIT approach, where a group of workers operate in a work station over which they have a high degree of self management. The role of both middle manager and supervisor changes from inspector/controller, to facilitator/coach. A much higher level of training expenditure is essential.

b) Examples of the job enrichment approach to motivation may be seen in Japanese car factories, or in western factories which have adopted the Japanese style of management. On an old fashioned line, a single model would be produced in long identical runs on a continuous line. Workers would be specialised to a fine degree, each undertaking one simple task as a vehicle reached them on the track. This enabled rapid production of large numbers of vehicles ahead of orders. Quality would be 'inspected in', by quality control officers, and workers timed by work study officers. Pay would be on a piece rate system, and there would be no incentive to ensure quality. Industrial relations would be confrontational.

Advances in computer and robotic technology have made possible a much more flexible system. Workers operate in groups in a work station over which they have control of task allocation (on a flexible basis), right down to housekeeping! A 'kanban' system is applied, where instructions are issued to the workstation by computer link, in response to, rather than in advance of, orders. Just In Time inventory control permits different variants of the model to be produced. The advantage is that great savings are made in inventory of 'buffer' stocks of parts and of completed vehicles. Costs of quality can be measured and eliminated, and a 'zero defects' target reached. The impact on workers is great. Motivation comes from having control over the pace and type of work task. Piece rates are abolished, and performance rewards are geared to unit of company performance. Quality circles are often a feature of this method, along with large numbers of suggestions from the workers for possible improvements. In the first year of operating this system, Rover Cars saved forty million pounds in inventory costs alone, whilst Toyota in five years received from its workers some 5000 suggestions for improvements, 98% of which were implemented.

FURTHER READING

Buckley, *Structure of Business*, 2nd edition, Pitman 1990:
    Chapter 13, Directing.
    Chapter 8, Developing a leadership style that works.
    Chapter 9, Using rewards as a leadership tool.
Hammond, *Business Studies*, 2nd edition, Longman Group 1991:
    Chapter 12, People and Business.
Jewell, *Business Studies*, Pitman 1990:
    Chapter 3, The External Environment.
Timm, Peterson, Stevens, *People at Work*, 3rd edition, West Publishing Company 1986:
    Chapter 3, An introduction to human needs and motivation.
    Chapter 4, Creating conditions for motivation.

CHAPTER

COMMUNICATION I

TYPES OF COMMUNICATION MEDIA

BARRIERS TO GOOD COMMUNICATION

COMMUNICATIONS NETWORKS

MODERN COMMUNICATIONS TECHNOLOGY

GETTING STARTED

Much of our daily life is spent in communication with family, friends, school or work colleagues, either in speech or in writing. We are also often receiving communications from others, whether on radio, TV or in print. Thousands of messages are being transmitted and received, some trivial and simple, some complex and important. For a number of reasons it is quite likely that some of these messages are misunderstood and misinterpreted.

In this chapter we set out the various types of communication mechanisms which are used in organisations, indicating their strengths and weaknesses and the factors which may cause communication to break down.

When something goes wrong in an organisation, it is likely that the person blamed for the problem will in turn blame a breakdown in communication. This would probably be correct, since 80% of management time is spent communicating with others in the process of controlling and directing the activities of the organisation, and there are many ways in which breakdown of communication might occur. The bigger the organisation, the more probable it is that lengthening lines of communication and the complexity of the structure of the organisation may cause messages to be diverted down the wrong channel, go astray or be misinterpreted.

ESSENTIAL PRINCIPLES

Within any organisation, effective communication is important for a number of reasons. For example:

- coordination of activities of different departments is only possible by effective communication.

- clear instructions are essential if workers are to understand what is required of them and to enable the activities of groups or workers to be integrated.

- relationships with clients, suppliers, bankers, unions, the community, tax authorities and so on will only be satisfactory if communications with them are clear, helpful and understood.

A number of characteristics are required for a communications system to fulfil these objectives. These are: clarity, simplicity, brevity and accuracy. This is so whether the communication is quantitative, or qualitative. *Quantitative communication* involves the transmission and interpretation of numerical information, for example sales figures, market research findings, financial accounts; this area is dealt with in Chapter 10.

In this chapter we are concerned with *qualitative communication*, using language, either spoken or written. Such spoken or written messages are complicated by the impact of non-verbal signals. Posture, gesture, dress and presentation, tone of voice, facial expression, eye contact, all deliver a message irrespective of the spoken message. In fact non-verbal signals may totally contradict the verbal message which is being presented. Psychologists suggest that 70% of all communication is of this kind. This may explain why meetings and negotiations do not always go according to plan, no matter how carefully the participants may choose their language.

TYPES OF COMMUNICATION MEDIA

Various types of communication media are available for use in an organisation. These are set out in Table 9.1.

verbal	face to face by 'phone by presentation by discussion
non-verbal	by gesture by posture by eye contact by tone of voice by physical appearance and presentation
written	by letter or fax by memo by report by visual aid (OHP slide etc) by noticeboards etc
numerical	by tables of data by bar charts by histograms by pie charts by graphs

Table 9.1 Types of communication media

Each of these types has advantages and disadvantages.

Face to face

Advantages:

- immediate impact (reinforced by appropriate non-verbal signals)

- misunderstandings may be instantly corrected

- receiver can instantly respond

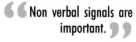
Non verbal signals are important.

Disadvantages:

- disagreement may produce instant conflict

- non-verbal signals (posture, eye contact, gesture, tone of voice, etc) may offer a conflicting message. This may be much stronger than the verbal message delivered

Phone communication

Advantages:

- as in the case of face to face conversation

Disadvantages:

- the absence of non-verbal signals makes the meaning conveyed by the transmitter of the message more difficult to receive
- a poor line and distorted sound may cause the message to be misunderstood

Presentations, speeches, lectures

Advantages:

- use of clear presentation techniques and clear language makes possible a strong one-way impact

Disadvantages:

- bad verbal presentation and lack of visual aids reduces impact dramatically
- bad acoustics may cause loss of important parts of the message
- the attention span of the audience may be too short to absorb the message, unless written summaries are provided
- there is little chance for clarification of important points

Written communications

Advantages:

- the message can be precisely presented
- the message is permanent and can be stored for future reference
- the written message may be supplemented with numerical evidence or other supporting illustrations

Disadvantages:

- incomprehensible language will destroy the impact
- verbosity will have the same effect
- if the message is too long, it may not be read in full
- careless typing or other reproduction may distort the message
- it is not easy to clarify difficult points

BARRIERS TO GOOD COMMUNICATION

At this point we need to develop the above idea a little further, by looking in a more systematic way at barriers to good communication. Despite the importance of good communication in any organisation, its creation and maintenance is often neglected. We all take language for granted, failing to realise that a given sequence of words may have totally different meanings to several recipients. There exist many barriers to good communication, but they may be grouped into those stemming from 'transmission', 'reception', 'manipulation' and 'distance'.

TRANSMISSION BREAKDOWNS

Why messages are misunderstood.

These may occur because of:

- Deficiencies in the language used. Reduced emphasis on the teaching of formal grammar in recent years may diminish the richness of vocabulary available and destroy meaning through loose construction.
- Technical language may be inaccurately used.
- Verbosity may obscure meaning in a flood of words.
- Archaic or colloquial conventions and expressions may obscure meaning.

RECEPTION BREAKDOWNS

These may stem from the following factors:

- The emotional state of the recipient may cause him or her to perceive a message as threatening, when it was intended to convey instructions or information. Wrong responses may ensue.
- Stereotypical attitudes (sexist, racist, etc) may cause an innocuous message to be misinterpreted.
- Excessive amounts of communications may cause information overload, or 'selective attention', resulting in important information being overlooked.

MANIPULATION BREAKDOWNS

These may arise when:

- An individual, for his or her own purposes, misdirects or misinterprets a message, in order to achieve some personal objective which runs counter to those of the organisation.
- A manager deliberately uses routine communications channels as a weapon with which to attack some rival in the company; this may be done by the number, type and direction of the messages. This sort of intimidation is commonly experienced by women managers working in a male environment. Thus manipulation of communications systems is a means of asserting power over others.

DISTANCE BREAKDOWNS

We have used this term to cover a number of related points:

- Geographical distance between any two plants in a group may limit the possible amount of face to face communication. This may lead to excessive reliance on other less direct methods which may be less effective.
- Status barriers. These may be critical, especially in UK firms. Strong class barriers may inhibit managers from listening to what workers have to say, or inhibit workers from attempting to express their point of view. Such barriers are reinforced by symbolic privileges, e.g. company cars, executive dining rooms, and so on. These are regarded with amazement by other cultures, especially the Japanese, who seek to dismantle such barriers and to encourage participation by the workforce through such devices as Quality Circles.

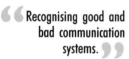 Recognising good and bad communication systems.

When you visit a company in connection with a project, or when you are looking at a case study, it is possible to use certain clues to discover whether the communications system in the organisation is working well or badly. Later in the chapter we will consider the types of networks which exist to convey communication in an organisation. Meanwhile here are some of the clues you might like to look for.

Symptoms of good communication

- High level of morale amongst the workforce.
- Cheerful and positive atmosphere in which decisions are made quickly and effectively.
- No signs of bullying or aggression.
- The operation is clearly under control.

Symptoms of bad communication

- Low morale, high sickness and labour turnover rates.
- High numbers of routine mistakes and excessive scrap product.
- Anxiety, expressed in an unwillingness to make decisions and accept responsibility.
- Aggression and hostility.
- Evidence of lack of control in the organisation.

It is unlikely that any organisation will achieve perfect communication, but there are a number of ways in which it might improve its results in this respect. For example:

- Ensure employee awareness of communication problems.
- Use more than one communication network within the organisation.
- Shorten the chain of communication.
- Seek ways of putting in place upwards communications systems such as staff meetings, suggestions schemes, quality circles, etc.
- Reduce status differences through open plan offices, common dining areas and car parks, etc.
- Encourage the use of good, simple language.
- Encourage instant feedback from recipients of messages.
- Use a variety of media to convey a message at all levels.
- Train employees, especially managers, in the use of language, and the importance of body language.

“Improving communication systems.”

COMMUNICATIONS NETWORKS

We have so far concentrated on the message and what may go wrong with it in terms of human error, or manipulation. But all this activity takes place within invisible but nevertheless real networks, either formal, or informal. It is to these that we must now turn.

FORMAL NETWORKS

“Organisation charts show lines of communication.”

We have already seen in Chapter 7 that in any business there exists an organisational structure which may be set out in the form of a tree diagram. This is intended to establish and convey a command structure, indicating lines of accountability, and relationships between departments. It also implies a system by which communication takes place for the reasons we have given. It also implies that the direction of communication is largely *down* the organisation, rather than upwards or across. In large organisations such communications channels may be slow or inefficient. The pattern of such communications

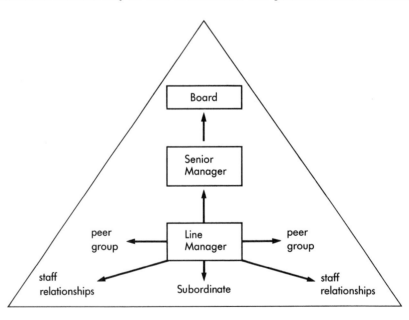

Fig. 9.1 The manager's communication network

may be simply expressed in diagrammatic form, as in Fig. 9.1. Here the pattern is seen from the perspective of the 'line' or middle manager, whose communications travel vertically up or down the organisation, horizontally to peers (equals in status) in other departments, or diagonally to staff one step down in other functions.

This model may be elaborated as in Table 9.2 in order to show direction, type, and content of communications travelling through the organisation.

INFORMAL NETWORKS

Every organisation also develops an informal communications network. Where the official

VERTICAL DOWNWARDS	TYPE	verbal newsletters memos notices staff meetings circulars
	CONTENT	instructions information (policies and procedures) appraisal company progress reports
VERTICAL UPWARDS	TYPE	progress reports suggestions grievance procedures consultation committees quality circle reports project team reports
	CONTENT	information to management
HORIZONTAL ACROSS	TYPE	cross functional teams formal/informal meetings memos requests for information
	CONTENT	solutions to problems development projects informal communication standard procedures
DIAGONAL LATERAL	TYPE	formal consultation meetings informal conversations
	CONTENT	fire fighting activities cross functional problem solving

Table 9.2 A model of communications channels

channels of communication are inappropriate to the needs of the organisation, then this informal system will assume great importance. Such informal networks arise through the social relationships which develop in all organisations, satisfying various human needs, for companionship, to relieve boredom, to gain more control over one's working life and to fill gaps left in the information available via the official communications channels. As with all gossip and rumour, the chances of information conveyed being inaccurate or damaging, will rise where the organisation is inclined to be secretive. In 'open' organisations, the informal network is less likely to be damaging.

> **Informal supplement the formal networks.**

Advantages of an informal network

- It operates faster than the official channels.
- Much of the information transmitted in this way is more accurate than you might expect.
- Staff managers tend to have a very efficient grapevine, keeping them in touch with what is happening throughout the organisation.
- It may be used by senior managers as a way of floating new plans which will affect working conditions, in a non-threatening way in order to obtain unofficial information on the likely response of the workforce.

Disadvantages of an informal network

- It may convey a distorted version of information which is confidential and which may provoke industrial relations problems unnecessarily.
- It may become semi-formalised into a 'sub-hierarchy', working behind official channels. Subordinates with access to key information may be used by ambitious managers as a source of information on which to base their own plans. These plans may run counter to the official plans of the organisation. In other words, it may become an important component in the power game within an organisation.

MODERN COMMUNICATIONS TECHNOLOGY

The explosion of Information Technology applications in all business fields has transformed the communications process. Some of the new technology is listed here.

These methods of communication are additional to those outlined at the beginning of this chapter.

“The impact of electronics.”

INFORMATION PROCESSING	microcomputer
	dedicated word processor
	computer memory storage of information
	database and spreadsheet for manipulation of data
	computer programmes to aid decision making, e.g. for linear programming exercises
	computer aided design
	software for producing graphics, forms, mailings, etc
INFORMATION TRANSMISSION	internal PC networks
	mainframe networks/workstations
	facsimile (fax) transmission of documents by 'phone
	teletext news and share prices
	viewdata, information receipt or transmission via 'phone network and TV receiver
	electronic mail messages posted via central computer
	electronic data interchange – computer to computer
	telex and teletex – printed message by 'phone line (superseded by fax)
	electronics funds transfer

Advantages of using the new methods

The advantages of using these new methods of communication may be summarised as follows:

- Reductions in cost, particularly in information storage and retrieval. There may be reductions in labour costs in these areas, as well as reductions in the overhead costs of office and storage space.

- Quality. Word processing may enable the reproduction of information, letters, memos, etc of better quality.

- Information which is stored may be more easily retrieved and processed.

- Greater access to information, e.g. financial, may permit more efficient management decision making.

“There are many advantages arising from new communications technology.”

- Computer-held information is more secure than a filing system.

- Computer Aided Design facilitates design functions.

- Sales presentations, seminar materials, etc may be more easily presented and of a higher quality.

- Information and funds may be more speedily transmitted between functions, plant subsidiaries and to customers or suppliers.

- Video and computer models may greatly improve training functions.

- Complex numerical information may be more easily and comprehensibly conveyed and manipulated.

Disadvantages of using the new methods

The disadvantages of using these methods, may also be considerable and often not recognised:

- Costs may increase, due to unnecessary duplication caused by running manual systems alongside computerised systems as a back-up in case of computer breakdown or misuse.

- Quality may be reduced. Where a WP operator is producing a letter, there is less imperative to get it right, because it can be corrected later, thus doubling the work involved. Keyboard skills have been diminished.

- Computers may 'crash' and lose critical information at a vital moment.

- Computer-held information may be accessed by outsiders for malicious reasons.

- Computer fraud, leading to syphoning off of funds is possible where the computer personnel have knowledge which enables them to outwit managers who are computer illiterate.

EXAMINATION QUESTIONS

1   Comment on the view that better communications in the business world will be the inevitable result of improvements in communications technology.   (AEB 1985)

2   One of the advantages small firms possess over large ones is good communications. Why does larger size tend to cause communications to deteriorate and what steps can be taken to ease the situation?   (AEB 1990)

3   Describe formal and informal communications systems. Examine the factors which would indicate when the formal communication system is breaking down.

(AEB 1985)

4   Many organisations suffer from poor communications. What are the principal barriers to good communications? How could the problems you have identified be overcome?   (London Overseas 1991)

TUTOR'S ANSWER

Question 1

There is no doubt that improved communications are necessary in the business world. There are a number of reasons why this is so. Key information must be available to managers in order that they may plan, organise, direct and control the activities of the organisation. Coordination of the activities of departments within the organisation is only possible if communications systems work. Clear instructions are essential if workers are to understand what is required of them and to enable the coordination of the activities of groups of workers. Similarly it is essential that the organisation communicates effectively with its clients and suppliers, as well as relating to external agencies which influence its activities, such as tax authorities, bankers and so on. It follows that improvements in the creation, transmission, storage and retrieval of information will facilitate better decision making and swifter response to events.

In the past twenty years there has been an explosion of improvements in the technology involved in these various aspects of communication. These may be conveniently divided into two groups, those involving the processing of information and those involved in its transmission.

Advances in silicon chip and electronic technology have enabled the development first of the mainframe computer and more recently the microcomputer or PC. In networked form the latter has come to equal the power of a mainframe, but at lower cost and with greater flexibility. This development has spawned a whole variety of communications possibilities, as previously unimagined quantities of information may be stored and conveniently retrieved without the waste of space and time involved in manual filing systems. Such information may be easily manipulated using database and spreadsheet facilities. Programmes may be developed to carry out routine business and accounting functions in vast numbers very quickly. Programmes may be developed to aid the design process in contexts as varied as designing a nuclear reactor to designing a kitchen. Programmes may be developed to use models such as linear programming to aid decision making, whilst simulations of business decision-making exercises may be developed for training purposes. Computers also have the power to greatly speed up and improve the quality of standard business communications such as letters (using a word processor), documents, graphics, mailshots, etc. All these possibilities relate to information processing functions.

Developments in information transmission are at an exciting stage. Access to either mainframe computers via workstations, or to a network of PCs, will speed up transmission of information within the organisation, cutting out the need for vast quantities of memos. Fax machines extend the power of the telephone as a means of business communication by permitting documents, such as sales orders, to be transmitted instantly, cutting out the delay of the postal system, or inexactitude of verbal messages by 'phone.

Electronic mail systems and electronic data exchange systems from computer to computer are able to speed this process up further still. Electronic funds transfer speeds up enormously the management of monetary transactions.

Apart from the obvious speeding up of transactions and transmission of data, these changes carry other potential advantages. There should be reductions in the overheads of the business and in the case of service activities like insurance and banking, speeding up of, and greater production efficiency in, the operations side of the business. The quality of communications and mass produced forms, letters, etc should be vastly increased. Greater access to 'real time' information should permit better business decision making, with less time lag effects. Stored material should be more secure.

At first sight these appear to be incontrovertible gains. However this may not be so. The application of the technology itself may produce snags. Fear of the system often leads organisations to duplicate information systems, retaining the old manual system alongside the computer system, or even failing to use the computerised system for critical functions because of fear of computer breakdown. This causes unnecessary duplication of effort, confusion and overstaffing, with attendant increases in costs. Furthermore, quality may be diminished by the power of the word processor. Since the operator knows what mistakes may easily be corrected, he/she will take less care to get it right first time. The manager or supervisor will then spend more, rather than less, time checking for mistakes, which will occur more frequently and require more costly rework than before. Computers have been shown to be fallible in other ways. The system may 'crash', losing vital information or causing long delays. They may be accessed or manipulated for fraudulent reasons by outsiders or by members of the firm. Computer fraud is difficult to spot. This danger is magnified by the vulnerability of computer-illiterate senior managers who may easily be hoodwinked by subordinates.

Even if it could be ensured that all these new possibilities were being efficiently used, there is still no guarantee that communications failure would not occur. Many of the principal reasons for communications failure are not connected directly to the technology involved, but might actually be worsened by over reliance on such technology. Thus inadequate language skills, vocabulary, jargon, inappropriate and confusing language conventions, may all cause failure of communication. Similarly the attitudes and emotional states of the communicators may cause breakdown, whatever medium is used. It will just happen faster, and possibly more frequently as a result of the loss of the direct human dimension. Better technology will not prevent the use of communications systems as a weapon in the office power game. Moreover new problems arise. The effects of prolonged use of VDUs is only just being recognised, but back problems due to wrong posture, eye problems due to watching the screen and consequent migraine, may all cause a decrease in efficiency and increased absenteeism. Additionally the presence of technology will do nothing to prevent breakdown in communication between levels in the organisation which result from matters of class, status etc.

Thus we may conclude that improvements in communication may result from the widespread use of new communications technology, but it is by no means inevitable that this will happen. Rather, there are good reasons to believe that the initial impact may be adverse.

STUDENT'S ANSWER

Question 2

> Start by indicating why small firms may have good communications.

> Why might this happen?

> Not necessarily.

There are a variety of reasons why larger firms are more prone to communication problems. The organisational hierarchy of large firms has more levels and the chain of command is longer. This not only means that vertical communication will be slower (as it may have to cross many levels) but there is also a greater opportunity for distortion of messages to occur before they reach their final destination.

Upward communication through the organisational hierarchy may suffer particularly in large firms. As there are more employees, the span of control is likely to be bigger. This means that each superior has to deal with information from his/her larger-than-average number of subordinates. He/she will restrict the information flow by passing only the information he/she considers to be the most important, further up the organisation hierarchy. (This is because his/her superior will also have several subordinates and can only cope with a limited amount of information.) In smaller firms, with smaller numbers of employees, the span of control may be less, therefore it is likely that the upward flow of information will not be restricted to such a high degree.

The human relations aspect of organisations must also be considered, as this is an important factor affecting communications. Small firms often tend to have a more personal informal atmosphere, where subordinates feel less intimidated by their superiors and are likely to communicate more readily with them. Employees may also feel more valued by small firms, as most small firms cannot afford to employ people unless they are vital to its successful operation. Employees are therefore more likely to believe that information they have for superiors will be taken notice of, and not dismissed. As a result they will be more forthcoming with information, thereby promoting upward communication.

Larger firms on the other hand may have a less personal atmosphere, subordinates may not feel so at ease with superiors and therefore may not want to or may not bother to give them information. If a larger firm has larger spans of control within its organisation, subordinates may feel they are 'one of the many' reporting to their superior and may feel their information for their superior may not be important enough to receive his/her proper attention. Also, those at the lowest levels of the hierarchy may perceive their jobs as being menial. They may therefore believe that even if they do give information to their superiors, it will be ignored and these factors may hinder or prevent upward communication.

Horizontal communication may also be affected by the size of the organisation. Within smaller firms there is less division of labour and less specialisation. As a result, functions very much overlap and horizontal communication across the same levels of the organisational hierarchy is more necessary. Within larger firms, horizontal communication may be reduced. As there is more division of labour and greater specialisation, departments tend to concentrate on performing their own function and do not interfere with other departments. Departments on the same horizontal level of the hierarchy of larger firms may feel they are competing with each other, which builds horizontal communication barriers.

To improve communication within larger firms, the organisational hierarchy may be flattened. By reducing the number of levels that information must pass through, the quality and speed of both upward and downward communication can be much improved.

Upward communication should be actively encouraged, at all levels. By making superiors more approachable and ensuring that employees are aware that information they pass 'upwards' will receive its due attention, subordinates will become more forthcoming with information. All employees at all levels within the firm should be made to feel they are valued members of the organisation and everyone has an important role. This will help to ensure that subordinates (particularly those at the lower levels of the organisational hierarchy) are not too intimidated or feel of too little importance to pass information upwards. Those at the higher levels of the organisation can play their part in improving upward communication, by seeming more approachable and available and mixing more with subordinates.

Horizontal communication should also be encouraged. Teamwork can be used to break down inter-departmental communication

Good! But could have had more impact as an introduction.

It is probably easier, as well.

Good!

But this has implications for the span of control.

New ideas should not be introduced in the concluding paragraph.

> barriers, e.g. by having teams consisting of members from each
> department working on a project together. Although larger firms
> do tend to suffer more communication problems than smaller ones,
> these difficulties can be minimised if the management is aware of
> them and takes the necessary steps to overcome them.

Tutor's comments

This is a thoughtful and well written answer. She might have offered some comment on communications media which are used, indicating how a change here in communications channels might improve things. She might have taken the opportunity before the last section to indicate the advantages of a team approach which encourages 'openness' at all levels. She could have said a little about the use of Quality Circles and Quality Improvement Teams as a means to motivate workers, flatten hierarchies and improve the upward flow of suggestions and information. She might, alternatively, have discussed other forms of worker participation.

This would be marked as a 'B' grade answer.

OUTLINE ANSWERS

Question 3

The formal communications system in an organisation is summarised in its organisational structure. This sets out the command structure and the inter-relationships between the departments within the organisation, both 'staff' and 'line'. It also indicates lines of accountability and implies the directions in which communication flows within the organisation. Such flows of communication may progress downwards, upwards, horizontally or diagonally.

Downwards vertical flows are usually in the form of verbal or written messages, contained in memos, notices or staff meetings. These messages convey instructions, information, progress reports and may involve formal appraisal procedures. Upwards vertical flows take the form of progress reports, reports from various committees, quality circles or project teams and may involve the reports of grievance procedures. They are used to convey information from lower levels in the organisation to management. Horizontal flows across the organisation take the form of the proceedings of cross functional problem-solving teams, formal or informal meetings within functions (e.g. sales meetings) or they may be responses or requests for information. They may or may not be formally reported and transmitted up or down the system. Diagonal communications between perhaps a line manager and a staff department supervisor may take the form of formal meetings or informal conversation. They often relate to 'firefighting' activities and cross functional problem solving.

It is difficult to draw an exact line between those communications activities which are formalised within the organisational structure and those which are informal. It is important that the formal system used matches the management style and corporate culture. If it does not, then informal networks between like-minded individuals will develop more than normal importance, and may be used to subvert the formal structures. Such informal networks will arise in any organisation due to social needs and to fill information gaps left by the formal system. They will be all the more important in an organisation which is authoritarian in style and excessively secretive. In an 'open' organisation such networks will be an important and beneficial bonus, making the organisation more effective. Its advantage is speed and its disadvantages are distortion and inaccuracy. It can become an important component in the power game played within the organisation.

Indications that the formal system is inadequate include the development of informal systems and the proliferation of rumour and inaccurate and damaging gossip. Major mistakes in supplying customer needs, e.g. wrong deliveries, late deliveries, loss of vital information, industrial disputes, stress-related illness and absenteeism are all symptoms of communications breakdown.

Question 4

The principal barriers to communication may be grouped under 3 headings:

a) organisational

- inadequate machinery for communication, e.g. lack of upward communication channels, downward message distortion
- information overload
- status
- selection of inappropriate medium

b) semantic

- people don't know or use the same words
- words have alternative meanings
- jargon

c) human feelings

- individual bias
- stereotyping
- inattention/selective attention
- change issues
- emotion (anxiety, fear, anger, trust)
- inappropriate body language
- deliberate manipulation

You would not be expected to detail all these points but should select examples from each of the broad groups.

It is unlikely that any organisation will achieve perfect communication, but it is possible to remedy many of the problems listed above. If you did not clearly link problem and solution you would be penalised.

Improvements in communication can be made by:

1 ensuring employees are aware of communication problems
2 using more than one communication net
3 minimising communication chain linkages
4 using methods of periodic and continuous upward communication, e.g. appraisals, staff meetings, suggestion schemes, grievance procedures
5 reducing status differentials, e.g. open-plan offices
6 selecting words with care, encouraging clarity of expression/simplicity of construction
7 encouraging feedback to determine comprehension
8 using different media to re-inforce message
9 encouraging recognition of cultural-social differences, prejudices, interdepartmental rivalries
10 training employees in relevant techniques of communication, e.g. listening, body language, not prejudging issues

FURTHER READING

Gregson and Livesey, *Management and the Organisation*, Heinemann 1983:
  Chapter 4, Communications in Principle.
  Chapter 5, Communications in Action.
Torrington and Weightman, *The Business of Management*, Prentice Hall International 1985:
  Chapter 7, Communication Structures.
Martin W. Buckley, *The Structure of Business*, 2nd edition, Pitman 1990:
  Chapter 15, Communication.
Susan Hammond, *Business Studies*, 2nd edition, Longman 1991:
  Chapter 13, Business Organisation and Communications.
Bruce Jewell, *An Integrated Approach to Business Studies*, Pitman 1990:
  Chapter 14, The way we do things around here.

COMMUNICATION II

PRIMARY DATA

SECONDARY DATA

DATA PRESENTATION

FREQUENCY DISTRIBUTION

MEASURES OF LOCATION

MEASURES OF DISPERSION

GETTING STARTED

Modern businesses not only produce goods and services but also vast amounts of data from areas such as sales, production, storage, transport, marketing, personnel, finance, etc. In its raw form, the data is unintelligible and would confuse rather than enlighten. In this chapter we discuss the sources of data, both primary and secondary. The choice of data nearly always boils down to one of cost – how can the relevant information be gathered for the minimum outlay in both time and finance. Where similar data has already been collected, but used for some other purpose, it is prudent to take advantage of its existence. However, sometimes the data does not exist in a secondary source and the firm must invest in some primary collection.

Once the data has been collected it must be processed and presented in a form suitable for the user, whether it be internally for management purposes or externally for shareholders or the general public. The merits and drawbacks of several forms of data presentation are examined in the third section. Where large quantities of data are involved it becomes useful to gather it in the form of a frequency distribution in order to make the data easier to understand.

In the final sections we explore how different sets of data can be described using measures of location and measures of dispersion. All of these techniques have been developed to make it easier for the users to analyse data, to identify trends and movements and therefore to assist in more effective decision-making.

ESSENTIAL PRINCIPLES

PRIMARY DATA

> Relevant information is needed for effective decision making.

Primary data is that data which has been collected with a specific purpose in mind. It is collected either by census or sample. A *census* is a survey which examines every member of the population whereas a *sample* is a small representative subset of the population. A census would be preferable from the viewpoint of completeness and accuracy but a sample is less costly in terms of time and resources. Whichever method is used the purpose of primary data collection is to gather relevant information to help understand and solve business problems. Good examples of primary data collection are the national opinion polls which periodically test the support for various political parties. A small, representative sample is identified and questioned. Obviously complete accuracy could only be obtained by asking all of the voting population, but this would prove too expensive.

SAMPLING TECHNIQUES

There are two basic problems to be overcome in sampling. These are deciding *who* to ask and deciding *how* to ask.

Who to ask

> Who is the target population?

For the sample to provide accurate information it must adequately reflect the whole population. There are six main ways of drawing such a sample from the population. The main characteristics of each type of sampling method are given in Table 10.1.

RANDOM SAMPLING

1 Each item selected has an equal chance of being drawn, i.e. it is generated in a random fashion.
2 The population is largely homogeneous, i.e. no way of distinguishing between items.
3 Allows the use of computer-generated random numbers.
4 Selection is unbiased.
5 A major drawback is that a population listing is required and the chosen items need to be located and questioned, or measured.

STRATIFIED SAMPLING

1 Used when the population has a number of identifiable attributes.
2 Populations stratified in this way are known as heterogeneous.
3 The sample must reflect the attributes among the population, e.g. the proportion of low, middle and high income earners.
4 Individuals within each strata may be selected randomly.
5 Results in a sample which is free from selective bias as it takes account of the significant attributes of the population.

SYSTEMATIC SAMPLING

1 The population is listed or physically present.
2 A random starting point is chosen.
3 From the starting point a systematic sample is taken, e.g. every 20th item.
4 Useful for homogeneous populations, e.g. items on a production line.

MULTI-STAGE SAMPLING

1 Population is spread over a wide geographical area which makes sampling expensive.
2 Divide area into regions and randomly select a small number of regions.
3 Taking sub-samples from selected regions proportional to the size of the regions.
4 Reduces the cost of collection but may suffer from bias if only a small number of regions is selected.

CLUSTER SAMPLING

1 A non-random sampling method for widely spread populations.
2 One or more geographical areas is selected and *all* the members of the population in that area are sampled, e.g. all engineering firms in one particular city.

QUOTA SAMPLING

1 Often used in market research.
2 A set number or quota of subjects with specific characteristics.
3 Interviewers must be highly trained as they are responsible for identification and selection.
4 A low cost, convenient sampling method particularly for stratified populations.

Table 10.1 Types of sampling

How to ask

A researcher may choose to use direct observation to obtain the required information. This would entail the costly procedure of viewing and recording the people, machines or items. A cheaper alternative is to seek other people's views through various forms of interview or survey. This allows the researcher to cover a wider area in a shorter period of time at a lower cost. The main forms of interview and their relative merits are given in Table 10.2.

PERSONAL INTERVIEW

1 Expensive but accurate.
2 Requires highly trained, unbiased interviewers.
3 Allows the use of questionnaires.

POSTAL SURVEY

1 Requires a well designed, unambiguous questionnaire.
2 Cheaper method than direct interview.
3 Low response rates unless suitable inducements given, e.g. free gifts, prize draws, etc.
4 Allows wide geographical area to be surveyed.

TELEPHONE SURVEY

1 Reasonably inexpensive.
2 Less clinical than a questionnaire.
3 Requires skilled researcher to overcome the natural reluctance of respondents to answer questions.
4 Possibility of bias if only a small proportion of the population have telephones.

DIRECT OBSERVATION

1 Often used on production lines, work study and traffic or pedestrian flows.
2 Most accurate form of data collection.
3 Labour-intensive and time-consuming, therefore expensive.

Table 10.2 Methods of primary collection

> Benefits must be weighed against costs.

Whichever method of sampling or interview is eventually chosen the benefits must justify the extra cost. An increasingly popular method of data collection is the use of questionnaires. If the data is to be informative and accurate the questionnaire must be carefully designed. The main features of a good questionnaire are given in Table 10.3.

The following points should be noted when designing a questionnaire:

Length: the questionnaire should be as short as possible.

Purpose: the title and preamble should state clearly the purpose of the survey

Questions: these should:
     a) be unambiguous
     b) be easy to understand
     c) not involve technical terms
     d) not rely on calculations or tests of memory
     e) not include leading questions which imply an answer
     f) not offend

Format: wherever possible use should be made of rating scales or tick boxes so that answers are categorised. The questionnaire as a whole should be clearly and simply set out and easy to follow

N.B. A questionnaire should be pre-tested in a pilot survey.

Table 10.3 Questionnaire design

SECONDARY DATA

Secondary data refers to the use of data for a purpose different to that for which the information was originally collected, e.g. a mail order firm may purchase a list of credit-card clients of a superstore in order to target likely customers.

It is important to understand the merits and drawbacks of the use of secondary data as well as an outline knowledge of the main sources of published secondary data.

> A clear understanding of the advantages and disadvantages is essential.

The first point to note is that secondary data can be generated internally as well as externally by other independent bodies. Internal data may include such items as stock lists, employee details, costings, work study surveys, etc. These specific primary collections may be used by others within the firm for a secondary purpose, e.g. employee addresses could be used to investigate the viability of a company bus service. More often than not the secondary data used is generated by an external body and in particular by the government's Central Statistical Office (CSO). The principal advantages and disadvantages are given in Table 10.4.

ADVANTAGES

1   Cheaper than financing own survey.
2   Often covers a wider geographical area.
3   Wide choice of statistical information.
4   Data is already partly processed.
5   Information and conclusions can be processed faster.

DISADVANTAGES

1   May not be acceptable quality.
2   Geographical or strata coverage may be inappropriate.
3   Definitions may be interpreted differently.
4   Data may be out of date.

Table 10.4 Advantages and disadvantages of secondary data

SOURCES OF SECONDARY DATA

Table 10.5 presents some useful sources you can use for secondary data.

TITLE	CONTENT
Annual Abstract of Statistics	Comprehensive coverage of economic, social and industrial life of the UK. The main reference book for statistical information.
Monthly Digest of Statistics	A monthly version of the Annual Abstract. Contains data on population, prices, wages, employment, expenditure production and output.
Economic Trends	A monthly compilation of the main economic indicators presented in tabular and chart form.
U.K. National Accounts (Blue Book)	The principal annual publication of the national accounts statistics.
Social Trends	An annual publication on a wide variety of social topics including population, households, education, income, health and social services.
U.K. Balance of Payments (Pink Book)	Annual publication of balance of payments statistics for the past ten years.
Employment Gazette	A monthly summary of statistics on employment, unemployment, vacancies, wages, prices and industrial stoppages.
Financial Statistics	A monthly statistical survey of government and company finance.
Other Sources	A variety of publications are available including the *Financial Times* (daily), *The Economist* (weekly), Bank Review and *The Times 1000*.

Table 10.5 Sources of secondary data

DATA PRESENTATION

Once data has been collected it needs to be presented in a suitable form. Many of these forms have a visual impact which makes it easier for the user to grasp the important features. There are three main forms of presentation each with its own advantages and disadvantages:

- Tabulation
- Graphs
- Diagrams

The visual image is important.

Tabulation

A *table* is defined as an arrangement of data in labelled rows and columns. The main purposes of presenting data in a tabular format are:

1   To present crude data in an orderly manner
2   To make it easier to identify trends
3   To summarise diverse information

❝ This applies to all business studies diagrams. ❞

Each table should include all that is relevant but exclude anything which is unnecessary. All tables must be clearly labelled, units marked and the source of data given, as in Fig. 10.1.

Of course you could go on to derive further tabular materials from the original tables. For example, you could convert the absolute numbers (millions) in the table into *percentages* of the total attending in each year, and so on.

ATTENDANCES AT THE MOST POPULAR TOURIST ATTRACTIONS

GREAT BRITAIN	MILLIONS					MILLIONS			
	1981	1986	1988	1989		1981	1986	1988	1989
Attractions with free admission					*Attractions charging admission*				
Blackpool Pleasure Beach	7.5	6.5	6.5	6.5	Madame Tussaud's	2.0	2.4	2.7	2.6
Albert Dock, Liverpool	.	2.0	4.2	5.1	Alton Towers	1.6	2.2	2.5	2.4
British Museum	2.6	3.6	3.8	4.7	Tower of London	2.1	2.0	2.2	2.2
Strathclyde Country Park, Motherwell	.	.	.	3.9	Blackpool Tower	.	1.4	1.5	1.5
National Gallery	2.7	3.2	3.2	3.4	Natural History Museum	3.7	2.7	1.4	1.5
Pleasure Beach, Great Yarmouth	.	.	2.3	2.5	Thorpe Park	0.6	1.1	1.0	1.3
Bradgate Park	1.2	1.2	1.2	1.3	Chessington World of Adventures	0.5	0.8	1.2	1.2
Stapeley Water Gardens, Cheshire	.	1.0	1.0	1.3	London Zoo	1.1	1.2	1.3	1.2
Tate Gallery	0.9	1.1	1.6	1.2	Kew Gardens	0.9	1.1	1.2	1.2
Glasgow Art Gallery and Museum	.	0.8	0.9	1.0	Science Museum	3.8	3.0	2.4	1.1

Fig. 10.1 Use of tables   **GRAPHS**

A *graph* is a line diagram which plots a series of values as points joined by straight lines. It is particularly useful for comparison purposes as shown in Fig. 10.2.

When drawing a graph make sure that it has the following essential information:

1   Title – clear and easily understood
2   Labelled axes
3   Source of information

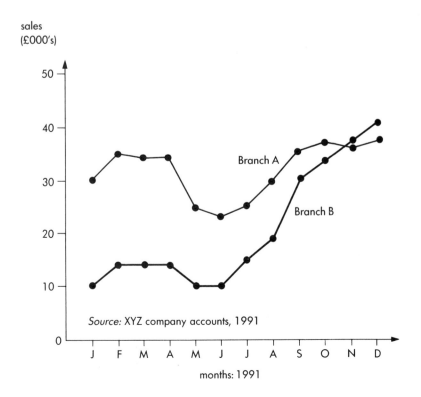

Fig. 10.2 Use of line graph

Advantages of line graphs

1 Easy to construct
2 Simple to understand
3 Trends are readily identified
4 Useful for direct comparison

Disadvantages of line graphs

1 Too many diagrams produce a confusing 'cobweb' of lines
2 Altering the scale of the axes can produce a misleading impression, e.g. in Fig. 10.2 if the 'x' axis measuring time is halved, the line becomes steeper – giving the impression that sales have risen faster

> Be aware of the 'abuse' of statistics.

DIAGRAMS

The principal aim of statistical *diagrams* is to give a quick visual impact in order to emphasise or re-enforce an argument. In this section we will consider three of the more popular diagram forms.

- Bar charts
- Pie charts
- Pictograms

Bar charts

There are three main types of *bar chart*:

1 Simple Bar Chart
2 Component Bar Chart
3 Multiple Bar Chart

A Simple Bar Chart is a set of non-joining bars of equal width whose height is proportional to the frequency it is representing. They can be drawn in a vertical or horizontal format and can show negative, as well as positive, values. The bars themselves can be shaded or coloured differently (see Fig. 10.3)

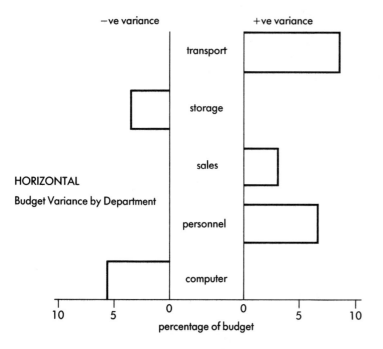
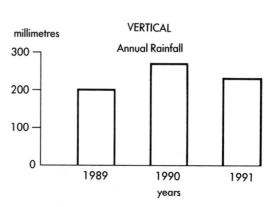

Fig. 10.3 Simple bar charts

A Component or Segmented Bar Chart is useful to illustrate a breakdown in the figures, e.g. the total sales of XYZ Co. could be broken down into sales by product (see Fig. 10.4). The constituent parts of each bar are always stacked in the same order with the height of each representing the individual frequencies.

A Multiple Bar Chart uses a separate bar to represent each constituent part of the total. These bars are joined into a set for each class of data (see Fig. 10.4). The data in Figure 10.4 can be represented in multiple bar chart form. (See Figure 10.5)

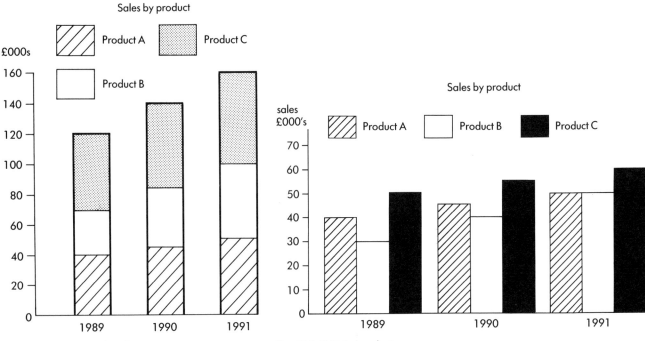

Fig. 10.4 Component bar chart

Fig. 10.5 Multiple bar chart

As a general guide it is best to use a component chart when class totals need to be represented. A disadvantage of this form is that it is difficult to compare components across classes. A multiple bar chart is best for comparing the components both within and across classes. Conversely it is difficult to assess totals with this method.

Pie charts

A *pie chart* is where a circle represents the total data and the sectors, drawn to proportion, represent the frequencies of the component parts. Fig. 10.6 shows the geographical distribution of the UK's export trade in 1989. Each sector of a pie chart must be constructed accurately. The size of each sector is found by calculating the proportion of the total for each sector then multiplying by 360 to obtain the angle of the sector from the centre of the circle, e.g. if one product accounted for sales of £60M out of a total of £300M its proportion would be $^{60}/_{300}$ or 1/5th, which when multiplied by 360 gives a sector with an angle of 72°. Pie charts are popular because they provide a dramatic and comprehensible form of display. However, they are laborious to construct (unless computer-generated) and are only effective for a small number of classes.

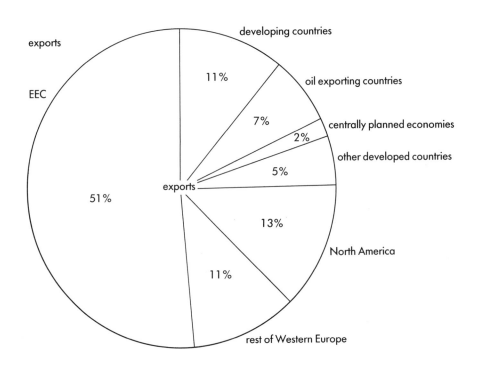

Fig. 10.6 Geographical distribution of UK exports, 1989

Data to be represented

Sales 1990   £36M
Sales 1991   £81M

Step one   Obtain the class totals to be represented

Step two   Choose a convenient radius for circle 1, e.g. let circle
               1990 have a radius of 2 cm

Step three   Insert the known data into the following equation

$$\text{Radius of circle 2} = \text{radius of circle 1} \times \sqrt{\frac{\text{Total 2}}{\text{Total 1}}}$$

$$= 2\,\text{cm} \times \sqrt{\frac{81}{36}}$$

$$= 2\,\text{cm} \times 1.5$$
$$= 3\,\text{cm}$$

Step four   Draw the representative circles

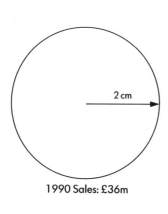

2 cm

1990 Sales: £36m

3 cm

1991 Sales £81m

Fig. 10.7 Multiple or proportional
pie charts

A further difficulty occurs with *multiple pie charts*. In this instance the areas of the circles must be proportional to the frequency totals, e.g. if one class total is four times as large as that of another, the area of the circle must be four times larger. Many students find this task difficult, but Figure 10.7 gives a straightforward step-by-step example.

Pictograms

A *pictogram* is a diagram which uses multiples of representative symbols to indicate the class totals. The symbol is carefully chosen to identify with the data in question, e.g. the size of a navy may be represented by ship symbols and an air force by the outlines of aircraft.

Figure 10.8 shows the number of students studying four 'A' levels at the Nowhere District College in 1991. It gives a simple, easily understood impression of the relative sizes. Unfortunately, for statistical purposes a pictogram is difficult to read accurately and awkward to construct for part totals, as shown in the numbers taking History in Fig. 10.8.

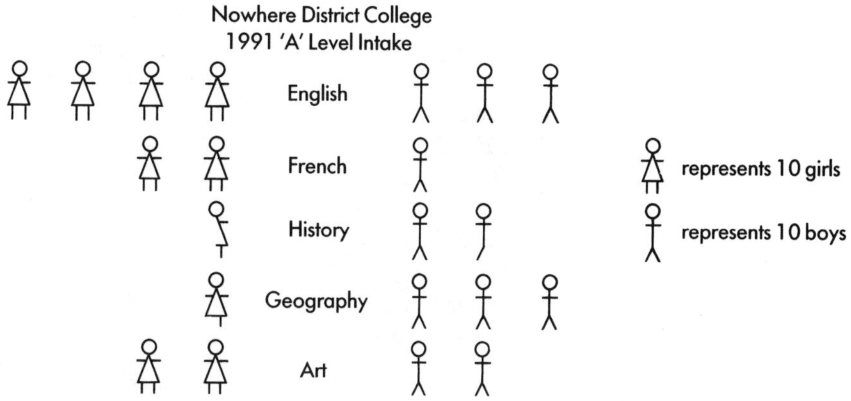

❝ Limited in its use. ❞

Nowhere District College
1991 'A' Level Intake

English

French

History

Geography

Art

represents 10 girls

represents 10 boys

Fig. 10.8 Use of pictogram

FREQUENCY DISTRIBUTION

ARRAYS, RANGES, MODES AND MEDIANS

The organisation and presentation of large quantities of numeric data is normally done using some form of *frequency distribution*. Data obtained from a survey or investigation is of little use unless it is organised into a logical, presentable manner. Before being organised the data is known as *raw* data. For example, the following heights were recorded of 20 'A' level male students:

> ❝Data needs to be organised before it becomes relevant information.❞

HEIGHTS (cm)

160	172	180	156
166	169	174	166
176	150	182	188
174	160	172	172
180	182	178	184

In this form it is difficult to see any pattern or trend. Some information could be extracted by putting the information in size order:

This is known as an *array*

150	156	160	160
166	166	169	172
172	172	174	174
176	178	180	180
182	182	184	188

From this we can extract the shortest student at 150 cm and the tallest at 188 cm. We can also see that the data has a *range* of values of 38 cm. The most frequently occurring item, the *mode*, is 172 cm and the value lying half way along, the *median*, is 173 cm (the middle value between the 10th item 172 cm and the 11th item 174 cm).

Simple frequency distribution

Where there are a limited number of data values it is preferable to use a *simple* frequency distribution as shown below.

The data being measured are the different types of vehicles using a local car park. A frequency is defined as the number of times a particular outcome or event happens during an investigation. In this case the frequencies are the numbers of vehicles in each category. It can quickly be seen that the car park is predominantly used by saloon cars and light commercial vehicles. However, where the number of classes and data values is large it is more appropriate to use a *grouped* frequency distribution.

VEHICLES USING LOCAL CAR PARK

Type of vehicle	Frequency
Saloon car	54
Estate car	11
Light commercial	25
Lorry	8
Others	2
	100

Grouped frequency distribution

The data is divided into groups or classes of values, each showing the number of items occurring in the group, e.g. the data on heights is shown below, grouped into classes of 5 cm.

GROUPED FREQUENCY DISTRIBUTION HEIGHTS OF MALE 'A' LEVEL STUDENTS (cm)

Heights (cm)	Frequency (Number of Students)
150 and under 155	1
155 and under 160	1
160 and under 165	2
165 and under 170	3
170 and under 175	5
175 and under 180	2
180 and under 185	5
185 and under 190	1
	20

Essential points to know about grouped frequencies are the following:

1 *Class limits:* these are the lower and upper values of the classes as shown in the distribution, e.g. in a distribution of test marks the classes were 10 to 19
    20 to 29
    30 to 39 etc.
    The lower limit of the first class is 10 marks and the upper limit is 19 marks.

2 *Class boundaries:* for statistical purposes this is where classes meet, i.e. a common point. In the example above the class boundaries of the 20 to 29 class would be 19.5 and 29.5. Where there is a gap in the values between classes the boundaries are fixed at the mid-point of the gap.

3 *Class interval or width:* the difference between the lower and upper class boundaries.

4 *Class mid-point:* the mid-point between the lower and upper class boundaries.

5 *Class numbers:* where possible the distribution should have approximately 10 classes, preferably of equal width.

6 *Open-class intervals:* these can be used at the extremes of the distribution, e.g. in the data on student height, 190 cm and over. Once the grouped frequency distribution has been formed it is easier to identify patterns. In the height survey it appears the distribution is bi-modal, i.e. there are two height groups which are the most common 170–175 cm and 180–185 cm.

Histogram

Many frequency distributions can be represented diagrammatically by means of a histogram. This is a set of joined vertical bars as shown in Fig. 10.9.

The essential features of a histogram are:

1 The bars represent a class and the width corresponds to the class width.
2 The bars are joined together at their true class boundaries.
3 The chart should have a title.
4 The 'y' axis represents the frequency, the 'x' axis the values being measured.
5 The class frequency is represented by the 'area' of the bar. Where the bars are of equal width the frequencies correspond to the height. N.B. If the class interval is twice the width, the height would have to be halved to keep the area proportional.

6 A line joining the mid-points of the top of the bars is known as a *frequency polygon* (see also Fig. 10.9).

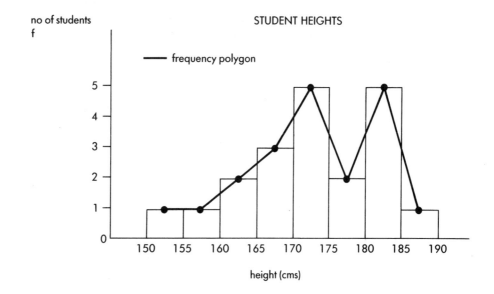

Fig. 10.9 Histogram and frequency polygon of student heights

MEASURES OF LOCATION

The reason for tabulating or grouping data is to make it easier for management to compare and analyse the sets of data in order to make more effective decisions. To help this process further we can calculate a number of statistical measures which convey the essential message of the data. Measures of *location* or averages are single values intended to represent or characterise the whole group of data. They are commonly used to give an approximate impression, e.g. the average life of a machine is six years or the average cost of an item is £2 etc.

THE ARITHMETIC MEAN

The arithmetic mean of a set of values is defined as the sum of the values divided by the number of values. The arithmetic mean is the most commonly used measure of central tendency. It is basically a value, in a set of data, around which all other values tend to cluster. The student must be able to calculate its value from simple data, a frequency distribution and a grouped frequency distribution as well as knowing the advantages and disadvantages of its use.

> An important measure of location.

Calculation from simple data

The value of the mean (symbol $\bar{x}$) is found using the formula:

$$\bar{x} = \frac{\Sigma x}{n}$$

where x = value of each item of data
Σ (sigma) = the sum of
n = the number of values

which is a shorthand method of writing

$$\text{The arithmetic mean} = \frac{\text{The sum of the values}}{\text{The number of values}}$$

Example:

	Mon	Tues	Wed	Thur	Fri
Daily sales (£)	420	560	630	580	810

Using the formula

$$\bar{x} = \frac{420 + 560 + 630 + 580 + 810}{5} = \frac{3,000}{5} = £600$$

The average daily sales are £600 and this represents a typical figure around which the rest of the data will cluster.

Calculation from a frequency distribution

Account must be taken of the frequencies, i.e. how many times a particular value occurs. In the following example a street trader sells five differently priced items for £2, £3, £4, £5 and £6. He sells 50 items during the day. It would be a mistake to say 'average price was £4, therefore the average takings was £200' because no account has been taken of the numbers sold of each item. The working below illustrates the correct calculation using the formula

$$\bar{x} = \frac{\Sigma fx}{\Sigma f}$$

where fx is the value of the item multiplied by the number of times it occurs.

Price of item (£) x	Number of items sold f	fx
2	5	10
3	3	9
4	18	72
5	10	50
6	14	84
	$\Sigma f = 50$	$\Sigma fx = 225$

$$\bar{x} = \frac{\Sigma fx}{\Sigma f} = \frac{225}{50} = £4.50$$

The average price of items sold is £4.50 and the average takings is £225.

Calculation from a grouped frequency distribution

In a grouped frequency distribution the individual values of the items are lost; therefore an estimate of their value must be made. This is done by assuming the items are evenly

> The mid-point is assumed to represent all items in the class.

spread throughout the class, therefore the mid-class point is representative of all items in the class. Once the mid-point has been determined the procedure is the same as for the frequency distribution. This can be applied to the grouped data on students' heights used earlier.

HEIGHTS (cm)	NUMBER OF STUDENTS	MID-POINT	
	f	x	fx
150 and under 155	1	152.5	152.5
155 and under 160	1	157.5	157.5
160 and under 165	2	162.5	325
165 and under 170	3	167.5	502.5
170 and under 175	5	172.5	862.5
175 and under 180	2	177.5	355
180 and under 185	5	182.5	912.5
185 and under 190	1	187.5	187.5
$\Sigma f =$	20	$\Sigma fx =$	3455

$$\bar{x} = \frac{\Sigma fx}{\Sigma f} = \frac{3455}{20} = 172.75\text{cm} = 173\text{cm}$$

The mean height of male 'A' level students is approximately 173 cm (to the nearest whole cm).

Advantages of using the mean

> Contrast these with the other measures of location.

1   It takes account of all the data.
2   As it is the mathematical average it can be used for more advanced analysis.
3   It is generally accepted as the standard average.

Disadvantages of using the mean

1   It may be distorted by extreme values.
2   The mean value may not correspond with an actual value, e.g. average number of children per family = 2.6.

THE MEDIAN

The median of a set of data is the value of the item which lies exactly half-way along the set when presented in size order.

Calculation from simple data

The process to determine the median is the same for all forms of data:

Step 1   Find the position of the median
Step 2   Read or estimate the value at the median position

Example: Machine output over 5-day period
Daily output   210   240   260   220   230

Step 1   Place in an array 210 220 230 240 260

Step 2   Find the middle position using the equation $\dfrac{n + 1}{2}$

where n = the number of values

$$= \frac{5 + 1}{2} = 3\text{rd item}$$

Step 3   Read the value of the 3rd item, i.e. 230 units. The median output = 230 units.

N.B. When there is an even number of items there will be *two* middle items. The median value is taken to be the average of these two, e.g. the data 4, 7, 8, 10, 13, 15 has a median value at position $\dfrac{n + 1}{2} = \dfrac{7}{2} = 3.5$
This is midway between values 8 and 10, therefore the median value is 9.

Calculation from a frequency distribution

> **First find the position, then read the value.**

The median is determined in the same way as earlier; first find the 'position' of the median, then read the median's 'value'. The only difference is that we construct a cumulative frequency column to help determine the middle value.

PRICE OF ITEM (£)	NUMBER OF ITEMS SOLD	CUMULATIVE FREQUENCY
x	f	cf
2	5	5
3	3	8
4	18	26
5	10	36
6	14	50
	$\Sigma f = 50$	

The position of the middle item is $\dfrac{n+1}{2} = \dfrac{50+1}{2} = 25.5$th

8 items have been sold for £3 or less and 26 items for £4 or less. It is obvious that items 25 and 26 were sold for £4 therefore the value of the 25.5th item is also £4.

Calculation from a grouped frequency distribution

When data is grouped, the identity of individual items is lost; thus there is no exact means of calculating the median. However, two methods are commonly used to estimate the median value; by *graph* or by *arithmetic interpolation*.

1   *Graphical method:* Using the data from our grouped frequency distribution earlier, the first step is to plot the *less than* cumulative frequencies (known as *ogive*) on a graph with the variable on the 'x' axis and the cumulative frequencies on the 'y' axis (see Fig. 10.10).

The position of the middle value is $\dfrac{n+1}{2} = \dfrac{20+1}{2} = 10.5$th item. Draw a horizontal line from the 10.5th position on the 'y' axis until it touches the ogive, then read off the median value on the 'x' axis. This gives a median value of 173 cm.

heights (cm) x	no of students f	cumulative frequency cf
less than 155	1	1
less than 160	1	2
less than 165	2	4
less than 170	3	7
less than 175	5	12
less than 180	2	14
less than 185	5	19
less than 190	1	20

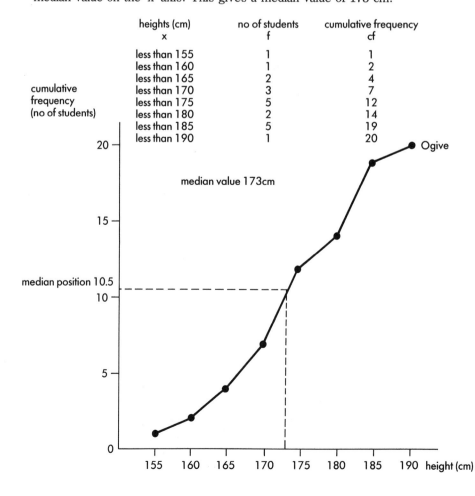

Fig. 10.10 The median by graphical method

66 An approximation is found. 99

2 *Arithmetic interpolation:* The first step is to identify the class that contains the median value. Using the cumulative frequencies (cf) a formula is applied which will provide a theoretical value for the median within that class. The formula assumes the items in the median class are evenly distributed along the class, and is given by:

$$\text{Median} = L_m + C_m \left[\frac{\frac{n+1}{2} - \text{cf to L}}{F_m} \right]$$

where L_m = lower class boundary of the median class
       n = total number of items
    cf to L = cumulative frequency up to the lower class boundary
       F_m = frequency of the median class
       C_m = class interval of the median class

Using the same data as for the graphical method:

The median position $= \dfrac{n+1}{2} = \dfrac{20+1}{2} = 10.5$th item

This item lies in the class 170–175 cm

Applying the formula:

$$\text{Median} = L_m + C_m \left[\frac{\frac{n+1}{2} - \text{cf to L}}{F_m} \right]$$

$$= 170 + 5 \left[\frac{10.5 - 7}{5} \right]$$

$$= 170 + 5 \ \ (0.7)$$

$$= 170 + 3.5$$

$$= 173.5$$

66 When is the median preferred to the mean? 99

Advantages of the median

1 The median may give a more typical value because it is not distorted by extreme values in the data.
2 It is not affected by uneven or open-minded class intervals.
3 It often corresponds to an actual value.

Disadvantages of the median

1 The median ignores all other items of data except the middle item.
2 With grouped data the median value can only be estimated.
3 It cannot be used for further statistical analysis.

THE MODE

The *mode* is the value that occurs most often or has the largest frequency.

Calculation from simple data

From the array of student heights used earlier in the chapter (see p.130) the most common value was 172 cm which occurred three times. The modal height is therefore 172 cm.

Calculation from a frequency distribution

The modal value is the item with the largest frequency. In the case of our street trader the modal price would be £4, since the largest number, eighteen, is sold at this price.

Calculation from a grouped frequency distribution

66 It is bi-modal when the two highest frequencies are equal. 99

A crude mode can be taken as the mid-point of the modal class which is the class with the highest frequency. In Figure 10.10 we have two modal classes, 170–175 cm and 180–185 cm, each with a frequency of five. This distribution is bi-modal with crude modes of 172.5 cm and 182.5 cm. However, an *interpolated mode* can be calculated using the formula

$$\text{Mode} = L + C \left[\frac{fA}{fA + fB} \right]$$

where L = lower boundary of the modal class
C = modal class interval
fA = frequency of the interval following the modal class
fB = frequency of the interval preceding the modal class

Applied to the data in Figure 10.10 this would give interpolated modes of 172 cm and 181.7 cm.

Advantages of the mode

1 It is easy to understand and to calculate.
2 It is useful where the most popular item is required, e.g. shoe size.
3 It is not distorted by extreme values.

Disadvantages of the mode

1 It does not take account of all values.
2 It may not exist or be unique, e.g. if all the items have different values.
3 It may occur at one of the extremes of a distribution.
4 It cannot be used for further statistical work.

COMPARISON OF MEASURES OF LOCATION

> Often required in exam questions.

The three measures of location help to describe the data. The mean is the most commonly used measure, particularly when further statistical analysis is to be carried out. However, the median may be more suitable where the distribution is distorted by extreme values, e.g. a few high-earners could distort the true picture of a 'typical' wage earned in a firm. When the most popular item in a range is required the mode is preferred, e.g. garment size, colour or style.

MEASURES OF DISPERSION

> A second means of describing the data.

In the previous section the data was described with reference to a form of 'average' to describe the central tendency of the distribution. Comparisons can be improved considerably by adding a measure which shows the 'spread' or *dispersion* of the data. For example, two salesmen could have the same average sales but differ quite markedly in the spread:

	Sales over 5-day period (£)				
SALESMAN A	90	110	100	120	80
SALESMAN B	20	210	130	40	100

Both have mean sales of £100, but Salesman A is more consistent on a daily basis than Salesman B. Dispersion can be measured in several ways such as:

1 The range
2 The interquartile range
3 Standard deviation

THE RANGE

The *range* is the numerical difference between the smallest and largest values in a distribution.

In the example above, Salesman A has a range of 120 – 80 = £40 in his daily sales, whereas Salesman B has a range of 210 – 20 = £190.

Advantages of range

1 It is easy to understand.
2 It is easy to calculate.

Disadvantages of range

1 It only takes account of the two extreme values.
2 It is easily distorted by an unusually high or low value.

THE INTERQUARTILE RANGE

The interquartile range is the numerical difference between the items in the central 50% of a distribution.

If the data is arranged in an array then the first (or lower) quartile lies one quarter of the way along and the third (or upper) quartile lies three-quarters of the way along.

The difference between the value found at these points is the *interquartile range*. The position of the quartiles is found in the same way as the median (which is known as the second quartile) using the formula

$$\text{1st quartile position (Q1)} = \frac{n + 1}{4}$$

$$\text{3rd quartile position (Q3)} = \frac{3(n + 1)}{4}$$

Example:

DAILY OUTPUT : WEEK 22

Day	1	2	3	4	5	6	7
Output (tons)	120	90	110	130	105	115	100
Arrange data in an array		90	100	105	110	115	120	130

$$\text{Position of Q1} = \frac{n + 1}{4} = \frac{7 + 1}{4} = \frac{8}{4} = \text{2nd item}$$

$$\text{Position of Q3} = \frac{3(n + 1)}{4} = \frac{24}{4} = \text{6th item}$$

The value of Q1 and Q3 are 100 and 120 respectively.

The interquartile range is $120 - 100 = 20$ tons

To calculate the interquartile range from a grouped frequency, follow the same procedure as that for the median, i.e. use either the graphical or arithmetical method but this time finding the values at the lower and upper quartile positions.

THE STANDARD DEVIATION

The *standard deviation* is the average deviation from the arithmetic mean of a set of data.

Calculation from simple data (symbol σ or 'little sigma')

Step 1   Calculate the arithmetic mean of the data, $\bar{x}$

Step 2   Find the differences or 'deviations' between each of the values in the distribution and the mean, $(x - \bar{x})$

Step 3   If we add up the deviations from the mean, the negative values will naturally cancel out the positive ones, resulting in a figure of zero. To eliminate the signs, therefore, we square the deviations, $(x - \bar{x})^2$

Step 4   Add up all the squared deviations, $\Sigma(x - \bar{x})^2$

Step 5   Find the average squared deviation by dividing by the number of values, n, thus obtaining $\dfrac{\Sigma(x - \bar{x})^2}{n}$

Step 6   The average squared deviation is known as the *variance* but it is in units squared. To get it back into the same units as the mean, take the square root of the average squared deviation $\sqrt{\dfrac{\Sigma(x - \bar{x})^2}{n}}$

The complete formula is therefore:

$$\sigma = \sqrt{\frac{\Sigma(x - \bar{x})^2}{n}}$$

where σ = the standard deviation
Σ = the sum of
$(x - \bar{x})$ = deviations from the mean
n = the number of values
$\sqrt{}$ = the square root

Example:

DAILY SALES (£)	DEVIATIONS FROM MEAN	DEVIATIONS
x	$(x - \bar{x})$	$(x - \bar{x})^2$
420	− 180	32,400
560	− 40	1,600
630	+ 30	900
580	− 20	400
810	+ 210	44,100
$\Sigma x = 3{,}000$		$\Sigma(x - \bar{x})^2 = 79{,}400$

$$\bar{x} = \frac{\Sigma x}{n} = \frac{3{,}000}{5} = £600$$

$$\sigma = \sqrt{\frac{\Sigma(x - \bar{x})^2}{n}} = \sqrt{\frac{79400}{5}} = \sqrt{15880}$$

$$\sigma = £126$$

The mean sales per day is £600 and on average the sales may vary from the arithmetic mean by £126.

Calculation from ungrouped and grouped frequency distributions

The calculation for frequency distributions follows the same pattern as for simple data but the formula must be adapted to take account of the frequency associated with each value. The new formula is

$$\sigma = \sqrt{\frac{\Sigma f(x - \bar{x})^2}{\Sigma f}}$$

An example of this formula in practice is given below for an *ungrouped* frequency distribution.

STANDARD DEVIATION FOR AN UNGROUPED FREQUENCY DISTRIBUTION

PRICE OF ITEM (£)	NUMBER SOLD		DEVIATION	(DEVIATION)^2	
x	f	fx	$(x - \bar{x})$	$(x - \bar{x})^2$	$f(x - \bar{x})^2$
2	5	10	−2.5	6.25	31.25
3	3	9	−1.5	2.25	6.75
4	18	72	−0.5	0.25	4.5
5	10	50	0.5	0.25	2.5
6	14	84	1.5	2.25	31.5
	$\Sigma f = 50$	$\Sigma fx = 225$		$\Sigma f(x - \bar{x})^2 =$	76.5

$$\text{mean } \bar{x} = \frac{\Sigma fx}{\Sigma f} = \frac{225}{50} = £4.50$$

$$\sigma = \sqrt{\frac{\Sigma f(x - \bar{x})^2}{\Sigma f}} = \sqrt{\frac{76.5}{50}} = \sqrt{1.53} = £1.24$$

The mean price of an item sold is £4.50 with an average deviation from the mean of £1.24. The use of this formula can be rather cumbersome, especially when the mean is an awkward number. For *both* ungrouped and grouped distributions an adapted, quicker method can be used with the formula:

❝A useful shorthand method.❞

$$\sigma = \sqrt{\frac{\Sigma fx^2}{\Sigma f} - \left(\frac{\Sigma fx}{\Sigma f}\right)^2}$$

This allows the student to calculate the standard deviation without needing to find the deviations. A worked example for *grouped* data is given below. Note that for grouped frequency, x is the class mid-point.

Although the numbers appear awkward the process is quite simple and careful use of a calculator should save valuable time.

> It represents all the items in the class.

STANDARD DEVIATION FROM A GROUPED FREQUENCY DISTRIBUTION

HEIGHTS (cm)	x	f	fx	fx^2
150 and under 155	152.5	1	152.5	23256.25
155 and under 160	157.5	1	157.5	24806.25
160 and under 165	162.5	2	325	52812.5
165 and under 170	167.5	3	502.5	84168.75
170 and under 175	172.5	5	862.5	148781.25
175 and under 180	177.5	2	355	63012.5
180 and under 185	182.5	5	912.5	166531.25
185 and under 190	187.5	1	187.5	35156.25
		$\Sigma f = 20$	$\Sigma fx = 3455$	$\Sigma^2 = 598525$

(columns labelled: MID-POINT FREQUENCY)

$$\bar{x} = \frac{\Sigma fx}{\Sigma f} = \frac{3455}{20} = \underline{\underline{172.75cm}}$$

$$\sigma = \sqrt{\frac{\Sigma fx^2}{\Sigma f} - \left(\frac{\Sigma fx}{\Sigma f}\right)^2}$$

$$\sigma = \sqrt{\frac{598525}{20} - \left(\frac{3455}{20}\right)^2}$$

$$\sigma = \sqrt{29926.25 - 29842.56}$$
$$\sigma = \sqrt{83.69}$$
$$\sigma = \underline{\underline{9.15cm}}$$

The mean height of students is 173 cm (to the nearest cm) and on average one would expect a deviation from the mean of 9.15 cm.

N.B. The most common fault of 'A' level students is to confuse the term fx^2 with the term $(fx)^2$ – remember, only x is squared and then multiplied by the frequency f.

Advantages of standard deviation

1   It takes account of all values in the distribution.
2   It can be used for further statistical work, particularly with reference to the normal distribution.
3   For distributions not skewed, we can state the following:
   a) 68% of the data should lie within one standard deviation of the mean;
   b) 95% of the data within two σs;
   c) 99% of the data within three σs.

> Compare with the other measures of dispersion.

Disadvantage of standard deviation

1   It can be distorted by extreme values.

SUMMARY

A manager can now describe a set of data with reference to its measure of central tendency and to its measure of dispersion. This allows different sets of data to be more easily compared and analysed.

EXAMINATION QUESTIONS

1 The owner of a UK company selling coats, dresses and hats is considering expanding by setting up another shop in Europe.

a) What commercial information should the owner seek before making any decision?
(4)

b) The pie charts below are taken from the company's reports and accounts for 1986.
   i) Discuss whether these pie charts satisfy the main principles one should always bear in mind when presenting data. *(4)*
   ii) Show that the total sales in 1986 were £45 million. *(3)*
   iii) Calculate the percentage increase in the sales value of accessories between 1981 and 1986. *(3)*
   iv) If total sales continue to increase by the same average amount over the next three years as they did in the five years 1981–1986, and sales of dresses increase by 40% in total over the next three years, what angle of a pie chart for 1989 would represent the contribution to total sales by the dress department? *(4)*

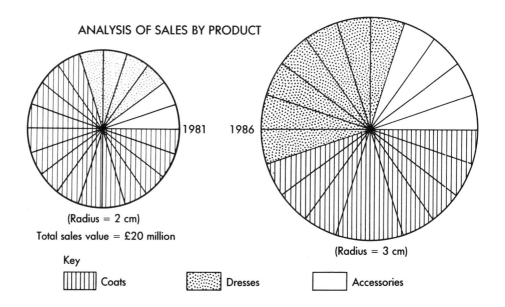

ANALYSIS OF SALES BY PRODUCT

1981

1986

(Radius = 2 cm)
Total sales value = £20 million

Key

Coats   Dresses   Accessories

(Radius = 3 cm)

c) The managers of the three departments each claim that their product is 'doing best'.
   i) How could each manager use the above pie charts to support his claim? (You are not required to undertake any calculations to answer this question.) *(3)*
   ii) Suggest an appropriate graphical method for displaying sales information. Give reasons for your answer. *(4)*

(UCLES 1987)

2 The data alongside has been obtained by the Marketing Manager of a Safari Park. The data relates to the number of miles travelled from home by people using the Park.

a) Construct a histogram to illustrate this data. *(12)*

b) According to the data, which of the groups contains the modal distance travelled to the Safari Park? *(2)*

c) What percentage of visitors travelled more than 50 miles to reach the Safari Park? *(3)*

d) State *two* methods that might have been used to collect this information. *(2)*

e) The above information is an example of 'primary' data. State and explain one advantage and one disadvantage of this over 'secondary' data. *(4)*

Frequency	Miles travelled to reach Safari Park
10	1–10
20	11–20
50	21–30
40	31–40
30	41–50
25	51–60
15	61–70
10	71–80

f) State *two* promotional methods that could be used to encourage more local people (i.e. those living within a 20 mile radius) to visit the Safari Park. *(2)*

3 a) Explain the differences between the following types of sample:
   i) random
   ii) stratified
   iii) quota *(6)*

   b) A firm wishes to fix a piece work rate for its employees and to do this it needs to know the average number of operations per person per day. Rather than make this calculation for all its staff, the firm decides to take a sample.
   i) Describe how the firm might decide on the kind and size of sample it would need. *(4)*
   ii) Discuss which of the measures of central tendency would be the most appropriate to use and explain why you think this is the case. *(4)*

   c) Suppose that workmen had previously been paid a flat rate of £25 per day, on the basis of an arithmetic average of 100 operations per day. Suggest why, and at what levels of operations, you might introduce bonus payments, if the results of the sample showed that the arithmetic mean was 100 operations, with a standard deviation of 30. (You may use the table below if you think this is appropriate.) *(5)*

Proportionate parts of the area under the normal curve				
Distances from Mean in terms of standard deviation in one direction	$0-1$	$1-1$	$2-1$	over 3
Proportion of area in above range	34%	14%	2%	Negligible

   d) Suppose a workman performed the following set of operations over a 10-day period:

   180,   180,   150,   130,   190,   200,   150,   160,   170,   180.

   What would you conclude about the workman and/or the sample results? Explain your reasons. (You may assume that the standard deviation remains at 30.) *(6)*

   (UCLES 1985)

TUTOR'S ANSWER

Question 1

a) The owner would require a combination of primary and secondary data in order to make any effective decisions. Primary data might include market research in the prospective European sites as well as an in-depth study of foreign competition. Secondary data should be available on European populations, incomes, exports from the UK and market penetration of rival firms. This type of information should enable the management to identify gaps in the market.

b) i) Data should be presented in a clear manner in order to make a good visual impact. They should be adequately labelled, drawn to scale and possess an informative key. The pie charts have all these attributes as well as a title. The only item missing is the source of the data.
   ii) The areas represent the total values and the ratio of the areas is proportional to these totals, therefore:

   $$\frac{\text{Sales 1981}}{\text{Sales 1986}} = \frac{\text{Area of 1981 circle}}{\text{Area of 1986 circle}}$$

   $$\frac{£20m}{x} = \frac{\pi r_1^2}{\pi r_2^2}$$

   where $r_1 = 2$cm and $r_2 = 3$cm

$$\therefore \frac{£20m}{x} = \frac{4}{9}$$

$$4x = £180 \text{ m}$$
$$x = £45 \text{ m}$$

Total sales in 1986 were £45 million.

iii) Sales value of accessories in 1981 = £2 m
Sales value of accessories in 1986 = £9 m

$$\text{Percentage increase} = \frac{\text{Change in sales}}{\text{Original sales}} \times 100$$

$$= \frac{7}{2} \times 100 = 350\% \text{ increase}$$

iv) Average increase in sales over the period 1981/1986 was

$$\frac{\text{Total increase}}{\text{No. of years}} = \frac{£25m}{5} = £5m \text{ p.a.}$$

Therefore sales in 1989 would be £60 m.

Sales of dresses in 1986 = $^{7}/_{20}$ × £45 m = £15.75 m

$\therefore$ sales of dresses in 1989 = $\frac{140}{100}$ × £15.75 m = £22.05 m

$$\text{The pie chart angle} = \frac{\text{sales of dresses}}{\text{total sales}} \times 360°$$

$$= \frac{22.05}{60} \times 360°$$

$$= \underline{132.3°}$$

c) i) The coats manager could claim that his department enjoyed the largest component of sales in the period 1981/86. The dresses manager could claim his area has seen the largest absolute increase in sales and the accessories manager could claim the largest proportionate increase in sales from 10% to 20%.

ii) An arithmetic graph would best show the absolute changes in sales which would be favoured by the dress and coat departments. However, the accessories manager may prefer a semi-log graph which shows proportionate change.

Another alternative would be to illustrate sales by a multiple bar chart or component bar chart depending on whether the aim is to stress the constituent parts or the totals.

STUDENT'S ANSWER

Question 2

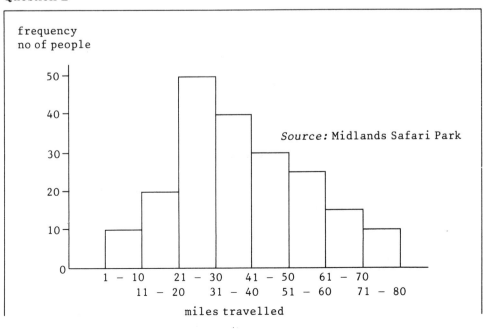

Fig. 10.11 Histogram of miles travelled to visit Safari Park

An acurately drawn, and clearly labelled histogram.

Correct definition and selection of the modal group or class.

Accurate reading of frequency table and conversion into a percentage figure.

Correct.

Correct. Perhaps 'secondary data' could have been defined here.

Correct.

a) See graph

b) The modal distance is the class with the highest frequency, i.e. 21–30 miles with a frequency of 50

c) Total frequency = 200
   Visitors travelling more than 50 miles
   = 50

   $\therefore$ percentage $= \dfrac{50}{200} \times 100 = 25\%$

d) Personal interview as people arrive at the gate.
   Questionnaire on arrival or departure.

e) One advantage is that the data is being collected for a specific purpose and the accuracy of collection is known.
   A disadvantage is that it is more costly than secondary data in terms of both time and money.

f) i) Placement of an advert in a local newspaper with a limited circulation.
    ii) Mail-shot to areas within 20 miles of the park.

Tutor's comments

An accurate answer which shows a good grasp of the principles of collecting and analysing data. Answers are brief, but are to the point of each part of the question. An A grade answer to a quite straightforward question.

OUTLINE ANSWER

Question 3

a) A straightforward description is required but emphasising the differences which largely concern whether the population is homogeneous or has certain attributes, as well as making the collection of data easier.

b) i) The sample must be large enough to be representative. It must be easy to collect and capable of analysis and conform to the constraints of time and money. It must also take account of the variety of staff and the differences in work-rate at different times of the day.
    ii) The main measures of central tendency are the mean, the mode and the median. The mean would lend itself to further statistical analysis whereas the mode would show the number of operations that most people achieve.

c) In this section use must be made of the properties of the standard deviation for a normal distribution. The limit for a bonus would depend on:
   i) the level of output the firm believe needs a special award
   and/or ii) the proportion of the workforce which should be rewarded.
   One standard deviation above the mean includes 34% of the workforce; therefore only 16% would achieve an output of 130 or more operations. If 130 is set as the bonus mark, roughly 1 in 6 workers will be rewarded and motivated.

d) The arithmetic mean of this worker = 169 operations. This is more than two standard deviations above the mean and would be achieved by less than 2% of all workers. Either the worker is exceptional or the sample results are not representative.

FURTHER READING

Harris and Powell, *Quantitative Decision Making*, Longman 1987 (Chapters 4, 5 and 6)

CHAPTER 11

THE MARKET

THE MARKET

DEMAND

SUPPLY

DETERMINATION OF MARKET PRICE

PRICE ELASTICITY

OTHER FORMS OF ELASTICITY

GETTING STARTED

A market can be defined as any economic activity designed to satisfy the needs of society. On one hand we have consumers who demand goods. On the other hand we have sellers who aim to satisfy demand by providing the required goods and services while at the same time, making a profit.

The needs or wants of consumers are unlimited but the resources to satisfy them are finite. Because of this dilemma, economic goods are considered to be scarce in relation to the demand for them. In other words, consumers must *choose* between the alternative goods available. The collective actions of all consumers determines the *market demand*. Sellers, too, are faced with the problem of scarce resources and must also exercise choice. Their collective action determines the *market supply*.

The interaction of the two market forces of supply and demand determines the *market price* for each commodity or service. In this chapter we explore the factors which influence the level and direction of demand and supply and how that, in turn, affects price and the quantity traded in the market in any given time period. It is important to understand the general principles which are involved so that any change in the economic environment can be analysed as to its effect on market conditions.

ESSENTIAL PRINCIPLES

THE MARKET

The market can be viewed as the area where individual decisions about buying and selling interact. On one side we have purchasers or consumers who wish to buy:

- single use consumer goods – food, cigarettes, alcoholic drinks, matches, etc.
- consumer durables – TVs, dish-washers, cars, furniture, etc.
- consumer services – health care, dry cleaning, beauty treatments, etc.

On the other side we have producers willing to supply these commodities who therefore must buy:

- factors of production – land, labour services, capital equipment, etc.
- producer services – insurance, banking, transport, telecommunications, etc.

"The interaction of supply and demand."

The interplay between these forces determines the market price of the product and the quantity bought and sold. It is important to understand what can influence both the demand side of the market and the supply side.

DEMAND

INDIVIDUAL AND MARKET DEMAND CURVE

The *individual demand curve* shows the quantity of a product a consumer would be willing *and able* to buy at various prices. We call this the 'effective' demand of the individual, since he or she can turn their wish to buy into reality. Figure 11.1 shows two consumers A and B and their individual demand curves for product X. At price £10, A is willing to buy only 2 items but B is willing to buy 4. When the price falls to £4, A wants 6 items and B wants 10. This demonstrates a 'law' of demand, namely that as price falls the quantity demanded rises (assuming all other variable influences remain unchanged). This is known as an *expansion* of demand. Conversely as price is increased the quantity demanded will fall or *contract*.

"An important law."

When we move *along* a demand curve, due solely to a change in the price of the product itself, we use the terms expansion or contraction of demand. If consumers A and B are the only consumers, their combined demand forms the market. We can devise a market demand curve by adding the individual demands at each price level. This is known as *horizontal summing*. At price £10 the total demand is 6 while at price £4 market demand is 16.

INCREASE OR DECREASE IN DEMAND

We have seen that if the price of the product changes, then we move *along* the given demand curve, with more or less of the product being demanded. However, sometimes the whole demand curve will *shift* its position due to changes in factors other than the price of the product. These factors are known as the *determinants of demand*. If one or more of the determinants, detailed below, changes then the entire demand curve *shifts*, either to the right or to the left (i.e. more or less of the product is demanded at each and every price) (see Fig. 11.2).

"The entire demand curve shifts."

At price P_1 demand is originally at Q_1 on the demand curve D_1D_1. An *increase* in demand shifts the demand curve to the right to D_2D_2 where OQ_2 is demanded at price OP_1. Similarly a shift in demand to the left to D_3D_3 causes a *decrease* in demand to OQ_3 at price OP_1.

When the demand curve *shifts*, due to a change in one or more of the determinants of demand, we use the terms increase or decrease in demand.

The determinants of demand

A *shift* in the demand curve (increase or decrease) is caused by a change in one or more of the following:

"Reasons why demand curves shift."

- *Changes in income:* an increase in real disposable income will normally cause the demand curve to shift to the right (increase) as consumers can now afford more goods and services. This may be caused by a reduction in taxes (government action) or by a rise in wages (producer action) or by individuals acquiring better-paid employment. A

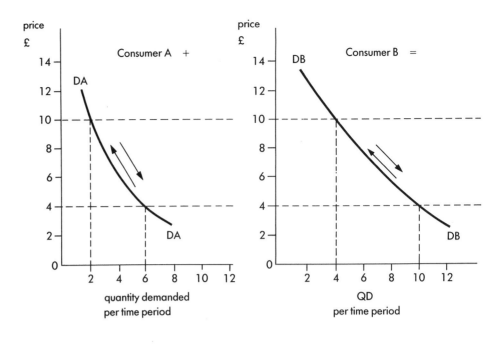

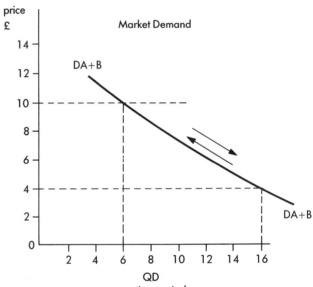

Fig. 11.1 Individual and market demand curves

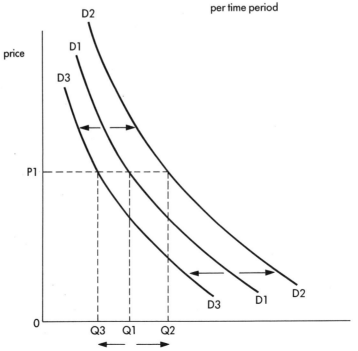

Fig. 11.2 A shift in demand (increase and decrease)

fall in real disposable income will, of course, cause the demand curve to shift to the left (decrease).

■ *Changes in taste and fashion*: a change in consumer taste in favour of a good will shift the demand curve to the right. After a period of time the fashion may subside and the curve shifts to the left. This is commonly observed with clothing, children's games and popular music.

■ *Changes in the price of substitutes*: many goods have close substitutes. A change in the price of a substitute may cause consumers to switch expenditure from one good to another, e.g. if the price of brand X soap powder is reduced it may attract custom away from brand Y even though brand Y's price has not changed. The demand curve for brand Y will then shift to the left.

■ *Changes in the price of complements*: many goods are jointly demanded, such as bread and butter, cars and petrol, computers and software etc. In this case a change in the price of one will affect the demand for the other, e.g. a rise in the price of petrol may cause a fall in demand for large cars.

■ *Changes in future expectations*: expectations about future price changes may affect demand in the present market, e.g. the increase in demand for tobacco products and alcoholic drinks prior to the expected tax rises in the budget or the increase in demand for a particular share in anticipation of a good dividend performance.

■ *Changes in population*: changes in the size and structure of a population will lead to significant changes in demand. For example, an ageing population will demand more facilities for retirement and better health care.

■ *Changes in the effectiveness of advertising*: the impact of an advertising campaign may persuade more consumers to purchase a product at its existing price.

SUPPLY

INDIVIDUAL AND MARKET SUPPLY CURVE

The total *market supply* of a product is equal to the combined totals of the *individual firms* making the product at that price; i.e. we obtain market supply by the *horizontal summation* of the individual firms' supply curves. In Fig. 11.3, Firm A is willing to supply 12 units at £10 but only 4 units at £4 while Firm B, which may be more efficient, is willing to supply 16 units and 8 units respectively. The total market supply at £10 is 28 units, obtained by adding together the quantities each firm is willing (and able) to supply at that price.

A change in the price of the product itself will result in a movement *along* a given supply curve. We use the terms expansion and contraction of supply in this case.

INCREASE OR DECREASE IN SUPPLY

The whole supply curve may *shift* its position, with more or less being supplied at any given price. A shift to the right (increase) or left (decrease) will be due to a change in one or more of the *determinants of supply* outlined below.

> The entire supply curve shifts.

In Fig. 11.4, a rightward shift in supply from S_1S_1 to S_2S_2 would cause the quantity supplied at price P_1 to *increase* from OQ_1 to OQ_2. A leftward shift in supply from S_1S_1 to S_3S_3 would cause the quantity supplied to *decrease* from OQ_1 to OQ_3.

Determinants of supply

> Reasons why supply curves shift.

■ *Changes in the price of inputs used in production*: a change in costs will affect the profit level; e.g. a rise in costs either reduces profit or forces a firm into a loss-making situation and eventual closure. The result would be a shift in the supply curve to the left (decrease), with less output being supplied at any given price. Conversely, a fall in costs will increase profit levels and encourage production, shifting the supply curve to the right (increase).

■ *Changes in the price of other goods*: some goods are jointly supplied, such as petrol and paraffin. A rise in the price of petrol will not only stimulate an *expansion* in the supply of petrol but also an *increase* (shift to the right) in the supply of paraffin.

■ *Changes in technology*: supply curves are drawn on the assumption of a given level of technology. Technological advancements could lead to better production methods and higher output levels for the same input. A larger quantity will then be supplied at each and every price because unit costs have fallen (i.e. an increase in supply).

■ *Changes in taxes and subsidies*: the imposition of indirect taxes (e.g. VAT) has the same effect as a rise in production costs, causing the supply curve to shift to the left. Similarly, a subsidy to the producer has the effect of reducing costs and shifting the supply curve to the right.

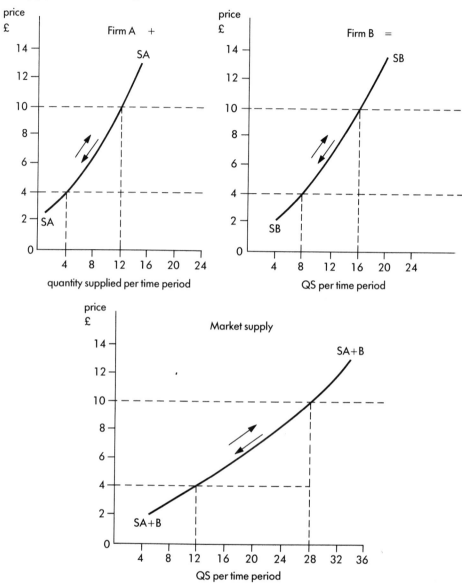

Fig. 11.3 Individual and market supply curve

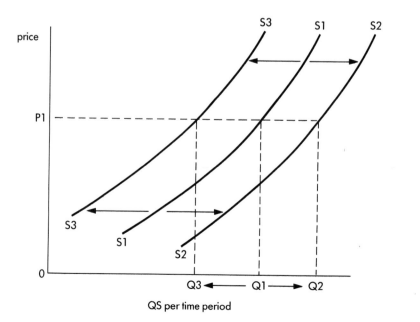

Fig. 11.4 Shift in supply (increase and decrease)

- *Changes in future expectations*: as with consumer demand, the producer may alter present behaviour in anticipation of future changes. The onset of recession in 1989 caused many manufacturers to cut production levels despite little change in current prices, shifting the supply curve to the left.
- *Changes in weather*: climatic changes can have a considerable impact on the supply of agricultural goods. Adverse weather can severely affect harvest and decrease supply, e.g. frost destroying much of the Brazilian coffee crop. Conversely, favourable weather may produce a bumper harvest and shift the supply curve to the right.

THE DETERMINATION OF MARKET PRICE

EQUILIBRIUM PRICE

In a free market system prices are determined by the interaction of supply and demand. In Fig. 11.5, supply and demand intersect at Price OP_1 which is considered to be the *equilibrium* price as the quantity supplied just satisfies the quantity demanded, OQ_1. At this price the market is in 'balance' (equilibrium) with no tendency for price to rise or fall. At Price OP_2 we have over-supply or a glut where excess supply could only be sold by reducing the price. At Price OP_3 demand is greater than supply and the shortage will cause consumers to bid up the price in an attempt to obtain the goods. Only at Price OP_1 is the market in a settled position.

> Equilibrium is a state of rest.

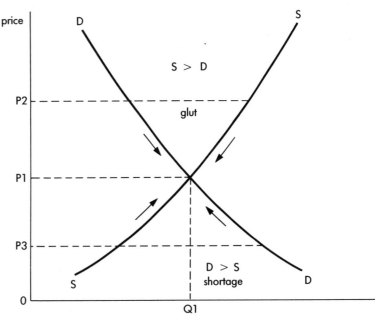

Fig. 11.5 Determination of market price

DISTURBING THE EQUILIBRIUM

The forces described above allow us to analyse the effects of changes in the economic environment on the equilibrium market price and quantity.

In Fig. 11.6 the demand curve has shifted to the right (increase). This could have been caused by a change in taste or fashion in favour of the product, rising real incomes, a rise in the price of a substitute or a fall in the price of a complement.

Irrespective of the cause, the result is a rise in equilibrium price from OP to OP_1 and in the quantity supplied and demanded from OQ to OQ_1.

In Fig. 11.7 the supply curve shifts to the left (decreases). This could be caused by a rise in indirect taxes, a rise in input costs such as labour or raw materials, or a more pessimistic view of the future by the producer. In this case equilibrium price rises from OP to OP_1, but this time the equilibrium quantity falls from OQ to OQ_1.

> External forces affect each business.

Each firm is affected by changes in the economic, political and social environment that can be analysed, through the use of supply and demand diagrams, to illustrate the impact of the change on the market. However, it is not only the *direction* of change which the firm needs to know but also the *magnitude*. This involves a study of the degree of responsiveness of supply and demand to changes in price, income or, in fact, any of the determinants. This is called the *elasticity* of a good. We will consider three stimuli: price, income and the impact of changes in the price of other goods.

> Elasticity means the responsiveness.

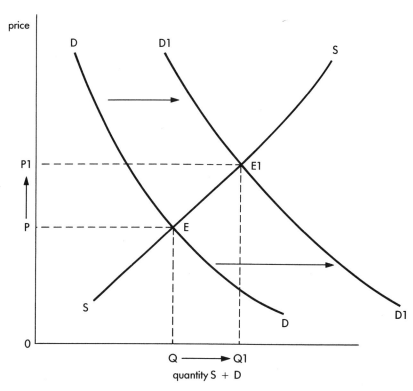

Fig. 11.6 Change in the equilibrium
position: a shift in demand
(increase)

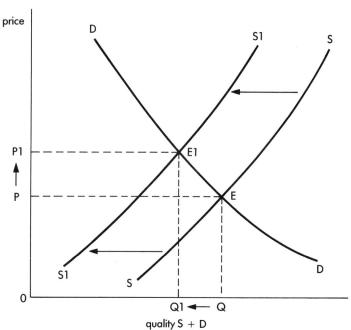

Fig. 11.7 Change in the equilibrium
position: a shift in supply (decrease)

PRICE ELASTICITY

Price elasticity is concerned with the responsiveness of supply and demand to change in *price*.

PRICE ELASTICITY OF DEMAND

Price elasticity of demand (PED) for a product measures the responsiveness of the quantity demanded following a change in its own price. It is calculated using the formula:

Important equation.

$$PED = \frac{\text{Percentage change in quantity demanded}}{\text{Percentage change in prices}}$$

or $\dfrac{\Delta Q_D/\text{original } Q_D}{\Delta P/\text{original } P}$

When talking about PED we are considering *movements along* a given demand curve. The formula may give values ranging from zero through to infinity. These values fall into a number of categories. (Note that we ignore the *negative* sign for elasticity in the following discussion.)

PED>1. Demand is *price elastic* if the PED value is greater than one. This means that for any given change in price the change in quantity demanded will be greater; e.g. if a retailer reduces the price of a commodity by 10% and the PED is estimated to be 3, then sales can be expected to expand by 30%. The greater the value of the PED, the more responsive is demand to any price change. Demand is said to be *infinitely elastic* if the PED value is infinity; i.e. a rise in the price of a product would lead to demand falling to zero, and vice versa.

PED<1. Demand is *price inelastic* if the PED value is less than one. This means that for any given change in price the change in the quantity demanded will be less; e.g. if petrol prices are increased by 5% and demand contracts by only 1% then the PED value would be 0.2, showing that the demand for petrol is inelastic.

PED = 1. Demand is of *unitary elasticity* if the PED value is exactly one. A given percentage change in price brings about exactly the same percentage change in quantity demanded; e.g. a 5% increase in the price of tomatoes brings about a 5% contraction in the demand for them.

> Price elasticity is important for determining the impact of price changes on revenue.

The importance of price elasticity of demand is in the impact of price changes on consumer expenditure and subsequently on producer *revenue*. Table 11.1 summarises the effect of price changes on revenue. It must be understood that price elasticity is not necessarily a fixed value, as it is influenced by many variable factors.

PRICE CHANGE	TYPE OF ELASTICITY	DESCRIPTION	EFFECT ON REVENUE
INCREASE	ELASTIC DEMAND	Q_D changes by a larger percentage than does price	FALL
	UNIT ELASTICITY	Q_D changes by same percentage as price	SAME
	INELASTIC DEMAND	Q_D changes by a smaller percentage than does price	RISE
DECREASE	ELASTIC DEMAND	Q_D changes by a larger percentage than does price	RISE
	UNIT ELASTICITY	Q_D changes by same percentage as price	SAME
	INELASTIC DEMAND	Q_D changes by a smaller percentage than does price	FALL

Table 11.1 Price elasticity and effect on revenue

Determinants of price elasticity of demand

The main factors which affect the value of price elasticity of demand are:

- *The number and availability of substitutes*: where there are several close substitutes, demand will tend to be more elastic as the consumer can easily switch to a similar product following a small price rise; e.g. the wide variety of brands of tea. The absence of substitutes removes competition and demand tends to be less elastic.

- *The time period*: when a price changes, not all consumers will be *aware* of the change. Therefore few will react in the short run and demand will remain much as it was. However, as time elapses more consumers revise their consumption patterns and demand becomes more elastic; e.g. if one brand of petrol is reduced it may go unnoticed on the first few days but eventually more and more motorists will switch brands as news of the price cut becomes general knowledge. Generally the demand for a product is less elastic in the short run but more elastic in the long run.

- *The proportion of income spent on the product*: demand will tend to be inelastic if the amount spent on the item is small; e.g. matches. A price rise of even 50% may then have little impact on our spending habits. Where, however, the commodity forms a large part of expenditure, consumers will be more willing to look for substitutes. Therefore in this case demand is likely to be more elastic; e.g. a rise in the price of beef may cause a shift in consumption toward mutton or pork.

■ *The degree of habit*: some goods are habit forming, such as tobacco and alcohol, in which case demand will tend to be inelastic.

PRICE ELASTICITY OF SUPPLY

A price change not only causes a response from demand but also a response in supply. The price elasticity of supply (PES) measures the responsiveness of the quantity supplied following a change in the price of the product. The formula for calculating the elasticity value is:

$$PES = \frac{\text{Percentage change in quantity supplied}}{\text{Percentage change in price}}$$

$$\text{or} \quad \frac{\Delta Q_S/\text{original } Q_S}{\Delta P/\text{original } P}$$

When talking about PES we are considering *movements along* a given supply curve. The following numerical values for PES might be noted:

PES = zero. This represents *perfectly inelastic* supply, i.e. any change in price has no effect on the quantity supplied.

66 Elasticity values can vary. 99

PES<1. Here supply is *inelastic* in that the percentage change in supply is less than the percentage change in price; e.g. a 10% increase in the price of cigarettes causes only a 1% expansion in supply. The PES value would then be 0.1.

PES>1. Here supply is elastic, i.e. it responds by a larger percentage following a price change; e.g. a 5% fall in the price of product X results in a 20% contraction in supply. The PES would then be 4.

PES = infinity. Here supply is *perfectly elastic* because a change in price leads to an infinitely large change in quantity supplied.

Determinants of the elasticity of supply

66 Factors affecting elasticity is important. 99

The elasticity of supply can be affected by changes in any one (or combination) of the following factors:

■ *The time period considered*: in the short run, supply cannot be expanded by any significant amount and therefore tends to be inelastic. A producer could use spare capacity or work overtime in order to expand output on a temporary basis, but large scale changes could only take place with new investment or the emergence of a new firm. This, by definition, can only take place in the long run.

■ *The ease of entry into the industry*: a price rise may attract new firms into the industry with the result that supply expands. The easier it is for new firms to enter the industry, the more elastic will be supply. However, if barriers to entry exist, then supply will tend to be inelastic.

■ *The availability of factors of production*: the more available are factors of production, the more elastic will be supply; and vice versa. The rise in the price of oil encouraged greater exploration of the North Sea but exploitation had to await the design, commissioning, building and establishment of oil rigs. In the short run, supply remained inelastic until new fields could be opened.

THE IMPORTANCE OF ELASTICITY

A knowledge of price elasticity is important to producers and government alike, for several reasons.

66 Practical applications of price elasticity. 99

■ Businesses wish to predict the impact of price changes on their sales revenue. Increasing the price of products with *price inelastic* demands will increase the firm's revenue. However, increasing the price of products with *price elastic* demands would have the opposite effect, and reduce the firm's revenue.

- The Government uses elasticity to estimate revenue returns from changes in taxation. Extra taxes on products with price inelastic demands produces an increase in tax revenue; e.g. taxes on tobacco, alcohol and petrol.

- A fall in the price of UK products may generate additional export demand (and revenue) for those products with price elastic demands.

- Estimates of price elasticity would enable governments to predict the impact on prices following either a change in supply (e.g. a bumper harvest) or a change in demand (e.g. following a food health scare). The incomes of primary producers (e.g. agricultural and mineral products) are significantly affected by even small changes in demand or supply because of their inelastic nature.

Although price may be the most important factor affecting supply and demand there are other determinants which can affect consumer behaviour.

OTHER FORMS OF ELASTICITY

CROSS ELASTICITY OF DEMAND (CED)

This is defined as the responsiveness of demand to changes in the price of related goods. The formula is:

$$CED = \frac{\text{Percentage change in demand for good A}}{\text{Percentage change in price of good B}}$$

> The sign of cross elasticity is important.

Cross elasticity of demand is associated with *shifts* in the demand curve. The nature of the shift will depend upon the relationship between Good A and Good B:

- If Good B is a *substitute* for Good A, then a change in its price will have the same direction effect upon the demand for Good A; e.g. a fall in the price of one brand of petrol will result in a fall (decrease) in demand for a rival brand. The cross elasticity value will be positive. The higher the positive value, the closer the goods are as substitutes.

- If Good B is a *complement* for Good A, then the cross elasticity value will be negative; e.g. a fall in price of compact disc players will cause a rise (increase) in demand for compact discs. Again the more complementary the goods are, the higher the negative value of the cross elasticity.

INCOME ELASTICITY OF DEMAND (YED)

This measures the responsiveness of demand to changes in consumer incomes. The formula is:

$$YED = \frac{\text{Percentage change in quantity demanded}}{\text{Percentage change in income}}$$

> Negative cross elasticity indicates an inferior good.

Income elasticity of demand is also associated with *shifts* in the demand curve. Those goods which have a positive YED value will see demand grow as income increases. Most goods will follow this pattern and have a positive value. Where the value is negative, it means that demand is moving in the opposite direction to income; e.g. as a population increases its standard of living and enjoys higher real incomes, the demand for basic staple foods may fall as consumers substitute goods of a higher quality. Goods with a positive value are known as *normal goods* and those with a negative value are called *inferior goods*.

OTHER FACTORS AFFECTING THE MARKET

So far in this chapter we have restricted the impact on supply and demand for a product to changes in price, income, time and prices of related goods. These are not the only factors which can affect market supply and demand. Action by the government (e.g. taxes and subsidies) and increasingly by the European Union also result in significant changes in consumption patterns. In the same way that elasticity measures responsiveness to price or income changes it can also be used to calculate similar responses to changes in advertising or taxation. It is essential for candidates to appreciate the wide range of possible determinants which together form and influence the market forces acting upon a commodity.

EXAMINATION QUESTIONS

1   a) Marketing managers need to know about elasticity. Why?   (*10*)
    b) If the Bank of England introduced a tighter monetary policy, what, in your opinion, would be the consequences of this for a firm producing video machines?   (*15*)
                                                                    (UCLES 1985)

2   Discuss how economic and other constraints might influence the exploration and development policy of an oil company.   (UCLES 1989)

3   Examine how an enterprise might alter its plans if a prolonged period of heavy unemployment is predicted.   (AEB 1988)

4   a) In 1990 Williams Ltd sold 60,000 hi-fi systems at £400 each. Average consumer income is expected to rise by 10% in 1991 as compared with 1990. The price elasticity of demand for hi-fi's is −0.5 and the income elasticity of demand is +1.2.
       i) Given the expected change in income between 1990 and 1991, calculate the expected change in sales volume and sales revenue   (*3*)
       ii) If Williams also cut price by 10%, what further changes to sales volume and sales revenue would result?   (*3*)
       iii) Explain and comment on your findings in i) and ii).   (*5*)
                                                          (UCLES 1991 Part Question)

OUTLINE ANSWERS

Question 1

a) The student needs to display a wide knowledge of the calculation and application of elasticity in this section. The marketing manager must estimate the impact of price changes, the effect of income changes and the reaction of competitors on the sales of the company's products. The application of price, income and cross elasticity would allow approximate sales forecasts to be made for a variety of marketing schemes. The student should explain each type of elasticity, give a relevant example and state the appropriate equation.

b) The second part is really an extension or practical application of the first part and should be tackled in logical stages. Firstly, explain what is meant by a 'tighter monetary policy' and how it affects interests rates, bank borrowing, bank overdrafts and hire purchase. Secondly, translate these measures into the impact on overall demand for consumer goods with particular reference to video machines, a consumer luxury. This will allow you to bring in income elasticity and the concept of elastic and inelastic demand. Finally, reference could be made to the impact on the firm's costs as higher interest rates and tighter credit will create an increased financial burden. Is it possible to pass this on to the consumer? Again there is scope for discussion of price increases in a luxury good with reference to price elasticity.

Question 2

This type of question allows the student to discuss a wide range of issues and how they may affect a company, in this case an oil company. A good starting point is the market demand and market supply for the various oil-based products, chiefly petrol. Petrol is demanded inelastically in the short run but supply can be prone to sudden shocks, e.g. Middle East war or a drilling rig disaster. The use of a supply and demand diagram would be appropriate to show the impact on price. Reference can also be made to other forms of energy which may compete with oil, e.g. hydro-electricity, solar, wave, gas, nuclear etc. Oil is traded in US $: therefore exchange rate movements would be a further constraint; a strong pound would reduce the sterling earnings of a UK-based oil company. The question specifically mentions 'exploration and development' indicating that the examiner would like some comment on risk and long-term planning. Exploration could involve the use of probability and expected values whereas development allows the student to discuss investment appraisal techniques. Finally, mention could be made of the role of technology. Oil exploration is at the forefront of science and any improvements in oil extraction or refining would have a significant impact on costs and profits.

TUTOR'S ANSWER

Question 3

Unemployment may be structural, frictional or seasonal but if it is heavy and prolonged it will have a significant impact on the level of aggregate demand. Whatever the cause, high unemployment will mean lower incomes and reduced discretionary spending. For the firm it may mean a future of falling sales, reduced revenue and declining domestic demand. With such bleak prospects the firm must re-assess its plans not only in the short run but also to take a longer term view of the market.

The firm, especially in the short run period, will become more self-conscious. The first areas to suffer will be those activities considered to be peripheral, e.g. philanthropic acts. Credit control will be tightened with reduced credit periods and more stringent follow-up of late payment. The firm may well try to delay paying its own creditors in order to improve the cash flow situation. However, if all companies are experiencing the fall in demand a vicious circle of late payment will be created which will favour the larger and more influential firms.

Another cost-cutting exercise is to de-stock. Excess stock can be sold through special discounts or promotions while production is reduced to slow down the in-coming stock. The financial cost of keeping stock is thus reduced. The plant will now be working at below full capacity, which may lead to a rationalisation of the inputs required. A major slice of production costs is labour, which may experience a ban on overtime working, a reduced working week, the shedding of part-time workers and – if need – be redundancies. The first three measures are easily achieved in the short-run but the question of redundancies is a more serious matter. It may only be contemplated as a last resort, as it will undermine confidence among the remaining labour force and lead to friction with Trade Unions. As well as damaging morale the redundancy payments may further weaken the firm's liquidity position.

As output falls, the fixed costs of the firm must be spread over fewer goods, thus reducing the unit profitability. This may cause the firm to review its marketing procedures in favour of more aggressive measures. This was seen recently in the motor trade during the 1990/91 recession. Another alternative would be to explore new markets particularly those overseas which are not affected by falling domestic demand. At home, the firm could look at alternatives to its present range in the hope that diversification may lead to a safer and wider base of operations.

An early casualty of recession may be investment plans. These could be postponed or even scrapped if the outlook is bleak, even in the long run. However, some firms take the opposite view and see falling demand as a spur to cut costs by investment in labour-saving capital equipment. Technologically advanced production techniques could give the firm a competitive edge over rivals and, if successful, allow it to dominate a larger section of the reduced domestic market.

Whatever the strategy adopted, most firms will experience financial difficulties in the short run. Cash flow problems may result in a run-down of reserves or, more likely, an increase in bank borrowing. This in turn will cause costs to rise and make the firm more vulnerable to closure and/or takeover. A period of restructuring may be allowed by the banks but in the final analysis funds will only be forthcoming if the prospect of long-term improvement is convincing.

Some firms may be able to obtain external assistance from central government regional funds, local government sponsorship or grants from the European Community. However, this type of assistance tends to be specific and investment orientated. Another option to closure is to merge or be taken over by a larger, more financially secure enterprise. Whatever option is chosen there will always be some firms who will not survive, while others will emerge leaner and fitter following a rigorous rationalisation programme.

STUDENT'S ANSWER

Question 4

> Good. Always write the equation in full.

> Should state the change in revenue as well as the new total!

> Presented in a logical manner.

> A good explanation of the relevance of income elasticity.

> Price elasticity is clearly explained. Good point – the reactions of competitors is an important influence on decision-making.

a) i) Sales revenue for 1990 = Sales volume × price
= 60,000 × £400
= £24,000,000

Assuming no change in price, an increase of 10% in incomes will result in:

$$\text{Income elasticity of demand} = \frac{\text{Percentage change in demand}}{\text{Percentage change in income}}$$

$$+1.2 = \frac{\% \triangle \text{ in demand}}{10}$$

$$+12 = \% \triangle \text{ in demand}$$

Expected sales volume will increase by 12%, i.e. an increase of 7,200 to a total of *67,200*.
Sales revenue for 1991 = projected sales volume × price
= 67,200 × £400
= *£26,880,000*

ii) A 10% reduction in price will give a new price level of £360. The impact of this is given by the price elasticity of demand figure of −0.5.

$$\text{Price elasticity of demand} = \frac{\text{Percentage change in demand}}{\text{Percentage change in price}}$$

$$-0.5 = \frac{\% \triangle \text{ in demand}}{-10\%}$$

$$5\% = \% \triangle \text{ in demand}$$

Demand will increase from 67,200 by a further 3,360 to a new level of *70,560*
Sales revenue for 1991 = sales volume 1991 × price
= 70,560 × £360
= *£25,401,600*

iii) As people's incomes rise, then assuming no price changes, so does their standard of living. Demand for most goods including luxury items like hi-fi's rises. An income elasticity of demand of 1.2 indicates that demand will change by a larger percentage than the change in income, i.e. demand is income elastic. In this case a 10% rise in income results in a 12% increase in demand for hi-fi systems. Williams Ltd. benefits by an increase in revenue of £2.88 million.

iii) A price elasticity of demand of −0.5 indicates the product is price inelastic and that demand will only change ½% for every 1% change in price. A reduction in price of 10% increases sales by only a further 3360. Unfortunately, this results in total revenue falling from £26,880,000 to £25,401,600, i.e. a drop of £1,478,400. Williams Ltd. would be better leaving the price at £400 subject to rival competitors not altering their prices.

Tutor's comments

This is a high quality answer showing a good grasp of the application of price and income elasticity to a practical situation. An A grade answer.

CHAPTER

MARKETING STRATEGY

MARKETING INFORMATION

MARKET RESEARCH

SALES FORECASTING

TARGET MARKETING (MARKET SEGMENTATION)

USEFUL BROAD CONCEPTS

INNOVATION AND PRODUCT DEVELOPMENT

MARKETING STRATEGY

MARKETING MIX

GETTING STARTED

The days when companies could quite happily operate on the basis of 'selling what they can make' are over, even for those in mass production industries such as car manufacturing. To a greater or lesser extent all companies must 'make what they can sell'. Marketing therefore becomes the central function in the organisation, undertaking the following activities:

- Identifying suitable markets.
- Identifying customer requirements (quality, design and price).
- Becoming aware of the organisation's ability to produce what the customer wants.
- Communicating customer requirements to the organisation.
- Working with other functions to ensure that requirements are met.
- Liaising constantly with customers.

The marketing personnel are therefore the eyes and ears of the organisation. Their aim must be to enable the organisation to target the right markets, within a long-term strategic plan. Marketing thus involves analysis, planning, and control with the ultimate mission of satisfying customer requirements. It is a dynamic activity, which should lead the organisation. In this sense marketing is both the philosophy of the business and the set of behaviours needed to make it effective. In the modern business environment an organisation, be it a major car company or a secondary school, must be market orientated, not production or even sales led.

A production-led company will emphasise the use of techniques to maximise output and minimise cost, with products designed to be standardised in order to achieve this objective. A sales-led company will emphasise product differentials, and advertising to create and retain market share, without reference to the needs of customers. A marketing-led company will, in the words of the Institute of Marketing, seek to 'identify, anticipate and supply customer requirements (quality design and service) efficiently and profitably'.

In this chapter we seek to set out the nature and process of decision making in marketing.

ESSENTIAL PRINCIPLES

MARKETING INFORMATION

 The link between marketing and other functions.

One of the prime functions of marketing personnel is to collect and analyse the information needed in order to identify the needs and wants of potential and present customers. This will also involve observation of the activities of competitors. It is also their function to use historical data to establish the past and current performance of the whole of their product range and to develop forecasts of potential future sales of current, modified or new products. This information is then analysed in order to assist the other functional departments, design, production, personnel and financial, in their task of managing the firm's efforts. The purpose of the marketing department is to act as the centrepiece of the business, enabling it to 'sell products which do not come back, to people who do'.

The techniques which are used are:

- Market research
- Sales forecasting
- Target marketing
- Benchmarking of competitors on product and price
- The product life cycle concept
- The 'Boston Box' concept

The purpose of these techniques is to collect and analyse three sets of information. These are set out in summary form in Table 12.1.

INFORMATION ON PAST PERFORMANCE	■ sales ■ market share ■ product life cycle ■ profit analysis
CURRENT MARKET POSITION	■ benchmarking competitors ■ product portfolio ■ market segments ■ customer satisfaction
FUTURE TRENDS	■ sales forecasts ■ new competitors ■ environmental and legal factors ■ new technologies

Table 12.1 Types of marketing information required

The analysis of the information generated will lead to strategic decisions at the highest level in the company as to the appropriate marketing strategy and the appropriate marketing mix needed in order to carry out that strategy.

MARKET RESEARCH

 The aim of market research.

This is a process by which information is collected and analysed on the basis of which marketing opportunities and problems may be identified. It will also be used to assist in the development of a strategy to deal with problems which have already been identified. Its function therefore is to produce information which will assist marketing personnel to make decisions. The data collected may be either primary (collection of new data) or secondary (data which already exists, either in the company or outside sources). Table 12.2 summarises the various types of market research which may be undertaken and indicates their uses.

 Market research may be undertaken by an outside agency.

These activities may be undertaken in-house, or by an outside advertising agency. In the latter case, product knowledge and confidentiality may be critical factors. It would not be sensible to use an agency which is also used by a rival company. The choice between in-house and use of agencies will be determined partly by cost considerations and the availability of the necessary expertise within the firm.

MARKET/SALES RESEARCH	■ estimate market size ■ identify market segments/characteristics ■ identify market trends ■ obtain information on present and past customers ■ information on competitors ■ sales forecasting
PRODUCT RESEARCH	■ generate new product ideas ■ product concept testing ■ product testing ■ test marketing ■ packaging research
PRICING RESEARCH	■ identify demand for the product ■ place price in relation to competition
COMMUNICATION RESEARCH	■ effectiveness of advertising ■ media selection research ■ copy testing ■ sales territory planning
DISTRIBUTION RESEARCH	■ warehouse location research ■ retail outlet location research ■ retailer type research

Table 12.2 Types of market research

MARKET RESEARCH METHODS

All these activities require that a scientific research method be used. Three broad approaches might be used:

■ sampling and survey techniques.

■ field experiments. This relates to those activities which are undertaken in the marketplace, such as product testing.

■ observation. This may range from sending buyers out to look at competitors' products in order to note their performance in the retail environment, to industrial espionage.

The results of such work must normally be presented in an appropriate format, summarising the statistics generated using measures of central tendency and dispersion.

SALES FORECASTING

Why sales forecasting is important!

This is an essential element in planning within the company. It is more than just predicting sales, but is also part of the financial planning process – identifying cash flows and potential profits. The aim is to avoid having 'slack', surplus capacity. It is thus the starting point of planning, for a new start-up company, or for a new product. There are two ways in which forecasting may be conducted:

■ Make a forecast for the industry and try to work out what share of that market the company may reasonably seek to win.

■ Forecast sales on the basis of historical sales data.

Forecasting may be short, medium or long term. *Short term* forecasts are intended for tactical reasons, for example to plan production requirements, cash flow etc.

Medium term forecasts are intended for business budgeting purposes to predict input costs, plant and manning requirements (one year ahead).

Long term forecasts 5 to 10 years ahead are intended for the purpose of strategic planning.

One technique (of many possible) is the use of moving averages applied to past sales figures, in order to establish trends. (For more detail of this technique, see Chapter 19.)

QUALITATIVE TECHNIQUES

Qualitative techniques may also be used in sales forecasting. The most important techniques are detailed below.

User survey

This involves asking customers about likely purchases, particularly of your product rather than that of competitors, for the forecast period. It may be undertaken by the salesforce. Alternatively, a sample of likely purchasers may be used.

It has a particular advantage where there is a relatively small group of organisational buyers, but this is rather rare.

Its disadvantage is that it cannot easily be used where the product is sold through retail outlets or where the purchase is complex, as in the case of kitchen furniture.

Jury method

This involves asking a committee of experts from inside and outside the company to consider their individual views and produce a combined forecast.

Its advantage is that expert opinion is collected.

> **All qualitative techniques have problems.**

Its disadvantage is that the views of the experts individually will vary widely and the committee forecast is likely to be an average figure, which may be misleading.

Salesforce composite

This involves each salesperson making a forecast for his or her own territory or sector, the results being summed to arrive at a composite figure.

The advantage is that the information comes from the people in closest touch with the market.

Its disadvantage is that the salespersons may be tempted to overestimate (in order to improve their own standing in the eyes of the sales manager) or underestimate (in order to be set a more attainable target for their own sales, thus enabling them to earn more bonus).

Product testing and test marketing

This is most useful where no previous sales data exists. The product is launched in a limited geographical area, thus allowing a simulation of a national launch.

The advantage is that for a fast moving consumer product (e.g. cough medicine), the pattern of demand is unlikely to differ by region and therefore test marketing is a very cost-effective way of arriving at sales forecasts.

The disadvantage is that the method is suitable only for consumer goods which are either brand new or substantially modified. A further disadvantage is that the first sale of such a product may be on a novelty basis and not repeated, leading to a forecast which is too optimistic.

TARGET MARKETING (MARKET SEGMENTATION)

This involves attempting to relate the characteristics of products to the requirements of potential customers. Modern markets often require more variety of specific product characteristics. Firms must, therefore, seek to target specific groups of customers, with particular requirements which the firm can meet. This could also be called 'niche' marketing, especially when applied to a new entrant to the market. The process of choosing a target market involves identifying

> 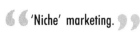 **'Niche' marketing.**

- market 'segments' – distinct groups of buyers.
- market targets – selecting one segment to be evaluated and targeted.
- product 'positioning' – in a particular 'niche' in that market segment.

Target markets may be identified in a number of ways.

DEMOGRAPHIC/SOCIO-ECONOMIC CHARACTERISTICS

The most commonly used characteristics are age, sex, income, family size, educational background or occupation. Table 12.3 shows one classification which is commonly used.

SOCIAL GROUP	SOCIAL STATUS	OCCUPATION	% OF POPULATION
A	Upper middle class	Directors Professionals Professors	3%
B	Middle class	Middle managers Lecturers	11%
C_1	Lower middle class	Supervisors, office and clerical staff	22%
C_2	Skilled working class	Skilled manual workers	32%
D	Working class	Manual workers	23%
E	Other	Pensioners, students, unemployed	9%

Table 12.3 Socio-economic groups

A company marketing a new range of upmarket kitchens through distributors who are allocated a specific geographical area may use the above socio-economic classification to survey the territory and establish the number of targeted socio-economic individuals. This will establish whether the distributor will have a sufficiently large client base to work on.

'CAUSAL' CLASSIFICATION

This is an attempt to establish why a specific group need the product. In the above example the company might want to research the rate at which houses change hands, the number of new households formed each year and perhaps the age profile of the housing stock. All of these will influence the potential demand for new kitchens. Thus a district containing large numbers of twenty-year-old detached properties, where the inhabitants are highly mobile and well-paid executives, who frequently change job and location, will generate more demand for quality kitchens than a stable population living in a small rural town.

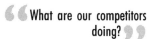

Target markets can be identified in several ways.

CLASSIFICATION BY HEAVINESS OF USE AND CONSUMER LOYALTY

If the product is regularly bought and has on the market already a number of strongly branded items, for example in the case of toothpaste, it will be difficult to establish a niche. Where the product is less strongly branded and sold more on quality and service, as in the case of kitchens, then it may be easier to establish a niche for a new entrant.

It is essential that the target market be evaluated in terms of costs and revenues.

A separate marketing mix will be developed for each target market.

BENCHMARKING OF COMPETITION

What are our competitors doing?

Before using the above analysis to 'position' the product it is vital to discover in some detail what key competitors are doing, both in marketing strategy, product development and price. This may be undertaken by desk research and by observational studies. For example, a mail order fashion and garment company may use one of its buyers to undertake a survey of the styles, qualities and price of comparable products offered in haute couture stores, in order to best guess the next fashion craze before seeking a supplier who can imitate those new designs.

USEFUL BROAD CONCEPTS

A company which has decided to appraise its strategic position within its marketplace, or a student required to analyse a case study, will find it useful to have to hand some broad concepts which will provide a perspective from which to examine the marketing information which is available.

SWOT ANALYSIS

You may already be familiar with this approach, which requires that a systematic appraisal be carried out of Strengths, Weaknesses, Opportunities and Threats which seem to be present in a situation. For example, a new entrant to a very competitive marketplace such as that for fitted kitchens, may have considered its position along the following lines:

- *Strengths:* low overheads, access to cheap materials and abundant labour due to a recession.

- *Weaknesses:* lack of specific knowledge of the marketplace and technical know-how on the part of the principals.

- *Opportunities:* the inefficient production, quality and marketing standards of one or more main competitors.

- *Threats:* the presence in the marketplace of a strong and fast-growing large competitor.

❝❝ SWOT'S – a brief example. ❞❞

This analysis would be developed in more detail, but you can see how helpful it could be in deciding on a marketing strategy. Access to sufficient marketing information will then allow the company to decide whether it can compete, and by what marketing strategy.

THE 'BOSTON BOX'

This model was developed by the Boston Consulting Group in the USA, and its purpose is to rate products according to sales growth and market share. It is most appropriate for a company which has been established for some time and has a wide product portfolio. It will enable senior management to use marketing information produced by the methods we have outlined above in order to optimise the product mix and to set objectives for each product in the portfolio. The model is set out diagrammatically in Fig. 12.1.

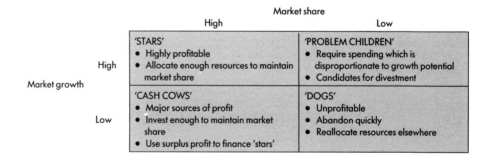

Fig. 12.1 The Boston Box

THE PRODUCT LIFE CYCLE

This is a most important concept for the Marketing Department of any company to have in mind as part of their strategic planning process over the long term. It suggests that as soon as a product enters the market it commences a life cycle, which can be measured or forecast. The life cycle will tend to be long for standard, commonplace items like soap or bread, but short in the case of high technology products like computers. The concept is a helpful management tool, in order to identify the correct strategy for each stage, the movement from one stage to another and the probable time scale of the whole cycle. This will permit a sound policy on the systematic and sequential introduction of new products. This will clearly have implications also for both Research and Development departments and for production. The concept is summarised diagrammatically in Fig. 12.2.

Criticisms of product life cycle

There is reason to believe that the concept of the product life cycle may be over used and

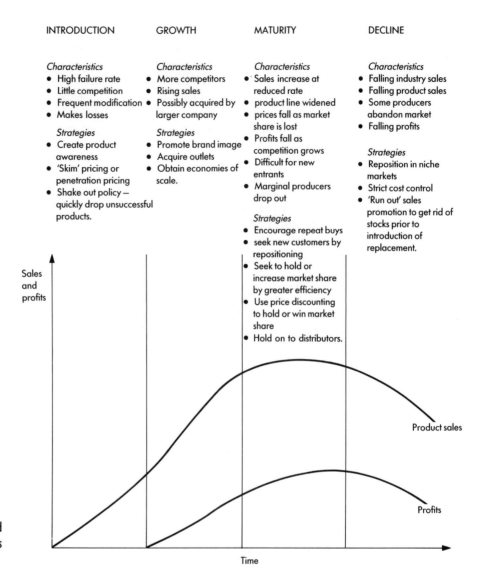

INTRODUCTION	GROWTH	MATURITY	DECLINE

Characteristics
- High failure rate
- Little competition
- Frequent modification
- Makes losses

Strategies
- Create product awareness
- 'Skim' pricing or penetration pricing
- Shake out policy – quickly drop unsuccessful products.

Characteristics
- More competitors
- Rising sales
- Possibly acquired by larger company

Strategies
- Promote brand image
- Acquire outlets
- Obtain economies of scale.

Characteristics
- Sales increase at reduced rate
- product line widened
- prices fall as market share is lost
- Profits fall as competition grows
- Difficult for new entrants
- Marginal producers drop out

Strategies
- Encourage repeat buys
- seek new customers by repositioning
- Seek to hold or increase market share by greater efficiency
- Use price discounting to hold or win market share
- Hold on to distributors.

Characteristics
- Falling industry sales
- Falling product sales
- Some producers abandon market
- Falling profits

Strategies
- Reposition in niche markets
- Strict cost control
- 'Run out' sales promotion to get rid of stocks prior to introduction of replacement.

Fig. 12.2 The product life-cycle and its various stages

become a self-fulfilling prophecy. It may lead to over-emphasis on the introduction and promotion of new products. The reasons for this criticism of the concept may be summarised as follows:

- the four phases are not clear cut.
- it is difficult to judge which phase a product is in at present.
- the phase may itself be determined by marketing strategies.
- many brands can be given new lives, thanks to modification (e.g. Mars ice cream bars) or intelligent promotion (e.g. the Mini car).
- some products appear to be impervious to the normal life cycle sequence (e.g. the board game, Monopoly).
- variations on an existing theme may reposition a product which appears to be in decline (e.g. the 'Discovery' version of the Land Rover).
- the current product is often capable of this kind of restoration at much less cost than the introduction of a new product.

Do products have a life cycle?

In view of the above criticisms of the concept, it should not be over-emphasised. There is much evidence to suggest that product modification may allow a company to manipulate the product life cycle to its advantage. For example, either product modification or a change in marketing strategy may enable a company to prolong the life cycle of a product and to turn it from a potential 'dog' into a continuing 'cash cow'.

Product modification

One or two examples will indicate what we mean. The Mars Bar has been the principal 'cash cow' for the Mars company for many years, but it is now threatened by a host of similar products from competitors. The company made use of the strong brand image of

'Mars Bars' in developing a modification, the Mars Ice Cream Bar, which would cash in on the marketing expenditure which had created this image. The Rover Car Company faced a similar problem with the Land Rover. Their response was to revamp and present the product in a format (the 'Discovery' version of the Land Rover) which was technically similar but matched the image presented by Japanese and German competitors. The Ford Motor Company was able, by judicious updating of the external appearance and internal specification, to prolong the life of the Cortina model for some seventeen years.

Changed marketing strategy

Another example from the car industry falls into this category. This is the Mini, which has achieved a new lease of life as a 'cash cow' by being moved from the 'niche' of basic transport (which is now dominated by competitors such as the Ford Fiesta and Rover's own Metro) to a smaller but lucrative niche market here and in Japan, as a 'fun' car, with a strong nostalgic appeal.

INNOVATION AND PRODUCT DEVELOPMENT

A company which is forward-looking will seek constantly to respond to the promptings of its marketing department in the process of developing new and improved products, in the search for new 'stars'. But a new product involves a vast commitment of resources, which must not be wasted. 'New' products fall into three broad categories:

- Innovative products. These are products which on introduction are completely new, as was TV in the 1940s or the personal stereo in the 1980s. These products are usually the result of a technological breakthrough.
- Replacement products. Again these are the result of technical developments which make an old product perform in new ways. For example, the jet engine revolutionised air transport.
- Imitative products. These are new to the company, but already available from competitors. This involves 'creative copying' of the ideas generated at great expense by other firms. An example would be the many variants now available at lower prices than the original Sony Walkman.

PRODUCT DEVELOPMENT

Product development involves seven steps:

- Establishing whether there is a customer 'need'; can the company afford to respond and can it do so profitably?
- Generation of ideas. This is likely to come from the Research and Development department, but may come from anywhere in the company, from the Chairman (as did the Walkman) down to a production line worker.
- Screening new ideas. This must be done systematically and take account of, for example, raw material or component availability, production capacity, distribution and the effect on existing product lines.

- Business analysis. This involves establishing whether the company can afford any required capital investment and find sources of finance and whether it can afford the necessary variable costs like labour. Can it carry the product to the break-even point?
- Product development. Producing and testing prototypes.
- Test marketing. This follows, rather than precedes, the decision to go ahead.
- Commercialisation. Developing a marketing strategy, e.g. whether to go for 'skim' pricing, or for market penetration.

In practice, few product ideas become commercial successes. Even large firms achieve a success rate of less than 50% and overall it is estimated that less than 3% of potential new products reach the commercialisation stage.

MARKETING STRATEGY

The analysis of the information generated by the marketing department in the context of the Boston Box, SWOTS analysis and the product life cycle concept, will lead to the development of a *marketing strategy*. This will be done in collaboration with other functional departments. It will enable management to arrive at key decisions as to which of the following strategies they might adopt, with regard to different elements in their product portfolio:

- market penetration
- market development
- product development
- diversification
- defence of market share

Thus a newly-established kitchen company might start by seeking *market penetration* on the basis of price and rapid delivery to the trade customers. It might then find that it can seek *market development* by supplying and fitting kitchens for retail customers. It may then find that it can increase its output and turnover by product development, perhaps by setting up a facility to manufacture kitchen furniture carcasses more cheaply than they can be bought in. Success in these fields may lead to *diversification* into bedroom furniture.

This process will involve the development of a suitable 'marketing mix'.

MARKETING MIX

Some aspects of the environment in which the company operates are outside its control. It can however use its *marketing mix* in an attempt to offset environmental uncertainty. The marketing mix is the set of ingredients which the firm uses in order to achieve its objectives. This 'mix' consists of the appropriate elements from within the 'four Ps' which are set out in Table 12.4

PRODUCT	product range product features product quality packaging
PRICE	price levels price discounts credit policy price strategy
PROMOTION	advertising spend advertising copy suitable media advertising scheduling
PLACE	channels of distribution stock levels delivery

Table 12.4 Marketing mix

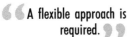
A flexible approach is required.

The marketing mix, once adopted, should not be set in concrete. The environment is volatile and the company should be prepared to constantly review and change its mix. For example, the fitted kitchen company referred to above will in the early stages of its development be concerned especially about pricing policy and delivery. It may not be able to afford much promotion and will have to rely on establishing a client base by word of mouth marketing (i.e. recommendation by one customer to another). Once it has reached break-even it may be able to develop new product features and improve quality. It may be able to afford to increase its sales by an advertising campaign. If it moves into supplying the contract market amongst builders, it may have to rethink its pricing policy to give and accept more trade credit. It may well, therefore, have to develop different elements in the 'four Ps' during its first year of operation, as the business develops.

We will look at the marketing mix in more detail in the next chapter.

EXAMINATION QUESTIONS

1 You are Marketing Manager of a firm selling polyunsaturated margarine. In its annual Budget, the Government has cut direct taxation. Soon afterwards a promotion

campaign is launched by the Butter Information Council and the Government forbids advertising which suggests that margarine is healthier than butter. In the light of these events, what changes would you consider in your marketing strategy?

(UCLES 1986)

2 Discuss elements beyond a firm's immediate control which may influence its marketing decisions.

3 a) How might the 'marketing mix' adopted by a large carpet retailer with many outlets, differ during its annual January sale, from that used for the rest of the year? *(12)*
   b) What are the benefits to companies of holding such sales? *(13)*

(UCLES 1989)

4 When emphasising the importance of customer orientation, Peter Drucker wrote:
   'The business enterprise has two and only two basic functions, marketing and innovation. Marketing and innovation produce results, all the rest are cost.' How would you reconcile this statement with the importance of production?

(AEB 1988)

TUTOR'S ANSWER.

Question 1

In this case study we are given certain information and must infer other items of information which are needed in order to establish a new marketing strategy.

1 Our firm makes and sells polyunsaturated margarine.

2 Its main competing product in the market is butter, which is in most respects a perfect substitute for margarine.

3 The main competitive advantage which our firm has for some years enjoyed is that margarine has been perceived as more healthy than butter, as a result of the campaigns by the medical profession to reduce the consumption of animal fats (in order to reduce the incidence of heart disease). This material has been used by manufacturers of margarine to gain an advantage over suppliers of butter. It has also enabled them to add value to and differentiate the product, thus bringing the price up to parity or better with butter. This has generated large profits.

4 The Government has increased disposable income in the economy which is available for consumption by reducing direct taxation (on income). However, food products are highly income inelastic in demand and the total amount of edible fat products such as butter or margarine bought is unlikely to be greatly affected by this increase in disposable income.

5 The 'Butter Information Council' has launched a campaign which suggests (on the basis of recent medical research) that butter may be more healthy than margarine.

6 The Government meanwhile has banned the use of advertising material which suggests that margarine is healthier than butter. Clearly the National Farmers' Union, a powerful political lobby, has been at work in Whitehall.

7 The impact of these events on the market for edible fats may be theoretically examined by the use of standard supply and demand analysis.

Fig. 12.3 describes the market for margarine. We have assumed that the change in disposable income has no discernable impact on the demand for edible fats. However, the impact of the Butter Council advertising campaign and the restrictions on the use of the health factor in the margarine industry, have brought about a change in tastes and a shift to the left in the demand curve for margarine. This has the result of reducing the demand for margarine from OQ to OQ_1 and simultaneously reducing the price from OP to OP_1. This would have a serious effect on margarine manufacturers, since the lower turnover (less sales at lower prices) may not be matched by an equivalent fall in costs of production. Thus profits would fall or disappear. The opposite case applies for butter manufacturers (see Fig. 12.4), since the demand curve would shift out to the right, producing a higher price and higher total quantity sold, with corresponding beneficial effects on profits.

8 The margarine manufacturer now needs to rethink his marketing strategy within the constraints imposed by these recent events and by consumer protection law and advertising standards, in such a way as to reverse the effects shown in Figs. 12.3 and 12.4. It will also be necessary to take account of the fact that both industries are

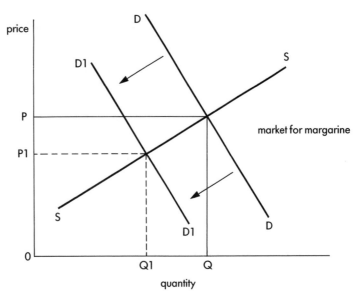

Fig. 12.3

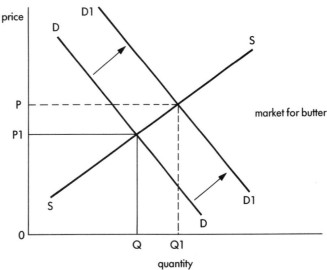

Fig. 12.4

oligopolist in structure. This means that large scale advertising and promotional expenditures are already necessary in order to maintain market share against other similar manufacturers, and to act as barriers to entry into the industry. This fact, combined with falling revenues for the margarine manufacturer (and the opposite for butter manufacturers) may impose budgetary constraints on what may be done.

Proposals for a new marketing strategy

In the light of the above analysis, the following proposals are offered:

1 Collaborate with other firms to form a 'Margarine Manufacturers' Council'. This would prevent an advertising war between margarine manufacturers simply to defend one firm's market share against the others in a declining market.

2 Such a council should then seek to develop a general marketing campaign to promote margarine as against butter. Since it is not permissable any longer to promote the health aspects of margarine, it will be necessary to develop some other aspect of margarine which will increase its appeal. For example it may be possible to capture the importance market amongst teenagers (who have great influence on mother's shopping habits) by stressing the 'fact' that margarine is less likely to cause skin blemishes than butter. Such a campaign might just be acceptable within the new rules.

3 Each firm might then promote its own specific products by adding value. This might involve product development by adding some new ingredient. Or it might involve adding value by changing the form and appearance of the packaging.

4 An alternative general thrust for a 'council' promotional campaign might be based on environmental issues. Whilst it is not permissible to directly attack the competing product, or its manufacturer, it might be permissible to use the known scientific 'fact' that cattle rearing causes damage to the ozone layer as a consequence of the emission

of methane gas by cattle in vast quantities! The less damaging nature of cultivation of groundnuts or oilseed rape might be stressed.

5   All the above strategies would be designed to restore demand for the product in general and to maintain market share for the specific firm, without the need for price discounting and a price war to maintain the share of one firm against the rest. Such a policy could only lead to the weaker producers whose costs are higher, and brand image less well established, to cease production.

6   Both at industry and firm level, in order to undertake this defensive strategy, there would need to be a further increase in already high marketing budgets. Thus cuts in production costs through redundancies and plant closure would possibly be required.

7   It would not be possible to gain any advantage by changing the channels of distribution.

Thus by consideration of the relevant aspects of the 'marketing mix', it might be possible to develop a defensive strategy in this industry, which is producing a product at the 'mature' stage of its product life cycle. If this is not done the product will cease to be a 'cash cow' and become a 'dog' in terms of the Boston Box model.

STUDENT'S ANSWER

Question 2

There are many factors which can seriously affect the strategic decisions made by a firm, including marketing strategy. Many of these factors are within the control of the firm. However there are a number of factors in the external environment of the firm over which it has no direct control. It may only react to or if possible foresee such events.

> Give some examples.

An external environmental factor which has become of increasing importance in recent years is the ecology and physical environment of the planet. Firms must react to the increasing public concern with environmental or 'green' factors. For example, products which harm the atmosphere or pollute rivers, whether through the production process or the use of the product, are frowned upon and even banned by law. This may seriously affect sales. Examples are: petrol and the increased trend towards lead-free fuel; fridges and aerosol cans which use CFCs which damage the ozone layers. Firms in these industries have had no choice but to develop new products which are ozone friendly. A sensible marketing strategy is impossible unless this is done. A firm must make sure that it is beyond criticism in this area, or its markets could dramatically collapse. Even McDonalds, the largest franchise operation in the world, has come under criticism over the destruction of rain forests to make room for cattle grazing. McDonalds deny that their farming methods harm the environment.

> In general this is true, but perhaps not for an individual firm.

> Too sweeping a statement.

> In many cases these 'externalities' are ignored by the firm unless regulated by the government.

A second external factor around which a company must develop its marketing strategy is the economic environment, which may dramatically and suddenly totally alter the face of the market. This for example is especially so in a recession, when disposable incomes fall sharply and demand for many products is sharply reduced. Companies which have undertaken a strategy of marketing a highly differentiated product in a niche market, at a high price, may be hard hit by falling incomes. Therefore, it is important to anticipate and plan for such changes in the economic environment.

> Good example!

Another important factor to be considered is your market share and the activities of your main competitors. It is obviously important to be competitive in terms of costs, product range and development and price, but it is also important to have a

> The firm can influence consumer behaviour though, through (for example) advertising.

> Not necessarily! Have Rolls Royce cars been reduced in price much during the 1989–92 recession?

marketing strategy which maximises your market share, or increases market penetration. In this case packaging and advertising will be important. No one will buy your product if they do not know it is there.

A further external influence on marketing strategy is the vagaries of consumer behaviour. It may be almost impossible to predict, given the complexity of human behaviour. The firm cannot control this factor, but must respond to it. If the general market trend is towards high price, high value added products, the firm must follow; if the trend is towards cheap bargains, again the firm must follow.

Therefore we can see that the factors are all on a national or international scale and the important ones are not necessarily those apparently within the 'business' field. The only solution is to anticipate and respond to these factors in planning and marketing strategy.

Tutor's comments

He has made the general point that there are many factors in the external environment of the firm to which it must respond and if possible anticipate. He has sensibly used four examples and given some indication of how they might affect a firm's marketing strategy, by quoting cases in point. The weakness of the answer is that he has not taken the opportunity to indicate his knowledge of the concepts involved in the development of a marketing strategy. Thus he might have brought in at the appropriate points some or all of the following concepts:

The main objectives of marketing strategy – market penetration, defence of market share, market development, product development and diversification.

He might have used the product life cycle and Boston Box concepts to indicate how a company might review its continued production of a product which is under temporary threat from external changes in the market.

He might have indicated that in a specific case, a firm would need to use the concept of the 'marketing mix' in deciding its response to change.

These developments would have given depth to the answer and it would have then been a high B or A grade, rather than as it stands a middle D to low C grade.

OUTLINE ANSWER

Question 3

The Marketing Mix of any company will be centred round the four 'Ps', i.e. Product, Price, Promotion, Place. If we assume that the multiple carpet store operator is seeking to cover the full range of product types through large retail outlets and is not involved in running small niche targeted outlets, then he is likely for most of the year to use the following marketing mix.

As regards the product, he is likely to stock a wide range of product types; woven, tufted, natural and artificial fibres, etc. He will offer a wide range of qualities and designs. His store will be laid out in such a way as to demonstrate the key features of the products offered; durability, colour suitability for different uses etc.

Pricing policy will reflect the target market(s) aimed at. A large store will offer a wide range of price levels for products from different makers, for different purposes. He will probably not offer, or at least stress, discounting as a sales device, and will have in-house or bought-in credit facilities available.

He will be likely to promote his product both through local and national advertising media, on the basis of a regular budgeted schedule through the year. If he is targeting the top end of the market he will emphasise quality, durability and style and will associate his products with a certain standard of living in the choice of advertising media and copy.

If he is a major high street retailer, he will seek to maintain sufficient stock to demonstrate all the product types he is offering, with the back up of an in-house warehousing and delivery facility. He will offer a fitting service in-house.

Conversely, at January sales time he is targeting a different segment of the market, viz. people who aspire to his level of style and quality but who are unwilling or unable to afford his regular prices. The thrust of his marketing strategy at this time of year will be based on value for money and price. If he has insufficient ends of range and surplus stock, he may buy in such goods or possibly slightly inferior products in order to offer an attractive range at low prices.

The advantages to the firm of January sales are numerous:

- It will sustain cash flow at an otherwise quiet time of year.
- It will enable him to 'run out' stock of designs which he wishes to dispense with.
- It will thus give him both space and cash with which to purchase the new season's designs.
- It may attract new customers with long-term buying potential, e.g. young married couples.

The successful operation of this strategy will depend on offering more than ends of ranges. It gives the opportunity to try out new designs and new producers and also of targeting new segments of the marketplace. It will require a different advertising campaign, in different media and in different form, stressing the main marketing thrust which is price and value for money. It may involve lavish expenditure, especially in times of recession, when customers are reluctant to buy. Discounts for cash will be important.

Overall it is an essential strategy for retailers in product areas where sales are highly seasonal, in order to keep cash flowing, albeit at reduced margins.

TUTOR'S ANSWER

Question 4

Drucker was one of the first business 'gurus' to stress the paramount importance of satisfying customer requirements. The 'Fordist' approach of mass manufacture of standard products on a production line basis, with minimum product variations was sufficient for the new consumer durable markets of the 1930s and is still a sensible approach to the production of products with a very long life cycle such as Coca Cola. This overstatement by Drucker is intended to draw our attention to the need to be able to respond much more rapidly to changing customer requirements, in an age when new technology permits rapid changes in the nature and purpose of the products themselves.

For a firm to remain profitable it must, of course, organise the production function efficiently; reducing unit cost to the minimum compatible with meeting customer requirements. The conventional production line is geared to produce output at the greatest speed possible, with quality 'inspected in' at the end of the line. The workforce is probably paid on the basis of piece rates measured by work study methods. The motivation for them is to work as fast as possible, irrespective of mistakes. The Production Manager is working in a management culture which requires him to ship the product out on time with little regard to waste and mistakes. Machinery is overused and undermaintained and unable to work to fine tolerances. Inventories of parts are very high, as a buffer against unusable items and line breakdowns.

This is now seen in well managed companies as a wrong approach. The demands of customers are changing. Many more variations must be produced and stock levels of parts, finished product and work in progress must be reduced. Computer-controlled machine tools make much greater flexibility possible, provided the workforce is trained to do several jobs operating in workstations rather than on a continuous line. The use of *Just in Time* (JIT) inventory management is possible and desirable. Components are delivered to the line direction on a daily basis to match an ever varying range of models which are being produced to order rather than for stock. Quality is the responsibility of every worker and at every stage, rather than being inspected in at the end of the line. The gains from this approach go straight through to the bottom line. In the case for example of Rover Cars, the introduction of JIT produced cost savings in the first year of some £40 million. Springram plc, producers of kitchen and bathroom furniture, have reduced scrap and waste levels to less than 1% of production through this approach. Similar improvements are possible on the service and delivery side of a business. By getting it right first time, it is possible to almost eliminate costs from warranty claims, as Japanese car makers have shown.

Production is therefore important, but in a different sense from before. These changes have been driven by a recognition that consumer needs have changed and that the production function must change in response. How then do successful companies know that they need to make these changes? They have listened to the marketing function, who in turn have recognised that they are the eyes and ears of the company, seeking to recognise the signals of changed customer requirements. They no longer see it as their duty to persuade the public to buy whatever the production people want to make. Their ability to articulate within the company the requirements of customers, also raises the importance of the design and research and development teams. The designer must design a product which is suitable for the market targeted, not just adapt an existing product. The research team must also start from customer requirements rather than what is intellectually satisfying for them. The true innovator, however, is the person who sees the possibility of producing a totally new product concept, using modern technology, which the customer does not know exists until it has been through its trials. The 'Sony Walkman' was a prime example. Akia Morita, Chairman of Sony, saw youngsters roller skating carrying noisy and cumbersome portable radios. He had seen details of a Bell Telephone patent for a new concept called transistors, which made miniaturisation of consumer electronics possible. He put the two together and produced the Walkman. His Board were horrified and Morita staked his job and reputation on the new product not only being possible, but also likely to produce £2 million profit in its first year. He is still in office!

These examples suggest that Drucker was right to stress the importance of the innovator and the marketeer. Their combined efforts enable new products to be developed and old ones, in the mature stage of their life cycle, to be given a new lease of life. Without these efforts, the production people would be out of a job.

FURTHER READING

Hill, *Marketing for BTEC*, Business Education Publishers 1989:
    Chapter 2, Analysing Markets.
    Chapter 3, Market Segmentation.
    Chapter 4, Marketing Research.
    Chapter 7, Developing New Products.
Cameron, Rushton and Carson, *Marketing*, Penguin 1988:
    Part 2, Markets and Customers.
    Part 4, Market Strategies and Planning.
Baker, *Marketing – An Introductory Text* (4th edition), MacMillan 1985:
    Chapter 6, Market Segmentation.
    Chapter 11, Marketing Research.

MARKETING IN ACTION

THE PRODUCT

PRICING POLICY

PROMOTION

DISTRIBUTION

GETTING STARTED

In the previous chapter we considered marketing from the strategic standpoint. We were concerned with the ways in which a firm decides what market it is intent on exploiting through market research, product development and target marketing. We used broad concepts such as the Product Life Cycle and the Boston Box as tools with which to establish overall marketing strategy. In this chapter we are concerned with the more practical aspects of marketing.

The key concept here is the Marketing Mix. This refers to the factors which may be adjusted in order to increase the appeal of our product to the customer. In this way we hope to see how the company might increase its sales. There are four aspects to the marketing mix:

- Product – Quality, features and facilities offered, colour, warranty and after sales service, size and packaging.
- Price   – Basic price, discounts, credit facilities.
- Place   – Distribution outlets, availability of the product.
- Promotion– Advertising, personal selling, sales promotion, direct mailing, publicity.

In this chapter, we examine each of these factors, from the point of view of the Marketing Department of a company which has to recommend to senior management ways in which their overall strategy might be achieved and any pitfalls which may arise. Whatever marketing tactics the marketeers might recommend will have cost implications and the available marketing budget will be a major constraint on what is possible. The extent to which it is a constraint will be very different in a large organisation such as Unilever (which may budget for an expenditure of up to 40% of its total costs on promotion of a product) compared with a small new start-up company, selling, say, kitchens in a very competitive market place. The approach adopted by two supermarket companies to the marketing mix might be quite different. For example, Sainsbury plc will emphasise quality, range of products and presentation, whereas Asda emphasises price. The search for a competitive edge is never ending and is critical to the survival of a commercial organisation.

ESSENTIAL PRINCIPLES

THE PRODUCT

66 **What is a product anyway?** 99

66 **Selling the benefits** 99

Most of us when we think about a product think of physical goods such as books, pianos, wines and cars. However, the marketeer also uses the term to cover services such as insurance, window cleaning and package holidays. Even people such as pop stars can be products in that we can buy their records or attend their concerts.

We can look at the product offered at three different levels. First we can identify a core benefit or service that the product gives. This is not necessarily as obvious as it seems. For example, when purchasing toothpaste is the consumer buying 'clean teeth' or the hope of being accepted by their peer group? Much promotion focuses on the latter point – selling the benefits not the features.

Secondly we can see that the core benefit/service has a number of tangible features which are deemed attractive by the purchaser. Taken together these create the 'tangible product'. These features may have a functional purpose (e.g. power-assisted steering on a car) or be purely aesthetic (e.g. metallic finish paintwork on a car). The tangible product may have as many as five characteristics (see Fig. 13.1).

Lastly we can consider the augmented product. This includes other services or benefits that may be obtained through the purchase of that product. It can include guarantees, delivery, installation and servicing.

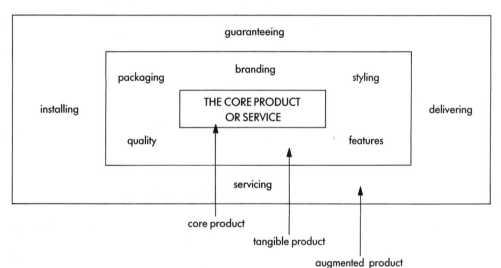

Fig. 13.1 Three ways of looking at the product

TYPE OF PRODUCT

All goods and services fall into one of two broad categories – consumer or industrial – which may be subdivided further. Note how different aspects of the marketing mix become important with different classifications of goods.

Consumer goods

66 **Products for the private consumer.** 99

These are products which are purchased by private customers, for their own use. They may be subdivided into four groups.

- *Convenience goods:* these may be staple goods (like bread), emergency goods (like sticking plaster) or impulse items (magazines for example). They are bought during regular weekly shopping expeditions and little effort is required except to choose between brand names. They are often called FMCG (fast moving consumer goods). The producer should aim to have his product displayed in as many outlets as possible. It will often be backed up by considerable promotional effort.

- *Speciality goods:* these are items which may require extensive search to find the 'right' product. They are used by the consumer to establish his or her public personality. In other words they are based on psychological rather than physiological needs (clothing, holidays and cosmetics are good examples). Exclusivity and design are the keys to choice, along with brand image. The price is relatively unimportant to the consumer.

■ *Unsought goods:* these are items which are not usually actively sought by consumers. They may be trivial (dried flowers) or meet important but unrecognised needs (e.g. life insurance). New products also fall into this category. Unsought goods will commonly need a lot of advertising and/or personal selling.

■ *Shopping goods:* these are major durable or semi-durable items, often expensive and whose purchase involves considerable research effort and price comparison. Some may be close to necessities (motor vehicles), or luxury items, which are bought on non-price characteristics (paintings, antiques).

Industrial goods

These are products which are bought by firms or organisations for their own use as imports into the production process. The market for industrial goods is very large as the following classification indicates:

> " Products for the industrial consumer. "

■ *Materials and parts:* raw materials may be either farm products (eggs, cabbage, etc) or natural products (oil, iron ore, etc). Price, quality and availability are the key aspects the seller has to emphasise. Prices may fluctuate widely according to availability and demand. Manufactured parts include those which have to be processed in some way and those which can enter the finished product as they are. The seller will emphasise price and reliability as key features. Advertising, packaging and branding are relatively unimportant.

■ *Capital goods:* these may take the form of buildings and plant or factory and office equipment (tools, computers, etc). Buildings and plant are purchased after long negotiations. Personal selling is important, as is the ability of the supplier to meet the technical requirements of the purchaser and provide an after sales service. Price and advertising are less important.

■ *Factory and office equipment:* as orders are small, buyers many and geographically dispersed, these items are often sold through middlemen. The market is extremely competitive so price, quality and after sales service are considered important.

PRODUCT MIX AND PRODUCT LINES

A product line may be defined as a group of closely related products which are sold to a specific customer group through similar outlets. For example, a car manufacturer does not just produce one basic model of a car, there are a number of variations based on engine size, paintwork and other extras. The total number of variations of the basic model car make up the product line. For the producer the correct length of the product line is difficult to gauge. He doesn't want to lose a sale through not having certain options available, yet there are certain costs associated with providing that option (stockholding and production are the most important). A similar quandary exists for the retailer.

> " The product portfolio! "

A product mix, sometimes referred to as the *product portfolio*, is the total number of product lines that a seller has to sell to the public. Most firms will have a number of different lines. A typical supermarket may carry as many as 20,000 different lines. The product mix may have a significant impact upon the survival and profitability of the firm. A broad product mix enables the firm to survive when one of its markets or product lines fails. However, the impact of good performers (in terms of profits) may be lessened by the poor performers. The trend in many firms at present is to reduce their product mix by divesting operations which are not compatible with their core activities. This enables them to maintain better control over their product portfolio.

PRICING POLICY

It is probably true to say that until the 1950s, price was the most important influence on buyer behaviour. Since that time non-price characteristics have become increasingly important in many markets. This has been the result of rising real disposable incomes as advanced economies grew, and increasing consumer sophistication and knowledge. Nevertheless, it is still critical for a firm to adopt the right pricing policy when deciding its marketing mix. In the 1990s there seems to be a trend back towards price as the most important factor in some markets. Thus for 10 years, the supermarket industry has been able to greatly increase its gross margins as customers shopped on characteristics other than price. The continued success of Kwik Save, and the entry of a German company, Aldi, into the market, with a strategy of returning to limited brand ranges, simple presentation and low prices, has activated a price war amongst the main UK supermarket companies.

The role of pricing

Pricing has two major roles:

- Price must be pitched at a level which enables the company to cover the costs of production, marketing, and the business overheads. It must also enable the company's profit objectives to be met, since profit is 'the price of staying in business'.

- Pricing is a key element in the marketing mix, but may not be the overriding factor. Decisions must take account of the nature and structure of the particular market.

THE ECONOMIST'S VIEW OF PRICING

The economist's view of the market has tended to over emphasise the role of price in determining demand for a product and has paid less attention to the influence of other aspects of the marketing mix, such as advertising. It has also tended to over emphasise profit maximisation as a business motive, whereas in fact most companies seek to maximise return on investment or market share, rather than profit. Nevertheless, the economist's model of the market may provide some useful insights.

In essence the model suggests that price will be dictated by the interaction of the forces of supply and demand (see Chapter 11). There exists some price where the wishes of producers and buyers are brought into equilibrium at a market price. Any attempt to artificially set a price in excess of this equilibrium price will leave an unsold surplus, whilst any attempt to fix a price below the equilibrium price will lead to excess demand. In the first case some producers with higher costs will leave the market and in the second case new producers will enter until the price returns to equilibrium. This may be shown most simply in diagrammatic form as in Fig. 13.2. As we saw in Chapter 11, forces other than price, such as advertising which changes consumer tastes, or changes in income, or changes in the price of substitutes, may cause a shift of the demand schedule to right or left, whilst the supply schedule may be similarly shifted by changes in resource availability and cost. Thus new market equilibrium prices may be generated.

> **Back to the price mechanism!**

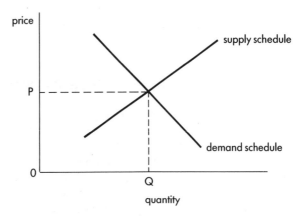

Fig. 13.2 Equilibrium price

The economist also looks at markets in terms of *market structure*. This is an attempt to analyse markets on the basis of the number and size of firms in an industry. The model is based on the condition of Perfect Competition, where there are many small producers, each too small to influence the market by its production decisions, each with similar costs, and each faced by perfectly elastic 'own elasticity of demand' for its specific product. In addition it is assumed that the products of all firms in the industry are homogeneous (identical) and that consumers have perfect knowledge of the market.

In this market structure, since all the firms are virtually identical and the product incapable of differentiation, then each firm is a *price taker*, i.e. it can only accept the price dictated by market conditions.

> **Price takers and price makers.**

In practice there are few markets which approximate to this condition. In reality most firms are able to differentiate their product from others, at least temporarily, to some degree. This gives the firm a chance to adjust its price, by making its product in a sense unique. In many markets the economies of scale available have enabled the growth of very large firms, competing in markets where there are only a few players.

An economist would define this situation as an *oligopolistic*. Here it is difficult to predict the pricing and output decisions of a firm. However, there are two broad situations we should consider. In some cases one firm is so dominant that its price is followed by all others. Here, competition between the firms is limited to non-price factors, e.g. claims regarding the product's attributes, packaging or after sales service.

A more likely situation is where at least two of the firms are of relatively equal strength. Here, a firm in determining its pricing policy will have to best guess its competitors' reactions. The oligopolist firm may reason that if it cuts prices its competitors will follow suit so as to avoid losing custom. However, if it raises prices the other firms will do nothing, hoping to gain customers driven away by the price increase. Thus the oligopolists' demand curve is relatively elastic for price increases but relatively inelastic for price cuts (see Fig. 13.3). This is often referred to as a 'kinked' demand curve.

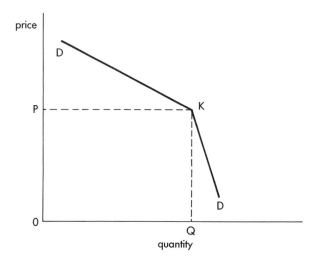

Fig. 13.3 Demand curve facing oligopolist

Obviously in such situations firms see little advantage in price changes – they lead to price wars which are often mutually destructive. In practice, there may be collusion over prices to be charged (though this is illegal in many countries) or a tacit agreement to follow the prices of the largest firm. In either situation this will be backed up by non-price competition, e.g. special offers, advertising, competitions. All these are aimed at enabling the firm to differentiate its product, win customer loyalty and create a brand image.

THE ACCOUNTANT'S VIEW OF PRICING POLICY

This is based essentially on costs. The influence of accountants on companies is considerable and it is not surprising that a number of variants on cost-based pricing policy have been produced. The most commonly used is cost-plus pricing. Here, the total unit costs of producing a product are calculated and a given percentage added on as a profit margin. This method is rather crude as it does not recognise that the proportion of fixed costs to be allocated to each unit will vary with output. The problem is compounded by the fact that the organisation may also achieve economies of scale through expanding output. Moreover, cost-plus pricing pays no attention to what customers are willing to pay. Nevertheless, accurate information on costs is vital to a firm for a number of reasons:

> *Cost based pricing policy.*

- the profit contribution of individual transactions can be measured.
- the most profitable products, customers or market segments, can be identified.
- the effect of changes in volumes of production on profit can be measured.
- it can be determined whether a product can be produced and sold at any price.

The careful analysis of fixed (overhead) costs and variable (direct) costs is therefore an important evaluative tool. In planning the introduction of a new product, or the establishment of a new firm, it is customary to seek to identify the *break-even point* (that level of output and sales where profit begins to be earned). This analysis, which is illustrated in Fig. 13.4 is very useful for the price decision maker in the firm:

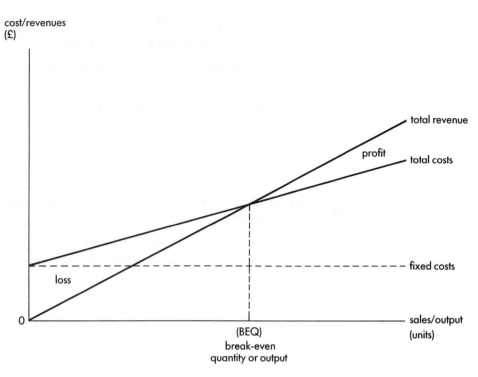

cost/revenues
(£)

total revenue

profit

total costs

fixed costs

loss

0

(BEQ)
break-even
quantity or output

sales/output
(units)

Fig. 13.4 Break-even ouput

- At outputs below BEQ the firm makes losses.
- At BEQ the firm breaks even (sales revenue = total costs).
- At outputs above BEQ the firm makes profits.

The slope of the total revenue line will be different at different unit prices, but the cost line will not vary with price.

Neither the economist's nor the accountant's model is sufficient as the basis for pricing decisions, since they take no account of the influence of the marketing mix on demand for the product.

The marketeer and pricing policy

We can summarise the views of the economist and the accountant as follows.

The upper limit to price is determined by demand, the lower limit is the cost of producing and distributing the product. The difference between these limits is called the area of 'pricing discretion'. The firm may be able to lower the bottom limit by careful attention to its operational activities. The efforts of the marketing department are directed at moving the upper limit upwards by increasing in some way the perceived benefits to the customer provided by the product. Competition, by lowering prices, is the last option and only possible if the product is in elastic demand. The marketeer aims to desensitise the customer to price, by various kinds of promotion, aimed at the targeted market segment. Nevertheless, it is important to have a general pricing strategy based on the answers to five questions:

> " The area of pricing discretion. "

- Should we price above or below the market average?
- Who are we competing with on price?
- Should we respond to competitors' price changes or not?
- Should we vary our prices, or aim for stability?
- Should we use price for promotional purposes?

> " Some pricing tactics. "

If unexpected and dramatic changes occur in the market place, e.g. a new entrant to the market, it will be necessary to consider short-term pricing tactics in response. The extent to which price as used is a key ingredient in the marketing mix will depend on the nature of the product, but it is fair to say that aggressive pricing as a prime marketing strategy is likely to prove damaging and self-defeating. Each stage of the product life cycle may require a different marketing mix and pricing policy. Thus in the launch of a new product there are two broad strategies available:

- *'Skim pricing'*: that is, taking advantage of the uniqueness of a totally new product by charging a very high price (as Sony did for the Walkman). The price may then be gradually lowered at successive stages of the cycle.

■ *Pre-emptive low price strategy:* where a new variant in an existing market is launched on very low prices and heavily promoted.

Other pricing strategies which are available include:

■ *Price discrimination:* between different customers for the same product, either by customer category, time of day, geographical area. This is used by British Rail on its 'InterCity' services.

■ *Price discounting:* may be used for bulk purchases or as a price cutting tactic by a retailer, or as a promotional aid.

PROMOTION

> " Informing and persuading the customer. "

Organisations undertake a variety of promotional activities in order to communicate with customers, with four objectives in mind:

■ To inform the public of the availability of the product.

■ To target a particular segment of the market and so 'position' the product.

■ To increase sales.

■ To stabilise sales.

The programme of activities undertaken to achieve these objectives is known as the 'promotional mix'.

THE PROMOTIONAL MIX

This term describes the procedures and policies adopted by the marketing department of an organisation. The elements within it may be combined in various ways and must be kept within the agreed budget. The promotional mix is made up of the following:

■ advertising
■ packaging
■ sales promotion
■ personal selling
■ merchandising
■ public relations

The decision as to the particular mix used will be determined by the nature of the product, and the targeted market. Advertising is usually referred to as 'above the line' promotion expenditure, whilst other promotional techniques are referred to as 'below the line'.

ADVERTISING

An organisation may use a variety of media in order to inform the potential customer that his product is available and what it can do for him. This form of advertising does not come under criticism since it is essential for customers to know of the existence and purpose of available products. Almost all advertising is, however, likely to be persuasive to a degree. That is, it goes beyond information provision, although that function may still be provided and seeks to persuade the customer that the company's product is better than its competitor's product in some way. The skill of the advertising copywriter lies in designing advertisements which are both visually attractive and which appeal to deep-seated consumer motivations, such as status or sex appeal. The objective of persuasive advertising is to use constant repetition of a message to create and perpetuate a brand image and customer loyalty. In this way market share is created, extended and maintained.

Other objectives of advertising are:

■ to attack a competitor's products (directly or indirectly) and attempt to increase market share at his expense.

■ to cooperate with producers of joint-use goods to suggest mutual approval, e.g. washing machines and washing powders.

■ to convey an image of the firm rather than the product or service.

■ to support a consumer's decision to buy *after* the purchase has been made.

The choice of media

This is very important. It will in the first place be limited by the advertising budget available. For example, few new firms would be able to afford a television advertising campaign.

The other determinants of choice of media are:

- *The market segment:* magazines, newspapers and TV stations will all appeal to different groups of readers and viewers. If the company advertising its product has a clear idea as to its targeted market, it will be able to identify the most suitable media.

- *The size of the market:* if the company is aiming at a national market, then it will choose a media outlet with national coverage. If it can only operate locally, it will choose the most suitable local media outlet (perhaps a local 'free' newspaper).

- *The nature of the product:* a very specialist consumer product (e.g. fishing tackle) will be best advertised in appropriate specialist magazines. A very specialist industrial product will be best advertised in a 'trade' magazine (e.g. school textbooks are best advertised in the educational press).

ENSURING THE EFFECTIVENESS OF ADVERTISING

This may be done in a number of ways:

- *pre-testing* on a representative sample of customers, in order to decide which of various alternative advertisements makes the biggest impact.

- *post-testing,* which seeks to establish the impact made by an advertising campaign after the event, by the use of 'recognition tests', by asking readers/viewers whether they have seen the advertisement. This may be developed further by use of an 'unaided recall test', where the respondent is asked to comment from memory on the details of an advertisement.

- *post-sale check,* where the customer who buys the product is asked where they heard of it. This is especially useful information for a new firm which is experimenting with different media.

Much advertising does little more than maintain market share. However, research has shown that this is an essential part of marketing strategy because brand loyalty is short lived. Thus in the case of fast moving consumer goods which are repeatedly purchased and where a number of alternatives are available (i.e. the firm's demand curve is elastic) it is important to maintain the product's profile in the customer's mind. In this sense the frequency with which advertising takes place will, in part, determine its effectiveness.

THE ETHICS OF ADVERTISING

Advertising raises a number of ethical questions. Some of these are:

- *False claims.* This is where the advertisement claims that the product can do something for the customer which cannot be proved. An example would be the claim that a patent medicine will cure the common cold, when it is known that no cure exists for this virus.

- Manipulation of the customer. This might be where the advertising uses deep-seated drives, such as sex, as a means to tempt customers to see a particular product as right for them (as in the use of pretty girls draped over a new model of a car – thus associating sexual success with a particular product). The customer is unaware that he is being manipulated.

> **When is advertising undesirable?**

- *Subliminal advertising.* This takes the previous point a step further. It is possible to flash a message advertising a product across a screen, in the middle of a film, so quickly that it is only picked up by the viewer's conscious mind. It is a form of brainwashing and is banned in many countries.

- *Knocking copy.* This is where an advertisement does not just proclaim the virtues of the company product, but actually does so by making unfavourable comparisons with a competitor's product. Although frowned on, this is done, especially in motor vehicle advertisements in the press.

- *Waste of resources.* It is alleged that excessive advertising, as perhaps in the case of washing powders produced by two firms in a duopoly situation, is a grotesque waste of scarce economic resources.

As a result of criticisms along these lines, an Advertising Standards Authority has been established in the UK. This body administers a Code of Advertising Practice. Its aim is to ensure that advertisements represent the product they promote in an unambiguous and fair way, both in the wording and impressions conveyed, by the advertising 'copy'. It will give advertisers advice as to whether proposed advertisements are within the guidelines and also deals with complaints from the public in cases where it is alleged that an advertisement is untruthful, misleading or offensive.

Protecting the customer.

OTHER FORMS OF PROMOTION

In addition to advertising, a number of promotional possibilities are open to an organisation. Which of them are chosen will depend on the size of the organisation, the type of product, the market segment chosen and the promotional budget available.

Public relations

This covers a wide range of activities, ranging from press releases (about a new product) which may be published without cost, through to sponsorship of artistic, sporting or educational activities. The aim is to keep the company's name in the public eye, by attaching the name to activities which appear to be socially desirable, or are of particular interest to their market segment. Another aim is to flood the media with 'good' news, in order to offset any unfavourable publicity which the firm might unwittingly attract. When this does occur, it is important that the public relations spokesperson puts the company point of view.

Personal selling

This is where a professional team of salespersons is employed to deal directly with customers. This has the advantage of providing a two-way communications channel, which helps the firm to ensure that it is meeting customer requirements, as well as simply increasing sales of the product. It also enables the firm to negotiate specific deals meeting the needs of different customers on price, service, modifications etc. This method of promoting a product is almost always employed in selling industrial goods. It is less common with consumer goods, except those which are 'unsought', such as life assurance or pensions contracts. In these cases the need is to educate the customer as to why he needs a product he had never thought about. This problem also explains the widespread use of direct sales teams to promote encyclopedias or double glazing by 'hard' sell techniques. In the case of some luxury products such as cosmetics, the manufacturer may supply promotion and sales teams to man counters in retail outlets like departmental stores. In this way they maintain control over the image conveyed.

The effectiveness of personal selling will be greatly enhanced if it is backed up by advertising campaigns and other sales promotion activities.

Packaging

Catching the customer's eye.

Packaging is an important part of the promotional function. The increasing importance of self-service stores has emphasised the need to display products boldly and attractively in order to create and maintain an impact in the customer's eye. This approach to marketing is especially evident at Christmas time but can also be seen in many easily identifiable products on supermarket shelves, e.g. Coca-Cola, Perrier, Daz, Toblerone.

Sales promotion

This is where a range of activities such as competitions, provisions of gifts, coupons and special price packages are used to boost sales. This has been evident in the promotion of petrol sales since the 1960s and has recently been used by car manufacturers to counter falling sales in recession. Gifts, training and trade exhibitions may be used to entice industrial customers.

Direct mailing

Direct mail involves sending information on company products to 'prospects' whose names are on databases of high potential purchasers of that type of product. Mailing lists can now be obtained for many classes of people and organisations and although the cost of obtaining the list and mailing these people may be higher than other forms of promotion, the people reached are far more likely to purchase. Direct mail has been used extremely successfully to market books, clothing and financial services. Charities, hospitals and schools have also used direct mail successfully to raise funds.

Branding

Here we are talking about a name placed on a product, which is used in the process of establishing the product in the market place and differentiating it from similar products of other manufacturers. This differentiation may be real or only exist in the perception of the customer. It will be established by clever advertising campaigns, which will also be used to keep the name constantly in view of the public. For this purpose the name may be linked with a logo, motto or situation.

By establishing a strong brand image, the company is in effect both shifting the demand schedule for the product to the right and making it steeper (more inelastic). It is then able to establish and maintain a price which is higher than that charged for identical products from different manufacturers. The premium on price in the case of Heinz baked beans over supermarket own label brands is a good example. The company may extend a strong brand name to cover a family of products, thus taking advantage of the original investment in promotion of the name. Again, 'Heinz 57 varieties' is a good example. Here the company name is used as the brand name. In the car industry names are chosen which reflect the characteristics and use of a particular model, thus smaller cars are now usually given 'fun' names, such as 'Panda'! Branding of products is very important since it has the following effects:

- differentiates the product
- aids identification
- causes customers to self-select the product repeatedly
- creates customer loyalty

DISTRIBUTION

“Channels of distribution.”

Distribution is the process of getting the product from the producer to the consumer. Most producers do not sell their goods directly to the consumer but go through one or more intermediate stages.

Decisions regarding distribution channels are very important. They affect other marketing decisions. For example, promotion and pricing policy will be markedly different where clothes are sold through chain stores rather than up-market fashion shops. Similarly the size and training of the sales force will vary according to whether they are selling to the trade or direct to the customer. Finally, selling through one distribution channel may prevent the company marketing its products through other outlets.

The main channels of distribution are shown in Fig. 13.5.

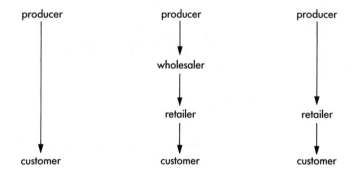

Fig. 13.5 Three major channels of distribution

DIRECT SELLING

Many industrial products are sold this way (particularly when there are only a small number of customers) as well as a number of consumer products, e.g. Avon, Tupperware, Singer Sewing Machines. A whole range of products are also sold through mail order, which is another form of direct selling. The major benefit arising from direct selling is that you can ensure the proper promotion of your product by a large, well trained sales staff, although this is a costly investment. However, orders for industrial goods may be so large that the cost per product unit sold may be negligible, while in consumer markets the producer may benefit from a higher profit margin. Direct selling, particularly of double glazing and financial services, has been heavily criticised for its use of high pressure sales tactics.

PRODUCER TO WHOLESALER

This is often chosen by smaller firms with incomplete product ranges. The wholesaler reduces the marketing effort for the producer by buying in bulk and selling in smaller lots to his customers. He also relieves the producer of some marketing costs such as stockholding, spoilage, pilfer or fashion obsolescence. However, the producer has no control over the outlets where his products are eventually sold (if they are stocked at all) and will generally obtain a lower profit margin. The traditional role of the wholesaler has declined. One attempt to offset this decline has been the establishment by the wholesaler of an exclusive service to independent chains of stores, e.g. Spar and Mace. Thus these independent retail outlets enjoy some of the benefits, e.g. discounts and bulk purchasing which would not normally be available to them.

PRODUCER TO RETAILER

There are many situations where wholesalers are an inappropriate channel of distribution. For example, where products are sold through chain stores specialising in a particular line(s) of products, the producer will be able to deliver in bulk. Such retailers, e.g. Asda and Currys, will often have strategically-placed warehouses where stock delivered is broken down into smaller lots for onward transmission to branches. Equally where retailers are geographically concentrated, a producer may find it easier (and cheaper) to supply them direct.

To ensure continuity of orders, the producer will need to employ a large costly workforce. Moreover he may find that large firms, e.g. Asda and Marks and Spencer impose onerous quality and delivery constraints upon him.

Where producers rely on retailers they have no direct contact with the customers. Additionally the retailer will probably be stocking competitors' products. In order to ensure his products are promoted properly the producer will often adopt a 'push-pull' strategy. The sales force will 'push' the retailer to promote their products properly, e.g. point of sale display perhaps encouraged with various forms of sales promotion. At the same time the producer will advertise his products hoping to 'pull' or attract the consumer to his products.

EXAMINATION QUESTIONS

1   As a marketing consultant, you have been asked for advice by a firm which has acquired the sole import rights for spectacle lenses made by an East European manufacturer. Prepare an initial report, explaining alternative possible distribution networks in the UK and appropriate methods for organising and remunerating the sales force.   (UCLES 1991)

2   You have been asked by the Egg Marketing Board to advise them about various forms of packaging. Write a report in reply explaining the main functions of packaging and how these relate to the other aspects of the marketing mix.   (UCLES 1988)

3   Outline the different pricing methods available to firms and consider when each might be used. Do such pricing methods imply that consumers have little or no influence on prices?   (AEB 1989)

4   It doesn't matter where a product is in its life cycle, advertising is always the essential factor in successful marketing. Discuss.   (London-Overseas 1991)

TUTOR'S ANSWER

Question 1

Report on alternative distribution networks for imported spectacles

From: J. Bloggs   Marketing consultant
To: A.N. Other   Managing Director, Spectacles Galore Ltd.
Date: 17/5/91

1 Purpose of the report

To offer alternative distribution network possibilities for spectacle lenses imported from Eastern Europe. The report considers briefly:

a) the nature of the market
b) existing preferred methods of distribution of such products
c) alternatives available to the company, with evaluation

2 The nature of the market

Recent legislation has introduced massive changes to the spectacle/ophthalmic advice industry. It was previously dominated by qualified opticians, who operated a cartel arrangement, by virtue of their sole right to undertake ophthalmic testing and the subsequent supply of spectacles to clients. As a result, the price of the finished product was unnaturally high, particularly where simple correction was needed, without highly specialised lenses. The market is now free for anyone to supply spectacles on a retail basis and the client has the right to obtain his or her prescription from an optician but purchase the spectacles to that prescription elsewhere. This opens up new possibilities for a firm which imports lenses from low cost countries. These opportunities are addressed here.

3 Existing distribution channels

At present, manufacturers of lenses (as distinct from frames) are supplying the product through either wholesalers or direct to opticians practising in a semi-retail environment. Such lens manufacturers are likely to be small scale and have a close relationship with their distributors, whether wholesale or the optician. Costs of production are unlikely to be minimised and the artificially high price available for standard lenses probably cross-subsidises the high cost of specialist prescriptions. This situation offers your company an opportunity. There are various ways in which it might be exploited.

For many users of spectacles, shopping for the product has changed. It is no longer a 'speciality good', requiring attendance at an optician's office, in a semi-medical environment. It has become an 'homogeneous convenience good', a necessity, required by many people, but infrequently bought, with an increasing emphasis on price as well as image and psychological need.

The lens however is only part of the spectacles and as such is sold to a manufacturer of the spectacles as an 'industrial component part'. These manufacturers are however operating in a totally changed environment, where the winner will be the one who can beat the competition on price and availability, rather than design and style. To gain a market edge he needs to attend to both aspects. If he can obtain standard lenses at a very favourable price, he can maintain a better standard on style and design than his competitor and so also retain an edge on price. It is these potential winners who we must first identify, and then seek to supply.

These successful companies will be likely to take advantage of the new environment by establishing chains of retail outlets, offering no more than the simplest eye test, geared to minor corrections, in order to make spectacles a more frequently bought fashion product, and to capture from the opticians the market for replacement spectacles.

4 Some alternative approaches to distribution

We are clearly targeting several types of company who are in, or likely to enter, this new growth market.

a) Spectacle manufacturers, who supply large volumes of straightforward spectacles to chains of genuine opticians such as Rayners, who already operate in a retail rather than medical environment.
b) Large chains of 'cheap and cheerful' spectacle shops, such as those recently opened.
c) Large retail chains who may be persuaded to enter this market by buying lenses cheaply from this company and having them fitted to frames manufactured on contract. Woolworths might be an example.

d) Large mail order companies who may be persuaded to adopt this strategy, e.g. GUS.

e) There may be scope for your company to undertake a joint venture with a frame manufacturer, in order to undertake direct mail order marketing yourselves.

5 Evaluation

All these possibilities appear to me to be worth investigating by your marketing department. I think they may well place them in the above descending order of viability and priority.

6 The sales force

It will be necessary for you to establish a sales force of sufficient size to seek leads, present the product and negotiate and close sales. This may be organised either:

a) on a geographic basis, by sales regions

or

b) on a basis of sectors

I think the latter would be more suitable in this case.

The package offered to this salesforce would have to reflect the paramedical nature of the industry, with strong ethical considerations. I would therefore recommend that high quality staff be sought and that they be rewarded on the following basis:

Salary – £15,000

Car – Ford Sierra or equivalent, full funded private mileage

Bonus scheme, related to sales performance, preferably of the company, or the department rather than the individual in order to encourage a team approach. Sufficient to offer an achievable target income of say £20,000.

BUPA and life insurance paid by the company.

I have discarded as inappropriate for ethical reasons all arrangements which smack of high pressure sales, e.g. commission only, direct selling techniques. You are looking to obtain a handful of top class accounts, after which the sales force would become in large measure 'Client Liaison Managers'.

STUDENT'S ANSWER

Question 2

> **Date, to, from? Set the scene!**

> **Is this a function of packaging?**

R E P O R T

THE MAIN FUNCTIONS OF PACKAGING

   i) Packaging is a communications medium. Many products are easily identified from a product's packaging on the supermarket shelf. Many companies keep the same package image for many years because of this reason.

  ii) Products are also identified by a BRAND NAME, this could be an abbreviation, logo or feature associated with the product. These brand names, if good, are often synonymous with reliability and quality, e.g. Marks and Spencers' St. Michael name. Note also that BRAND NAMES should be tested before the final image is selected.

 iii) The final package choice is also influenced by cultural, political and social considerations — not just commercial ones. For example, in certain countries some colours are associated with death — white in many Far East countries or purple in Latin America.

  iv) Features of the packaging should be used to stimulate sales.

   v) Packaging should PROVIDE PROTECTION to the product against spoiling, damage, pilferage and contamination.

  vi) Packaging should OFFER CONVENIENCE in the handling, storage and dispensing of the product.

 vii) With more supermarkets around, packaging is more

thoughtfully considered, especially the artwork and design of the label and colour impact. Here the customer is involved in the 'moment of decision'; packaging is therefore an effective method of communication.

"Good!"

PACKAGING IN RELATION TO THE MARKETING MIX

The marketing mix consists of the four Ps:
  Product
  Price
  Place
  Promotion

However, another variable, PACKAGING, is sometimes added but as it is under promotions it is sometimes included in the communications mix.

Packaging plays a vital part of promotion. It is often the image or the packaging of the product which is seen on the television, billboards or any other advertising medium.

Each part of the mix is selected according to importance; some elements can be more important than others, especially in certain areas of the country.

"This needs to be developed – give an example."

The elements are interdependent (alter one and the others change).

The marketing mix fulfils its role by profitably finding, creating and keeping customers. Customers are extremely influenced by packaging at the 'moment of decision' and are knowledgeable on brand image. The marketing mix element promotion is necessary to establish what a consumer requires, thus the right packaging can be produced.

VARIOUS FORMS OF PACKAGING EGGS

As eggs are a delicate product one must consider a packaging that will allow protection. Of course mediums like bags, cartons or boxes could be used but the most practical is the egg box, for the following reasons:

  i) It can be stored and transported easily due to its
     rectangular shape.
 ii) The box can be designed to cushion the eggs and separate them
     from each other.

What materials should be used? In today's environmental market, plastic is out — recycled cardboard is in. The logo colour and name should stand out amongst all the other egg cartons to make it different and not just one of the crowd.

The company should also advertise the QUALITY of the product to outshine its competitors.

CONCLUSION

Consideration clearly must be given to the packaging for these reasons:

   i) It affects 'the marketing mix'
  ii) It must be functional
 iii) It has to be environmentally sound
  iv) It has to be convenient
   v) It needs to build up an image

As promotion and packaging are so closely interlinked it is very important to have the correct advertising strategy showing an image of the product. A dull carton would never attract the customer's attention.

The box should be functional. Its main concept should be to

protect the eggs in a convenient way. Also a box is easier to
transport.
    The box should be made of recycled materials. This is a good
selling point in the 'green 90s'.
    The box should carry a memorable logo to attract customers at
the decision moment and also for it to be kept in mind as the egg
to buy.

Tutor's comments

This is a good answer, which should qualify for a low B or high C grade. It is a slightly unusual question in that packaging is a part of the marketing mix which is less commonly referred to in examination questions. Nevertheless, this student has been able both to place packaging within the marketing mix, which could be expected from an average candidate, and has also been able to develop in some detail the reasons why packaging is so very important for much of modern business. She has also used a sensible and appropriate format, which brings out very clearly her key statements. She has also been able to apply her ideas to the situation given.

OUTLINE ANSWERS

Question 3

Any company must have a policy for pricing its products. This must take into account on the one hand the dictates of the market (i.e. the factors influencing the demand schedule and supply schedule for the industry) and on the other hand the desire of the firm to generate profit. The firm must take into account three key matters; the cost of production, the demand for the product and the activities of the competition. The degree to which the firm may achieve greater freedom in its pricing policy depends on its success through marketing strategies and product development in differentiating the product from those of competitors.

Cost-orientated pricing may be either a standard mark up percentage or a target return on capital. *Mark up pricing* is common where many products are offered for which individual pricing would be complex and costly. It involves adding a fixed percentage to unit cost. *Target return pricing* involves setting a price which should give a desired rate of return on capital. This is common in public sector organisations. The following formula may be used:

$$\text{Price} = \frac{\text{Desired percentage return} \times \text{investment}}{\text{Volume of product sales}}$$

Demand-orientated pricing may take several forms. 'Skim' pricing is used when launching a new and unique product, relying on the customers who are willing to pay high prices for something new. As competitors enter the market, the price is lowered or the product changed. Japanese consumer electronics firms commonly use this practice. Penetration pricing involves setting a very low price, to obtain market share rapidly, perhaps in a 'mature' market. Price sensitivity is also critical here, which relates to price elasticity of demand and awareness of substitutes. Psychological pricing plays on human irrationality; £1.99 sounding much cheaper than £2; high quality perfume at a low price will not sell. Price discrimination may be used in some industries, e.g. British Rail. This is possible where the market is segmentable.

Competition-orientated pricing is aggressive in nature, although in recession it may be defensive. Some firms may follow the lead of competitors who are bigger. Retail stores may use loss leaders, i.e. offering some basic branded products at below cost in order to attract customers who then spend more on high mark up items. Discount pricing is the chief market strategy of some companies. For example this has always been the policy of Woolworths. Tendering by sealed bid is common in the construction industry.

Pricing policy becomes more complex where a range of products if offered based on one design, as in cars. It will be necessary to establish price for each variant on the theme, both in relation to the range of prices on competing products on offer and between the models in the range (and their immediate competitors) and in relation to the company's other model ranges. In general terms, pricing policy must be seen in relation to decisions about the complete marketing mix and the companies stated 'mission'.

The implication of this discussion seems to be that consumers have no control over prices. The degree to which they do so in reality depends on the structure of the market. In an industry which is close to perfect competition, for instance printing, the consumer has much choice and the firm may have no option but to be a price taker. In markets where a firm has a degree of monopoly power, permanent or temporary, by virtue of either its control over availability of the product throughout the market, e.g. a water company, or briefly as a result of a promotional campaign which has differentiated the product successfully, or where a firm has produced a new and unique product, e.g. the Sony Walkman, then the consumer has little or no power over prices, there being no available substitute. In more general terms a recession may cause the collapse of demand over a whole market, forcing producers to cut prices unwillingly, as in the case of the UK car industry in 1991.

Question 4

Different elements in the marketing mix will be appropriate at different stages of the product life cycle. This means that decisions have to be made by a company with regard to the four Ps as may be appropriate to the stage in the life cycle.

In the introduction stage of a new product these decisions might be as follows: offer a basic product, use cost plus or 'skim' pricing policies, build a selective distribution network, build product awareness by informative advertising and a heavy sales promotion to entice customers to try the product. Thus a new entrant to the fitted kitchen market might use a pricing policy geared to costs but undercutting competitors as a result of low overheads. It might aim to attract a few regular trade users whilst building gradually its retail market. Advertising would be simple and basic, stressing price and possible rapid delivery and good service.

In the *growth stage*, it may be possible to extend the client base by such policies as offering extensions to the product. In the case of the kitchen company above, perhaps by manufacturing better than standard quality carcasses. It may seek to extend its range of trade outlets, whilst seeking retail distributors on a commission basis, or possibly by franchising. It may seek contract markets in the building industry. It would do this by direct marketing, using a sales force. It may seek to extend its direct retail market by heavier advertising on a wider geographical scale.

In the *maturity stage*, when the company has penetrated as much of the market as is possible with the resources available and in the light of the competition's activities, it may seek to diversify, developing new products, or products which aim at a different market segment in quality terms. Thus at this stage the company might seek, in the kitchen example, to franchise its retail distribution and to develop a range of bedroom furniture which is compatible with its mainstream activities. This strategy would involve heavy persuasive advertising, stressing quality and style rather than price. This might encourage brand switching and develop a brand image for the company.

In the *decline phase*, it might be necessary to phase out weak brands or items, phase out marginal outlets, reduce advertising, stressing low price once more and perhaps use a 'run out' approach, by renaming the products available. It is however necessary in a market like fitted kitchens, to prolong the life cycle of your product. This may be achieved by product modification, in this case by producing a new range of facias to apply to the carcasses.

It is clear that the role of advertising will change as the product life cycle proceeds. It is only one element in a whole series of decisions which must be made in developing the marketing mix. It is not *the* essential factor, but it must be correctly matched with the effects of the other decisions about product, place and price.

FURTHER READING

Hill, *Marketing for BTEC*, Business Education Publishers Ltd. 1989:
     Part 2, 'The Marketing Mix', Chapters 5–13.
Cameron, Rushton, Carson, *Marketing*, Penguin 1988:
     Part 3, 'The Technology of Marketing'.

CHAPTER

PERSONNEL MANAGEMENT

MANPOWER PLANNING

RECRUITMENT

WAGE POLICY

EDUCATION AND TRAINING

EMPLOYEE LEGISLATION

MODERN EMPLOYMENT TRENDS

GETTING STARTED

Any organisation depends for its success on the efforts of its employees. They will differ in terms of abilities, aspirations and motives. They are more unpredictable than any other input into the production process. In some businesses the cost of employing workers may be as high as 75% of total costs. Not only must they be paid a wage, but the employer also has to accept other liabilities in law which are very costly. He must pay National Insurance contributions on behalf of each worker, conform to the provisions of the Health and Safety legislation, pay redundancy money when releasing a worker with more than two years' standing in the firm and may be required to pay compensation should he be successfully sued in an Industrial Tribunal on a claim of unfair dismissal, or failure to observe the provisions of the Equal Opportunities legislation. It is therefore not surprising that care has to be paid to this function.

The Personnel function undertakes a range of responsibilities which we will deal with in this chapter. These are: manpower planning; recruitment; wages and salary policy; training and development and employee legislation.

A further important function which is the responsibility of this department is *Industrial Relations*, which is dealt with in detail in the next chapter. The department may also be responsible for advising the company on ways of motivating workers to higher levels of activity and commitment. Comments on motivation will be found in Chapter 8.

From the point of view of the company and its overall performance, it is important that the personnel function is able to reduce certain potential costs. These would arise from excessively high levels of absenteeism, labour turnover and industrial disputes.

Since all management is largely people management, it follows that these responsibilities are also undertaken in part by 'line' management. The personnel manager's responsibility is to make sure that line managers act with consistency and equity. This is not always easy, since traditionally personnel managers are seen as 'soft' on the workers, their function having originally stemmed out of the welfare movement early in this century. In recent years the personnel function has been taken more seriously and is now often referred to as Human Resources Management (HRM).

The distinctive characteristics of HRM are:

- more sophisticated techniques, for example psychometric testing to establish the abilities and personality of workers.

- concern for resource maximisation, for example through management development programmes.

- more involvement in strategic business decision making.

- the use of 'human asset accounting', which attempts to assign an accounting value to human resources and to assess their depreciation or appreciation values. This brings HRM into the calculation of the 'bottom line' for the first time, leading to a longer term view in the utilisation of the workforce.

ESSENTIAL PRINCIPLES

MANPOWER PLANNING

The company must ensure that it is able to meet its future objectives by having available the correct mix of human resources. This requires planning, based on an awareness of two basic factors:

- The external environment of the firm (economic, social and political as well as demographic).

- Current strengths and weaknesses of the organisation and the strategy based on that position.

The principal elements in the process of generating a corporate manpower plan may be shown diagrammatically as in Fig. 14.1.

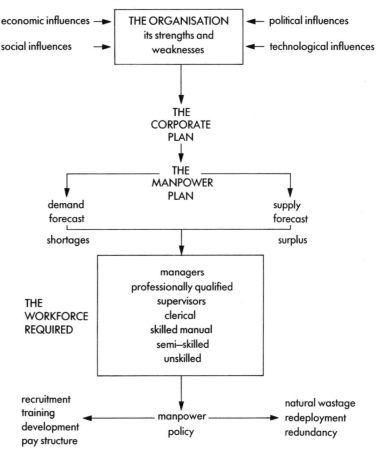

Fig. 14.1 Generating a corporate manpower plan

The firm's ability to meet its manpower requirements will depend on the demand and supply side factors in the labour market. What is the current demand for the types of labour employed by the firm? What are the firm's requirements in relation to that market place? For example, the current growth in demand for part-time female workers may cause problems if the firm is say a large hotel, dependent on such workers. What is the supply side position both inside the firm and in the wider labour market? The hotel in our example may face a heavy turnover of part-time younger women workers and find it impossible to replace them because of the 'demographic time bomb' effect of the fall in the birth rate in the 1970s. It thus has a problem on both demand and supply side, the labour market condition being what it is. It will have to either pay higher wages, or seek alternative sources of labour amongst the unemployed males, women returners or pensioners. All will have cost implications through retraining requirements. If the firm has been prudent in predicting these conditions and has also predicted correctly other important factors set out below, it will be able to maintain an adequate staffing position.

MANPOWER PLANNING INFORMATION

- retirement rates over next few years
- percentage of new workers who can be retained

- percentage loss of workers to other jobs
- need for new highly qualified staff
- new needs dictated by change of product or technology or expansion

It is therefore possible to produce a forecast as to where within the company shortages and surpluses are likely to occur. A manpower plan may then be drawn up in order to avoid the problems created by those shortages and surpluses. It should be possible to meet the requirements of the organisation with minimum cost to the company and friction amongst employees by suitable policies of recruitment, training, redeployment and redundancy.

LABOUR TURNOVER

This a very important element in manpower planning. A certain amount of turnover is good for an organisation for various reasons:

- a stagnant workforce becomes complacent
- new blood is essential if the company is to respond to changes in its environment
- it is the only way to avoid an ageing workforce

There are three groups of reasons why workers leave an organisation:

- management action, i.e. redundancy or dismissal for poor performance or disciplinary reasons
- involuntary departure, i.e. due to death, illness, pregnancy, marriage, partner's career
- voluntary departure, i.e. leaving for another job as a result of dissatisfaction with pay, conditions of service, nature of the job or alternatively career advancement purposes

A high level of voluntary departures is worrying.

Dissatisfaction amongst employees should be of great concern to management, since it suggests that something is seriously wrong with the company if this occurs too frequently. It may indicate poor morale or possibly that a competitor is offering more attractive terms. The rate of turnover can be expressed in the form of a percentage rate. Although such statistics should be treated with caution, a comparison of the current turnover with that of earlier periods may highlight problems which need to be addressed. The formula is:

$$\frac{\text{number leaving} - \text{unavoidable departures}}{\text{average number employed}} \times 100$$

There are a number of costs to an organisation which can be identified as arising from an excessive turnover rate. For example:

The costs of high turnover.

- lost production whilst a post is vacant
- lost production during induction training of new employee
- cost of recruitment and training
- undermined morale as a result of the break up of work groups
- cost of errors and mistakes by the new trainee
- payment of overtime or bonuses to other workers in order to maintain production until a new person is recruited and trained

The role of the personnel manager is to identify trends in labour turnover and to seek to adopt policies which will reduce the rate to an acceptable level. Strategies which might be used to achieve this objective are:

Strategies for reducing labour turnover.

- improve selection and induction process
- make sure that employees are fully utilised
- improve working conditions
- job enrichment schemes, which give the worker greater scope to decide how to carry out his or her tasks
- provide an internal promotion ladder
- review the pay structure (this is often a major constraint)

RECRUITMENT

Since the organisation depends on a flow of new recruits to replace those lost through departures, recruitment is central to the work of the personnel function. It must through its own activities, possibly supplemented by the use of outside agencies, seek to identify the company's needs exactly and find appropriate recruits. The first task it must undertake is *job analysis*.

JOB ANALYSIS AND JOB DESCRIPTION

All the relevant facts relating to the vacant job must be identified. The information will be obtained from existing records, discussion with the present job holder, or by direct observation of the job. A *job description* may then be written up outlining the content of the job. The items included would be:

- *Basic details:* title and grade of the job and the department concerned.
- *Job summary:* outlining the purpose of the job, identifying main, secondary and occasional tasks and the standards to be maintained. Information on social and work environment.
- *Responsibilities:* clarifying the position in the organisational structure. Identify subordinates for whom the new employee will be responsible and seniors to whom he or she will report.
- *Conditions of employment:* salary, holiday entitlement, hours of work, pension scheme, welfare and social facilities, trade union membership arrangements.
- *Training:* indicating training arrangements to induct the recruit and bring him up to the required standard.
- *Promotion:* career structure and opportunities for advancement within the organisation.

> **Information included in a job description.**

This job description will form the basis of the recruitment advertising and training programmes. It may also be used in wage and salary administration.

JOB SPECIFICATION

Job descriptions are also used as the basis for *job specifications*.

> **A definition.**

A job specification sets out the characteristics sought in candidates for the job. These will include:

- *Physical characteristics:* age, health, appearance
- *Attainments:* academic standards, professional qualifications, training
- *Experience/knowledge:* positions held, knowledge gained
- *Aptitudes:* mechanical, verbal, ability to work under pressure
- *Domestic circumstances:* ability to work away from home, ability to relocate, etc

A job specification also identifies the qualities of the person most likely to fit into the organisation.

THE RECRUITMENT PROCESS

The actual task of recruitment may be directed towards internal recruitment sources within the firm, or to outside candidates, from competitors or compatible operations in another industry. The process may be carried out entirely in house or may be partly or wholly delegated to an outside recruitment agency. Sources outside the company from which candidates may be drawn include the following:

> **Sources of new employees.**

- careers office
- job centres
- employment agencies
- headhunters
- links with higher education, further education institutions or schools
- informal networks, e.g. 'old boy networks'

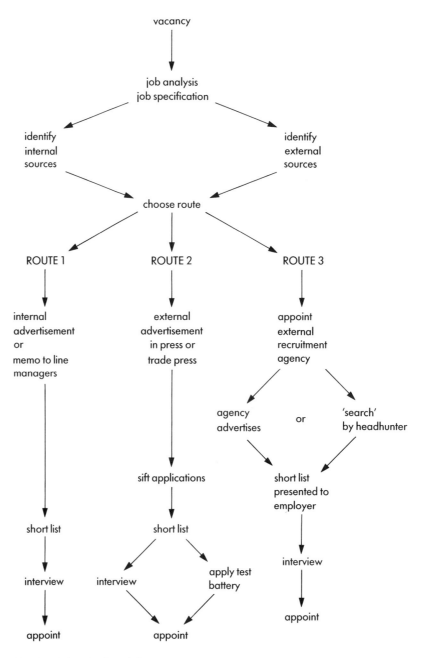

Fig. 14.2 The recruitment process

■ national and local advertising

■ redeployment from other subsidiaries within a group

The process may be represented diagrammatically as in Fig. 14.2.

If the job description and job specification have been carefully constructed, the advertisements (where used) may be worded in such a way as to screen out unlikely or fringe candidates, thus saving time. The initial sift of application forms or letters, will concentrate on relating the *curriculum vitae* of the candidate to the job specification. Many more fringe candidates will be excluded here and a short list drawn up of the most likely candidates. References will be taken up from previous employers and personal referees. At this point some of the remaining candidates may be discarded. The remaining short list of two or more candidates will then be invited to interview. This is possibly the weakest link in the chain, since it is easy to be misled in this situation where immediate impressions may override reason. This is why the modern trend is to subject candidates to aptitude tests (psychometric testing) in order to obtain a more scientific appraisal.

From Fig. 14.2 it can be seen that the firm may choose one of three 'routes' through which it might make an appointment. The route it chooses will depend on the level and nature of the job. Routes 1 and 2 will most commonly be used for the selection of wage paid and lower grade salaried workers and junior managerial posts. The external recruitment agency is most likely to be used for higher level managerial appointments and the 'headhunter' only for the highest level jobs where the salary exceeds £30,000 per annum. At this level the person best suited for the post might not even apply and may have to be sought and persuaded confidentially to allow himself to be considered.

WAGE POLICY

As we have seen, wages and salaries comprise a large percentage of the costs of any organisation. In service industries this is particularly important, since labour costs may be 75% of total costs. Wages policy therefore has as its aim the attraction and retention of staff of the right quality, at a cost that the company can afford. Despite attempts in enlightened companies to give all employees 'staff' status in order to remove 'them and us' attitudes, it is still customary to think of two categories, wage paid and salaried staff. The prime differences between the two groups in the conventional organisation are:

- manual workers are paid a weekly wage, often in cash
- clerical, professional and managerial staff are paid a monthly salary
- manual workers have shorter holiday entitlements
- manual workers are on a week's notice, whereas staff are on one month's or more notice
- incentive payments to manual workers are in the form of piece rates on production, whereas for staff they may be an annual bonus, or in other forms such as share options for senior managers
- staff are given various privileges and benefits, ranging from separate dining rooms to company cars, as 'perks'

> Typical distinctions between waged and salaried workers.

In Chapter 8 we discussed the various ways in which workers are motivated. Obviously pay is an important motivator, if not always the most important one. Other motivators are:

- security of employment
- comparative income, wage differentials in relation to similar workers
- status – where an occupation is highly valued by society, good quality entrants will not be deterred by low pay
- group acceptance – it is important to be accepted in a group and this feeling of belonging to an exclusive team may override money considerations
- job satisfaction – interesting and challenging work, with prospects of advancement, will to an extent override pay considerations

CALCULATING THE REMUNERATION PACKAGE

The remuneration package offered (pay plus 'perks'), reflects external and internal considerations.

External considerations include:
- a nationally negotiated wage settlement
- rates paid by competitors
- other job opportunities available in the area

Internal considerations include:
- a system of payments which reflects the value of the job to the organisation
- a system which is perceived by employees to be fair and just

Internal considerations are met by means of a job evaluation. Each aspect of the job is considered and is allocated a value according to the complexity. The values obtained are summed to arrive at a value for the job and workers will find themselves allocated in a certain salary band.

Although this method of salary grading is designed to give a semblance of objectivity it is not a very scientific approach and it may ignore the perception of the worker. Factors which are emphasised by management may not be considered important by the employee. Employees are also inclined to forget that it is the job, and not themselves, that is being graded.

METHODS OF PAYMENT

Three basic alternatives are available:

Flat rate scheme

This provides for a basic rate per period of time worked (hour, day, week, or month). Time worked beyond the agreed number of hours qualifies for overtime payments at a higher rate. Salaried workers may have to accept time off in lieu of overtime. This system is appropriate where payment cannot or should not be related to output, as in teaching or warehouse work. An element of incentive pay is possible, including for example bonuses for good timekeeping or long service. Merit awards may also be used for exceptional performance but may depend on an appraisal system.

> Imagine paying policemen by results!

Incentive schemes

Such schemes are also known as piece rates. They are calculated by using work study techniques. The logic is that the worker is paid a low basic rate plus payment by the 'piece', that is, the amount produced. It is supposed that such schemes will increase productivity through the desire to earn more pay. Unit costs will thus be reduced, which benefits the company, as does a reduction in the amount of supervision required (but this is offset by the need for greater quality control checks). Unfortunately such schemes in reality cause much conflict between worker and employer and between workers. Workers will seek to manipulate the rate measured by the Work Study officer, in order to lower the 'standard' rate and so increase bonus. Piece rate workers often depend on flat rate workers who supply them with materials, or maintain machinery for them, and these workers will resent their lower pay. One possible remedy is to work on a basis of group incentives, but this is technically difficult. It does, however, overcome the problem of the resentful flat rate worker by including him in a team (but there is still plenty of scope for friction between workers).

Measured day-work

This method seeks to bridge the gap between flat rate and incentive schemes. The employer and employees agree a level of output which the employee believes from experience to be capable of being maintained. The employer agrees to pay the employee on the basis of this output regardless of short-term variations in output. The advantage to the worker is a stable and predictable wage and to the employer predictable productivity at a more easily calculable cost, provided that he strives to reduce delays and breakdowns to the minimum. However, wage differentials are highlighted and difficulties may arise in disciplining workers who are treated on a basis of trust.

EDUCATION AND TRAINING

Large companies have separate training departments, but in small and medium-sized firms, the Personnel Manager is responsible for this area. It is generally believed that UK companies are very backward in this respect. Many prefer to 'poach' workers already trained from more far-sighted companies which have schemes of training and apprenticeship in place. Well managed companies use training to obtain a number of competitive advantages, rather than seeing it as an extra overhead. They see a well trained workforce at all levels as having a number of advantages:

> Company training has several advantages.

- improved quality
- reduced 'costs of quality' (see Chapter 21)
- reduced labour turnover
- increased flexibility
- motivating the workforce

Some companies have taken this philosophy to extreme lengths, for example Ford UK, who despite the recession, offer to employees of *all* levels, vouchers worth some £100 each year to spend on any kind of training or education, from quality assurance to flower arranging. They believe that a mentally alert workforce performs better.

TRAINING STRATEGY

An effective system of training will cover the whole organisation, at all levels. It is now recognised that the first contact a customer or client has with the firm is likely to be with personnel at a lower level in the organisation.

> **Training must be undertaken at all levels.**

Visiting clients will be subconsciously influenced by the atmosphere and cleanliness of the office/shop/workplace – this is the responsibility of the janitor. Alternatively, they will be influenced by the telephone manner of the receptionist, in particular, the promptness and courtesy in responding to calls. This is the responsibility of the office manager, whose staff will need training. Setting up training programmes, whether for line or staff personnel, cannot be effectively provided on a haphazard basis. It must be planned in a systematic way between the personnel and/or training manager and the appropriate functional managers. It is essential to identify deficiencies to be remedied and improvements to be made, on the basis of the measured performance requirements of each job. Schemes of training must be developed at various levels in the organisation and stages in the employee's career including:

Induction

The induction of new employees into the firm and the specific job is extremely important as it helps the employee settle down in their new job.

Apprenticeship/trainee scheme

The induction and then development of basic skills for a trade or office skill in young entrants to the workforce.

Operative level

Training in the specific skills required, either on the job or at a training centre. The emphasis today is on training operatives in a range of skills, to provide flexibility for the organisation (but it also increases the employee's value in the wider labour market).

Supervisor level

The emphasis is on interpersonal skills, team leadership and problem solving, since specific job skills can be taken for granted.

Management development

Such training is seen as increasingly important and is mainly academic in content. It may be undertaken in various ways: short courses ranging from several days to two weeks' duration; part-time post-experience courses in management centres attached to higher education establishments; full-time one year courses at management centres; distance learning for Diploma or Degree courses. Most of these courses lead either to professional qualifications such as Membership of the Institute of Marketing or an MBA or Diploma in Management Studies.

The development of training programmes will usually be delegated to either the Personnel Manager or a Training Officer. His role will be to:

- consult with all functional departments to discuss specific training needs
- develop and implement in-company training programmes
- liaise with colleges, polytechnics and universities in the development of company linked and sponsored training programmes (in the case of large firms) or to adapt company training programmes to fit ready made courses available at local colleges (smaller firms)
- advise employees on available college courses, etc
- maintain training records as an aid to future recruitment programmes and promotions

The process of training development may be expressed in diagrammatically as in Fig. 14.3.

EMPLOYEE LEGISLATION

The personnel function must ensure that the company complies with all law which relates to employment. In these matters they are responsible to the Company Secretary, who has a legal obligation to ensure compliance.

CONTRACT OF EMPLOYMENT

All workers are entitled to a written statement of the main elements of the contract, that is

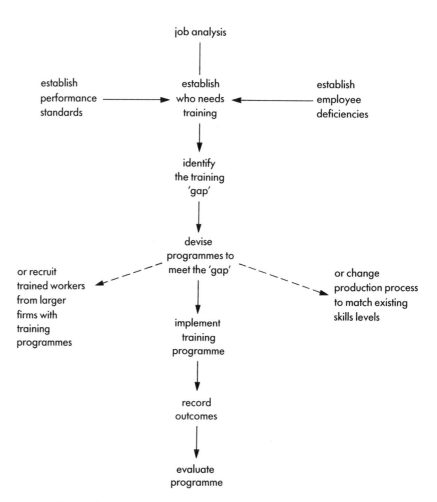

Fig. 14.3 Developing a training programme

the terms and conditions of employment, to which is probably added a brief job description. The full contract will include requirements stipulated by the Company Rule Book and also any agreements reached through collective bargaining. Terms may also be implied into the contract by common law. Obligations of the employer include:

- to pay wages when they are due
- to make only authorised deductions
- to provide work
- to take reasonable care for the safety of employees

Obligations of the employee include:

- the duty of obedience
- to take reasonable care in their job
- to act with honesty and integrity

ANTI-DISCRIMINATION LAWS

Various forms of inequitable treatment of employees are now illegal. These include, principally, where men and women are treated differently by the employer, or where people are treated differently according to ethnic origin. These principles were established by the Sex Discrimination Act of 1975 and the Race Relations Act of 1976. Discrimination against disabled persons is now frowned upon and it is required that firms of over 20 employees should employ a quota of 3% from groups with disabilities.

HEALTH AND SAFETY

Employment legislation.

The Health and Safety at Work Act of 1974 requires firms to formulate a written safety policy. It also places an obligation on employees to obey safety regulations. A Health and Safety Committee must be established in any workplace with more than 25 employees. It must include representatives of the workers. A Health and Safety Inspectorate exists to enforce the Act.

GRIEVANCE AND DISCIPLINARY PROCEDURES

These are not required by law, except in so far as the issues in this area may well lead to a charge of 'unfair dismissal' and an expensive appearance before the Industrial Tribunal. The personnel department will therefore be charged with the establishment of procedures in these areas, in consultation with the unions.

MODERN EMPLOYMENT TRENDS	The rapid changes in technology and the degree of economic volatility in the world in recent years have combined with increasingly sophisticated consumer tastes, to place much greater demands on firms. Flexible manufacturing systems, based on the use of computer-controlled machines, has made small batch production viable. This is so, even in standardised mass production systems such as those developed in the vehicle industry. This means that it is essential to have a flexible workforce, operating in groups on semi-autonomous workstations rather than a 'line' in the old sense. Flexibility in this case means that each worker is able to do several jobs, which in turn involves more and better training. Unions in the UK are often seen, rightly or wrongly, as resistant to such changes.

A NEW EMPLOYMENT STRUCTURE

Employers are responding to the need for flexibility in the wider sense of being able to respond rapidly to changes in patterns of demand and levels of demand. They are doing so by developing a completely new employment strategy. This new format can best be shown diagrammatically as in Fig. 14.4.

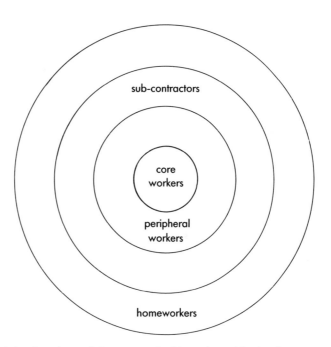

Fig. 14.4 A flexible workforce

In this model the functions of the groups inside and outside the firm are as follows (all of them are activities which would formerly have been done within the firm and on its own premises):

Core workers

- small in number
- well paid
- highly trained
- well educated
- permanent contract and career path within the firm

A flexible workforce.

These will be the employees, at all levels, whose activities are vital to the continuation of the firm in its main line of business, at minimum production levels. They are expected to switch jobs and locations, thus providing an element of 'functional' flexibility.

Peripheral workers

- less job security or career paths
- full-time, part-time or temporary contract
- often female

These workers may be in any part of the firm, e.g. extra production line staff, packers, etc at times of high levels of demand, or even sales staff paid by commission only. Many workers, especially females, are happy with this arrangement which gives them choices about when and where they work. Employment agencies now exist which specialise in supplying temporary staff. Labour turnover tends to be high which gives an element of 'numerical' flexibility.

Subcontractors

Small subcontractors have always been used for specific tasks but their use has now gone much further. Activities of a specialist nature which were formerly done 'in-house' but which were not part of the core business are now being put out to contractors. These contractors may be the former employees who used to provide the service 'in house'. Examples of this are catering and 'housekeeping' functions, market research and recruitment. This greatly reduces the overhead costs of expensive 'staff' appointments.

Networking

Ironically, this is in a sense a return to the early days of the industrial revolution, when many industrial processes which had not yet been mechanised were 'put out' to domestic hand workers. This practice has continued in some industries, for example the stuffing of envelopes for mail order companies. However, the recent advances in communication technology (see Chapter 9) such as fax and computer links have made it possible to locate specialist functions such as programming, administration, financial control and sales, wherever the overhead is lowest. Thus some local authorities in London have now relocated their administration in northern and midland towns to obtain the lowest overheads. Other companies have begun to allow some of their staff to work from home, meeting only occasionally for briefing and training. This again cuts the overhead dramatically and also enables able women, at home with children, to continue with their career or to rejoin the workforce. It has also been found to result in higher productivity.

EXAMINATION QUESTIONS

1 Analyse the role of the Personnel Department in a large organisation.   (AEB 1986)

2 Discuss how systems of wage payment may sometimes conflict with quality standards.   (UCLES 1987)

STUDENT'S ANSWER

Question 1

A good introduction, which emphasises the importance of this function.

The role of the Personnel Dept in a large organisation has assumed greater importance in recent years. This is because it has been recognised that people are a firm's most important and expensive resource. It is important that the personnel department carries out certain functions very professionally and efficiently. Personnel management is now better paid and requires formal professional training. This has been made even more important by legislation in recent years. These laws have greatly increased the 'on cost' of employing a person and have created a number of legal pitfalls which must be avoided because they can prove to be very expensive.

The first function of personnel is to recruit the right people. This means that personnel must undertake 'job analysis' of every post in the firm, in order to make sure that jobs are filled by the right people who can actually do that job properly. From the job analysis the personnel manager can work out a 'job specification' which makes clear where the job fits into the organisational structure. It will also specify in detail the specific parts of the job. To match this personnel will draw up a 'person specification', indicating the personal qualities and the qualifications required. After that point, when vacancies arise, personnel can go ahead and invite applications by advertisement, seek references, short list and interview likely candidates. For senior posts the company might prefer to appoint an outside executive search consultant, who will contract to produce a short list of people who were not necessarily applying for jobs.

Once the firm has its staff, it is up to personnel to plan the manpower requirements of the firm, taking account of labour turnover in the firm or industry, the future requirements of the firm and the external circs such as population changes which affect the number of suitable candidates likely to be available.

It will be up to the personnel department to interpret the wishes of senior management in terms of the wages and salary policy of the company. They must consider matters to do with security of employment, comparative income between groups of workers, status symbols and perks. Decisions have to be made about incentives. Is the firm going to use performance related pay schemes and if so what type? Does the system require any form of regular appraisal and if so how is it to be conducted and by whom?

A very important role for personnel is in planning and implementing training, although in large firms this might be delegated to a separate Training Manager. This will be an essential means of ensuring that long term manpower needs are fulfilled and perhaps of retaining key workers who might otherwise leave the firm. Training will have to be provided at several levels, induction, apprenticeship schemes, operative level, supervisor level and management development.

Perhaps the most difficult area for personnel now is in making sure the firm does not fall foul of the law, whether UK law on Employment, Equal Pay, Equal Opportunities, employment of disabled people, contracts of employment, Redundancy laws and in the future the effects on labour mobility of EC 1992 and possibly the Social Charter.

In a large organisation working on numerous sites and with many different groups of employees belonging to separate unions it is likely that industrial relations will be a separate department. However, the work of the two departments obviously overlaps and will require coordination.

Tutor's comments

This is quite a well written answer which systematically covers the main points (nb. abbreviations such as 'Dept' and 'circs' should be avoided). It would have been better had the candidate developed the points made in more detail, with examples to stress the point. Otherwise, it is a good C grade answer.

OUTLINE ANSWER

Question 2

All workers are offered a 'remuneration package', worked out by the personnel function within the company's corporate manpower plan. It is customary to differentiate between weekly paid wage-earning line employees and salary earning 'staff' employees. It is assumed here that the question refers only to wage-earning employees in 'line' functions within the firm.

A number of considerations will determine the wage system used, and the level of payments made. External considerations include: wages paid by competitors, other job opportunities available in the area and any nationally negotiated wage settlement, which forms the baseline on which the wage payment system must be built. Internal considerations are: the need to reflect the value of the job to the firm in terms of productivity. There is also the need for the system to appear to be just and equitable to the workers in order to avoid conflict and industrial disputes. A job evaluation system will place a numerical value to the company on a job, which will be easier to do in some jobs than others. A decision must be made as to the type of payment to be used.

Three basic alternatives are available in the case of weekly paid workers. A flat rate may be used. This provides a basic rate per period of time worked, measured in hour, day, week or monthly units. Time worked beyond this agreed number of hours at a given rate qualify for overtime payments at a higher rate. Bonuses may be paid or awards, on the basis of good timekeeping, or exceptional performance. Such schemes are convenient for jobs where output is not easily measured. The advantage for the worker is that he earns a consistent and known wage each week. The disadvantage to the company is that the worker has an incentive to spread his work over time, in order to ensure overtime opportunities, which often are essential for him to maximise his earnings. This increases company costs, through inefficiency and low productivity.

An incentive scheme may be set up. Commonly in a production environment this will take the form of 'piece rates'. The essence of this system is that a Work Study Officer will undertake 'time and motion studies', both to establish the best way in which to do the job and to evaluate a 'standard time' for doing the job. The worker is paid perhaps 75% of what he should produce in a week on the standard time as a basic rate and any output he achieves beyond that qualifies for 'bonus' payments, by the piece. The advantage to the firm is that productivity and output should be maximised. The benefit to the worker is that by working fast he can maximise his income. However, conflict may arise with 'indirect workers', who assist him in some way but are paid on flat rates. They have an incentive to work slowly, whilst the man on piece rate is frustrated by being slowed down. Conflict also arises over the setting of the standard times and bonuses. It is a recipe for industrial disputes.

A system of measured day work might be seen as more suitable in some environments. This seeks to bridge the gap between flat and piece rates. A level of output is agreed between employer and employees which can reasonably be maintained. The employer agrees to pay on this basis, irrespective of short term fluctuations in output. The worker gains the advantage of a stable and predictable wage and the employer gains predictable productivity and costs. This system has the effect of highlighting wage differentials and may again cause conflict.

Any combination of these systems which includes any form of bonus payment related to production, will have implications for quality control and assurance. Production lines producing standard items on this basis are likely to harbour considerable 'costs of quality'. That is, there will be large volumes of scrap and rework produced in the search for output at any price. Overwork of machines and inadequate attention to maintenance is also likely to cause scrap and to cause mistakes which damage machines, causing in turn costly machine downtime. In order to cover for all these faults, it will be necessary to carry large buffer stocks of parts and components, increasing inventory costs. 'Inspecting in' quality at the end of the line and discarding scrap is in itself a costly exercise.

Japanese companies and western companies which have imitated their 'total quality approach', have sought to eliminate the costs of non-conformance to specification and have implemented 'Just in Time' or 'Kanban' management of inventories. Suppliers must be prepared to deliver on a daily basis, the parts necessary for an ever changing flow of small batches of product. Scrap and rework are eliminated and costs reduced by as much as 40%. In order to achieve this success these companies have abandoned piece rate systems in favour of high basic rates, plus bonuses paid annually in relation to company profits. High levels of training are offered and workers are encouraged by lifetime employment contracts, to train and to involve themselves through 'Quality Circles' in a search for 'continuous improvement'.

FURTHER READING

Appleby, *Modern Business Administration*, 5th edition, Pitman 1991:
   Chapter 9, Human Resource Management.
Buckley, *Structure of Business*, 2nd edition, Pitman 1990:
   Chapter 19, Personnel.
Cumming, *Personnel Management*, 5th edition, Heinemann 1985:
   Chapter 1, The Personnel Management Function.
   Chapter 4, The Employment Function.
   Chapter 6, Aspects of Employment.
   Chapter 10, The Training Function.
   Chapter 19, Health and Safety.
Graham (Revised; Bennet), *Human Resources Management*, 6th edition, M & E Handbooks 1989:
   Chapter 12, Manpower Planning.
   Chapter 14, Recruitment and Selection.
   Chapter 17, Labour Turnover.
   Chapter 22, Wages and Salaries.
   Chapter 23, Safety and Conditions of Employment.

GETTING STARTED

In a capitalist economic system relationships between workers and employers are frequently in conflict. In theory at least, the employer seeks to extract from his employees the maximum work for as little pay and as little security of employment as possible. Conversely, employees seek the maximum reward for their efforts, with as much security of employment and safety at work, as possible.

In view of these differing perspectives and requirements, a system needs to exist by which compromise and agreement may be reached. This is what we mean when we talk about industrial relations in the widest sense. It is best seen as a process which continues all the time in any organisation. The way that the process works and the institutions through which it is conducted will differ in each society, as will the legal framework imposed by governments and within which it must be conducted. What is certain is that the relationship between workers and employers is *symbiotic*. That is, they need each other and are interdependent on each other. Thus the process must be conducted in one way or another.

In advanced economies, labour costs may be a very high proportion of total costs in an organisation. In service sector industries this cost (including National Insurance contributions, the cost of safety at work provisions, etc) might be as high as 75% of total cost. In this sort of climate industrial relations is a very serious concern for both employer and employee.

Given this conflict of interest within a symbiotic relationship, it was inevitable that both workers and employers should have sought to combine their resources in organisations designed to conduct this relationship. Hence the development in capitalist economies over the last 200 years of trade unions on the one hand and employers' associations on the other. In this chapter we will look briefly at the development of these organisations and the methods which they have developed to conduct their relationship in an orderly way. We shall also look briefly at some of the alternative approaches to this fundamental problem which have emerged over the same period. These all involve some degree of industrial democracy, or worker participation in decision making and even ownership of firms.

The basic concept with which we are concerned in this chapter is *collective bargaining*. This is the process by which workers, through their unions, negotiate changes in pay and working conditions with their employers, who are represented by employers' associations.

ESSENTIAL PRINCIPLES

THE EMPLOYER'S VIEW

The employer's objective is to maximise output at minimum unit cost and to prevent disruptions to the production process. To achieve this objective he needs some way of negotiating pay and conditions of work for his employees. He seeks maximum flexibility of working practices and the highest possible level of motivation for his employees to work hard for the company. Elsewhere in this book we outline the various techniques available for this purpose (see Chapter 8). The responsibility for making these arrangements falls to the Personnel Department in conjunction with other functional managers. Adjustments to these arrangements which management may wish to introduce will have to be negotiated with the employees. This is sometimes also the responsibility of the Personnel Manager, although in a very large firm there is normally an Industrial Relations Manager to carry out this function.

The employer must also comply with laws relating to the employment of labour. These include the provisions of the Health and Safety Act and the various Employment Acts. The responsibility for ensuring that these laws are complied with to the satisfaction of Government Inspectors, the Inland Revenue Department and the Social Security Department, lies with the Company Secretary. However, in the case of any dispute, the Personnel Department will be involved.

THE WORKER'S VIEW

The vulnerability of individual employees led to the development of trade unions. These are organisations of workers which exist to protect the interests of workers, individually and collectively in the fields outlined above. The ultimate power of trade unions in carrying out these functions lies in their members' legal right to withdraw their labour. Thus the individual worker sees his union as providing protection against exploitation by employers.

THE VIEW OF THE STATE

In advanced economies the State has long accepted the right of both workers and employers to organise themselves in order to conduct their mutually necessary relationship. In the UK, governments have seen their duty as being to set out a framework of laws within which the dialogue may be conducted with minimum disruption to those members of society who are not party to disputes. In the years up to 1979, the law gradually evolved in such a way as to give considerable immunities in law to the trade unions. Since 1980 the law has been dramatically revised and has greatly reduced the strength of the union movement. Conversely since 1945, successive governments have introduced 'protective' legislation which provides *individual* workers with considerable protection on safety matters, equality of opportunity and employment and redundancy.

> 'Protective' legislation has increased.

The beginnings of the trade union movement may be traced back to the earliest days of the industrial revolution in the late 18th century. Work was being concentrated into factories rather than being done by independent craftsmen in the home. Conditions of work were bad and the earliest combinations of workers were as much concerned with the joint provision of welfare benefits for members as with tackling the employers head on. However, once the Combination Laws were repealed in 1824, workers could act against employers within the law. The first recorded full scale strike occurred in 1825 amongst the worsted industry workers in the West Riding of Yorkshire. The story of the next hundred years is of the gradual removal of legal restrictions on what unions might do. It was also a period when changing economic conditions and industrial technology led to the emergence of trade unions in a growing range of industries and occupations. This culminated with the appearance of unions amongst white collar workers in both industry and public service occupations. By the 1970s the union movement was an important political as well as economic, force. It was sometimes argued that trade unions had been granted too many immunities in law and had too much power. This was said to be damaging the ability of the

> The history of trade unionism.

UK to compete in foreign markets, due to high labour costs, inflexible working practices and excessive disruptions.

By 1980 some 50% of the workforce were members of a union; a record number. However, despite an increase of approximately 2 million in the workforce (including many part-time workers) in the 1980s, by 1990 membership had fallen from 12 million to 8.4 million. This was a result both of deep recession and unemployment and the increasing constraints imposed on unions by law. It is claimed that the decline in the unions' power has resulted in a number of effects on the economy and the business environment. These include:

> **The impact of recession, unemployment and legal constraints.**

- less excessive growth in money wages
- less cost push inflation
- rapid labour productivity growth
- less overmanning in manufacturing industries
- rapid decline in days lost through strike action
- less protection for workers from unscrupulous employers

OBJECTIVES OF TRADE UNIONISM

Several objectives pursued by the trade unions can be classified, some economic and some more general and political. For example:

Industrial objectives

- to improve pay, working conditions and status of employees
- to obtain protection against unfair employment practices and arbitrary management decisions
- to create organisations and attract funds, which makes it possible to take action against employers with a reasonable chance of success
- to attempt to obtain some influence in the decision making process of firms.

Political objectives

These have been pursued by the unions through their association with the Labour Party from its earliest days, and they include:

- full employment
- improved social security provisions
- a voice in national decision making in a pluralist society
- improved public, social and health and education services
- public control, ownership and planning of industrial activity, through nationalisation or regulation

In the pursuit of these objectives by the union movement, a number of different types of trade union developed, whose more specific objectives may differ and possibly produce inter-union conflicts. Such conflicts, for instance may occur over the demarcation line between functions undertaken by workers in different unions. Blurring of boundaries between skilled and unskilled functions as technology changes is a common cause of such disputes. This is seen by employers as a necessary move to greater flexibility. To the union it is 'deskilling' and destructive of jobs. Moreover it is likely to reduce pay levels and to undermine the recruitment base for the union.

> **The decline of multi-unionism.**

In recent years employers have sought to get rid of 'multiunionism', where in a large firm (e.g. Ford of UK) there may be as many as twenty unions in a factory. Instead the employer seeks to achieve a single union agreement and if possible a no-strike agreement. At the very least, the employer would seek to reduce the number of unions present in his factories. The movement in this direction has caused much animosity between unions, and the EETPU (electricians' union) was expelled from the Trades Union Congress as a result of its pursuit of single union deals.

THE TRADES UNION CONGRESS (TUC)

As we have seen earlier in this chapter, the trade unions have sought to work together as a movement in order to achieve wider objectives. The TUC was formed as early as 1868, originally as a forum for craft unions, which were the first to develop. There are at present over 100 member unions, representing some 8.4 million workers. It is mainly concerned with general questions which affect trade unions, both national and international. It participates in discussions on matters relating to the economy as a whole through participation in bodies such as the National Economic Development Office (NEDO). The importance of this function as a pressure group is now much less than it was before 1980 since the Conservative Governments of this period have chosen to largely exclude the TUC from influence on the national stage.

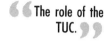 **The role of the TUC.**

Between meetings of the Annual Congress, it is represented by the General Council, which has no power to call strikes, or stop them, but it can offer advice on disputes to member unions, or to employers.

TRADE UNIONS AND THE LAW

It has been pointed out earlier in this chapter that since 1980 changes to the law have greatly changed the climate in which unions have to operate. These changes are summarised below.

Employment Act 1980

- secret ballot, to be funded by the state, required on strike action
- secret ballot for union elections and changes of rules
- illegal to use a 'closed shop' to deny workers union membership
- secondary action by members not involved in a specific dispute leaves them liable to action for damages

Employment Act 1982

- closed shop to be approved by a 'substantial majority' in a ballot of the affected workforce
- where no ballot has been held in a closed shop, anyone dismissed for refusing to join the union may claim 'unfair dismissal' in an Industrial Tribunal hearing
- removes union immunity from action for damages, where acts are committed on behalf of the union which, if committed by an individual, would be actionable

Trade Union Act 1984

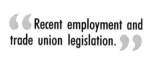 **Recent employment and trade union legislation.**

- where a strike has not been authorised by secret ballot, the union is liable for civil action for damages by the employer

Employment Act 1988

- union members have the right to prevent their union from striking where no ballot has been held
- members have the right not to be disciplined by the union for refusing to take part in such a strike

Code of Practice on Secret Balloting 1990

- has no legal basis itself, but its provisions are admissible evidence in a court of law
- unions should consider whether to call for strike action where there is a low turnout in the ballot
- independent scrutiny of ballots is encouraged to prevent abuse

Employment Act 1990

- limits unofficial action
- makes all forms of secondary action illegal
- should shop stewards call for a strike, the employer may ask the union to repudiate the strike call

■ if the union rejects the strike, the employer may dismiss any unofficial striker one day later

■ if the union does not repudiate a call for unofficial strike action by shop stewards, it may face a court action for damages

EMPLOYERS' ASSOCIATIONS

A definition.

An employers' association is an organisation of employers which sets out to influence, assist or control the industrial relations decision-making progress of member firms. It may also be active in trade matters on their behalf, though this function is sometimes undertaken by a separate trade association. In some cases federations of employers' associations have been formed to act collectively on labour issues.

Small firms are often not members of such associations and some large firms prefer to retain independence, in order to negotiate their own agreements and not be tied to national decisions which might reduce their ability to improve labour productivity. An association may maintain a common strike fund to assist employers hit by disputes and withdrawal of this facility may be used as a disciplinary measure.

In the area of industrial relations, employers' associations carry out two functions:

1   they represent members' interests in dealing with trade unions – negotiating national wage agreements and conditions of employment
2   they handle disputes between member firms and unions

In most cases the agreed national wage is a basic figure which may be supplemented by local agreements on incentive pay, etc.

Like the TUC, the employers' associations represent members' interests on a wider level, to government, EC, etc and also supply information services to members. There are over 300 such associations.

There are also other associations which represent the view of industrial leaders on the wider stage and which are influential in government policy making.

THE CONFEDERATION OF BRITISH INDUSTRY (CBI)

This organisation was formed in 1965. Whilst it has no direct role in industrial relations as such, it is very influential on both government and industry. Its regular surveys of business confidence, for example, are monitored by trade unions as a guide to what the market can stand in the way of pay rises at a particular time. It offers views to government and the public generally on important issues, including industrial relations. It claims to be politically neutral.

Employers' pressure groups.

THE INSTITUTE OF DIRECTORS

This is open for membership by any director of a limited company (as against the company itself being a member in the case of the CBI). It also acts as a pressure group, lobbying government on industrial issues of the day. It is less politically neutral than the CBI.

COLLECTIVE BARGAINING

This is the process of negotiation about wages and conditions of work when undertaken by groups of workers (rather than individual workers) and employers. It is undertaken by unions or groups of unions with employers (often represented by an employers' association). This system of bargaining accounts for about 75% of all employees' pay, including the bulk of public sector workers, where even 90% of managers, professionals and non-manual workers are covered by such negotiations. Only a minority of such workers in the private sector are covered in this way.

Collective bargaining may take place at several levels:

■ in the workplace, between shop stewards and management
■ at the level of the company, between union(s) and management
■ at the level of the industry, between groups of unions and groups of employers.

Company and workplace agreements are usually concerned with piece rates and other incentive payments, which supplement a national agreement. These wider national agreements have become less important in the private sector in recent years, but where they exist they act effectively as a lower benchmark on which local agreements may be built. The more informal system of bargaining at plant or firm level, covers a wider range of issues. Company level bargaining is now often the preferred approach, whilst recession has so weakened the workers' hand that in the recession-hit 1980s 'no bargaining' situations became common. In the public sector national agreements are still the norm, but this is gradually being changed. For example, in the case of teachers' pay, Local Management of School budgets, combined with changes in the national rules on pay, have allowed greater freedom for the use of incentive allowances.

66 National agreements are becoming less important. 99

THE ROLE OF THE STATE

Whilst the state has sought to avoid being directly involved in collective bargaining, except in the public sector where it is (directly or indirectly) the employer, it has, over the years provided two systems which seek to deal with specific situations. Thus since 1912 there have existed Wages Councils for certain industries and since 1974 there has been a service of conciliation and arbitration available to break deadlock in national negotiations.

66 A limited role. 99

WAGES COUNCILS

66 'Minimum wage legislation'. 99

These are established by law in certain industries where it is difficult for workers to be organised and where their position in negotiation is weak (e.g. catering workers, shop workers and agricultural workers). They are established to fix minimum wages for the industry. They do involve negotiations with employers and unions, but they also include independent members to break any deadlock and their awards are legally binding and are enforced by an Inspectorate. In recent years the government has weakened Wages Councils by removing their statutory control over minimum wages for juvenile workers.

ADVISORY CONCILIATION AND ARBITRATION SERVICE (ACAS)

This body was established in 1974 in order to assist industry and unions to solve industrial relations problems. It seeks to act through voluntary cooperation and is free. Its main functions are:

- provision of conciliation services. That is, bringing the two parties to a dispute together where deadlock has occurred and seeking to assist them in reaching an agreed solution. Approximately 80% success is achieved.

66 The role of ACAS. 99

- Mediation is provided where conciliation has failed. The two sides remain separate, and a neutral third party is provided to act as go-between until grounds can be reached on which the two sides can come together to negotiate.

- Arbitration. This is offered where other measures have failed to bring agreement. A neutral third party will hear evidence from both sides before handing down a binding decision. This service is provided by the Central Arbitration Committee (set up in 1975) which also deals with trade union recognition problems and equal pay issues.

OTHER LEGISLATION AND DIRECTIVES

Legislation passed by the UK Parliament and Directives from the Commission of the EC, provide a floor for workers' rights and may thus also influence the collective bargaining process. Some examples include:

Health and Safety laws

These may have the effect of imposing strict rules on employers about the conduct of their business which otherwise the unions would have to fight for. By law all workplaces with above 25 employees must have a Safety Committee which will include union representatives. Its function is to ensure that safety rules, for example about safety clothing and machinery guards, are complied with by the employer, who is subject to inspection by government.

66 'Protective' legislation. 99

Anti-discrimination laws

These may require that women receive equal pay for equal work, that racial discrimination in employment is illegal and that all workplaces above a certain size must employ a given percentage of disabled workers.

Employment Acts

These require that all workers be provided with a contract which states clearly their job description. They also provide the right to seek justice from an Industrial Tribunal in the case of alleged unfair dismissal.

All these and other laws provide statutory rights which otherwise the unions would have to fight for. In this sense, despite recent weakening of the bargaining power of unions, their members are better protected than ever before.

DISPUTES AND STRIKES

INDUSTRIAL DISPUTES

These occur when a dispute arises between an employer and one or more employees. Officially under current law, a 'dispute' can only officially exist between a worker and his *own* employer. At workplace, firm and national level there exists 'machinery' through which disputes may be settled. That is, there has to be an agreed set of 'procedural rules' which dictate the stages through which the dispute goes. These in themselves may cause disputes, especially when one side feels that the other has unilaterally ignored or broken these rules.

The purpose of these procedural rules is to provide a means by which 'substantive rules' may be agreed upon. These are the terms on which a dispute is settled, be it about wages, or a disciplinary matter affecting only one worker.

The potential for disputes exists at all times in any organisation and the process of industrial relations is a continuing one. It only becomes news when it breaks down. A dispute may arise over any of the following matters:

- pay
- conditions of work
- contracts of employment
- allocation of work
- discipline in the work place
- breaches of procedural rules

INDUSTRIAL ACTION

These are measures taken by workers or employers in pursuit of a dispute which has not been amicably settled via the normal procedural rules. They are actions taken in order to win concessions from the other side and they include the following which fall short of an all-out strike:

- Overtime ban. A refusal to work hours beyond those in contract.
- Work to rule. Workers follow their employers' rules so precisely that they are deliberately inefficient.
- Go slow. Workers deliberately work slower than is customary.

These measures are very effective in certain kinds of business, and have the advantage of not costing either the workers or the union anything much in lost wages or strike pay. They are most used in the public sector such as British Rail or the Post Office.

Strikes

A strike is where workers withdraw their labour completely. This measure is designed to force the employer's hand through loss of production and vital orders. It is the ultimate weapon of the workers, although in recent years its use has been curtailed by legislation. Thus unofficial 'lightning strikes' are now banned by law.

As you can see from Table 15.1, the effects of strikes are always damaging to the economy as a whole and to the individual consumer. However, there are reasons why the unions, and even the employers may feel that a strike is advantageous to them. The latter point may seem a little odd, but the miner's strike of 1984/5 was an example of a strike which benefitted the employer much more than the striker and it was suggested at the time that it was deliberately engineered by the Coal Board, together with the Government. An employer could also benefit from a strike in a recession by cutting wage costs and running down excess stocks.

66 Strikes may benefit employers. 99

The consequences of strikes

These may be summarised as follows:

EFFECT ON	DAMAGING EFFECTS	BENEFICIAL EFFECTS

Employers	Loss of output
	Reduction in sales/revenue
	Loss of customers
	Cash flow problems
	Harm to reputation
	Disruption of work
	Permanent loss of worker
	   cooperation
		Cut surplus stocks
		Cut wage bill
		Improve cash flow
		Get rid of trouble-makers
		Impose more favourable contract of
		   employment

Customers	Inconvenience Shortages	
The Economy	Loss of exports Import penetration Decline in tax yield Additional claims on social services Loss of confidence in sterling	
The Strikers	Reduction in income in short term Threat to jobs long term Domestic stress	Rise in long term income if they win and/or better employment contract

Other Firms	Reduction in income in the area
	   reduces trade
	Difficulty in buying essential inputs
		Damage done to competitors who
		   suffer the strike

Table 15.1 The consequences of strikes

INDUSTRIAL DEMOCRACY

This is a general term to describe a number of theories about the government of industry and schemes for reorganising industrial management. It involves some degree of decision-making power by workers, or their representatives. The history of the idea may be traced back to the late 19th century and in the UK to the work of a group called the *Guild Socialists*. After the First World War, reformers, influenced by their ideas, generated a number of schemes to bring about new machinery for the conduct of industrial relations. In the UK the most recent consideration was the report of the Bullock Committee in 1977. This saw no contradiction between boardroom representation of workers and the normal process of collective bargaining. However, the Committee was not able to agree on a format for bringing about greater representation of workers on boards of companies. Furthermore, as a result of opposition from both employers and unions the idea was quietly shelved.

This failure is symptomatic of the inability of British industry and unions to achieve greater worker participation in decision-making beyond that already available on the limited range of issues through collective bargaining (which is in essence confrontational rather than cooperative in nature). Nevertheless worker participation is regarded as normal in Germany (see Table 15.2) and is seen there as a major reason for their industrial success. In different ways the Japanese have also achieved worker involvement, but without formal representation on boards. They too have achieved great industrial success by harnessing worker co-operation in the enterprise.

Joint Consultation.

Current thinking in the UK is that Joint Consultation is the way forward. The objective is to provide a two-way communication channel which would permit:

- management to inform employees of the firm's progress, plans and policy
- workers to have a say in decisions which affect them

In Germany the law requires that:
- every company with over five employees must have a work's council to resolve disputes within the firm.
- every firm with over 100 employees must have an economic committee which meets to discuss any matters which may adversely affect worker interests such as mergers, changes in technology and production methods, company structure. Work's councils are responsible for resolving conflicts occurring in the economic committee.
- where the company employs over 2,000 workers, a two-tier board provides for representation of workers at that level. An upper supervisory board comprised of worker and shareholder representatives (five each) plus an independent member agreed by both. The lower board is made up of management representatives.

Table 15.2 Worker participation in Germany

- suggestions to be made by workers for increasing productivity
- development of greater understanding between the two 'sides' of industry

MODELS OF INDUSTRIAL DEMOCRACY

It is possible to identify a number of ways in which industrial democracy could be achieved. For example:

Worker control

Where the workforce is the sole source of authority, even though the enterprise may be owned by the state. This model is inconceivable in the UK.

Worker co-operation

Here the workers both own and control the enterprise. Total involvement in decision making is only possible up to about 24 members, after that some delegation to specialist managers is unavoidable and direct democracy is lost. Consequently most examples are small. Large scale co-operative activity is, however, possible as illustrated in the Mondragon area of Spain where 20,000 workers are employed in a variety of co-operative ventures.

Worker directors

Representatives of the workforce sit on the board. Unless they have equal representation, as in Germany, the worker director is likely to be accused of having no power and only being a token representative. Worker directors are not expected to have involvement with detailed operational decisions, they are concerned with policy making.

Collective bargaining

As practised in the UK this is, in a way, industrial democracy in that the employer gives up sole decision-making rights over important areas of the business.

Employee participation (or involvement)

This has been the approach adopted in the UK. It moves away from the worker having decision-making powers and reduces his input to influencing, rather than making, decisions. The aim is to harness the energy and knowledge of the workforce for the benefit of the company and to give the worker a sense of involvement in the future of the business. This is closer to the Japanese approach than the European. It is also believed that this level of involvement will improve industrial relations generally. The approach may be based on formal joint consultation machinery, or on the creation of semi-autonomous work groups with considerable control over the daily operation of work stations. Workers in such groups are 'empowered' to allocate tasks amongst the group, order materials, control the flow of production, undertake routine maintenance and housekeeping activities and monitoring of quality standards. They may also voluntarily join *Quality Circles* which meet regularly in company time in order to seek ways of improving the production process or product (see Chapter 20). More formal joint consultation machinery could be seen as irrelevant and time-wasting by both sides, since the workers have no real decision-making power or authority. Trade unions may also see such schemes as threatening to their role as representative of the workers' interests, through collective bargaining of the traditional kind.

Employee ownership

Some interesting experimental schemes have emerged in recent years in the UK. Some companies (ICI for example) have, for many years, offered annual bonuses to permanent employees in the form of company shares, to increase commitment to the firm's interests. Since no decision-making or even consultation process is involved, these schemes are useful but not radical. A more exciting experiment was the 'employee buy-out' of National Freight when it was privatised. In this case only employees were allowed to buy shares in the new company. The increased involvement of the workers combined with charismatic leadership produced a remarkable turn round into profit.

EXAMINATION QUESTIONS

1   Differentiate between the role of a foreman and a shop steward. Would the qualities required for the effective performance of each role different significantly?   (25)
(UCLES 1987)

2   'The main obstacle to change in manufacturing industry in the UK is still multi-unionism whereby each group of workers is represented by different trade unions.' Discuss.
(25)
(UCLES 1989)

TUTOR'S ANSWER

Question 1

The foreman (referred to in manufacturing environments as 'supervisor') is an employee charged with the responsibility for controlling and monitoring the work of other employees. Given the assumption of a 'span of control' extending to at most six workers, the ratio of foremen to workers is likely to be 1–6 approximately, in a traditional factory environment. The foreman is accountable to a line manager, several of whom in turn report to a Production Manager. The foreman's task is to ensure that workers fulfil work targets set by the Production Manager. They are likely to have a degree of role uncertainty since they have little authority in their own right. Their cultural loyalty is likely to be to former fellow line workers, of which they were one themselves originally but their official loyalty must be to management objectives. They are therefore usually on the receiving end of criticism from both sides, workers seeing them as agents of the boss and managers as members of the workforce. In a modern factory environment, based on Total Quality approach, their role has changed significantly. They must be better trained and are seen as facilitators and coaches of the team of workers under their supervision. They have more authority devolved to them and are faced with a new source of stress, since they may take time to become accustomed to this degree of responsibility.

In contrast the shop steward represents the workers directly in their relationship with managers and in all negotiations on industrial relations problems, be they over pay, working practices and conditions, safety welfare, etc. They are elected by colleagues within union membership in a workplace. In a large factory there will be a shop stewards' committee composed of representatives of each workshop and led by a Convenor, who is the chief mouthpiece of the workers' point of view. Their efforts in negotiation within the factory supplement the work of the union on a wider front in collective bargaining procedures. Under current trade union law they are less able to act independently and perhaps irresponsibly without reference to Regional or National trade union officials. Thus they are less able to call for lightning strikes or other industrial action. Their role has therefore also become more that of facilitator conducting an ongoing dialogue with management, in some cases being given time (and resources) off the job to do so. Where more than one union is present in a plant (multi-unionism), as is often the case in the UK, a joint shop stewards' committee may exist, to pursue workers' claims collectively in negotiation with management.

The qualities required for these two roles will differ sharply, especially in an old-fashioned factory environment with a very confrontational style. The foreman will be chosen by management with certain characteristics in mind. It will be expected that he is very experienced in the tasks in his work area, but not necessarily specifically trained by the firm for his new role. He will be chosen because he is seen as reliable, i.e. likely to put the firm's interests first at all times, no matter how disadvantageous this may be for the workers. It is likely that the employer will look for a man with some authority amongst his workmates, either through experience and skill, or personal strength and leadership skills. He is likely therefore to be conformist, authoritarian but subservient to management. He is likely to be an older employee and not to be a keen union man.

In total contrast the shop steward is elected by his work mates, not chosen. In a plant with a tradition of activism, he is likely to be radical, anti-authoritarian and possibly have socialist principles. He may or may not be a skilled and effective worker, but he is likely to be self-educated at least sufficiently to challenge the employer on matters of employment law, etc. In a more apathetic plant, he may be reluctantly 'volunteered' by his workmates, being the one least strong enough to say no. In the 1970s when union activism was at its height some large manufacturing firms took the view that it made sense to conduct a dialogue with shop stewards, on the basis that it was easier to negotiate with one worker representative than hundreds of individuals. In this situation, it is likely that the shop steward, given time and facilities by the employer to undertake this role as worker representative, becomes in a sense a member of 'management'. He may then become nearer in character to the foreman and in his role. The key difference remains that the essential skill for the foreman is to lead, or manage workers to achieve targets which they may resent and to organise and direct their efforts. The shop steward must above all be a good negotiator, preferably with leadership skills.

In a modern factory run on Japanese lines, with either no union presence or a single union and possibly with a no-strike agreement in place, the roles of the two converge. Indeed, the shop steward becomes irrelevant most of the time, since the workers have greater control over their working lives and the foreman has become coach and facilitator.

OUTLINE ANSWER

Question 2

This quotation overstates the case. There are many obstacles to necessary change in British industry, of which multi-unionism is one, but perhaps not the only or main one. The changes needed in much of British industry centre around the need to be more competitive both in export and domestic markets. To achieve this competitiveness various changes are required. Products need to be more competitively priced and thus greater control over production costs is required. This may require more investment in modern computer-controlled and robotic machines. The 'short termism' of the UK banking system may inhibit firms from taking the long term view necessary for this change. Short term returns are also more important to large institutional shareholders. The control of inventory costs by use of Just in Time (JIT) may well involve this sort of long term capital investment. As markets become more sophisticated and consumer requirements more exacting and varied, so competition on non-price factors such as delivery, service and above all quality, become more important. These changes may only be achieved through a major cultural change in the organisation. The flexibility required of the workforce and the control of wage costs in an inflationary climate, do require changes in industrial relations practices. This is where multi-unionism becomes a problem.

Multi-unionism is the presence in a firm or plant of a number of potentially competing unions, together with the use of collective bargaining on an industry scale. It makes negotiations very difficult for the employer, since apart from the problems of the annual pay round, there may arise disputes over demarcation between jobs (which inhibits flexible working), pay differentials between groups of workers and disciplinary matters. The recent move towards single union agreements and the decline in the power of the union movement through legislative changes, have reduced the problem. However, the process of achieving single union agreements may be difficult and in the short term damaging to the company. There may therefore be some reluctance on the part of management to attempt the change. In other cases management may feel that divisions between unions in the plant make them easier to control than a powerful single union would be.

FURTHER READING

Cumming, *Personal Management*, 5th edition, Heinemann 1985:
    Chapter 14, The Framework of Industrial Relations.
    Chapter 15, Labour Relations at the Workplace.
Graham (revised: Bennett), *Human Resources Management*, 6th edition, M & E Handbooks 1989:
    Chapter 25, Industrial Relations.
Griffiths and Wall (eds.), *Applied Economics*, 4th edition, Longman:
    Chapter 20, Trade unions, wages and collective bargaining.

GETTING STARTED

Accountancy has been defined as 'the process or art of recording and verifying accounts'. This in itself is not very informative. More helpful would be to view accountancy in much broader terms as a database of information about the activities of an organisation which is expressed in monetary terms. In Chapter 10 we saw how statistical information could be presented in a suitable format for a specific purpose. Accounting information can be viewed in exactly the same way. It must answer three important questions:

- What information is needed?
- Who is the information for?
- What form should the information take?

This approach should help students overcome the mental barriers which often come down at the mention of 'accountancy'.

The information required is concerned with profits, growth, liquidity and solvency which is needed in order to help effective decision-making. The role of the accountant is to record and account for transactions over a period of time and to communicate or report the resulting information.

Who requires the information? Two groups, one internal and one external, are interested in the performance of an organisation. The internal group is comprised of the owners, the managers and the employees. Owners, both existing and potential, want to know how their investment has performed and what its future prospects are. Managers require financial information in order to review the success of past decisions and to help formulate and control future plans. Finally, the employees are interested with respect to job security and the company's ability to meet pay claims. The external group includes the government and creditors. The government requires financial information to verify tax liabilities, and creditors are interested in order to assess the credit-worthiness of the organisation.

With all these needs to satisfy, what form should the information take? The volume and detail of business information is so immense that whatever form is chosen it must be condensed. In this chapter we will look at the three principal statements; the Balance sheet, the Income statement (or Profit and Loss Account) and the Funds flow statement.

Accountancy has two distinct branches; one accounts for what has happened in the past. This is the role of financial accounting and will be the content of this chapter. The other, cost and management accountancy, aids the planning and control of present and future events. This is covered in Chapter 18. Chapter 17 will deal with the analysis and interpretation of accounts as well as the controversial issues dealing with depreciation and stock valuation.

CHAPTER 16

FINANCIAL ACCOUNTING

THE REGULATORY FRAMEWORK

THE DOUBLE-ENTRY SYSTEM

THE BALANCE SHEET

PROFIT AND LOSS STATEMENT

FUNDS FLOW STATEMENT

ADDITIONAL STATEMENTS

ESSENTIAL PRINCIPLES

THE REGULATORY FRAMEWORK

The production of financial accounts is largely governed by three sets of influences; accounting concepts, accounting conventions and legislation. These have been developed over the years so that different accountants producing accounts for different organisations in various activities can do so using similar methods.

ACCOUNTING CONCEPTS

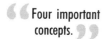 *Four important concepts.*

There are four basic assumptions which underlie the production of a set of accounts.

- *Going concern:* the organisation is assumed to be an enterprise that will 'continue in business for the foreseeable future'. In practical terms this means valuing assets at cost on the assumption they are worth at least that amount. If a business were planning to close down, the most important information would be *realisable value* (value if sold) of the assets, which might be less or more than cost, e.g. machinery and land.

- *Consistency:* this means adopting the same procedure every time for recording and measuring items. If this were not followed the comparison of accounts from one period to another would be meaningless.

- *Accruals or matching concept:* this concept recognises revenues and costs as they are *earned* or *incurred* rather than as money is *received* or *paid*. The income statement is prepared for a uniform time period and the accountant must ensure that revenues and expenses of activities undertaken in that period are matched within that period.

- *Prudence or conservatism:* this concept is designed to balance the natural optimism of the businessman! It encourages the accountant to be prudent by recognising revenue only when it is realised in an acceptable form whilst providing for all expenses and losses as soon as they are known. For example, if a company gives a potential customer a quotation for some building work, the amount quoted could not be treated as a sale. When a sales invoice is eventually raised, the 'sale' can be recognised.

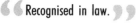 *Recognised in law.*

These four concepts are so fundamental that the Companies Act of 1985 has afforded them statutory force, insisting that they are complied with by all limited liability companies.

ACCOUNTING CONVENTIONS

Many conventions have been adopted over the years as tried and trusted 'rules of thumb'. Five principal ones are:

Five important conventions.

- *Objectivity:* as far as possible accounts should be based on facts which are measurable and can be independently verified.

- *Separate entity:* the company is recognised as a legal 'person' in its own right entirely separate from its owners and managers.

- *Money measurement:* all company assets and liabilities are measured in a common unit, money. Intangible assets such as goodwill and management skill which are of value to the company are left out of the accounts, as they cannot accurately be measured in money terms.

- *Historic cost:* all items are valued at cost. Where items fall in value through use they are depreciated or written down in value. Note however that freehold land and buildings are *revalued* at intervals, with the surplus or deficit on revaluation being reflected in the accounts.

- *Double-entry:* all transactions involve two sides: giving and receiving. This is acknowledged in the double-entry system of book-keeping where the acquisition of funds is balanced by the use made of them.

LEGAL AND OTHER REQUIREMENTS

Some concepts and conventions are so fundamental that they have been incorporated into legislation and/or the code of practice of the professional accountancy bodies.

■ Companies Acts 1985 and 1989. These acts dictate certain criteria which all limited companies must adhere to in the preparation of their published financial information statements. The company accounts must be verified by an independent audit.

SSAP's and FRS's.

■ Statements of Standard Accounting Practice. These statements have been issued by a consortium of the main UK accounting bodies (including the Institutes of Chartered Accountants). They cover various aspects of accounting which may historically have been (or still remain) contentious or controversial, e.g. depreciation, stock valuation, taxation etc. From 1992, they will gradually be replaced by Financial Reporting Standards (FRS's).

All these influences, concepts, conventions and legislation are concerned with ensuring that the information statements present a 'TRUE AND FAIR VIEW' of the organisation and its performance.

THE DOUBLE-ENTRY SYSTEM

Assets = Liabilities.

As stated earlier, there are always two parties involved in a transaction, a giver (a provider of resources) and a receiver (a user of resources). This dual relationship is at the heart of recording business transactions and is typified by the 'accounting equation'. This equation states that all Assets (Uses of funds) must be balanced by an equal amount of Liabilities (Sources of funds). This is best explained by way of a simple business example.

Example.

XYZ Co is established by shareholders with an issued capital of £10,000.
By convention we write liabilities on the left-hand side and assets on the right-hand side.
The preliminary entries will be:

Liabilities (Source of Funds)	Assets (Use of Funds)
£	£
Shareholders' Funds 10,000	Cash 10,000

In the first week of trading this company is involved in the following transactions:

■ A £3,000 van is bought for cash

■ £5,000 stock is bought on credit

■ £1,000 is paid to suppliers

■ A bank overdraft is used to pay a further £2,000 to creditors.

How do these transactions affect the accounting equation? The purchase of the van will increase one asset, vehicle, by decreasing another asset, cash, leaving the equation still in balance. The acquisition of stock on credit will increase an asset, stock, by £5,000 but at the same time create a liability, creditors, also by £5,000.

A part-payment to suppliers of £1,000 will reduce the asset of cash and also reduce liability of creditors by that amount. Finally, the raising of an overdraft will increase one liability, bank overdraft, in order to reduce another liability, creditors. The double entry system will now produce a record as in Table 16.1.

LIABILITIES	(£)	ASSETS	(£)
Shareholders' Funds	10,000	Cash	6,000
Creditors	2,000	Stock	5,000
Bank overdraft	2,000	Vehicles	3,000
	14,000		14,000

Table 16.1 Simple balance sheet

These transactions illustrate the four possible ways a balance sheet can be affected by the double-entry system. A summary of these is given in Table 16.2.

Essential to understand the effect of transactions.

TRANSACTION		EFFECT
Cash purchase of vehicle		Asset –
		Asset +
Credit purchase of stock	Liability +	Asset +
Part-payment of suppliers	Liability –	Asset –
Part-payment of creditors by means of bank overdraft	Liability–	
	Liability +	

Table 16.2 Impacts of double entry system on balance sheet

How then do we account for a profit or a loss? If the stock of £5,000 is sold for £8,000 then the asset side will increase by a further £3,000, the profit from trade. But who does the profit belong to? The answer is the shareholders whose claim on the business (the shareholders' funds) would rise by the amount of the profit, thus restoring the balance of the accounting equation. A loss on trade would have the opposite effect, reducing assets and reducing shareholders' funds.

The principle of double entry is applied to all the accounting records of an organisation. For examination purposes students must remember that each transaction will affect the accounting equation in such a way as always to remain in balance.

THE BALANCE SHEET

The Balance Sheet is a statement of the financial position of an organisation at a given date.

It shows the organisation's resources on that date in terms of what it owns and what it owes, i.e. its assets and liabilities. Money and resources have been provided by the owners (shareholders) and creditors which have been invested in various assets. The organisation is responsible for repayment or safekeeping of these funds. The money owed to creditors is known as *Liabilities* and that of the owners as *Shareholders' Funds*. In this section the student should become familiar with the contents of the Balance Sheet and its presentation.

> A snap-shot of the company's position on one particular day.

CONTENT OF THE BALANCE SHEET

> Where do the funds come from; how are they used?

In simple terms the Balance Sheet is made up of two elements, a source of funds and a use of funds. The source of funds is normally divided into two sections, Shareholders' Funds and Liabilities, while the use of funds details the assets acquired. This can be summarised in Table 16.3 using the traditional horizontal format.

> Traditional Balance Sheet layout.

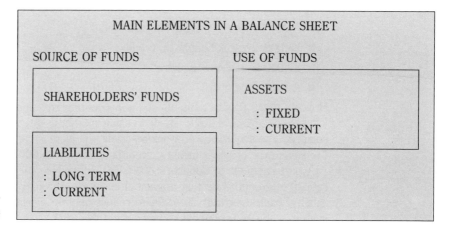

Table 16.3 Horizontal format for balance sheet

As can be seen, each section can be further divided to provide more and more detail. This is further itemised in the section below.

Shareholders' Funds

This is the permanent capital of the organisation, as its primary role is to provide finance towards the running of the business. It can take many forms, the most common of which in limited liability companies are:

- *Ordinary Share Capital:* represents funds invested in the company in return for part ownership of the company. Often referred to as 'equity'. The total number of shares allowed to be issued is called the *Authorised Share Capital* which may differ from the number actually sold, the *Issued Share Capital*. Each share has a nominal value, usually 25p.

- *Reserves:* These can take three forms; share premiums, revaluations and retained profits. Share premiums occur when a company issues shares which are sold for a price higher than their nominal value. Revaluations take account of assets (usually land and buildings) whose current value is greater than the historic cost because of inflation. Retained profits are those profits which the company directors have decided not to distribute as dividends but to retain in order to finance future operations.

Retained profits account for approximately 60% of the financial requirements of UK companies.

Liabilities

A liability represents any monetary amount owed by the organisation to another party. As we have seen, Shareholders' Funds is one form of liability, the other forms being termed long-term liabilities and current liabilities, each of which can be further divided into component parts.

> At least 12 months before repayment is required.

- *Long-term liabilities:* these are borrowings which are not due to be repaid for at least 12 months. They comprise long-term bank loans and *debentures*, which (for public limited companies) are borrowings from the public and are listed on the Stock Exchange in the same manner as ordinary shares. Long-term loans may often be secured against the company's assets.

> To be paid within 12 months.

- *Current liabilities:* these are debts which require payment within 12 months of the balance sheet date. They comprise four main types:

    1 *Creditors:* this covers goods and services received which have yet to be paid for.
    2 *Bank Overdraft:* this occurs when the bank allows the company to withdraw funds in excess of its present balance. They are legally repayable 'on demand' and are therefore included as a current liability, even when such arrangements may last for a longer period.
    3 *Taxation:* this comprises the corporation tax levied on the current period's profits which is due for payment in the next year.
    4 *Dividends payable:* an amount of profit set aside to cover the proposed final dividend. Once it has received approval at the company's A.G.M. it can be paid to shareholders.

Assets

These are items owned by the business and can be of two forms; tangible and intangible. Intangibles include such things as management skills or the goodwill of the customers and as such are not normally shown in the Balance Sheet. The tangible assets are broadly divided into fixed and current assets.

> Remain in their present state for long term use.

- *Fixed assets:* these are the long-term resources of the business which are designated to be used for more than one accounting period. They include such items as property, plant and machinery, fixtures and fittings, office equipment and vehicles.

> Constantly changing their form.

- *Current assets:* these comprise short-term resources which will be used up or change their form during the next 12 months. When current liabilities are deducted, the resulting total is often referred to as *working capital* or *circulating capital* because they constantly change form from cash to stock to debtors and back to cash again. This is the life-cycle of the business. The constituent parts will be stocks (raw materials, work-in-progress and finished goods), debtors (amounts owed to the company) and cash (both cash in hand and cash at the bank).

Presentation of the balance sheet

Table 16.3 illustrates the traditional layout of the balance sheet which is presented in a *horizontal* form. The components are always listed in reverse order of liquidity, i.e. the least liquid asset, or longest-term liability, is at the top and the most liquid asset, or shortest term liability, at the bottom.

> Modern Balance Sheet layout.

Table 16.4 is an example of the contemporary *vertical* format where liabilities are listed below assets (or vice versa). The only other difference is that current assets and current liabilities are grouped together to produce a net difference known as net current assets or working capital. When this total is added to Fixed assets we have *Net Assets Employed*, which is more informative than 'total assets' because a large proportion of stock may be owed to creditors or be financed by a bank overdraft.

PROFIT AND LOSS STATEMENT

The Profit and Loss Statement (sometimes called the Income Statement) shows the revenues and expenses and the resulting profit or loss for a given period of time (normally a year). The student must understand clearly the accountant's use of the terms revenue, expenses and profit as well as appreciating the format of the profit and loss statement.

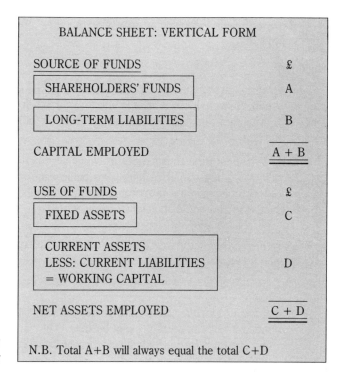

BALANCE SHEET: VERTICAL FORM

SOURCE OF FUNDS	£
SHAREHOLDERS' FUNDS	A
LONG-TERM LIABILITIES	B
CAPITAL EMPLOYED	A + B

USE OF FUNDS	£
FIXED ASSETS	C
CURRENT ASSETS LESS: CURRENT LIABILITIES = WORKING CAPITAL	D
NET ASSETS EMPLOYED	C + D

N.B. Total A+B will always equal the total C+D

Table 16.4 Vertical format for balance sheet

REVENUE

> A presentation of the performance of the company over a period of time.

Definition: Revenue is the total exchange value of the goods or services of a business which have been transferred to a customer in return for cash or some other asset, e.g. debtors. The following important points need to be known about revenue:

- The 'Realisation Concept' in accounting recognises a sale (hence a claim to revenue) on acceptance of legal liability for payment by the buyer. Revenue can be in the form, therefore, of either cash payments or amounts owing (debtors).

> Revenue ≠ Receipts.

- Revenue is not the same as receipts. Revenue refers to the *income earned in that financial period*, whereas receipts may include earnings from other periods.

- Revenue is always stated exclusive of any taxes, e.g. Value Added Tax.

EXPENSES

These represent the amounts charged against profit in respect of goods and services consumed during an accounting period.

- The 'matching principle' or 'accruals concept' states that from the revenues of a period must be deducted all the expenses of the benefits used in producing that revenue. In a similar way to revenue and receipts, expenses are not the same as *payments*. Expenses refer only to those costs associated with the goods or services sold in the period, whereas payments may include items from previous periods, or advanced expenditure for costs to be incurred in later periods.

> Expenses ≠ payments.

- Direct or product costs are those costs which can be accurately attributed to and identified with specific goods, e.g. raw materials, direct labour and some production overheads.

- Indirect or period costs are those overhead expenses which are not easily identified with a given output but refer to a period of time, e.g. selling and administrative costs.

- Product and period costs referring to items sold in an accounting period are known as revenue expenditure.

PROFIT

> Profit = Revenue – Expenses.

In its simplest form profit is the excess of revenue over expenses. If expenses are greater than revenues then a loss (i.e. negative profit) results. However, there are many different definitions of profit which can be best appreciated with reference to the presentation of the Profit and Loss Statement.

PRESENTATION OF THE PROFIT AND LOSS STATEMENT

The overall statement can be divided into three parts:

■ the trading account

❝Three important stages.❞

■ the profit and loss account

■ the appropriation account

The trading account

This details the sales revenue of the period less operating expenses to give a trading or operating profit as shown in Table 16.5. Much of the detail given in Table 16.5 would be omitted from published accounts (i.e. those accounts sent to shareholders etc.) but would be included in even greater detail for statements prepared for internal use.

THE TRADING ACCOUNT

			£
SALES REVENUE			A
LESS Cost of Goods Sold			
Materials	B		
Direct Labour	C		
Production overheads	D		
	B+C+D	=	E
GROSS PROFIT		A−E =	F

Table 16.5 Trading account

The profit and loss account

The profit and loss account starts with the gross profit, deducts overhead expenditure (e.g. selling and administrative expenses) to arrive at an operating profit and then adds any income from non-operating sources, e.g. interest and dividends from financial holdings to arrive at a total profit figure. From this total is deducted interest (the cost of financing the firm's operations). The final figure is the profit before taxation (often known as the 'net profit'). The layout is given in Table 16.6

THE PROFIT AND LOSS ACCOUNT

			£
GROSS PROFIT			A
LESS Selling expenses	B		
Administrative costs	C		
	B+C	=	D
TRADING (OPERATING PROFIT)	A−D	=	E
ADD: NON-OPERATING INCOME			F
TOTAL PROFIT BEFORE INTEREST AND TAX	E+F	=	G
LESS: interest			H
PROFIT BEFORE TAX	G−H	=	I

Table 16.6 Profit and loss account

The appropriation account

The appropriation account shows how the Profit is distributed or 'appropriated'. Some of the profit earned will be appropriated by the government as taxation. Part of the remaining after-tax profit will be distributed to shareholders in the form of dividends. The balance remaining is retained in the business to help finance future operations. This retained profit belongs to the shareholders and is added to Shareholders' Funds in the Balance Sheet under the section *Reserves*. The retained profit (or loss) is therefore the link between the Balance sheet of one period and the next; a profitable year adds to the wealth of the business but a loss reduces the net worth of the business.

THE APPROPRIATION ACCOUNT

		£
PROFIT BEFORE TAX		A
LESS TAX		B
PROFIT AFTER TAX	A–B =	C
LESS ORDINARY DIVIDENDS		D
RETAINED PROFIT (LOSS)	C–D =	E

Table 16.7 Appropriation account

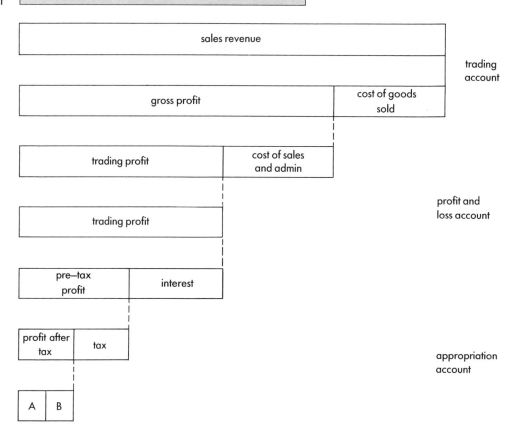

Fig. 16.1 Profit and loss statement

A = retained profits   B = ordinary dividends

Dividends are an appropriation of profits, *not* an expense against profits.

N.B. a common mistake of students is to view dividend payments as an 'expense'. They are not an 'expense' to be charged against profit but a distribution of profit already earned. Figure 16.1 shows the format for an overall Profit and Loss Statement combining the three accounts. This is how the results are normally published although not all the detail is revealed.

FUNDS FLOW STATEMENT

A company must be able to pay its short-term debts.

The main long-term objective of a business is to make a profit but in order to do this it must remain solvent in the short-term. The business must possess adequate liquid funds (cash in hand, at the bank or cash equivalents less liabilities due within the year) in order to finance its current operations. Rapidly growing firms often suffer from 'over-trading' i.e. accepting more business than it can adequately finance. If a firm does not possess sufficient funds to meet its short-term commitments, such as payments to suppliers and the bank, it can be forced to close. It is vital, therefore, for a firm to keep a close control of the flow of funds in a period so that it ensures the anticipated outflows are adequately covered by anticipated inflows. The Funds Flow statement details from where the sources of funds were obtained and how they were used or applied.

The main sources of funds are:

Sources of funds.

- Net profit (suitably adjusted for non-cash expenses such as depreciation, which does not result in an outflow of cash)
- Issue of new shares (extra Shareholders' Funds)
- Raising of long-term debt or loans

- Sale of fixed assets or investments

The main application or use of funds are:

- Purchase of new fixed assets
- Payment of dividends

66 Use of funds. 99

- Payments of taxes
- Repayments of debt
- Covering operating losses

The total sources of funds less the total of uses of funds will give the net increase or decrease in funds during the year and represents the overall change in working capital such as stock, debtors, trade creditors and cash. In other words, it will account for the difference between the Balance sheet at the beginning of the period and that at the end. A typical Funds Flow statement is shown in Table 16.8

FUNDS FLOW STATEMENT

XYZ Co. Ltd.
(1991)

	1991	
	(£'000)	(£'000)
SOURCES OF FUNDS		
PROFIT BEFORE TAX	30	
Add: Depreciation	10	
		40
Share issue proceeds	20	
Long-term loan	10	30
		70
USES OF FUNDS		
Taxation paid	15	
Dividends paid	10	25
New fixed assets purchased	5	
		30
NET INCREASE IN FUNDS IN YEAR		40
NET INCREASE IN WORKING CAPITAL		
Stocks	30	
Debtors	20	
Creditors	(5)	
Cash	(5)	
		40

Table 16.8 Funds Flow Statement

In the example XYZ Co. Ltd. has obtained extra funds of £70,000 from internal sources (Profit) and external sources (share issue and loans). £25,000 has been used to pay tax and dividends due during the year while £5,000 has been spent on acquiring new fixed assets. This net increase in funds of £40,000 is matched by a £50,000 build up in stocks and debtors, a £5,000 increase in credit available from suppliers and a £5,000 reduction in cash holdings.

The use and advantages of Funds Flow statements are:

- they indicate the solvency (or insolvency) of a business
- they indicate where improvements could be made in working capital
- they indicate resources available for capital investment
- they can be used as a basis to forecast future liquidity requirements in the next financial period

CASH FLOW STATEMENTS

From March 1992, public companies have been required by a Financial Reporting Standard to present a *Cash Flow Statement* instead of a Source and Application of Funds Statement. This places far greater emphasis on the cash inflows or outflows in an accounting period.

An example statement is shown in Table 16.9.

SANDAL PLC		
Cash flow statement for the year ended 30 April 1992		
	£000	£000
Net cash inflow from operating activities		4,765
Returns on investment and servicing of finance		
Interest received	2,435	
Interest paid	(56)	
Dividends paid	(1,890)	
Net cash inflow from returns on investments and servicing of finance		489
Taxation		
Corporation tax paid	(1,546)	
Tax paid		(1,546)
Investing activities		
Payments to acquire fixed assets	(857)	
Receipts from sales of fixed assets	280	
Net cash outflow from investing activities		(577)
Net cash inflow before financing		3,131
Financing		
Issue of ordinary share capital	200	
Repayment of debenture loan	(40)	
Net cash inflow from financing		160
Increase in cash and cash equivalents		3,291

Table 16.9 Cash Flow Statement

ADDITIONAL STATEMENTS

66 Need to be read in conjunction with the numerate information in the accounts. 99

As well as the Balance Sheet, the Income Statement and the Funds Flow or Cash Flow statement an annual report to shareholders should also contain:

- *A Directors' Report:* a short written statement providing a commentary on the company's current position and any important changes envisaged in the near future. It will also include the recommended dividend together with any changes in the board of directors.

- *A Chairman's Statement:* a broader outlook at factors affecting the company in the past, present and future. It may include items such as political events which are likely to have an impact on company affairs.

- *An Auditor's Report:* this is required by law and will declare if the accounts have been prepared according to accounting practice and whether they give a 'true and fair view' of the company's financial position.

- *Notes to the Accounts:* a more detailed explanation of certain items in the accounts such as changes in fixed assets, shareholders funds or long-term liabilities.

- *Statistical Tables:* a summary of the main accounting information over the past five or ten years.

In addition, the report might contain an Added Value Statement, which is an alternative method of showing the wealth created by the business. The difference between the final sales value and the original bought-in materials and services is the valued added by the firm. It is a simpler means of showing the wealth available for distribution to the four interested parties, shareholders, employees, government and the company itself.

EXAMINATION QUESTIONS

1 TCH's financial director has been examining the most recent published accounts available from Egypta, and these are shown below. The figures suggest that the lowest bid price based on present asset valuations would be 200p per Ordinary Share, a price arrived at by distributing the Ordinary Share Capital plus *reserves* between the total shares on issue. Specialist advice has been obtained, and it would seem that Egypta's premises could well be under-valued, and even the most conservative estimate adds £100,000 to the most recent balance sheet valuation. It is thought that the present stock valuation is far too pessimistic about allowances for deterioration, and thus could be increased by 10% from present figures. Against this, the firm is over optimistic about provision for bad debts, debtors being over-stated by 5%. Egypta's methods for the treatment of depreciation on plant were felt to be rather harsh by industry standards (no doubt a reflection of their having to re-equip after a major fire in the factory in mid-1989 which reduced profits for that year). The assets in question could probably be valued at 10% above present book figures. Patents and *goodwill* are almost certainly over-valued, the former being worth only half of its present level because of recent technological changes, and the latter being worthless, and thus should be written off. All of these adjustments would cause the present 200p lowest bid price to be revised.

EGYPTA plc:
BALANCE SHEET AS AT 31st MARCH 1990

	£'000s	£'000s
Fixed Assets		
Premises at cost	600	
Plant (after depreciation)	2,400	
		3,000
Goodwill		100
Patents		100
		3,200
Net Current Assets		
Current Assets		
Stocks	1,300	
Debtors	1,900	
Cash and Marketable Securities	100	
	3,300	
Current Liabilities	2,000	1,300
Net Assets Employed		4,500
Financed by:		
Shareholders' Funds		
£1 6% Preference Shares	500	
£1 Ordinary Shares Fully Paid	1,000	
Reserves	1,000	2,500
Long Term Liabilities		
12% Secured Loan Stock (2005/2008)		2,000
Net Capital Employed		4,500

Using the specialist advice referred to in the text, produce a revised balance sheet to show Egypta's worth, and thus calculate a new equity-based share price. (*10*)

(UCLES 1990 part of case study)

2 a) In what ways would accounting information, when prepared for internal management, differ from that compiled for the use of other interested parties?

(*15*)

b) What kind of information would a supplier require of a new customer ordering £1 million worth of raw materials on a regular basis? (*10*)

(UCLES 1986)

3 a) What does an accountant understand by the term 'liquidity'? (*5*)

b) Outline a method by which a firm might predict future liquidity problems and explain how these may be averted. (*10*)

(UCLES 1988 part question)

STUDENT'S ANSWER

Question 1

EGYPTA PLC: REVISED BALANCE SHEET
as at 31 March 1990

	£000's	£000's
FIXED ASSETS		
Premises	700	
Plant	2,640	3,340
Goodwill		0
Patents		50
		3,390
NET CURRENT ASSETS		
Current Assets		
Stock	1,430	
Debtors	1,805	
Cash and Marketable Securities	100	
Total	3,335	
Less Current Liabilities	2,000	1,335
NET ASSETS EMPLOYED		4,725
Financed by:		
Shareholders' Funds		
Preference shares	500	
Ordinary shares	1,000	
Reserves	1,225	2,725
Long Term Liabilities		2,000
Net Capital Employed		4,725

> **Excellent layout.**

> **The value placed on the business by the bidder.**

The equation used to determine the bid price was:

$$\text{Bid price} = \frac{\text{Ordinary share capital} + \text{reserves}}{\text{No. of issued shares}}$$

$$= \frac{1000 + 1225}{1000}$$

$$= \frac{2225}{1000} = \text{£}2.225 \text{ per share}$$

New bid price = 222.5p per share

OUTLINE ANSWERS

Questions 2 and 3

2 a) In this section the student should identify the differences between internal and external users giving examples of both groups. Having identified groups such as management, employees, owners, creditors, government and consumers there should ensue a discussion of the information needs of the different parties. Stress must be placed not only on the type of information presented but also the detail. For certain external purposes information is mandatory in order to comply with either the Companies Acts or the accounting profession's Statement of Standard Accounting Practice and Financial Reporting Standards (SSAPs and FRSs).

   b) This question requires an application of the general comments made in the previous section to the needs of a supplier of high value equipment. The supplier will be interested in assessing the degree of risk involved and the customer's financial standing. Its current net asset position could be obtained from the Balance Sheet and its past trading record by analysing the Profit and Loss Account. A great deal of attention will be placed on the Funds Flow Statement to assess the ability of the company to generate sufficient funds to avoid working capital problems. The application of various ratios (see Chapter 17) would be appropriate.

3 a) Liquidity is the ability to meet bills and claims as they fall due. In order to do so the firm must have sufficient current assets, i.e. cash or assets which can be converted quickly to cash, to meet current liabilities. A number of ratios (see Chapter 17) could be applied to test the level of liquidity, e.g. the current ratio and the Acid Test ratio.

   b) The method required is a forward Cash Flow statement. The student should describe or use a table to present an opening cash position, projected revenue, expenditure, borrowing, etc. and the resultant cash position. This will indicate the likely cash needs of the business or cash available for investment. The second part of the question requires a discussion of the various forms of raising short-term finance and/or delaying payment. This should include overdraft arrangements, stock reduction, delaying payment to creditors, debtor payment encouragement and the growing popularity of factoring. If the liquidity problem is seen as long term then a description of restructuring the company's capital should be included.

FURTHER READING

Taylor and Hawkins, *Quantitative Methods in Business* Nelson 1983:
   Chapter 4, Income Statement.
   Chapter 5, The Balance Sheet.
   Chapter 6, The Funds Flow Statement.
Myddleton and Corbett, *Accounting and Decision making* (3rd edition) Longman 1987:
   Chapter 4, The Balance Sheet.
   Chapter 5, The Profit and Loss Account.
Harvey and Nettleton, *Management Accounting* Mitchell Beazley 1983:
   Chapter 7, Financial Accounts.
   Chapter 8, Funds Flow Analysis.
Norkett, *Financial Accounting* Longman 1985:
   Chapter 3, An Accounting Framework.
   Chapter 8, The Added Value Statement.
Griffiths and Wall, *Applied Economics* (4th edition) Longman 1991:
   Chapter 2, Company accounts and the assessment of company performance.

ANALYSIS AND INTERPRETATION OF ACCOUNTS

GETTING STARTED

This chapter covers the interpretation of financial accounts and the various methods for dealing with depreciation, stock valuation and inflation.

The first section is devoted to *ratio analysis* which many students find complicated and difficult to apply. There is no easy route to understanding them. The best practice is to apply the ratios to different sets of accounts and to try to understand the reasons for any differences. Always ask yourself two questions. What am I trying to measure? Which ratio(s) will provide the answer? A good answer will always qualify the use of ratios with reference to their limitations.

In the second section we will discuss the various methods of assessing how to depreciate assets and how to value stocks. Depreciation and stock measures are important because of the direct effect they have on the reported profit figure. Two firms with identical sales revenue, fixed assets and physical stock levels, could declare entirely different profits depending on their choice of depreciation valuation methods and stock. Therefore it is important for the student to understand the basic difference in the methods and what effects those differences can have on final profits.

A thorough understanding of this and the previous chapter should enable the student to undertake simple Balance Sheet and Profit and Loss calculations as well as to give some interpretation of the results thus obtained.

ESSENTIAL PRINCIPLES

**ANALYSING
FINANCIAL
STATEMENTS**

Several interested parties such as management, employees, investors and creditors may want to interpret the year end financial statements. This is principally done using business ratios to compare this year's performance with that of previous periods and the performance of other similar companies.

On their own the ratios are largely meaningless. For example, is the statement that 'annual profits have grown by 10%' a satisfactory one? In isolation it may appear so, but what if in the same year prices have risen 15%, the company has increased its capital by 20% to generate the extra sales, a rival company of similar size had achieved a 22% profit increase and the industry average was 14%! A very different picture of the performance would emerge. What is required is a means of comparison. For *internal* comparison purposes the ratios for the current year can be compared to the same ratios relating to previous years. For *external* comparison purposes the ratios of one company can be compared to those of similar companies through organisations such as the Centre for Inter-Firm Comparison, a non-profit body established in 1959 by the British Institute of Management.

❝ Ratios allow comparison; internally and externally. ❞

There are a bewildering number of ratios to choose from, but for examination purposes they can be divided into two categories:

- Investment ratios to satisfy the interests of shareholders;
- Management ratios.

The latter can be sub-divided into *financial ratios* to analyse the firm's ability to meet its debts and *operating ratios* which aim to measure the performance and profitability of the organisation. This is illustrated in Figure 17.1.

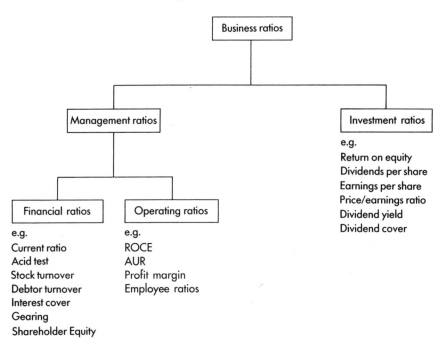

Fig. 17.1 Ratio analysis

❝ What is the ratio measuring? ❞

It is important from the outset that the student is clear what each ratio is trying to measure. The examiner is probably more concerned with a logical approach and a systematic use of ratios rather than with the numerical accuracy of the calculations.

OPERATING RATIOS

Operating ratios measure how well or how efficiently the company's resources have been used. Profitability is used as a measure of operating performance firstly in relation to the amount of investment in the company (total capital employed or net assets) and secondly to the sales revenue for the period. In general the higher these ratios are the better, as they indicate a high level of profits.

Return on capital employed (ROCE)

❝ The primary ratio is a measure of profitability. ❞

This is also known as the 'Primary ratio', as it relates the profit made to all the capital sums invested in the organisation (shareholders' capital, reserves and long-term liabilities).

$$ROCE = \frac{\text{Net profit (before tax and interest)}}{\text{Total capital employed}} \%$$

(or alternatively)

$$ROCE = \frac{\text{Operating profit}}{\text{Net assets}} \%$$

To improve this ratio the company must either increase profits or reduce the capital used. These elements, profit and assets, are analysed by breaking down the primary ratio into two secondary ratios, the asset utilisation ratio (or asset turnover) and the profit margin ratio.

Profit margin ratio (also known as return on sales ratio, ROSR)

> **Ratios help to raise questions rather than provide answers.**

This ratio can be compared to previous years' figures. A fall in this figure is caused by either prices being too low or costs being too high. This would trigger further investigations, especially into the various cost elements. The profit margin ratio can be further sub-divided to look at the relationship between administration costs, selling costs and sales, etc.

$$\text{Profit margin} = \frac{\text{Operating profit}}{\text{Sales}} \%$$

Asset utilisation ratio (AUR, or asset turnover)

The AUR reflects the level of intensity with which assets have been employed. The higher the ratio the better.

$$AUR = \frac{\text{Sales}}{\text{Net assets}}$$

The three ratios are inter-related in the following way:

ROCE = profit margin × asset turnover

or,

$$\frac{\text{Operating profits}}{\text{Net assets}} = \frac{\text{Operating profit}}{\text{Sales}} \times \frac{\text{Sales}}{\text{Net assets}}$$

Different industries will display different characteristics of profit and turnover. For example, a large food retail chain may have a ROCE of 15% obtained by low profit margins of 1.5% but a high asset turnover of 10. Conversely a heavy metal company could have the same ROCE of 15% but with profit margins of 10% and an asset turnover of 1.5. Each industry will display different norms.

Employee ratios (productivity)

A final measure of performance may be arrived at by analysing the results with respect to the labour force used. These give an idea of the productivity, i.e. the output or contribution per employee. (Value added refers to the monetary gain to the business caused by the conversion of raw materials and other goods purchased into a saleable product.)

$$\text{Sales per employee} = \frac{\text{Sales}}{\text{Number of employees}}$$

$$\text{Profits per employee} = \frac{\text{Operating profit}}{\text{Number of employees}}$$

$$\text{Value added per employee} = \frac{\text{Value added}}{\text{Number of employees}}$$

FINANCIAL RATIOS

Many businesses collapse not because they are unprofitable but through a lack of liquidity, i.e. cash to meet their debt commitments. Management must keep a careful watch on both the short and long-term positions to ensure the company remains solvent.

> **Lack of liquidity is a major cause of business failure.**

SHORT-TERM SOLVENCY OR LIQUIDITY

Short-term solvency involves a number of 'tests of liquidity' applied to the working capital elements of cash, stock and debtors.

Current ratio

This measures how well a company's short-term assets cover its liabilities. The ratio must be at least 1, thus indicating the company can cover its debts but it is preferable for most companies to have a ratio somewhere between 1.5 and 2. However, it shouldn't be too high, as working capital tied up in cash cannot be used for more productive purposes.

$$\text{Current ratio} = \frac{\text{Current assets}}{\text{Current liabilities}}$$

Acid test ratio

A better test of liquidity is the acid test, which uses only those current assets that are easily converted into liquid funds (cash and debtors). It ignores stock which may prove difficult to convert to cash without offering a significant discount. In general the acid test should be approximately 1 but it can vary significantly from business to business. For example, supermarket chains may have a ratio as low as 0.3, due to having high creditors figures but virtually no debtors.

> 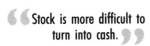 **Stock is more difficult to turn into cash.**

$$\text{Acid test ratio} = \frac{\text{Current assets} - \text{stock}}{\text{Current liabilities}}$$

Stock turnover

This measures the efficiency of stock management by indicating how many days' cash is tied up in stocks.

$$\text{Stock turnover} = \frac{\text{Stock}}{\text{Sales}} \times 365 = \text{No. of days}$$

Debtors turnover

In a similar way to stock turnover this measures how quickly debtors are paying their bills, i.e. the average collection period. In both this and the previous measure a company would be more solvent if they were kept to a minimum.

$$\text{Debtors turnover} = \frac{\text{Debtors}}{\text{Sales}} \times 365 = \text{No. of days}$$

Interest cover

The final liquidity measure is the interest cover. This is the extent to which the organisation's profit is taken up with the need to pay interest on long-term loans. In the last recession many firms suffered when profits fell below the level required to service high borrowings, e.g. Sock Shop.

$$\text{Interest cover} = \frac{\text{Operating profit}}{\text{Interest}}$$

LONG-TERM SOLVENCY

Here the concern lies with the ability to pay both current and long-term liabilities and is shown in the relationship between debt and equity, i.e. the resources provided by outsiders and shareholders. Two ratios are used to indicate long-term solvency.

Gearing ratio

This measures the capital structure or the relationship between long-term liabilities and the total capital employed. High capital gearing may indicate dangerously high interest payments. This may not be a problem if earnings and profits are secure and expanding as in the boom years of the early 1980s. However, if the level of economic activity falls, the high interest payments become an increasing burden.

$$\text{Gearing ratio} = \frac{\text{Long-term liabilities}}{\text{Capital employed}} \%$$

Shareholders' equity ratio

This shows the relationship between funds supplied by shareholders and the total capital employed. A high proportion is usually acknowledged as indicating a strong financial position, whereas a low proportion would indicate an over-dependence on outside provision of capital.

$$\text{Shareholders' equity ratio} = \frac{\text{Shareholders' equity}}{\text{Capital employed}} \%$$

INVESTMENT RATIOS

The investor is interested in three principal issues:

- The security of the investment
- The future value of the investment
- The future income from the investment

To this end the investor uses a number of ratios which explore the relationship between share prices, earnings and yields.

Earnings per share (EPS)

This serves as a good indicator of the management's use of the investors' capital. It is also used to determine the price/earnings ratio.

$$\text{EPS} = \frac{\text{Profit (after tax and interest)}}{\text{Number of ordinary shares issued}} = \text{p. per share}$$

Price/earnings ratio (P/E ratio)

The P/E ratio may be taken as an indicator of investor confidence as the market price reflects the market's anticipation and estimation of future returns. The higher the ratio the more confident the market is that the level of earnings will be maintained or improved.

$$\text{P/E ratio} = \frac{\text{Market price per share}}{\text{Earnings per share}}$$

Return on equity

This shows the rate of return after all costs, including tax and interest, have been met on the funds provided by the shareholders (both share capital and reserves).

$$\text{Return on equity} = \frac{\text{Net profit after tax and interest}}{\text{Shareholders' funds}} \%$$

Dividend cover

This ratio provides a guide to the company's ability to maintain its current level of dividends. Conversely it also indicates the proportion retained by the company for re-investment.

$$\text{Dividend cover} = \frac{\text{Profit after tax and interest}}{\text{Dividends}}$$

Dividend yield

This compares the dividends paid by the company with the share's market price.

$$\text{Dividend yield} = \frac{\text{Dividends per share}}{\text{Market price per share}}\%$$

SUMMARY

Table 17.1 provides a quick reference table for the main ratios. However, the best means of learning the ratios is to apply them to a set of accounts and to interpret their meaning.

OPERATING RATIOS

1	Return on Capital Employed	$= \dfrac{\text{Operating Profit}}{\text{Net assets}}$
2	Profit margin	$= \dfrac{\text{Operating Profit}}{\text{Sales}}$
3	Asset turnover	$= \dfrac{\text{Sales}}{\text{Net assets}}$
4	Employee ratios	
	4.1 Sales per employee	$= \dfrac{\text{Sales}}{\text{Number of employees}}$
	4.2 Profit per employee	$= \dfrac{\text{Operating Profit}}{\text{Number of employees}}$
	4.3 Value added per employee	$= \dfrac{\text{Value added}}{\text{Number of employees}}$

FINANCIAL RATIOS

5	Current ratio	$= \dfrac{\text{Current assets}}{\text{Current liabilities}}$
6	Acid Test	$= \dfrac{\text{Current assets} - \text{stock}}{\text{Current liabilities}}$
7	Stock turnover	$= \dfrac{\text{Stock} \times 365 \text{ days}}{\text{Sales}}$
8	Debtor Turnover	$= \dfrac{\text{Debtors} \times 365 \text{ days}}{\text{Sales}}$
9	Interest cover	$= \dfrac{\text{Operating profit}}{\text{Interest}}$
10	Gearing	$= \dfrac{\text{Long-term liabilities}}{\text{Capital employed}}$
11	Shareholders Equity Ratio	$= \dfrac{\text{Shareholders equity}}{\text{Capital employed}}$

INVESTMENT RATIOS

12	Return on equity	$= \dfrac{\text{Net profit after tax}}{\text{Shareholders funds}}$
13	Dividends per share	$= \dfrac{\text{Dividends}}{\text{Number of shares}}$
14	Earnings per share	$= \dfrac{\text{Profit after tax and interest}}{\text{Number of shares}}$
15	Price/Earnings ratios	$= \dfrac{\text{Market price per share}}{\text{Earnings per share}}$
16	Dividend yield	$= \dfrac{\text{Dividends per share}}{\text{Market price per share}}$
17	Dividend cover	$= \dfrac{\text{Profit after tax}}{\text{Dividends}}$

Table 17.1 Ratios

THE USE OF RATIOS

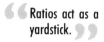

Ratios act as a yardstick.

Ratios used internally can provide a useful yardstick with which to evaluate performance. Comparison can be made with past years to see if the company's performance, measured against itself, is improving. However, without external comparisons, this could lead to complacency on the part of management, who must make sure that the company's performance is not only good with respect to its own past performance but also good in relation to its competitors. An external comparison can help motivate management and provide indicators for further improvement. However, ratios are not a panacea for all management problems and they should be used cautiously.

LIMITATIONS AND PROBLEMS

A common examination question.

- Ratios are only as reliable as the data they are based on.
- Some ratios are dependent on figures which are themselves subjective, e.g. stock.
- Inter-firm comparisons are difficult because of:
    - i) different year-ends
    - ii) different product mix
    - iii) different accounting methods
    - iv) different company objectives
- Ratios are based on historic information. As economic conditions can change quickly, there is no certainty that what has happened in the past will occur again in the future.
- Ratios use only information expressed in *financial terms*. Business information about the market and likely competition would be required to obtain a more complete picture.

DEPRECIATION

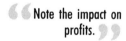

Depreciation is defined as the process of spreading the cost of a fixed asset over its useful life.

THE NEED FOR DEPRECIATION

Note the impact on profits.

If no allowance is made for depreciation during an asset's useful life, profits will be *overstated* until the time when the asset must be sold or replaced. In that year the profits will be *understated*, as the total cost of the use of the asset will be charged against that year's earnings. Therefore, a more systematic method is required to 'spread' the cost of the item fairly over the asset's useful life.

The matching principle also requires that the expense of assets should be 'matched' against the benefit which the assets produce. The expense of the fixed asset is called 'depreciation' and is charged like other expenses to the Profit and Loss Account. The adjusted value of the asset or 'written down' value is shown in the Balance Sheet.

DETERMINATION OF A DEPRECIATION POLICY

Four factors need to be considered in deciding a depreciation policy:

- The acquisition cost
- The estimated useful life
- The residual value
- The method of depreciation to be used

Acquisition cost

This should include not only the purchase price but also the cost of acquiring and locating the fixed asset. This will include items such as legal costs, transport charges, installation fees and non-recoverable taxes. During the life of the asset any repairs are treated as expenses and charged to the Profit and Loss Account, but improvements can be 'capitalised' and added to the current value of the asset in the Balance Sheet.

Estimated useful life

This is limited by four factors:

- The physical wear and tear, e.g. a car deteriorating with mileage travelled.
- The passage of time, e.g. a lease on a building for 30 years.
- Technological obsolescence – new advances in technology may produce a cheaper, more productive replacement, e.g. advances in computer hardware.
- Market obsolescence – the item which the asset is helping to produce may go out of fashion or be replaced before the end of the asset's physical life, e.g. cutting tools in car manufacturing may be made redundant by model changes.

Some of these factors may be hard to assess, so the accountant should apply the rule of conservatism (prudence) and apply the shortest period of economic life.

Residual value

This is the saleable value (or scrap value) at the end of the asset's economic life. It is often difficult to assess, especially for long-lasting assets. Where the residual value is small relative to the original cost it is often regarded as zero for depreciation purposes.

Method of depreciation

Whichever method is used the same total depreciation is charged over the same time period. The only difference is how the depreciation expense is spread over the useful life. In general where the asset provides equal benefits or service over its economic life the *straight-line* method of depreciation is used, e.g. a desk, a lease on a building, a patent on an invention etc. The *reducing balance* or declining balance method is used where it is considered the asset is more useful or productive in its early life, e.g. a vehicle.

TWO METHODS OF DEPRECIATION

Straight-line method

The expense of depreciation is charged in equal portions, using the equation:

$$\text{Depreciation charge p.a.} = \frac{\text{Original cost} - \text{residual value}}{\text{Useful life in years}}$$

For example, a machine costing £10,000 has an estimated useful life of 4 years and a residual value of £2,000. The annual depreciation charge would be:

$$\frac{10,000 - 2,000}{4} = \text{£2,000 p.a. for four years}$$

The value of the asset would decline in a straight line from £10,000 to £8,000 to £6,000 to £4,000 and to £2,000 in the year of sale.

The straight-line method has two main advantages:

- it is easy to understand
- it is easy to calculate and record

However, the method's disadvantage is that it may not reflect the way assets lose value in the real world.

Reducing balance or declining balance method

This method allocates a fixed percentage of the written down value as an annual expense. Therefore a larger proportion of the cost is allocated to the earlier years. The rate of depreciation is calculated using the equation

$$\text{Depreciation rate} = \left(1 - \sqrt[n]{\frac{\text{residual value}}{\text{cost}}}\right) \times 100$$

where n = useful life in years

Applying this method to the example used above, the rate would be:

$$\left(1 - 4\sqrt{\frac{2,000}{10,000}}\right) \times 100$$

$$= 33\%$$

A tabulated comparison of the two methods is given in Table 17.2 and the net book values in graph form in Figure 17.2.

	STRAIGHT-LINE		REDUCING BALANCE	
	Depreciation	*Net value*	*Depreciation*	*Net value*
YEAR	£	£	£	£
0		10,000		10,000
1	2,000	8,000	3,300*	6,700
2	2,000	6,000	2,200	4,500
3	2,000	4,000	1,500	3,000
4	2,000	2,000	1,000	2,000
TOTAL DEPRECIATION	£8,000		£8,000	

Table 17.2 Comparison of depreciation methods.

* rounded to the nearest £100

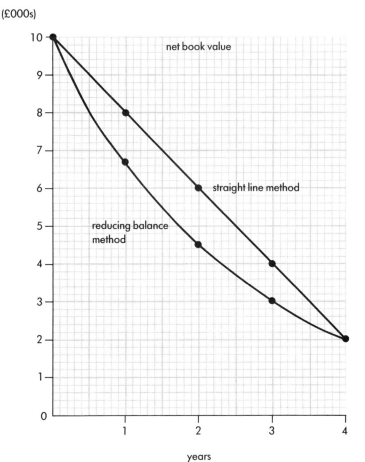

Fig. 17.2 Comparison of depreciation methods (graph form)

The reducing balance method results in much larger amounts of depreciation being charged to the early years, but overall, both methods charge the same total of £8,000.

The advantages of the reducing balance method are that:

■ it takes into account the greater benefit obtained from most assets in their earlier years;

■ it balances the fact that repair and maintenance charges increase with the passage of time;

- it reflects more accurately the real life value of assets.

The main disadvantage is that it may leave a small amount of depreciation not accounted for in the final year, in which case it is added to the final year's allocation.

Whichever method is used, the student must appreciate the impact on profits. The straight-line method will have an equal impact on the profit figure, whereas the reducing balance method will reduce profits in the earlier years of an asset's life but boost them in the latter period. Remember also that depreciation is a provision, i.e. profits set aside to match the loss in the asset's value by the end of its useful life. Depreciation therefore does not result in a cash outflow from the business.

> " Depreciation does not result in an outflow of cash. "

STOCK VALUATION

As with depreciation there are several ways of valuing stock. Different methods can result in different profit results being reported in the periodic accounting statements. In general it is best to adopt the conservative approach and accept the valuation of stock which is the lowest. By the term 'stock' we mean not only the store of finished goods but also any raw materials and work-in-progress.

BASES OF STOCK VALUATION

Let us assume a trading business buys and sells finished goods and at the end of an accounting period wishes to place a money value to each item in stock. Three of the possible ways of valuing the stock are:

Net realisable value (NRV)

This is the estimated net income from the sale of the stock, i.e. selling price minus selling costs. This method is usually chosen when the stock is valued at below its purchase price. In other words a loss is anticipated on the goods because the stock:

- is damaged
- is out-of-date
- has deteriorated
- is no longer demanded

An example is a retail outlet's stock which is approaching its legal sell-by date.

Historic cost

This uses the original purchase price as its base and is still the most common form of stock valuation. However, in times of inflation, a firm may be holding stock of the same item bought at different times and different prices. This presents a problem at the end of an accounting period in deciding which stocks are remaining, those bought first or those bought most recently. This is even more of a problem for a manufacturing concern where work-in-progress not only has a historic purchase cost but an allocation of direct expenses and overheads. In principle the accountant will observe the convention of using 'historic cost or net realisable value, whichever is lowest'.

> " Lower of cost or net realisable value. "

Current replacement cost

This method adopts the view that the cost of using an item of stock, irrespective of when it was originally purchased, is the cost of replacing the item. Therefore, stock should be valued at current purchase prices. This has the advantage of matching current purchase costs with current selling prices. The main disadvantage is that since some of these prices have to be estimated, the system is more subjective. Note that this method is unacceptable under conventional (historic cost) accounting principles.

> " More subjective. "

STOCK VALUATION AND PROFIT

Example

An electrical retailer has two identical hi-fi systems for sale, one bought at £200 and one bought later at £300. The current selling price is £500. When the retailer sells a system his reported profit could be:

- £500 − £200 = Gross profit of £300 and closing stock £300

- £500 − £300 = Gross profit of £200 and closing stock of £200
- £500 − £250 = Gross profit of £250 and closing stock of £250

Note the impact on that period's profits.

Each of these methods is technically acceptable, with the first example using the FIFO (first in, first out) approach, the second using the LIFO (last in, first out) approach and the last using an average cost method. The method chosen will therefore affect the level of profits recorded in the current period and the value of stock to be used in the next period. The FIFO and LIFO methods are popular examination question subjects and are detailed below.

FIFO AND LIFO

FIFO (first in, first out) is based on the assumption that the stock purchased first will be the first sold. In most businesses this reflects what happens in practice. The advantage of this method is that the stock remaining is valued at current prices and gives a realistic value of stock for the Balance Sheet. The disadvantage is that the profit is calculated using current selling prices but past purchase prices. In a business with a rapid turnover, such as a supermarket, this would not present a problem but would do for a business with a slow stock turnover, e.g. heavy engineering. This method does not meet the accounting objective of matching current costs with current revenues, with the result that profit will be overstated in the current period but stocks valued realistically.

Compare FIFO and LIFO's advantages and disadvantages.

LIFO (last in, first out) is based on the assumption that the most recently purchased stock is used first. This achieves the matching principle but leaves stock being valued at out-of-date prices.

EXAMINATION QUESTIONS

1 a) What do you understand by the term 'gearing' and how might it be measured?
   (5)

   b) How might a finance house use gearing ratios when considering an application from a medium-sized manufacturing company for a loan of £5,000,000 for expansion purposes? *(10)*

   c) What alternative source of funds might the firm examine? *(10)*
   (UCLES 1987)

2 'Ratios extracted from one company's accounts are virtually useless without additional information'. What other information would you need in order to make them valuable?

   (AEB 1989)

3 A machine costs £20,000 to purchase. It has a useful life of 5 years and a residual value at the end of this period of £3,000.
   Depreciation figures, using the Reducing Balance Method, are as follows:

Year	Depreciation Provision (£)	Net Book Value (£)
1	6,315	13,685
2	4,321	9,364
3	2,957	6,407
4	2,023	4,384
5	1,384	3,000

   a) Explain the term 'depreciation'. *(3)*

   b) Suggest *three* factors that influence the useful life of an asset. *(3)*

   c) Calculate the annual depreciation provision using the Straight Line Method. *(3)*

   d) Compare the Reducing Balance Method with the Straight Line Method of depreciation. *(6)*

e) On a graph, show the annual Net Book Value for each of the following methods of calculating depreciation:
   i) the Straight Line Method, and
   ii) the Reducing Balance Method. *(7)*

f) Why is depreciation a provision rather than an expense? *(3)*

(AEB 1989)

OUTLINE ANSWERS

Question 1

a) In this section the student should define gearing as a measure of financial risk. It measures the proportion of debt to equity finance. Explain what is meant by a 'high' geared company and a 'low' geared one.

b) The examiner is looking for the application of the gearing concept to a practical example. Use the gearing ratio of long-term liabilities to capital employed and the interest cover ratio to explain the likely impact of servicing an extra debt of £5m. Discuss how lenders would react to high and low gearing and interest cover figures.

c) An explanation of at least three of the following alternatives:

Ordinary shares	Sale and leaseback
Preference shares	Hire purchase
Mortgages	Factoring

Question 2

The student should be aware that this question is not solely about ratios and how they are calculated. This is a common examination fault. The essay is principally about the limitations of ratios and asks specifically for examples of information other than ratios. The candidate who stresses that ratios must be analysed in context with other information and provides examples will score highly. Other information can include items such as size of company, type of market, extent of competition, industrial relations, economic outlook, future plans, accuracy of figures, etc. Each of the points should be developed with reference to ratios, e.g. the impact of an impending recession on profitability ratios. Stress should be placed on the use of ratios as indicators for further investigation rather than as answers to problems.

STUDENT'S ANSWER

Question 3

An example would be a useful addition.

a) Depreciation is a means of making a provision for the cost of using a fixed asset over the duration of its economic life.

b) The useful life of an asset is influenced by:

Good, concise answer.

- The physical wear and tear the asset undergoes e.g. mileage done by a vehicle.

- The state of technology which may produce a cheaper more efficient alternative before the asset has worn out.

- Product obsolescence whereby the asset becomes out-of-date because the product which it helps to make is no longer demanded.

c) Annual charge $= \dfrac{\text{original cost} - \text{residual value}}{\text{useful life in years}}$

$= \dfrac{20,000 - 3,000}{5}$

$= £3,400$

d)

	REDUCING BALANCE		STRAIGHT LINE	
Year	Depreciation	NBV	Depreciation	NBV
0		20,000		20,000
1	6,315	13,685	3,400	16,600
2	4,321	9,364	3,400	13,200
3	2,957	6,407	3,400	9,800
4	2,023	4,384	3,400	6,400
5	1,384	3,000	3,400	3,000
	17,000		17,000	

The reducing balance method allocates more of the cost to the earlier years whereas the straight line method allocates a uniform amount per year. The total allocated is the same.

e)

(£000s)

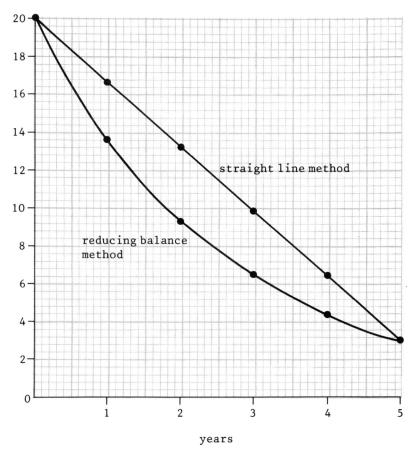

> Axes, origin and graph clearly labelled.

Fig. 17.3 Graph of net book value

f) Depreciation is a provision because it is setting aside some of the company's current profits to reflect the use of the asset over its life. Although not a cash expense (it does not mean that money leaves the business), the annual depreciation is treated as an expense in the Profit and Loss Account, thereby reducing the profit for the year.

Tutor's comments

A well structured answer with a high degree of accuracy and clear presentation.

18

MANAGEMENT ACCOUNTS

GETTING STARTED

Chapters 16 and 17 examined the role of financial accounting in keeping a true and fair record of the assets, liabilities and activities of a business. Company and fiscal legislation requires the financial accountant to produce regular reports for the owners, such as a Profit and Loss Account and a Balance Sheet, in order to fulfil the stewardship function. These reports are usually intended for external consumption. In this chapter we look at the role of management accounting which aims to provide management with quantitative and financial information for better decision making and is, therefore, principally for internal consumption.

The emphasis of management accounts is to adopt a wide approach to planning and control, not only providing information on actual costs and revenues but also on expected costs and revenues. This enables projections to be made and future plans detailed in a numerate form. Management accounts aim to record, analyse, interpret and finally report to management on cost and revenue data. In the first half of the chapter the importance of costs is first examined and then combined with revenues to help produce forward plans and estimates in breakeven analysis. The second half is devoted to the control aspect, where actual costs are compared to expected costs and the resultant variances analysed. The student must keep an overall view of the role of management accounts in that they aim to provide the necessary data for better decision making and control by management.

THE IMPORTANCE OF COSTS

THE CLASSIFICATION OF COSTS

COSTING METHODS

BREAK-EVEN ANALYSIS

BUDGETARY CONTROL

THE BUDGET PROCESS

STANDARD COSTING AND VARIANCE ANALYSIS

ESSENTIAL PRINCIPLES

A cost is the monetary value of all economic resources used in the production of a good or service. The classification and analysis of costs is a valuable aid to running a business organisation. Cost information can be used for:

- *Financial control:* the implementation of well-designed cost control systems can help management to monitor the financial implications of production. Profit is equal to sales minus costs, and as costs are generated by the firm itself, it is important to control them. Every £1 saved in costs adds a further £1 to profits.
- *Planning:* a study of cost behaviour with respect to output changes enables management to estimate the outcome of future production plans. This includes comparing product profitability and departmental performance.
- *Pricing:* costs provide one of the ingredients in the highly complex process of pricing finished goods. They may also be used for the valuation of raw materials and work-in-progress.
- *Decision-making:* cost factors help in the assessment of alternative courses of action which face the business in the future, including expansion plans.

Control of costs is important.

Cost–plus pricing.

For these reasons the student should understand how costs can be classified and then used in the formation of costing techniques.

There are several ways of classifying costs, each method looking at costs from a different angle. Four such methods analyse costs by function, by type, by behaviour and by time.

FUNCTION

This method groups costs according to the functional department which incurs them, such as production, sales, distribution and administration. Each of these departments would have one or several *cost centres* (i.e. locations or functions which are readily identifiable and against which costs can be charged). The *cost unit* is the actual product or service being produced, e.g. in car manufacture the vehicle would be the cost unit whereas for a car-hire firm it may be the rental-mile.

TYPE

Costs can be classed into two types, direct and indirect:

- *Direct costs:* these are costs which can be directly identified with the item or service being produced such as raw materials and labour specific to the task, e.g. the cotton cloth used in making a shirt and the machinist's time to cut and sew it.
- *Indirect costs:* these are also known as Overhead Costs and are all those costs incurred in the organisation which cannot objectively be allocated to specific output, e.g. rent, insurance, supervision etc.

Allocation of overheads is often subjective and arbitrary.

Direct costs are also known as *prime* costs and when added to *overhead* costs they form the *total cost* as illustrated in Table 18.1.

BEHAVIOUR

Fixed only for a given range of output.

Over a given range of production or time some costs tend to be unaffected by the level of output, e.g. factory rent. This type of cost is known as *fixed* cost. It is important to realise that they are 'fixed' or unchanging only over a range of output and a given time-span. For example, in Fig. 18.1(a) they are constant over a range of 2,000 units. To

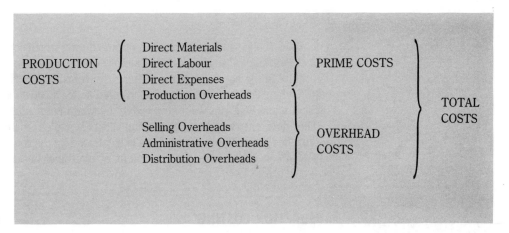

Table 18.1 Types of Costs

produce more than 2,000 units extra factory space must be added thus 'stepping up' the fixed costs as in Fig. 18.1(b).

Other costs do change with variations in output and are known as *variable* costs, e.g. raw materials used in each product. When the variable costs are constant over a given output range the cost curve will be linear, as in Fig. 18.1(c).

A third category could be added called *semi-variable* costs, which comprise of a fixed element and a variable element. This may apply to items such as power, telephone, water, etc. where there is a fixed charge for rental and minimum usage with an added usage charge thereafter. This type of cost is shown in Fig. 18.1(d).

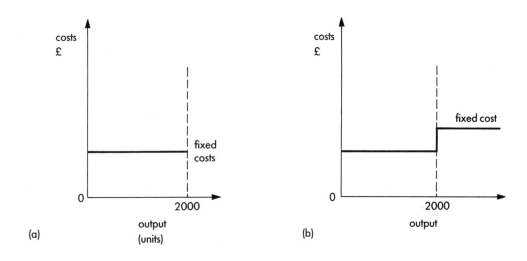

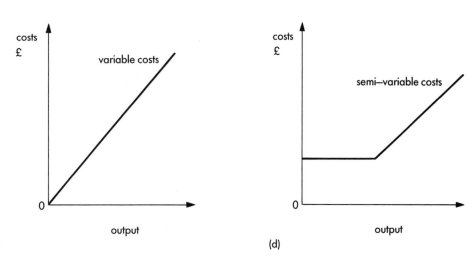

Fig. 18.1 Cost behaviour

TIME

The 'short run' period is that amount of time during which some of the factors of production cannot be changed, e.g. the size of factory or the supply of skilled, experienced workers. Therefore in the short run some of the costs remain fixed. The 'long run' is defined as the period when all factor inputs can be changed hence all costs are variable. The time span of short run and long run will differ widely between companies and industries.

The different ways of classifying costs enables management to apply different approaches to problem solving. This is illustrated by the following costing methods, one of which is concerned with the treatment of overhead costs and the other with marginal costs.

COSTING METHODS

ABSORPTION COSTING

One classification of costs is into direct and indirect costs. Direct costs are easily identified with individual products and present little difficulty. Indirect costs, however, relate to the running of the business as a whole in order to facilitate the production process. These overhead costs need to be allocated to the products in order to establish a 'full cost' per item so that a selling price can be set which not only covers cost but also ensures a satisfactory profit. To do this each unit of production must be allocated a share of the overheads or indirect costs, so that the total overheads are 'absorbed' by the output of the firm, hence the term *absorption costing*. This becomes a difficult procedure when the business produces several different products. What is required is a method which ensures that the allocation of overheads is reasonable and appropriate. This is done by a four-stage process:

> **All costs must be covered eventually.**

Allocation of overheads to cost centres

> **An important step-by-step guide to cost absorption.**

The business is divided into several cost centres, e.g. production centres and service centres. These are often geographical areas responsible for costs specific to that area, e.g. fabrication shop, assembly shop, spraying department, stores, transport, administration etc. (A cost centre could also be a particular machine, process or person.) Overheads which relate solely to one cost centre are allocated to that centre.

Apportionment of overheads

Some overheads apply to the business as a whole and not specifically to one cost centre, e.g. rent of the property. These general overheads must be 'apportioned' on an appropriate basis as in Table 18.2

TYPE OF OVERHEAD	BASIS OF APPORTIONMENT
Rent	Areas occupied by each cost centre
Electricity	Area or number of appliances
Insurance	Capital value of equipment
Heating	Volume occupied by cost centre
Personnel	Number of employees
Power	Average machine usage

Table 18.2 Apportioning overheads

Re-apportionment of overheads

As all overheads must eventually be absorbed by the product, the service overheads must be re-apportioned to the product cost centres, again using a reasonable basis, e.g. warehousing overheads could be apportioned to products depending on the volume of each product stored, or maintenance overheads according to time spent in each production area. At the end of this process *all* overheads will have been allocated to production.

Absorption of production centre costs into products

The cost centre overheads must now be charged to the cost units being produced by the cost centre. This is done by dividing the cost centre overheads by the base unit for that period to produce an *Overhead Absorption Rate (OAR)*.

$$\text{OAR} = \frac{\text{Cost centre overheads}}{\text{Cost centre base units}}$$

For example, the fabrication shop may have overheads of £50,000 per month and a monthly production of 2,000 units. The OAR would be £2.50 per unit. If the shop were making several different products it may prefer to use labour hours as its base unit so that the OAR was expressed in £ per labour hour, and then absorbed by the product according to the time taken for fabrication of each type.

Use of the OAR

The OAR can be used to establish budgets for future production periods which will be discussed later in the chapter. It can also be used for pricing purposes as shown in the following example.

Example:
A company produces two goods, 1,000 units of A and 400 units of B each month. Materials cost £1 per unit for A and £2 per unit for B. Each require 30 minutes labour charged at £8 per hour. The total overheads are £4,200 p.m. If a mark-up of 20% on costs is required what prices should be charged for A and B?

$$\text{OAR} = \frac{\text{Total overheads}}{\text{Total units}} = \frac{£4,200}{1,400} = £3 \text{ per unit}$$

Cost Statement for A and B £'s

	A	B	Total
Direct materials	1,000	800	1,800
Direct labour	4000	1,600	5,600
Prime costs	5,000	2,400	7,400
OAR (£3 per unit)	3,000	1,200	4,200
Total cost	8,000	3,600	11,600

Cost of A = £8 per unit and cost of B = £9, therefore prices are

A = cost + 20% = £8 + £1.60 = £9.60
B = cost + 20% = £9 + £1.80 = £10.80

Advantages of absorption costing

- Makes manager aware of total costs
- Provides full costing for pricing purposes
- OAR can be used for budgeting

Disadvantages of absorption costing

- Different apportionment criteria can produce different costs for products, which may distort decision making
- Apportionment is partly arbitrary and therefore subjective

MARGINAL COSTING (CONTRIBUTION COSTING)

This costing method adopts the view that in the short run fixed costs cannot alter and have to be borne anyway, whatever the level of production or sales in that period. The variable costs, which can be accurately allocated, are termed the *marginal costs*. The difference

between the marginal costs and the selling price is the *contribution* towards the fixed costs. No attempt is made to apportion fixed costs with this method. The total contribution is set against the fixed costs. If the contribution is greater than the fixed costs a profit is realised; if not then a loss is made. This is illustrated in Table 18.3.

Product A contributes £30,000, product B £15,000 and product C £35,000, which is sufficient to cover the fixed costs of £50,000 and leave a profit of £30,000.

N.B. A common mistake among students is to confuse contribution with *profit*. Profit is that part of contribution which is left after the fixed costs have been covered.

Marginal Cost Statement: XYZ Co. (£000's)

Product	A	B	C	Total
Materials	10	15	20	45
Labour	10	5	10	25
Marginal costs	20	20	30	70
Sales income	50	35	65	150
Contribution	30	15	35	80
Fixed costs				50
Profit				30

Table 18.3 Marginal cost statement

Advantages of marginal costing

- Easy to calculate
- Difficulties of apportionment avoided
- Able to assess the contribution of each product or department and the sales mix
- Allows marginal cost pricing to be adopted for special orders (see below)

Disadvantages of marginal costing

- For long-term pricing, overheads need to be taken into account, otherwise prices might be fixed at a lower level than is necessary to cover total costs.
- It may give the impression that fixed costs are divorced from production, or are less important than variable costs.

Marginal cost pricing

A common examination question.

The concept of contribution allows management to assess the effects of accepting a special order which at first appears to be a loss maker. For example XYZ Co. produces product D which has a marginal cost of £4 per unit, an OAR of £2 and normally retails at £8 per unit. A customer wants a special order of 5,000 units of D but is only willing to offer £5 per unit. At first glance this should be rejected as the £5 does not cover the average cost of £6 (marginal costs plus OAR). Using marginal costs, however, the order can be presented in a different way:

	£
Selling price	5
Marginal costs	4
Contribution	1

A firm must consider the impact of the special order on its regular customers.

Since all the additional costs (variable costs) of £4 will be covered, each unit will make a contribution of £1 giving a total of £5,000. As fixed costs have already been absorbed by current output the contribution will increase profits by £5,000.

This policy only applies to orders additional to normal output and where spare capacity exists. It should only be accepted if it is temporary in nature and does not affect regular output and sales. This type of pricing policy is often adopted in order to:

- keep plant in continual operation
- obtain greater market penetration
- make full use of the regular workforce

It is often used in industries which suffer seasonal variations such as the hotel trade and tourism. Off-peak pricing aims to cover variable costs and make a contribution to unavoidable fixed costs.

BREAK-EVEN ANALYSIS

TR = TC.

Break-even analysis (or cost-volume-profit analysis) makes use of the division of costs into Fixed and Variable in order to determine the minimum output where all costs are just covered by revenue, i.e. the break-even point where Total Revenue (TR) equals Total Costs (TC). This provides a minimum output which the firm must achieve in order to avoid a loss and to start making a profit. The break-even point can be found either by calculation or by graph form.

By calculation

To break-even, all costs must be covered, i.e. TR = TC.

TR = TC at break-even output (B/E)
therefore
B/E output × selling price = Fixed cost + B/E output × Variable cost

re-arranging the equation

$$\text{B/E output} = \frac{\text{Fixed cost}}{\text{Selling price} - \text{variable cost}}$$

but
Selling Price – Variable cost = Contribution

$$\therefore \text{Break-even output} = \frac{\text{Fixed cost}}{\text{Contribution per unit}}$$

For example, a company sells its product for £8 and the variable costs are £3 with fixed costs totalling £12,000. Current sales are 3,000 units.

$$\text{B/E output} = \frac{\text{Fixed cost}}{\text{Contribution}}$$

where contribution = SP – VC = £5

$$\text{B/E output} = \frac{12,000}{5} = \underline{2,400 \text{ units}}$$

By graph

TC = FC + VC.

The break-even point is found by plotting the total cost and total revenue curves as shown in Figure 18.2.

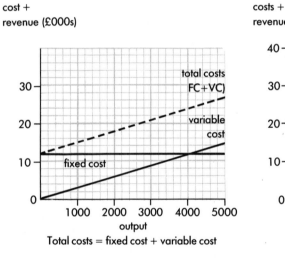

Fig. 18.2 (a) Break-even analysis   Fig. 18.2 (b) Break-even point

The firm currently sells 3,000 units; therefore it has a *margin of safety* of 600 units, i.e. sales can fall by 600 units before the firm starts to make a loss. (Alternatively the margin of safety can be expressed as a percentage of current sales, i.e. 20%.)

As the fixed costs are covered by the first 2,400 units (2,400 × £5 contribution = £12,000) the contribution from the remaining 600 units is all profit, i.e. 600 × £5 = £3,000.

Total cost is made up of fixed cost and variable cost as shown in Figure 18.2 (a). Total revenue is the output multiplied by selling price. The break-even point is shown in Figure 18.2(b) at the intersection of the TR and TC curves. Current sales of 3,000 units gives a profit of £3,000 and a margin of safety of 600 units.

Assumptions of break-even analysis

- The selling price remains constant over the given range of output.
- Costs vary in a linear manner.
- There is a constant sales mix where more than one product is sold.
- Fixed costs remain fixed over the given range of output.

Advantages of break-even analysis

- Enables the break-even point to be determined – an important minimum target.
- It shows the relationship between costs and revenue and the rate at which profits increase with sales.
- Margin of safety shows by how much sales can fall before the company becomes a loss-maker.
- Useful for showing the impact on profit and the break-even point when changes in price or cost occur.
- Levels of profit/loss at any level of output can be read from the graph.

Disadvantages of break-even analysis

- Useful only in the short-run situation where the assumptions hold true.
- Linearity may be an over-simplification.

BUDGETARY CONTROL

Good management involves not only reviewing past performance and the progress of current work but also looking ahead to the future requirements of the business. The market is constantly changing with the arrival of new products, new technology, new competitors and new demands from the consumer. A successful business is one which can identify and anticipate market changes and plan accordingly. To do this the organisation requires two types of plan, one long-term which sets out the strategic objectives of the firm, and one short-term which details the tactical objectives for the coming financial period.

A constant review of the firm's performance and future plans.

Long-term plans are expressed in general terms and cover periods of at least five years. They illustrate the expected growth in the market, the company's target market share and the anticipated profit levels. Plans of this nature are often prepared on a 'rolling' basis where another year is added as the current period lapses.

To achieve the long-term strategic objectives the business requires a series of tactical plans which are normally devised on an annual basis. These plans have their own set of objectives which must be compatible with the long-term objectives and provide a step towards their eventual attainment. The annual plan will be devised in much greater detail and take account of recent forecasts concerning economic activity, inflation, costs and revenues for the coming period. The detailed plan of action is usually referred to as the *budget*.

A budget is a plan quantified in monetary terms, prepared and agreed in advance, showing the expected income and expenditure over a given period of time.

The main purpose of budgetary control is to plan and control the organisation's activities. The budget is a *plan for action* in the next financial period. It can be used to delegate responsibility to departments and allow senior management to concentrate on investigating major deviations from the plan. This is the principle of *management by exception* and forms one of the main controls on the business. Performance is constantly monitored against the budget plans and feedback is an important part of the budgetary process. At the end of the period the budget is evaluated and managers' performance appraised against the agreed objectives and targets. This appraisal may then form the basis of the next budget plan.

Feedback is an integral part of the budgeting process.

The student needs to emphasise that the budgetary control process is about:

- setting agreed objectives
- planning
- control
- evaluation

THE BUDGET PROCESS

SETTING OBJECTIVES

It is the function of top management to outline the organisation's short-term objectives for the coming period and to communicate them to all other management areas. The objectives will not be concerned only with profit maximisation but with a whole range of topics which are complementary to the organisation's long-term strategic objectives.

Short-term objectives may include:

- *Profit:* a designated return on capital employed
- *Market penetration:* the launch of a product into a new market area
- *Market share:* a target percentage of the market
- *Product development:* research and development into product improvement, new technology or new products
- *Staff development:* internal and external training of current workforce
- *Productivity:* introduction of new techniques and working practices to achieve a desired work-rate
- *Industrial relations:* to review current working relationships with Trade Unions and evaluate existing agreements

It is important to appreciate that some of these objectives will be difficult to quantify but the organisation must be concerned with quality as well as with quantity in the overall plan.

The outline objectives are often communicated by top management to a budget committee made up of the heads of the main functional areas (sales manager, production manager, etc) who in turn interpret and communicate these to all departmental managers and supervisors. The departments will themselves set their own objectives within the overall framework and submit detailed proposals back to the budget committee for discussion, possible alteration and mutual agreement. This method of setting agreed objectives and plans is a combination of the 'top-down' approach where senior management provides the general outline and the 'bottom-up' approach where lower-level managers detail what is feasible and realistic. The budget is a plan for the whole organisation and therefore requires teamwork to achieve the desired goals. The objectives of the managers of individual departments should be consistent with the overall objectives of the firm and not in conflict with them. This is known as *goal congruence* where all employees are pulling in the same direction, satisfying their own interests while achieving the aims of the organisation.

PLANNING

Budgeting is a management function and not simply an accounting function. All levels of management should be involved at some stage in the setting of the budget proposals. The overall responsibility for the coordinating and final publication of the budget will be with the budget committee or budget officer, but the budget should be prepared at departmental level. The budget officer (probably a management accountant) will collate the various departmental budgets into a master budget. Detailed below is a typical budget procedure which may be followed by a firm concerned with the selling and marketing of its own manufactured goods.

Sales budget

This is normally the starting point for all budgets as market demand is often the key or limiting factor. The sales department's estimate of likely market share acts as a major constraint on all the other functional areas. It will take account of past order levels, market research, trend analysis and the extent of competition for each of its products. The outcome of this budget is then the benchmark for the other departmental budgets.

Marketing and distribution budget

The cost of achieving the planned sales level is estimated by product and geographical area. This will include details of sales staff required, commissions, transport, distribution costs and advertising.

Cost of production budget

This budget will detail the production and storage capacity needed to achieve the agreed output. The production manager will need to assess the current level of capital equipment to determine if the target is feasible, not only as a total but also with respect to time. The cost of production budget sets down the production schedule and is a combination of the following three working capital budgets:

- Materials budget – the quantities and quality required, the source of supply and the unit price.
- Direct labour budget – the agreed pay rates and productivity schedules.
- Production overhead cost budget – all indirect production costs.

Administration budget

This will include all expenses not covered by sales or production and will include all other overheads, research and development costs and, if not already accounted for, its capital budget.

The master budget

Departmental budgets need to be co-ordinated.

The subsidiary departmental budgets are amalgamated into a master budget by the budget committee. At this stage there may exist some conflicts or contradictions which can be solved by coordinated action between the respective departmental managers.

The agreed master budget will then be translated into three parts:

- A 'cash budget', which details the cash flow and cash requirements to determine deficiencies and surpluses so that appropriate action can be taken.
- A 'profit and loss' budget which indicates the planned level of profits.
- A forecast balance sheet which predicts what the published balance sheet will look like at the end of the financial period.

Budgets must be achievable and realistic in order to be a valid plan of action.

When approved by the Board of Directors the master budget and its constituent parts are communicated to all departments. The budget becomes the plan for the forthcoming period and it is the responsibility of management to ensure that it is made to happen.

N.B. The agreed budget is a plan of action and not merely a forecast or estimate.

CONTROL

Control is based on the concept of management by exception, i.e. the investigation of items which deviate from the agreed budget. This is done by comparing the actual costs with the budgeted costs to identify an over-or-under-expenditure. The differences are known as *variances* and their investigation as *variance analysis* (see p. 250 for detailed treatment of variance analysis).

The financial period will be divided into several shorter periods for control purposes. These are normally monthly but can be shorter or longer as the case demands. The budget reports aim to identify areas where remedial action is required so that further divergencies from budget are avoided.

Where actual costs are greater than budgeted costs the term *unfavourable* (or *adverse*) is used and where actual costs are below budget the variance is favourable. The opposite is true of revenue variances, where favourable variances occur when the actual sales are above budget.

Variances act as alarm bells to warn management.

The aim of variance analysis is to highlight areas requiring immediate attention. Obviously not all variances will be investigated as some may be extremely small, but where the variance is large either in percentage terms or monetary terms, the situation is reviewed.

Constantly changing environment.

Once a variance has been investigated and its cause identified, remedial action can be taken. However, not all causes may be capable of solution, e.g. a permanent change in market demand, in which case the variance provides information which can be fed back into the planning stage for alteration to proposed activity and sales levels. The budget process should be dynamic rather than mechanistic.

EVALUATION

The budget provides a series of yardsticks or standards against which performance can be measured. It is important therefore, that these standards:

- have been mutually agreed by all levels of management

Budgets must be flexible.

- are attainable and fair
- are adjustable in the light of unforeseen changes

At the end of the period the past budget plan is reviewed and assessed to see if the original objectives have been met.

The actual performance can be evaluated with the use of *ratio analysis* (see p. 226). This starts with the application of the primary ratio to evaluate the return on capital employed. If the budgeted return is not as expected the analysis can be extended to the secondary ratios to measure profitability and asset utilisation, and so on down the pyramid of ratios until the principal cause is identified. Solutions to the problem can be incorporated in the next budget plan.

Ratio analysis can be useful in three ways as an indicator of performance:

- in absolute terms relative to targets set by management at the beginning of the financial period
- in relative terms to the past performance of the organisation
- in relative terms to the performance of similar firms in the same business, i.e. competitors

Ratio analysis is only useful, however, if the assumptions underlying the budget remain constant. Unfortunately the economic world is full of variables, some of which will be critical to each firm's performance. Critical variables might include inflation, the cost of money, market demand, cost of raw materials, etc. over which the firm may have little control. Evaluation, therefore, must be done in the context of the original assumptions and in a framework of what was possible under the given circumstances.

STANDARD COSTING AND VARIANCE ANALYSIS

This is a control technique based on the analysis of variances between actual costs and standard costs.

The system requires the following stages:

ESTABLISHMENT OF STANDARD COSTS

The standard cost of a product or service is the total cost of labour, materials and overhead apportionment as determined in advance of the production process. This entails an investigation of the best production methods, the most appropriate materials and the best source of supply with regard to both reliability and price. The final standard cost figure acts as a yardstick against which performance can be measured. It can also act as a motivator in that it engenders cost consciousness among employees and provides realistic, mutually agreed goals.

A standard cost specification for a heavy duty printed carton is shown in Table 18.4.

An important definition.

A standard to achieve.

PRODUCT : CARTON "X"		
Material costs	p.	
Card	40.6	
Tape	6.8	
Ink	2.7	
Total Material costs		50.1
Labour costs		
Machine operator	22.2	
Finisher	8.1	
Total Labour costs		30.3
Variable overheads		2.6
Fixed overheads		4.0
TOTAL COST		87.0p.

Table 18.4 Standard Cost Specification

DETERMINATION OF VARIANCES

> "A favourable variance results from a reduction in costs and/or increases in revenue and profit when actual is compared to standard."

> "Variances are caused by changes in price and/or volume."

Periodically the actual costs of production are compared with the standard costs laid down in the budget. Variances occur where the actual and standard costs differ, an excess cost being termed a positive (+) or adverse variance and an underspend as a negative (−) or favourable variance. There are two main types of variance, those relating to prices and those relating to volume. Unfortunately, most variances are combinations of both, which means that the review must separate out the two influences in order to identify the major cause. Price and volume variances are applied to all expense areas as well as to the revenue area of sales. Some of the main variances are given below.

Material variance

Material costs result from a combination of price and quantity used. Any difference could be caused by either a price or usage variance.

- Material price variance is the difference between the actual and standard price per unit of material multiplied by the actual quantity used.

  (Standard price − actual price) × actual quantity used

- Materials usage variance is the cost difference caused by more or less efficient use of the material. Its total is given by the difference between the actual and standard quantity used multiplied by the standard price.

  (Standard quantity − actual quantity) × standard price

Labour variances

- Labour rate variance measures the differences in labour cost caused by variations in the rates of pay. It is·calculated from the difference between the actual and the standard labour rate per hour multiplied by actual hours worked.

  (Standard rate − actual rate) × actual hours worked

- Labour efficiency variance is the difference caused by labour taking less or more time to complete the task. It is given by the difference between the actual hours taken and the standard hours allowed multiplied by the standard rate per hour.

  (Standard hours − actual hours) × standard wage rate

Sales variance

In order to explain profit variances, the sales must be analysed as well as the costs.
Sales can vary because of change in

- the quantity actually sold
- the price actually paid

Sales volume variance represents the difference in sales caused by the actual volume being different to the projected volume. It is calculated using the standard profit margin.

  (Actual sales − standard sales) × standard profit margin

- Sales price variance represents the difference in profit caused by selling at a non-standard price. It is calculated using the difference between actual and standard price multiplied by actual quantity sold.

  (Actual price − standard price) × actual quantity sold

The mechanics of variance analysis is quite straightforward. What is important is the interpretation of the results, i.e. whether positive or negative variances are favourable or not. The student's answer to Question 1 should prove a useful guide to examination technique.

EXAMINATION QUESTIONS

1 OP Ltd produces one product for which a standard costing system was introduced at the beginning of this year. The following standards were calculated for one unit of the company's products:

i) standard price of direct material   £0.45 per kilo;
ii) standard quantity of direct material   12 kilos per unit;
iii) standard direct labour   £2 per hour;
iv) standard number of direct labour hours   10 per unit.

a) Explain the meaning of each of the above terms (i–iv).   *(4)*

b) Discuss the ways in which the standards may have been set.   *(4)*

c) The company budgeted to produce 10,000 units during May 1985 but, in fact, produced 8,000 units, with the following results:
Direct material bought and used [94,000 kilos] £48,880
Direct labour used [84,000 hours] £189,000
From the given figures calculate:
  i) the standard cost per unit of output,
  ii) the actual cost per unit for May 1985,
  iii) the total cost variances.   *(6)*

d) Define the following terms, and calculate from the given figures:
  i) the material usage variance,
  ii) the material price variance.   *(6)*

e) Explain why the use of "standard costs" is considered to have advantages over the comparison of actual costs with past costs.   *(5)*

(UCLES 1985)

2 The following information relates to a company producing one single product:

Fixed costs	£50,000
Direct material costs	£5 per unit
Direct labour costs	£9 per unit
Variance overheads	£2 per unit
Selling price	£20 per unit

a) i) Using the above figures compile a table of costs and from this draw a chart to show the minimum number of units of the product which the company must sell to break even.   *(13)*
  ii) On your chart indicate the expected profit if sales were 25,000 units.   *(2)*

b) Market research has indicated that in the next period potential sales of 25,000 units at the current selling price, or 32,000 units if the selling price were lowered to £18 per unit are likely. Which strategy would you expect the firm to adopt, and why?   *(6)*

c) Why do businesses prepare break-even charts and what are the limitations of such charts?   *(7)*

(NISEAC Specimen Paper 1991)

3 a) What is meant by Full Cost Pricing?   *(5)*

b) In what circumstances would you advise the use of Marginal Cost Pricing, and why?   *(5)*

c) Why is the profit earned on a product important?   *(15)*

(UCLES 1985)

STUDENT'S ANSWER

Question 1

a) The standard price of direct material is the expected and estimated cost per kilo of material for the forthcoming production period. The standard quantity of direct material is the estimate amount of material required, on average, to make a unit of the product. The standard direct labour is the approximate cost per hour of the type of labour used in making the product. The standard number of direct labour hours is the projected time needed to make a unit. In all these examples

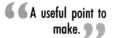
A useful point to make.

the figures are estimates and not actual but they are what one expects on average to occur.

b) The standard price of material could have been calculated by reference to past invoices and costs adjusted for the rate of inflation. The quantity of material needed could be estimated initially from the specification of the product design with later adjustment for wastage in the production process. The latter information would come from the work study department. Labour costs can be found from current labour charges with any adjustment for likely wage negotiations during the forthcoming production period. The final standard would involve the work study team, firstly in 'method study' to compare existing methods with proposed methods and secondly in 'work measurement' to establish the exact time required by a worker to complete the task.

> **A concise answer to a section where students often over-elaborate.**

> **Logically set out at each stage.**

c)   i) The standard cost per unit
      = standard cost of materials + standard cost of labour
      = $(12 \times 0.45) + (10 \times 2)$
     Standard cost per unit = 5.40 + 20 = £25.40

   ii) Actual cost per unit
      = actual cost of materials unit + actual cost of labour unit

   $$= \left(\frac{48,880}{8,000} + \frac{189,000}{8,000} \right)$$

   = 6.11 + 23.625
   Actual cost per unit = £29.735 = £29.74

   iii) Cost variances (£'s)

Cost variances (£'s)	Standard*	Actual	Variance
Direct Material	43,200	48,880	(5,680)
Direct Labour	160,000	189,000	(29,000)
			(34,680)

   A total adverse variance of £34,680 or £4.34 per unit

   * Direct Material = $(8,000 \times £5.40) = £43,200$
     Direct Labour = $(8,000 \times £20) = £160,000$

d)   i) The material usage variance is the difference between the actual quantity used in production and the standard amount allowed for that production, converted into monetary terms by using the standard price.
     (standard usage − actual usage) × Standard price per unit
      = $(96,000 - 94,000) \times 0.45$
      = $2,000 \times 0.45 = £900$ favourable

   The material usage variance is favourable to a total of £900 because less material was used than originally estimated.

   ii) The material price variance is the difference between the actual price paid for the quantity used and the standard price that should have been paid for the quantity used.

   Actual price $= \dfrac{£48,800}{94,000} = 0.52$

   (Standard price − actual price) × actual quantity
      = $(0.45 - 0.52) \times 94,000$
      = £6,580 adverse

   The material price variance is adverse by £6,580 because the actual price paid per unit was greater than the standard price.

e) The use of past costs can be misleading because they only show

> what has been achieved and not what can be achieved. Standard costs allow management to set criteria for both procurement and use of materials, labour and overheads. Efficiency standards can be built into the production plan and variance analysis provides essential monitoring and information feedback. Standard costs can also act as a motivator in that it engenders cost consciousness among employees.

❝ Overall this was a good answer from a candidate who has displayed accurate use of variance equations. ❞

Tutor's comment

TUTOR'S ANSWER

Question 2

a) i)

TABLE OF COSTS

Output (Units)	Fixed cost (£000's)	Variable* cost (£000's)	Total Cost (£000's)	Total revenue (£000's)	Profit (£000's)
5,000	50	80	130	100	−30
10,000	50	160	210	200	−10
15,000	50	240	290	300	10
20,000	50	320	370	400	30
25,000	50	400	450	500	50
30,000	50	480	530	600	70
35,000	50	560	610	700	90

* Variable cost = Direct material cost + direct labour cost + variable overheads
= £5 + £9 + £2 = £16 per unit

The break-even point is at 12,500 units, which is the minimum the company must sell to avoid a loss (see chart).

ii) Expected profit for sales of 25,000 is £50,000.

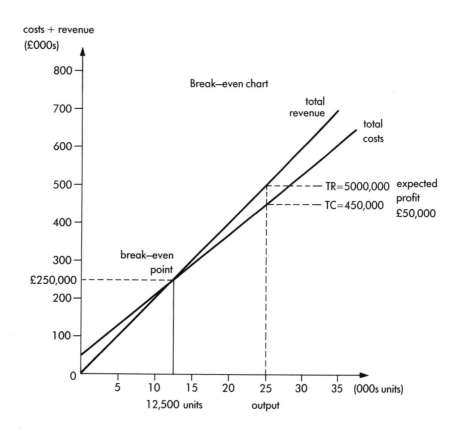

Fig. 18.3 Break-even chart

b) Sales of 25,000 at the current selling price would give a profit of £50,000.
   At 32,000 units and a selling price of £18 per unit:

Output	FC	VC	TC	TR	Profit
32,000	50,000	512,000	562,000	576,000	14,000

The lower price would result in increased sales but the resultant increase in costs would mean a lower profit of £14,000. The firm should keep its current selling price of £20 per unit.

c) Break-even charts are prepared in order to determine the output level at which profits will start to be earned. They can also be used to indicate the margin of safety, i.e. how far sales can fall from current levels before they reach a loss-making position. Finally, they can be used to estimate levels of profit from different levels of output.

The main limitations of break-even charts are that they:
   i) assume all costs can be categorised as fixed or variable, i.e. semi-variable costs are not included.
   ii) assume costs and revenue behave in a linear manner.
   iii) assume that all production will be sold within the trading period.
   iv) are only as accurate as the information on which they are based.

OUTLINE ANSWER

Question 3

a) A brief description is required of the pricing method based on adding the required profit level to the total production costs. Mention should be made of the division of total cost into direct costs and overheads and how the allocation of overheads is largely arbitrary. This method may be used as a starting point for pricing goods because no account has been taken of market conditions.

b) Start this section by defining and briefly explaining marginal cost pricing, i.e. basing the price on variable costs in order to make a part contribution towards fixed costs. This method could be used when a firm is operating at below full capacity, to make full use of its workforce or as a means of penetrating a new market.

c) Discussion of costs and prices naturally leads to an examination of profit. The student should not only describe the main reasons for earning a profit but also make some judgements as to their relative importance. The principal reasons are to provide a means of financing working capital, to provide a reserve of finance for future investment, to improve the capacity of the company to raise external finance, to act as a measure or yardstick of success, and to act as a motivator towards greater efficiency. In the final analysis a firm will not survive without profits.

FURTHER READING

Powell, *Production Decisions* Longman 1987:
   Chapter 6, The Contribution Costing Approach.
Myddleton and Corbett, *Accounting and Decision Making* Longman 1987:
   Chapter 10, Costs and Budgets.
Harvey and Nettleton, *Management Account Accounting* Mitchell Beazley 1983:
   Chapter 4, Break-even Analysis.
Norkett, *Management Accounting*, Longman 1982:
   Chapter 3, Basic Costing.
   Chapter 8, Budgeting Systems.
Daff, *Cost and Management Accounting* Woodhead Faulkner 1986:
   Chapter 6, Absorption and Marginal Costing.
   Chapter 7, Budgets and Budgetary Control.

GETTING STARTED

In Chapter 16, we noted that a funds flow statement showed where business finance had come from and how the business had used those funds. The aim of this chapter is to take a closer look at how businesses raise finance and how they decide to invest the money in specific projects.

All businesses need finance and capital. It is needed to finance the purchase of fixed assets – sometimes called investment capital. It is also needed to finance raw materials, stocks and debtors – commonly termed working capital.

The financial structure of small firms tends to be relatively simple. The owner finances the business through savings and borrowings from relatives, friends and banks. Larger firms have a far more complex financial structure raising money through share issues, borrowing nationally and internationally, long term as well as tapping various sources of medium and short term finance.

Long term finance is money raised for a period in excess of five years. It may be permanent – that is it remains available for company use as long as it is needed, or fixed term – repayable to the lenders at the end of a specified period. Medium term finance are borrowings for one to five years, whilst short term finance is anything up to one year. This classification is important. For example, long term financial needs should be met from long term, not short term, finance for otherwise the firm may find itself in difficulties when trying to renew that borrowing at the end of the loan period.

Capital investment requires the firm to commit money now, with the expectation of returns sometime in the future. As large amounts are involved and the impact of these decisions on the future of the firm is critical, careful appraisal of such investments is necessary. In this chapter we will turn our attention first of all to the different methods which may be used to assess the suitability of different capital projects.

SOURCES OF FINANCE AND INVESTMENT APPRAISAL

INVESTMENT APPRAISAL

APPRAISAL METHODS

INTERNAL SOURCES OF FINANCE

PERMANENT FINANCE

NEW ISSUE SHARE CAPITAL

LONG TERM FINANCE

CAPITAL GEARING

MEDIUM TERM SOURCES OF FINANCE

SHORT TERM SOURCES OF FINANCE

FINANCE FOR SMALL BUSINESSES

INVESTMENT APPRAISAL

ESSENTIAL PRINCIPLES

The level of a firm's profits depends upon the success with which it is able to use its assets, both human and non-human. Future profitability therefore depends on how successful the firm is at consolidating its existing assets and planning for expansion and improvement. These long-term decisions about new investment are part of the capital budgeting process where capital expenditure is analysed, planned and financed. Capital investment decisions are part of strategic decision making and help determine the future success or failure of a business. It is important that you understand the importance of investment decisions, the various types and the decision-making process as well as the various techniques for appraising different investment projects.

IMPORTANCE OF CAPITAL INVESTMENT DECISIONS

Capital investment decisions can be critical to a firm's future because they:

66 Uncertainty is an important factor (in investment appraisal decisions). 99

- involve a long-term commitment of substantial capital sums.
- are almost impossible to reverse without accepting a significant loss.
- contain a greater element of uncertainty – it is much more difficult to predict long-term changes in the market with any great degree of accuracy, e.g. what will be the consumer demand level for the product in five years time? What effect will tax changes have on demand? etc.
- not only affect the future profitability but may also affect the firm's very existence.

TYPES OF CAPITAL INVESTMENT

Capital investment is the expenditure on fixed assets with the view to making a profit over and above the original cost of the investment. Capital investment may take several forms such as:

66 Investment appraisal is used in many different situations. 99

- The replacement or acquisition of long term assets, e.g. plant and buildings.
- The expansion of capacity in an existing production line.
- The expansion into a new product line or into a new market area, e.g. exports to Eastern Europe.
- A special project aimed at affecting the future earning potential, e.g. research and development in a new manufacturing process or an advertising campaign.
- Investment in another firm either as a minority shareholder, merger or takeover.
- Investment in cost-saving equipment to reduce operating expenses.

THE CAPITAL INVESTMENT DECISION-MAKING PROCESS

Whichever method is used to appraise the future value of investment projects, the decision-making process should contain the following elements:

- The search for possible capital investment projects.
- Identification of the financial costs and benefits of the alternative projects.
- Assessment of the profitability of each alternative.
- Consideration of any non-quantifiable and non-financial factors.
- Selection of project, bearing in mind the risks involved and the finance available.
- Implementation of the investment decision
- Feedback: close monitoring and review of the progress of the project.

APPRAISAL METHODS

To help assess the profitability of different projects a firm can use one or more appraisal methods, all of which must take account of:

- The future stream of benefits or savings expressed in cash terms.
- The cost outlay required to effect the investment.

The four most common methods of investment appraisal are:

- Accounting Rate of Return (ARR)
- Payback
- Net Present Value (NPV)
- Internal Rate of Return (IRR)

Each of the first three methods is described below using the following example.

Example.
A firm is considering the purchase of a new machine and is faced with a choice between Machine A and Machine B, both costing £120,000. The estimated future cash flows and costs are:

	MACHINE A (£000's)	MACHINE B (£000's)
Initial Investment cost		
Year 0	120	120
Net Cash Flow		
Year 1	30	60
2	30	50
3	40	40
4	60	36
5	50	20
6	30	10

For the purposes of the example, we have assumed that the net cash flow has taken into account depreciation of the asset and that the machines have no residual value at the end of Year 6.

ACCOUNTING RATE OF RETURN (ARR)

This method expresses the average annual profit of a project as a percentage of the initial capital outlay. In comparing alternative projects, which are mutually exclusive, the project with the highest ARR will be chosen.
Example:

	MACHINE A (£000's)	MACHINE B (£000's)
Investment Year 0	−120	−120
Net cash inflow		
Year 1	30	60
2	30	50
3	40	40
4	60	36
5	50	20
6	30	10
Total cash inflow	240	216
Total net profit	240−120 = 120	216 − 120 = 96
Average annual profit		
over 6 years	20	16

$$ARR = \frac{\text{Average annual profit}}{\text{Initial investment}}$$

$$ARR \text{ machine A} = \frac{20}{120} \times 100 = 16.66\%$$

$$ARR \text{ machine B} = \frac{16}{120} \times 100 = 13.33\%$$

On the basis of ARR, Machine A would be preferred.

Advantages of ARR

- It is simple to calculate.

- It takes account of all cash flows.
- It is easy to understand.

Disadvantage of ARR

- It ignores the timing of cash flows. In the above example Machine B produces much of its net cash inflow in Years 1 and 2, whereas Machine A becomes more profitable in its later life. The extra £50,000 which Machine B earns over Machine A in Years 1 and 2 could be invested which, if taken into account, may alter the relative merits of the two machines.

PAYBACK

This method shows how long a period it will take before the original capital investment is 'paid back'. In this case the project with the shorter payback period would be chosen.

	MACHINE A (£000's)		MACHINE B (£000's)	
	Net cash flow	Cumulative cash flow	Net cash flow	Cumulative cash flow
Year 0	−120	−120	−120	−120
1	+30	−90	+60	−60
2	+30	−60	+50	−10
3	+40	−20	+40	+30
4	+60	+40	+36	+66
5	+50	+90	+20	+86
6	+30	+120	+10	+96

Payback for Machine A occurs in the 4th year. Only £20,000 of the £60,000 earned in Year 4 is required to complete the payback. Assuming linearity of cash flow, £20,000 is earned after a third of the year, therefore the exact payback period = 3⅓ years.

Similarly Machine B is paid back a quarter of the way through Year 3; therefore, the payback period is 2¼ years. Using this basis Machine B would be chosen.

Advantages of payback

- It is easy to calculate and simple to use.
- It is easy to understand.
- It takes account of how quickly the firm recoups its investment and is therefore, a useful measure of risk.
- It is useful in periods of rapid technological change when capital equipment can quickly become obsolete.

Disadvantages of payback

- It ignores all cash receipts after payback.
- It takes no account of the overall, long-term profitability of a project.

NET PRESENT VALUE (NPV)

NPV takes account of the timing of cash flows. It recognises that a given sum of money received now is worth more than the same sum received in the future, the reason being that the sum can be invested today to yield a return. For example, £100 invested now at an interest rate of 10% would be worth £110 in one year's time and £121 in two years' time. In other words £121 received in two years has a *net present value* of £100. Cash flows received at different times need to be adjusted to take account of the time value of money. This adjustment of future cash flows into present values is known as the *discounted cash flow* (DCF) technique. The equation to calculate any present value (PV) is given by:

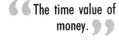The time value of money.

$$PV = \frac{An}{(1 + r)^n}$$

where An = the future cash flow in a given period
r = the discount rate expressed as a decimal
n = the time lapse

Example:
What is the present value of £100 received in three years' time when the interest rate is 10%?

$$PV = \frac{100}{(1 + 0.1)^3} = \frac{100}{1.331} = £75.13$$

The discount rate used is normally the opportunity cost of the initial investment capital which may be the present rate of interest obtained by depositing the money in the bank. (Also known as the 'exchange rate over time' as it determines the relationship between the amount invested now and a sum in the future.)

The NPV method discounts all future cash flows to present values and then compares the total present value of all cash inflows with the present value of all cash outflows.

The project with the highest positive PV would be chosen (any project with a negative PV would be rejected).

Assuming a 10% interest rate is available as an alternative use of £120,000, we can calculate the NPV of the two machines. The discount factors can be obtained from a PV table. The present value of any particular future cash flow is calculated by multiplying the net cash value by the appropriate discount rate. The NPV is the sum of all the individual cash outflows and inflows.

	MACHINE A (£000's)			MACHINE B (£000's)		
Year	Cash Flow	Discount Factor	PV	Cash Flow	Discount Factor	PV
0	−120	1.0	−120.00	−120	1.0	−120.00
1	30	0.909	27.27	60	0.909	54.54
2	30	0.826	24.78	50	0.826	41.30
3	40	0.751	30.04	40	0.751	30.04
4	60	0.683	40.98	36	0.683	24.59
5	50	0.621	31.05	20	0.621	12.42
6	30	0.564	16.92	10	0.564	5.64
		NPV =	+51.04		NPV =	+48.53

Machine A produces a positive NPV of £51,040, whereas Machine B has a positive NPV of £48,530. As the investment is mutually exclusive, Machine A would be chosen.

Advantages of NPV

- It takes account of all cash flows.
- The timing of cash flows is taken account of.
- It is reasonably easy to use.

Disadvantage of NPV

- It is not always easy to choose an appropriate discount rate.

INTERNAL RATE OF RETURN

This is another method using DCF, where the aim is to determine which project will produce the highest rate of return over its life.

COMPARISON OF THE METHODS

DCF methods of estimating the profitability of capital projects are considered to be superior to payback and average rate of return. ARR ignores the timing of the returns while payback ignores the cash flows after payback. Despite these problems firms may still choose to use more than one method. Whichever method is used, they all depend on the accuracy of the cash flow forecasts which is, in itself, often unreliable. As there are many contributing factors which can change over time one must accept that the cash flows are subject to a wide margin of error.

Capital investment appraisal provides only one facet of the total picture, that of the

Cash flow forecasts are often unreliable.

financial outcome. There are other non-financial and non-quantifiable considerations to be taken into account before a final decision is made:

- reactions of shareholders to the project.
- reaction of the financial sector if the project is profitable, but only in the long term.
- how does the project fit into the company's overall objectives?
- are there any political considerations, e.g. does success depend on the level of spending in the defence sector or on the NHS?
- how will the workforce react to the project?

> Non-financial factors may affect decisions.

INTERNAL SOURCES OF FINANCE

By far the greatest part of business investment in the UK is financed from sources internal to the firm. Indeed there are major advantages arising from internal financing because no interest payments have to be met, nor is any repayment necessary. However, reliance on internal finance does have its problems. In particular, if a business fails to generate the level of profits it has anticipated, its investment programme will be disrupted. A similar effect is caused by the decline of profits in a recession. Another problem which arises in inflationary periods is that depreciation provisions may be insufficient for the replacement of capital stock. Thus without external sources of finance a firm may actually contract rather than maintain or expand its current operations.

RETAINED PROFITS

Businesses are not required to distribute all their profits and many plough back a high proportion of their profits into the firm. Tax legislation encourages this by not charging income tax on the retained profits. (If the profits were distributed the recipients would have to pay tax.)

DEPRECIATION PROVISIONS

These are amounts of profit set aside to record the usage of fixed assets. However, as depreciation provisions do not result in an outflow of cash the funds can be used to finance current investments.

SURPLUS ASSETS

Many firms own land and buildings which are not used to their full capacity. The leasing or sale of such property can generate finance for current investment. Even where such property is not surplus to requirements it may be used to raise finance by a method known as 'sale and leaseback'. The company enters into two contracts at the same time:

> The best sources of finance are often 'internal'.

1 To sell the property (probably to an institutional investor).
2 To lease the same property back for a period of up to 100 years.

This method has the advantage of releasing funds locked up in fixed assets for other uses whilst guaranteeing long term occupation of the premises.

CURRENT ASSET CONTROL

Better inventory and credit control will reduce the levels of stocks and debtors, thus providing finance for investment.

PERMANENT FINANCE

A limited company can raise money by issuing shares. A person who buys shares becomes a part owner in that firm and is entitled to share in the profits of that company.

There are various forms of share capital. The *nominal* or *authorised* share capital is the amount of money a company can raise by selling shares. It is stated in the company's Memorandum of Association. Not all the authorised share capital is necessarily sold, however. The portion that has been sold is termed the *issued* share capital. Alternatively, a company may 'issue' or sell all its authorised share capital but just demand that a proportion is paid for now. For example, a company may issue shares at £3 each but only ask shareholders to pay 50p for the time being.

Companies often issue different classes of shares with different rights. This is so as to appeal to different groups of investors. The two main classes of share we will consider are ordinary and preference.

ORDINARY SHARES

Ordinary shareholders bear the ultimate risk within the business. They share in the profits after all other claimants, e.g. Preference Shareholders, Debenture holders, Inland Revenue, Creditors, have been paid. In years when profits are good their dividend will be high, but in bad years they may receive nothing at all. For this reason ordinary shares are often called 'risk capital'. Ordinary shares are also often referred to as *equity capital* because each ordinary share has the same rights and entitlements as any other ordinary share.

> **The major classes of shares.**

Ordinary shares will normally have voting rights at company meetings. Thus it is the ordinary shareholders who, by voting at the Annual General Meeting, appoint the Board of Directors and ultimately control the company.

PREFERENCE SHARES

As the name suggests, these shares receive priority when compared with ordinary shares. Preference shareholders will receive payment of dividend and repayment of capital (upon liquidation of the company) before ordinary shareholders. This obviously makes them less risky than ordinary shares.

Preference shareholders will normally be entitled to a fixed percentage dividend at the end of each year. Some, but not all preference shares, have voting rights. Due to taxation reasons, very few companies issue preference shares nowadays.

NEW ISSUE SHARE CAPITAL

Where a public company requires more finance it may raise this through the issue of more shares to the general public. (Compare this to the situation faced by the private company which cannot advertise to the public to buy its shares.)

Companies wanting to issue shares will normally use an issuing house (or Merchant Bank) to undertake the administration involved in the issue. The issuing house may also agree, for a fee, to 'underwrite' the issue or take up those shares not purchased by investors. This guarantees the share issue's success.

A new issue may take the following forms:

OFFER FOR SALE

> **Methods of raising share capital.**

The whole issue is sold to an issuing house (usually a Merchant Bank) who then re-offer it to the public at a higher price. It is the most popular form of share sale, used by all the 'privatised' companies, and newcomers to the Stock Exchange.

Detailed information of the company's activities, its track record and its future prospects is provided, together with an invitation to apply for shares. Large companies may take several pages in a national newspaper to inform the public of the share offer details. The cost of such issues is very high, thus it is only feasible where large sums of money need to be raised.

ISSUE BY PROSPECTUS

The formalities are the same as for an offer for sale, but the shares are sold direct to the public by the company. It is used very infrequently.

ISSUE BY TENDER

Where the issue price cannot be determined easily, the public may be invited to make bids (or tenders) for shares. Shares are allotted to investors at that price which ensures all shares are taken up. From the company's viewpoint the major disadvantage is that it is unable to predict the price and therefore, the total funds it will obtain, though it will set a *minimum* offer price.

PLACINGS

Where the small size of the company or the amount of capital required precludes an offer for sale, the issuing house will approach city institutions, e.g. pension funds, life assurance companies, who might be interested in holding shares in this kind of business. A high rate of return (and, therefore, a low purchase price) will be required by these investors to offset the lack of marketability of the shares.

RIGHTS ISSUES

New shares are offered to existing shareholders in proportion to their present holding. The 'offer price' is normally less than that quoted for existing shares on the Stock Exchange. The shareholder has the option of either taking up the offer, or selling the 'rights' on the Stock Exchange. Many of the costs associated with other methods of share issue are avoided with a rights issue.

LONG TERM FINANCE

Long term loan capital may take the form of mortgages or debentures. The distinction between the two is that a mortgage is a debt owed to a single lender whilst a debenture is a loan obtained from a number of people (or organisations). The following points apply to both mortgages and debentures:

Key features of loan capital.

- Loans are normally secured against property or other assets of the company.
- Loan interest payments are an expense to the company and must be paid in full before any dividends to ordinary or preference shareholders.
- Lenders are not members of the company and therefore have no say in the running of the business.
- Default on loan interest or capital repayments entitles the lender to terminate the loan agreement.

From the lender's viewpoint such loans are advantageous because their loan is secure and their interest guaranteed, even if the company fails to make a profit.

Long term finance also has advantages from the company's point of view:

- Inflation means that the real cost of making interest payments will decrease over time. Similarly the principal, when repaid, will be worth less (in real terms) than the amount borrowed.
- The present system of taxation recognises interest as an expense incurred in earning profits. Thus debt interest is paid out of pretaxed income whereas share dividends are paid out of taxed profits. In other words, it costs the company more to give shareholders the same return as debenture holders.

CAPITAL GEARING

As we have seen, long term finance can be satisfied by issuing shares or raising loan capital. The relationship between equity and loan capital is termed the *gearing ratio*. There are various ways gearing can be measured, but generally a company will be described as *highly* geared when it has a high proportion of fixed interest capital compared with ordinary share capital. Low gearing occurs when a company makes little use of fixed interest capital. The effect of gearing on a company is shown by the following example (Table 20.1). Companies A and B have raised the same amount of capital but in different ways. Company A makes little use of fixed interest capital – we can say it is low geared with a ratio of 1:9. Conversely Company B, with its greater use of loan capital, is highly geared having a ratio of 9:1.

In situation 1, both companies – after paying the debenture interest – have a residue available for ordinary shareholders which is equivalent to a 10% return on capital.

In situation 2, profits have increased by £10,000. The impact on Company A with its

	COMPANY A (£'000)	COMPANY B (£'000)
Ordinary shares	900	100
Debentures (10%)	100	900
Total long-term finance	1,000	1,000
Situation 1		
Profit	100	100
Debenture interest	10	90
Residue available to equity shareholders	90	10
As a % return on ordinary share capital	10% $\left(\dfrac{90}{900}\right)$	10% $\left(\dfrac{10}{100}\right)$
Situation 2		
Profit increases by 10%		
Profit	110	110
Debenture interest	10	90
Residue available to equity shareholders	100	20
As a % return on capital	11%	20%
Situation 3		
Profits decline by 10%		
Profit	90	90
Debenture interest	10	90
Residue available to equity shareholders	80	NIL
As a % return on capital	9%	NIL

Table 20.1 The impact of gearing upon profitability

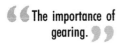

The importance of gearing.

greater use of equity capital is to raise the return to shareholders by 1% to 11%. However, in Company B the profits have to be spread between far fewer shareholders. Thus the impact of this profit rise is far greater. The return on capital has doubled from 10% to 20%.

In situation 3 though, where profits fall by £10,000 the return to ordinary shareholders in Company A falls from 10% to 9%. However, for Company B, the reduction in profit means that the shareholders will receive no return on their capital this year. Summarising, we can say that profit fluctuations will have a smaller impact on a low-geared firm than a high-geared firm. High gearing benefits firms in prosperous times, but in a recession, when sales and profits fall, the very existence of the firm may be at risk through an inability to service (pay interest on) its loans.

MEDIUM TERM SOURCES OF FINANCE

Medium term finance is generally accepted to be between one to five years long. It should be used for investment projects which will generate sufficient funds within that period to pay interest and repay capital.

BANK LOANS

Although banks have traditionally preferred to lend short term, they have in recent years modified their practices. Finance is now available for periods of up to 20 years; however the majority of lending is concentrated in the 1–5 year range. The agreement entered into between the banker and borrower will cover items such as interest charged (normally quoted as a percentage over market rate), security and repayment.

HIRE PURCHASE

Hire purchase companies are normally finance houses who specialise in bridging the financial gap between the seller of goods, who wants payment now, and the buyer who wants to pay by instalments. The hire purchase company will purchase the goods from the vendor and then enter into a hire purchase (HP) agreement with the would-be purchaser.

In effect an HP agreement is two contracts. The first is an agreement to hire plant or equipment for a particular period. The second is an agreement to purchase the item at the end of the period. No security is required on the agreement because legally the goods remain the property of the hire purchase company until the second agreement has been concluded. Where the hirer defaults on repayments on the goods it is possible for the hire purchase company to repossess the goods.

From the borrower's point of view the great advantages are that there is no need to provide security and that the asset can be used to generate funds and pay for itself. Also, as the instalments are fixed the firm can budget for the payment that becomes due. The major drawback is the cost – it can be twice as expensive as bank borrowing.

LEASING

The distinction between leasing and hire purchase is that under a leasing agreement the goods never become the property of the lessee or hirer. In effect the lessee is paying for the use of a piece of equipment for a specified length of time. Today it is possible to lease many items of equipment ranging from aircraft to dental equipment. The major advantages of leasing are:

- no large outflow of cash, as payments are spread over the life of the lease
- no need to provide security
- rental is paid from income generated by asset's use
- rental is an expense which may be offset against tax
- rental is fixed and can therefore be budgeted for
- it is advantageous where changing technology may rapidly make assets obsolescent

SHORT TERM SOURCES OF FINANCE

BANK OVERDRAFTS

Banks still regard themselves primarily as lenders of short term finance for items such as seasonal trade or for a specific contract. Bank overdrafts are flexible. It is basically an agreement to overdraw a current account up to a specified amount. Interest is charged on the balance outstanding at the end of each day's trading. However, the major disadvantage is that the banker can terminate the agreement at any time causing (in some cases) severe financial difficulties for the borrower. In practice this will not happen without good reason and although many overdrafts have a time limit of 6 to 12 months they are often renewed, thus providing the firm with a semi-permanent source of funds.

TRADE CREDIT

In most businesses goods are purchased on credit. The supplier invoices the purchaser for the sum due and allows him a period – normally 30 days – credit. It is possible to extend this period of credit, merely by not paying. Many firms anxious not to lose custom, will tacitly accept the delay in payment. For growing firms short of working capital this may be a major source of funds. However, beware! Bankers regard delaying payments as one of the first signs of financial difficulties. Moreover, delaying payment may allow the supplier to apply to the court for the winding up of the company, leading to liquidation.

FACTORING AND INVOICE DISCOUNTING

Delayed payment may cause particular difficulties to small or medium sized firms. Yet it is just these firms which may find their debtors (particularly large firms) taking an extended period of credit. Factoring and invoice discounting remedy this problem as the firm is able to sell all or part of its debtors. In effect, a credit sale has been turned into a cash sale!

With invoice discounting the business receives 75% of the value of its invoices immediately – the remainder, less bad debts, when they are paid.

Factors actually purchase the book debts, take over their administration and assume the risk of non-payment. The factor will deal directly with debtor customers.

Both factoring and invoice discounting provide immediate cash for the business and don't affect the borrowing potential of the firm. Invoice discounting also has the advantage of not revealing to the customer that book debts have been discounted – historically a sign of immediate bankruptcy.

FINANCE FOR SMALL BUSINESSES

Large and medium-sized firms with good profits and prospects have few difficulties in obtaining the funds they require. However, for over half a century it has been recognised that small firms, partly through ignorance and partly through the unavailability of sources that are open to large firms, are forced to rely on retail banks for most of their external finance. For that reason attempts have been made to provide other sources of finance to smaller firms.

VENTURE CAPITAL

This can be defined as the provision of finance to growing companies. The finance may be used for:

- start up capital – to develop/market a product
- second round capital – to expand a product range
- development capital – to develop a new range of products or diversify by merger

There are over 100 firms providing this form of finance. In return for finance the growing company may have to agree to restrictions on the distribution of profits, the appointment of non-executive directors and changes to management. For the financier, although the risks are great, so also are the potential rewards.

UNLISTED SECURITIES MARKET (USM)

Smaller firms not ready for a full listing on the Stock Exchange may raise cash for expansion and create a market for their shares through the USM. The procedure for raising capital is a simplified form of that for obtaining a listing on the Stock Exchange. The cost (less than £100,000) is significantly less than for the Stock Exchange. There are approximately 500 firms trading on the USM.

GOVERNMENT AID

Since 1980 the government has introduced many measures, a number of them financial, to aid smaller firms. The Loan Guarantee Scheme enables bankers to lend to small firms in situations where, in other circumstances, they would be reluctant. Under this scheme 70% of the loan is guaranteed by the government if the borrower pays a 2½% premium to the DTI.

Under the Business Expansion Scheme, risk capital investors in unquoted companies are allowed income tax relief on the investment at their highest rate of tax.

EXAMINATION QUESTIONS

1   Read the following information and answer the questions below.
    Machines Ltd. is about to choose between three projects.
        Project A is for the purchase of a new machine;
        Project B is for a promotional campaign;
        Project C is for the rationalisation of a part of the production department.
    The cost and expected returns for each project are as follows:

	PROJECT A	PROJECT B	PROJECT C
Initial Cash Outlay			
Year 0	£10,000	£10,000	£10,000
Cash Inflow			
Year 1	£1,000	£4,000	£3,000
2	£2,000	£3,000	£3,000
3	£3,000	£3,000	£3,000
4	£3,000	£2,000	£3,000
5	£3,000		£2,000
6	£3,000		£1,000

Present Value of £1 receivable at the end of a number of years at 10%						
After	*1 year*	*2 years*	*3 years*	*4 years*	*5 years*	*6 years*
PV of £1	£0.91	£0.83	£0.75	£0.68	£0.62	£0.56

a) What is the Net Cash Flow for Project C? (2)

b) i) Calculate the Net Present Value of each project using Discounted Cash Flow methods. (11)

   ii) On the basis of your calculations in b) i), which project should be selected? (1)

c) Suggest and explain *four* factors that might be taken into account when making an investment decision. (8)

d) State *three* different methods of financing the purchase of capital equipment. (3)

(AEB 1988)

2 Your firm has decided to make a takeover bid for a firm supplying you with raw materials. The question arises whether you should offer equity capital or cash.

a) What factors should be taken into account when making the decision to offer equity capital or cash? (15)

b) What might be the financial consequences for the shareholder of the company being taken over? (10)

(UCLES 1986)

3 More small businesses fail through lack of liquidity than through lack of profitability. Explain why this statement is likely to be true and suggest ways in which firms might attempt to avoid such failure. (25)

(UCLES 1991)

TUTOR'S ANSWER

Question 1

a) Net cash flow for Project C (£000's)

Year 0	−10
1	3
2	3
3	3
4	3
5	2
6	1

Net cash = + 15 −10

Net cash flow = +£5,000

b)

Year	Discount Factor	PROJECT A		PROJECT B		PROJECT C	
		Cash Flow (£000's)	PV	Cash Flow (£000's)	PV	Cash Flow (£000's)	PV
0	1.0	−10	−10	−10	−10	−10	−10
1	0.91	+1	0.91	+4	3.64	+3	2.73
2	0.83	+2	1.66	+3	2.49	+3	2.49
3	0.75	+3	2.25	+3	2.25	+3	2.25
4	0.68	+3	2.04	+2	1.36	+3	2.04
5	0.62	+3	1.86			+2	1.24
6	0.56	+3	1.68			+1	0.56

$$\text{NPV} = 10.4{-}10 \qquad 9.74{-}10 \qquad 11.31{-}10$$
$$= +0.4 \qquad -0.26 \qquad +1.31$$
$$\text{NPV} = +£400 \qquad -£260 \qquad +£1,310$$

Project C should be chosen as it has the highest NPV

c) One fact to take account of is the firm's belief in the future. It must take into consideration forecasts about demand, costs, inflation, taxation, etc. in order to create a picture of the future market.

A second factor is the alternative projects available. This is where the various investment appraisal techniques can be used to decide which one is most profitable given due consideration to the cash flows.

Another factor is the investor's attitude to risk. Investment decisions are often on a large scale; therefore it is important to recognise the firm's attitude to risk and project uncertainty.

The final factor is finance. Firstly, is the finance available internally or must the firm use external sources? The cost of the finance is not the only problem as one must also consider how it affects the firm's gearing and its liability to future interest payments.

d) Capital equipment can be financed by:
1) outright purchase – using internal funds or a term loan from the bank
2) leasing – paying for the use of the equipment but without buying it
3) hire purchase – using a finance company where payment is made over a period time by a deposit plus instalments

OUTLINE ANSWERS

Question 2

Your introduction should discuss briefly the reasons for such a takeover bid. These could include to secure supply sources for the future, to control the market or achieve economies of scale.

a) You should consider the impact on the firm of offering cash or shares. For example the issue of shares may have implications for the control of the company and future dividend policy. Alternatively the take-over company may feel that this current share price does not reflect the underlying value of their firm (this could be for many reasons, e.g. state of the economy or industry) and thus be unwilling to issue shares.

In the takeover bid there may be shareholders in the 'raw material' company who do not wish to be associated with the new firm. An offer for cash would be attractive to them as it would save them the costs of selling through the Stock Exchange. However, offering cash may leave the firm short of working capital (unless the firm being taken over has substantial cash reserves). Cash could be raised by the issue of debentures but this would have implications for capital gearing – particularly if the firm was subject to marked fluctuations in business activity.

The existence of other bidders may also affect the decision to offer cash or shares for the firm being taken over. If other bidders have a better profits record or are perceived to have better prospects, it may be better to offer the cash alternative rather than shares.

b) To a certain extent the financial consequences of the takeover will depend upon the future prospects of the combined firm. Shareholders will have to gauge whether the large firm is more, or less, risky than their original investment. Generally speaking though, raw material industries are seen as more cyclical than other industries and a business with a diversified product base will achieve more stable profits.

Existing shareholders in the firm being taken over will also have to look at the new firm's gearing ratios (to assess risk) and dividend policy (to assess future returns on their investment). More generally they are now subject to the policies of the takeover firm and this will obviously impact upon profits, share prices and the security of their investment.

Question 3

You should first define liquidity and explain its relationship to working capital. You should give examples of how it might be measured, e.g. current and quick ratios. Better candidates may also mention stock and debtor turnover ratios. You should make the point that working capital requirements should be a part of the *long term* capital of the firm.

The first part of the question asks you to explain why small firms fail through lack of liquidity rather than profitability. You should trace the impact of a fall in business activity upon the liquidity position of a small firm, e.g. falling sales, increased stock levels, debtors taking longer to pay their debts (especially large firms), creditors demanding payments more quickly. As working capital requirements increase, the firm may be unable to pay its debts as and when they become due, even though it is still trading profitably. Moreover, the reaction of short term lenders exacerbates this position because they wish to reduce, rather than increase, their lending to a firm in this position.

The second part of the question asks you to suggest ways in which firms might attempt to avoid such failure. First you might suggest that the small businessman should be more aware of the environment in which he works, watch for signs which indicate a downturn in business activity and adjust his activities accordingly. You could suggest various forms of 'longer' term financing which might be available to the small firm, e.g. Venture Capital or the government-backed BES. Alternatively, the firm might consider leasing rather than buying fixed assets, thus releasing funds for working capital. As a final comment, you might suggest that the firm expands more slowly, relying on retained profits for an increase in long term capital.

FURTHER READING

Middleton, *Financial Decisions* 2nd edition, Longman 1987:
    Chapter 4, Long term investment projects.
    Chapter 5, Types and Sources of Finance.
Ogley, *Business Finance* Longman 1981:
    Chapter 4, The capital needed at the start of a private sector company.
    Chapter 5, Main types of securities issued by companies.
    Chapter 6, Capital structure and gearing.
    Chapter 7, Working capital.
Mott, *Accounting for Non Accountants* Pan 1984:
    Chapter 14, Capital Investment Appraisal.
Buckley, *Structure of Business*, 2nd edition Pitman 1990:
    Chapter 22, Sources of Finance.

20

PRODUCTION I

THE PRODUCT

LOCATION

ORGANISATION OF PRODUCTION

SCALE OF PRODUCTION

PRODUCTION CONTROL

GETTING STARTED

Production, whether of goods or services, is concerned with the organisation and transformation of resources such as manpower, materials and finance to produce a saleable item. The *production* function encompasses long-term decisions about new technologies, new markets and new products as well as short- and medium-term decisions concerning stock management, quality, manpower, training, production levels, cost control, etc.

These decisions must be based on accurate factual data which is available both from outside the organisation and internally from its own control systems. The collection and analysis of this data also uses resources, so the production manager must always bear in mind the benefits of more information against the costs of gathering it. This point is often overlooked by students.

The ultimate goal is to produce a product which is desired by the market at a cost which makes the organisation profitable, i.e. to 'optimise' output through the efficient use of its resources. However, the production function cannot obtain this goal in isolation but must interact with the other sub-systems in the organisation. *Marketing* provides valuable information about market needs, not only in the present but also future forecasts. *Personnel* helps in the provision and handling of human resources and *finance* provides essential control and planning systems as well as the means for current and capital expenditure.

This chapter is about the decision-making process as applied to the *production* area to solve the problems of what to produce (the product), how best to produce (organisation), how much to produce (scale) and how best to monitor production (control). The problem of *where* to produce (location) is then discussed.

The 'production control' area allows us to look at some quantitative techniques which are available as useful tools to help make the production manager a more effective decision-maker.

ESSENTIAL PRINCIPLES

The *product* is any good or service that a business sells in order to make a profit. The product may be large (a multi-million pound oil-rig) or small (pencil, paper-clip, peanut). It can be a physical item (book, car, dress) or a service (hair-cut, bus-ride, hotel accommodation). Many products are combinations of both, where the retailer sells a physical item such as a gas cooker but also expects to offer associated services such as delivery, installation, repair and maintenance. Whether products are a good or a service, they all exhibit three major features:

- pressure to change
- a finite life-cycle
- conflicting requirements of the product

PRESSURE TO CHANGE

This can be generated internally within the company by advances in technology. The role of the Research and Development department is to constantly examine the product to see how improvements can be made, costs reduced or quality enhanced. This innovatory function generates pressure for change ranging from minor modifications of existing products to the complete design of a replacement. Most pressure, however, comes from external sources emanating from three areas:

- changes in consumer taste
- actions of competitors
- economic forces

Pressures for change.

Changes in consumer taste

The market is dynamic in that consumer preferences are constantly under review. The fashion industry not only changes from season to season but from year to year. Items which are fashionable in one period may very quickly become obsolete. A similar pattern can be observed with most consumer durables, e.g. walkmans, skateboards, computer games, etc.

Actions of competitors

The threat of competition and loss of market share.

The launch of a new or improved product by a close competitor may well threaten one's own market share. This will inject a sense of urgency to respond with similar or alternative improvements. In recent years the car industry has exhibited this type of behaviour with respect to features such as electric windows, power steering, sun-roof and central locking, which instead of being 'extras' have now become 'standard' as each manufacturer attempted to enhance its own basic model.

Economic forces

External influence of government.

Changes in the economic climate can severely alter the life-span of a product. The boom period of the early 1980s led to a rapid expansion in the housing market and the subsequent demand for household furnishings, double glazing, conservatories, etc. The optimism and high demand exhibited in these areas quickly evaporated in the period of high interest rates from 1988 onwards. Even a well-designed, efficiently made product may suffer from changes in a government's fiscal and monetary policy or from fluctuations in the exchange rate which affects the competitiveness of rival foreign firms.

A FINITE LIFE-CYCLE

Four stages in the life of a product.

Changes in consumer taste, the actions of competitors and the general economic climate all ensure that a product has a finite life-span. Each product, if successful, graduates from a development stage, through growth to maturity and eventually into decline (Fig. 20.1). This concept is developed more fully in the marketing section (see Chapter 12). It is sufficient to recognise three factors which follow from this:

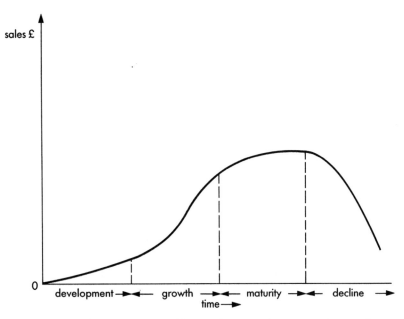

sales £

0

development →←— growth —→←— maturity —→←— decline —→

time→

Fig. 20.1 The product life-cycle

- The time-span for each stage will vary from product to product and may alter quite dramatically, e.g. the demand for eggs and beef following the salmonella and BSE outbreaks.
- A constant search for 'new' products must be undertaken to eventually replace those in the growth and maturity stages.
- The impact on the cash flow of the business.

The *development stage* results in an outflow of funds which will not be recouped until some point in the *growth stage*, if at all. Many products die at the development stage or never fulfil the company's aspirations when launched, e.g. Sinclair's C5 city-car. It is hoped that a product in the *growth/maturity* stages will help fund development of new products to guarantee product succession.

A 'new' product can be anything ranging from a revolutionary untried item (the video camera) to modifications of existing products (e.g. a new model Ford Sierra with different styling and added features). In the past companies tended to be product orientated where new items were designed in-house and presented to the consumer on a 'take-it or leave-it' basis. Greater competition and a more discerning customer has meant that companies must be market orientated and produce a good which satisfies a perceived or created consumer want. This is the reason why the production and marketing functions must work in close harmony so that a product is developed which will have a viable economic life.

> Market-led production.

REQUIREMENTS OF THE PRODUCT

Each product must satisfy the following criteria:

> Important product considerations.

- Functionally sound
- Capable of economic production
- Aesthetically pleasing

Functionally sound

The product must be suitable for the perceived purpose. For example, a car advertised as an 'off-road' vehicle will be expected to perform satisfactorily in conditions of mud, snow and rough terrain. Failure to do so will render the product unacceptable to the market.

Economic production

The design of the product must enable the production function to operate at as low a cost as possible so that the end-product can be presented to the consumer at an acceptable price. An acoustic engineer could create an audio system with near perfect sound reproduction but the cost would be prohibitive for the majority of consumers.

Aesthetically pleasing

In the modern market the customer not only wants a functional item but also one that is attractive. The flowing lines of the modern family saloon is as much to do with aesthetic appeal as it has to do with aerodynamics and efficiency. A music-centre is as much a piece of furniture as it is an audio system.

This balance between these criteria is the concern of value analysis. This is a formalised decision process to help improve product designs by determining the optimum mix of factors.

THE DESIGN PROCESS

Each new product, whether it be designed from 'bottom-up' or be merely a minor modification requires production to follow a design process. The process goes through the following stages:

An important sequence in production.

- *The idea:* a change which is described in a draft specification outlining purpose, material, reliability, performance, appearance, safety features and cost.
- *Testing:* the concept is assessed using a combination of scale models, mock-ups or mathematical models.
- *Prototype:* a full-scale working model.
- *Production specification:* a detailed breakdown of the production requirements eventually leading to a test production run and the testing of samples in the market.
- *Production:* only after this exhaustive process is 'new' product launched onto the market. However, the design process does not end with manufacture but continues by monitoring all feedback from both the operating plant and marketing to look for further improvements and adjustments.

LOCATION

Production takes place when labour, capital, raw materials and energy are combined to produce a commodity which is then distributed to its market. The choice of *location* may help to minimise the unit costs of this production. Location plays an important part not only for new firms about to set up but also for existing firms on the verge of expansion. There are many factors which influence location, some of which conflict (for example, the wish to be near bulky raw materials but at the same time to be near the final market). The best solution is, therefore, an optimisation of interest, weighing up the relative importance of each of the following economic influences as well as taking note of non-economic factors such as government legislation.

The search for an optimum solution.

ECONOMIC FACTORS AFFECTING LOCATION

The availability of land

The amount of land required depends on the size and type of business and the demands of the production process. Some firms require large flat areas (e.g. oil refineries and chemical plants), while others require remote locations (munitions factories and nuclear power stations). Service industries prefer to be close to large conurbations and may only require a small area, whereas a hypermarket would like the same proximity to population but desire much larger premises. The topography and the load-bearing properties of a site may also be a location determinant.

The physical requirements of the site.

The availability of labour

Labour is paradoxically one of the least mobile factors due to a host of reasons ranging from family ties to property prices. A firm may be looking for two types of labour, either or both of which could influence location.

The quantity and quality of labour.

- plentiful supply of cheap unskilled labour
- a highly skilled and experienced labour force

Locating away from the former would entail a firm incurring high transport costs or high inducements to persuade labour to travel or re-locate. Where the latter category is not available the firm incurs high training costs.

An important factor today is the history of labour relations in the area. Firms are keen to see if organised labour has a tradition of militancy or co-operation.

The availability of raw materials

It is self-evident that some firms are closely tied to their raw materials, e.g. quarrying and coalmining. The importance of raw materials as a locating factor has diminished with the continued improvement in transport and the greater use of lighter, less bulky materials. Plastics and alloys have replaced steel and wood as the principal materials of manufacture. Despite this trend raw materials are still a significant factor for those firms whose process is bulk-reducing such as sugar-refining, brickmaking and sawmills. The high cost of transport acts as a deterrent to all high bulk, high weight, low value products. Another sector influenced by raw materials is that dealing with perishable goods. Canning and freezing firms tend to locate close to production areas, e.g. Bird's Eye in the farming area of East Anglia. Companies relying on the import of bulky items may prefer a location close to a port, whereas the import of low bulk, high value items such as diamonds will exert little influence on location.

> The accessibility of raw materials.

The availability of services

All firms require a source of energy, water, drainage and waste disposal. In the past the pull of energy exerted a tremendous influence, first resulting in locations near to fast flowing rivers and then near to the coalfields. In most developed economies energy is widely available and does not exert a locating influence; however, in third world economies it is still a major factor.

> The provision of adequate services.

Access to water and other services will create an added cost to an undeveloped site remote from existing systems.

The availability of transport

The distribution system becomes important when either the raw materials or the finished goods are heavy and bulky. In this case the firm must compare the cost of the raw material transport with that of servicing the market. Some products, for example, fragile items like glass or perishables such as fruit may well need specialist transport. The ready access to a rail or sea terminal or close proximity to the motorway network may also be influencing factors. This is especially important but it also coincides with nearness to market, as evidenced by the M4 corridor link into London. Bulk-gaining processes require good transport links, e.g. soft drinks and furnishing.

> The transport network.

Proximity to the market

The most powerful influence in modern times has been the ready access to the market. London and the south-east has experienced rapid growth as many new and established firms have migrated to the large, lucrative conurbation. The opening of the Channel Tunnel may well cause a further shift to the south or even into northern France in order to take advantage of a wider European market.

> The demands of the market.

Other influences

- The availability of specialist further education which can provide essential training, e.g. motor engineering in the Midlands and textiles in Lancashire.
- Close proximity of similar businesses to provide technical or support services.
- A suitable climate for those involved in agriculture and horticulture.

NON-ECONOMIC FACTORS AFFECTING LOCATION

The role of government

A major non-economic influence has been central and local government. They influence location either by encouraging firms to establish in designated areas to help alleviate unemployment and under-utilisation of resources (e.g. schools, hospitals) or constrain it by regulation.

> Constraints and incentives.

Incentives

Since 1945 the government has promoted the location of new firms in areas of deprivation by offering a range of financial incentives which included:

- low rental sites
- purpose-built factories
- re-settlement of key workers
- grants for plant and machinery
- tax allowances
- management advice and consultancy

Originally these were available in designated Development Areas, Special Development Areas and Intermediate Development Areas, but recently this type of help has been assigned to Enterprise Zones and inner-city areas. Help is also available from the European Community as part of the regional aid scheme.

Constraints

The 1947 Town and Country Planning Act gave government the power to restrict building. An Industrial Development Certificate is required for all buildings over 5,000 sq. ft. in London and the south-east and for buildings over 10,000 sq. ft. elsewhere. Amendments to the Act in 1962, 1968 and 1971 have provided further powers to restrict land use, refuse planning permission and to create development-free areas. This 'carrot and stick' approach enables government to exert a considerable influence on location but well short of actually directing it.

Social influences

A growing influence which firms must take note of is the emergence of private pressure groups who wish to alter or deter development and location of firms for a variety of reasons:

The role of pressure groups and environmental concerns.

- Protection of wild-life and natural habitats
- Environmental concern, such as pollution
- Safety reasons, hence opposition to nuclear power stations, munition factories and the processing of toxic waste
- Selfishness – the 'not in my backyard' syndrome

Conclusion

Despite all these economic and non-economic influences, location can still take place for accidental reasons to do with place of birth or a liking for the area. Even when approached in a pseudo-scientific manner to achieve the lowest location cost per unit, changes in the social, political and economic climate, both locally and nationally may turn an advantageous site into a liability. Retailers dependent on passing tourist traffic are evidence of this when a new by-pass diverts the trade away from the once ideal site.

ORGANISATION OF PRODUCTION

The production process may be one, or a combination, of three different types; job, batch or flow production.

Important definitions.

Job: manufacture of a unique item from beginning to end as a result of an individual order.

Batch: manufacture of a quantity of similar items where a batch of products is processed through a given stage before the entire batch is moved to the next process.

Flow: manufacture using a mass-production line where the product moves continuously from one operation to another without stopping.

The type of production actually chosen largely depends on two major factors:

- The nature of the product
- The size of the firm and its market

THE NATURE OF THE PRODUCT

At one extreme is *job production*, where a customer has ordered a single item, often of a complex nature or unique design, e.g. a luxury liner, an extension to a house or a commissioned work of art. This type of product requires individual attention, a range of skills and is regarded as a 'one-off' with little chance of a repeat order. At the other extreme is *flow production*, which makes an identical, standard product in vast quantities. In this case the product is formed by the assembly of its constituent parts in a continuous process, e.g. car assembly, TVs. In between these two extremes is *batch production*, where a reasonably standardised item is manufactured in pre-determined quantities dependent on the state of the market, e.g. the demand for bread throughout the week and at the week-end.

As the product becomes more standardised it can be broken down into simple components which then allows the application of more specialised labour and machinery. This enables a firm to move from unit or job production towards batch and flow methods, depending on the market demand for the item.

THE SIZE OF THE FIRM AND ITS MARKET

The *size* of a firm also has an influence on the production method used. A small firm tends to accept only small orders with short production runs. An example of this would be a local builder who contracts to build individual houses to specific design requirements. As the firm grows it has the resources to finance and produce 'batches' of similar products. For building, this may be represented by a national company producing a limited range of houses on different sites throughout the country.

❝The importance of the size of market and the size of firm.❞

Mass production is only contemplated for those goods whose demand is perceived as being large, regular and long-lasting. The investment in plant, machinery, labour and stocks means that only the largest firms serving a national or international market can envisage using 'flow' production on a large scale.

CHARACTERISTICS OF THE DIFFERENT PRODUCTION METHODS

	JOB	BATCH	FLOW
PRODUCT	– unique item – wide variety of individual orders	– a number of standard items aimed at the market rather than individual consumer	– mass production of an identical standard product
LABOUR	– high technical expertise of the operator – craft skill – versatile	– specialists – less emphasis on technical skill	– limited range of tasks – low level of individual skill
MACHINERY	– general purpose facilities	– special purpose machine tools, jigs and fixtures	– highly specialised plant and machinery
LAYOUT	– fixed position – minimal movement during construction	– sub-divided by process e.g. fabrication, welding, painting etc	– sub-divided by product using continuous flow methods
MARKET	– individual orders – repeat orders unlikely	– market orientated – steady demand for variable quantities	– large scale regular, long-term demand
EXAMPLES	– machine tools – ocean liner – channel tunnel – bridge – motorway	– furniture – loaves of bread – pottery – brewing beer – pharmaceuticals	– washing machines – car assembly – TV's – audio equipment

Table 20.1 Characteristics of production methods.

	JOB	BATCH	FLOW
ADVANTAGES	– product tailored to consumer needs – easy to isolate problem areas – greater involvement of workforce – job satisfaction	– lower unit costs because of increased scale of production – use of more specialist machinery – able to calculate and use standard costs	– very low unit costs – high output rate – use of low skilled, easily trained labour
DISADVANTAGES	– high degree of technical expertise required – wide range of machinery needed – machinery often idle – flexible workforce – high cost per unit – repeat orders unlikely	– long production time – lost production during 're-tooling' between batches – high stock levels waiting between processes – ties up capital	– any breakdown affects total output – little job satisfaction – workforce could suffer from boredom when doing a monotonous operation – high capital investment

Table 20.2 Advantages and disadvantages of production methods.

The principal characteristics and advantages of the three methods cover the product, its market, the labour and machinery required and the production layout. These are compared in Tables 20.1 and 20.2. As the volume of production increases from job towards flow production a number of other points become important.

Materials handling

As production increases this must become more efficient to ensure the correct items arrive at the required time at the requisite work station.

Maintenance

This becomes more critical when 'down-time' results in the loss of increasing numbers of the product. For a mass-production line maintenance must be preventative as well as corrective to ensure continuous output.

Quality control

This must be built-in to the production process. It would be wasteful only to check the item at the end of a long and expensive production run. In-line process control is needed so that the item is checked at each stage of production without significantly affecting the flow of production.

In the final analysis the production method chosen will depend on the optimisation of the various advantages and disadvantages. The present and future market size, the state of technology, the product design and the level of employee skill all contribute toward the eventual decision.

A mix of influence.

SCALE OF PRODUCTION

Significant reductions in costs can be achieved through economies of scale.

The question of the *scale* of production brings into question the advantages and disadvantages of increasing the level of output. If a change in the scale of production leads to a more than proportionate change in output then the firm experiences increasing returns to scale. The effect of this is to reduce unit costs (average total costs), thus allowing the firm to either reduce price and become more competitive or to enjoy a larger profit margin or in fact a little of both. The main causes of such economies can be grouped into five categories, namely technical, marketing, financial, managerial and risk-bearing.

TECHNICAL ECONOMIES

New technology

A larger scale of output may allow new technology to be used which reduces operating costs per unit, e.g. larger fishing vessels can use radar to locate shoals of fish.

Increased dimension

A larger-scale plant costs proportionately less to build than smaller one, e.g. doubling the dimensions of a storage tank or warehouse results in an 8-fold increase in volume (storage capacity) but only a 4-fold increase in surface area (materials to build it).

Division of labour

Greater scope for the increased use of division of labour and the application of specialist machinery.

Integration of processes

Linking processes in a large scale operation can reduce storage, handling and transport costs as the product moves in an uninterrupted fashion from one process to another, e.g. the steel industry significantly reduced fuel costs by linking iron-smelting to steel fabrication, thus saving on re-heating between the two processes.

Fixed costs

High fixed costs can be spread over larger production runs thus reducing the fixed cost per unit.

Gearing economies

Large scale operations can make full use of all capital equipment by gearing the process in the optimum ratio. For example, a process using two machines X and Y, with capacities of 200 and 300 per day respectively, would require a daily output of 600 in order to synchronise all machines. In this case 3 machines of type X and 2 of type Y would produce the optimum combination. It is likely that small firms may not be able to afford such a capital commitment.

Research and development

Only the largest of firms can afford to finance expensive research facilities. However, the rewards of technological breakthroughs can be enormous and lead to an increased market share.

MARKETING ECONOMIES

Purchasing

The large scale purchaser of raw materials and components can often achieve benefits such as larger discounts, larger credit periods and prompt delivery.

Selling

The use of its own representatives rather than selling through agents may increase the effectiveness of a firm's marketing strategy.

Advertising

> Lower cost per unit.

Using the national media (television, radio and newspapers) may be more costly but if it leads to a more than proportionate increase in demand it becomes cost effective. The higher advertising costs are shared between a larger output, thus reducing costs per unit.

FINANCIAL ECONOMIES

- larger firms have more assets and are often considered less of a risk by the financial sector; hence they can negotiate loans at more favourable rates.

- large firms have access to more sources of finance which can prove to be less costly, e.g. issue of shares to the public.

MANAGERIAL ECONOMIES

- specialisation of management: the division of labour applied to management allows the employment of specialists in the fields of finance, purchasing, production, marketing and personnel.

- large firms are able to invest in sophisticated computer systems to handle the increase in data more effectively and efficiently.

RISK-BEARING ECONOMIES

The growth of conglomerates and multi-nationals.

Diversification can lead to greater security by not being reliant on one product, market, consumer or supplier. A range of products can be developed and marketed internationally so that recession in one area does not adversely affect the whole organisation.

DISECONOMIES OF SCALE

Limitations to the continued growth of firms.

Despite these economies there is a limit to the gains from growth. Eventually further economies will no longer be available and the firm will have reached its optimum level of capacity. Expansion beyond this point will result in diseconomies of scale as the organisation becomes more complex. This will appear as:

- Greater problems in co-ordinating activities as numbers of people increase, especially where output is performed in different geographical locations.
- The chain of command lengthens, which may cause delays in communication.
- The decision-making process slows down and the firm is less able to react quickly to market changes.
- There is more difficulty in motivating and monitoring large numbers of people.
- There is growth in the bureaucracy of the firm with established procedures and protocol. This may dampen employee initiative and innovation.

These diseconomies would lead to falling returns to scale and increasing costs per unit. The optimum size is dependent not only on the size of output but also, the state of technology. As science progresses the optimum production process of today may very quickly become outdated. The development of the silicon chip and its application to industry demonstrates how processes can be radically affected over a short period of time. The modern car assembly plant now relies more on robotics than on labour-intensive production lines.

PRODUCTION CONTROL

Production planning and control is concerned with converting sales forecasts or orders into a realisable manufacturing programme, i.e. ensuring that all orders can be met by the target dates within the agreed costs limits. A production plan will determine the scheduling and loading of jobs as well as detailing the material requirements. Once the plan has been approved and accepted it is important to monitor the progress of work from the beginning of the production process to the final delivery of the finished article to the consumer.

Two important parts of this monitoring process concern the control of stock and the control of quality.

THE CONTROL OF STOCK

Stock control is an important area within the production function as it attempts to reconcile two conflicting aims. On the one hand the firm needs a supply of various stocks for the following reasons:

Essential to have sufficient stocks.

- A stock of raw materials and work in progress: these need to be readily available so that the production sequence is not interrupted by shortages. Also bulk purchases can take advantage of discounts.
- A stock of finished goods: to act as a buffer between customer demand and the often erratic supply from the production process.
- A stock of tools and spare parts: for the maintenance of essential plant and machinery.

On the other hand, stock represents cash tied up in either the production process or goods on the shelves. The financial department would like to keep stocks to a minimum in order to release as much capital for other uses. The production and marketing departments would like to see adequate levels of stocks to ensure against breakdown, down-time or late delivery. The purpose of stock control is to find the optimum level of stocks which reconciles these two views.

THE COST OF STOCK

There are two main categories of costs; those associated with ordering and holding stock and those associated with running out of stock.

Inventory costs include the following:

- Acquisition or order costs – the cost of clerical and administrative work in raising an order, the transport inwards and its inspection on arrival.

- Handling or carrying costs: insurance
  storage costs (staff, equipment, handling)
  deterioration
  obsolescence
  security

- Financial cost: this is the opportunity cost of having capital tied up. For example, a firm holding an average of 100 tonnes of stock at a price of £400 per tonne would have £40,000 tied up in stock. If the firm is to make a return on assets of 20% the opportunity cost of such a stock level could be taken as £8,000 p.a. (average stock value × ROA). Lower stock levels would release capital and reduce costs. This could be achieved by having more frequent deliveries, but the saving on the opportunity cost must be balanced against the extra acquisition and holding costs.

STOCK-OUT COSTS

These are difficult to quantify but include:

- stock-out of raw materials and work-in-progress. This would result in machine and operator idle time and possibly the need for overtime payments to catch up on missed production.

- stock-out of finished goods may result in
  i) missed orders from occasional customers
  ii) missed delivery dates which could lead to deterioration in customer/supplier relations
  iii) incurring of penalty clauses for late delivery
  iv) the loss of the firm's reputation and goodwill

- stock-out of tools and spares:
  increase in downtime of machinery and loss of production

The total cost of holding a certain level of stock is therefore a combination of these two cost elements. As shown in Figure 20.2 a high level of stock means a low stock-out cost but a high stockholding cost and vice versa. The objective of a good stock-control system is to reconcile these two costs to determine the *optimum stock level* which minimises total costs and at the same time satisfies the firm's policy concerning the acceptable risk of running out of stock (stock level OQ_0 in Figure 20.2).

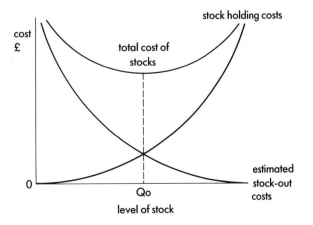

Fig. 20.2 Total cost of stockholding

STOCK POLICY

A stock or inventory policy is based on the answers to two simple questions:

- How much to order – the re-order quantity
- When to order – the re-order level

Economic order quantity (EOQ)

The optimum quantity.

In order to determine the optimum quantity at minimum cost we need to relate the acquisition cost and the holding costs at different order levels. Acquisition costs fall as the order quantity increases but the holding costs increase as more stock is held. The *economic order quantity* is where the cost of holding stock is just equal to the cost of raising and expediting an order. It can be calculated using the equation:

$$\text{EOQ} = \sqrt{\frac{2PD}{C}}$$

Where P = Acquisition cost
D = Annual demand
C = Storage cost per unit p.a.

The re-order level

This is the level of stocks, which when reached, signals that a replenishment order should be made. In order to calculate the level we require the following information:

- *average usage*: the number of stock items used per period of time.
- *lead time*: the interval between raising an order and the goods being available on site. (N.B. this is not the same as delivery time. Lead time or procurement time is made up of ordering time, delivery time and receiving/inspection time.) The lead time will depend on the reliability of suppliers. An examination of suppliers' records can determine the average lead time for each item of stock.

Example:
Assuming a usage rate of 20 items per week and a lead line of 3 weeks, the re-order level would be:
Re-order level = usage × lead time
= 20 × 3
= 60 units

Extra stocks as insurance.

When stocks reach 60 units a new order should be placed which will take 3 weeks to arrive, in which time the existing stock will be just enough to cover the usage rate of 20 per week. This assumes that the delivery will be exactly on time and that usage will be 20 per week. Any increase in usage or delay in delivery will produce a stock-out; therefore most firms also carry a safety or buffer-stock. This is the minimum stock level held to cover any possible deviation in the average demand and supply.

A stock model

Fig. 20.3 shows a *stock model* assuming that:

- The lead time is constant
- The usage rate is constant
- The goods arrive just as the minimum stock level is reached

From the model we can identify the salient points of a good inventory control system.

Important points and definitions.

- *A minimum stock level*: to act as a buffer against variations in supply or demand.
- *Economic order quantity*: the quantity which keeps total stock costs at a minimum.
- *Maximum stock level (Minimum + EOQ)*: the level above which the holding costs outweigh the advantage of holding stock.
- *Re-order level*: a signal to replenish stocks.
- *Lead time*: the time lapse between ordering goods and their replenishment.

This is an ideal situation which would not normally occur in practice for the following reasons:

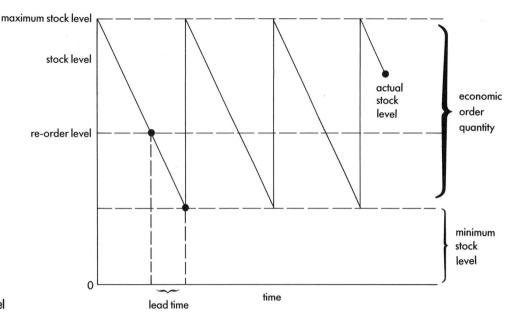

Fig. 20.3 Ideal stock model

- stock usage – often irregular and in discrete quantities particularly where batch production is used.
- lead time – suppliers may have variable delivery times dependent on production, transport and labour problems.
- demand for the finished goods – may be erratic and influenced by changes in consumer taste, fashion, taxation, government policy, threat of war, etc.

A more realistic stock situation is given in Fig. 20.4. Whatever the circumstances, the stock controller must attempt to reconcile the different demands placed upon stocks and seek the optimum policy.

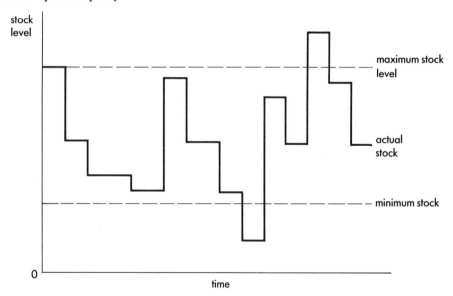

Fig. 20.4 Realistic stock model

QUALITY MANAGEMENT

The traditional approach

Quality has been seen as:

- 'the attribute of meeting required specification'
- 'reliability of product over a required period of time'

The achievement of quality has been seen as a matter for control by management of a process which it is assumed must always contain the probability of variability around the required specification. This variability is expected as a consequence of machine and tool wear, faulty materials and human error. This mindset leads to the need to decide on the degree of variance from specification which is likely to be acceptable to customers. The emphasis thus tends to be on achieving production targets at the expense of a degree of waste and scrap and rework which is thought to be acceptable to the producer. Control of quality therefore becomes a matter of inspecting in quality after the event, rather than ensuring quality in advance.

Quality control

Quality control has three aspects:

- *Supplier quality assurance.* A procedure for monitoring bought-out materials which are inputs into the production process. This process of monitoring depends on a detailed product specification, and willingness of the supplier to accept monitoring and appraisal of his own production process.

- *Post-mortem product inspection.* Usually undertaken by a Quality Control Department which is seen (wrongly) as being 'responsible' for quality. Inspection is based on a sampling system, which must be able to identify and collect the following data: sample size; acceptance number; acceptable quality level; lot tolerance % defective; producer's risk; consumer's risk. The system must be able to discriminate between acceptable and unacceptable quality. The information generated by single or double sampling plans, will be used to decide whether or not a batch of products is acceptable.

- *Process control.* Where quality control is undertaken during the production process rather than post-production, control charts may be used. These are used to establish the degree of variance occurring within the process, in order to determine when random and unexpected variations in quality are occurring, which may be solved by remedial action, e.g. replacement of a worn tool. Minor variance within an agreed acceptable range of tolerance either side of specification is accepted.

Quality and efficiency

The above approach to quality control, by inspecting in quality after the event, and accepting a degree of waste, is usually associated with batch and flow production systems, based on the 'economic order quantity'. This production method is usually to be found in large plant, producing standardised products in huge quantities. In such plant efficiency is sought by using Work Study and Method Study.

Work and method study

Method study seeks to establish *how* a job should be done. Work measurement seeks to establish how *long* the job should take. It also leads to job evaluation to establish how much a task is *worth* in pay.

- *Method study.* This seeks to establish the following:
    i) Improved procedures and processes
    ii) mprovement of the layout and design of the workplace.
    iii) Improvement in the use of manpower, plant equipment and materials.
    iv) Improved working environment.
    v) Improved specification and design of the product.
    vi) Improvements in application of human effort, and reduction of fatigue.

This end is achieved by systematic analysis, select–record–examine–develop–install–maintain the system. This method is based on the use of an operation (flow) process chart, using a set of generally accepted symbols. This records all activities in sequence; a string diagram may then be used to experimentally discover possible improvements to the flow, stemming from the discovery of obstructions to the free flow of the process. The solution proposed must be practicable, economic, acceptable (to the workers) and within the Health and Safety laws.

- *Work study.* This is an attempt to establish the work content of a specific task. Its aim is to reduce ineffective time, and establish the correct time for the job. It may be seen by workers as a way of minimising the time spent on the task at the worker's expense. It is also intended to establish the optimum work load for a worker or machine, and to produce useful information for budgeting and costing. It is often also used to provide the basis for a system of payment by results, usually known as 'piece work'. Since work study is used in the latter way, it is seen by workers as part of the apparatus of management control, based on the assumption the workers are only

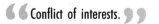

Before or after production?

Sampling reduces costs of inspection.

Not all solutions are workable or acceptable.

Conflict of interests.

motivated to work effectively by punishment and reward. As a result workers will see the Work Study officer as an 'enemy' to be outwitted, by seeking to manipulate the measurement by misleading him to record a slower 'correct' timing for a task than they can achieve. In this way the worker regains control over his work pattern, and earning power, and from management's points of view the exercise becomes worthless and counter-productive. Disputes about work study and incentive payments and between workers on piece rate and their colleagues on daily rates, help to produce confrontational industrial relations, as for example in car factories in the 1970s.

The modern approach

In this approach, quality is defined as 'conformance to customer requirements'. This includes design, conformance to agreed specification and reliability. The achievement of quality is here seen as a matter for assurance rather than control. It is the responsibility of all workers and managers, not just a Quality Department. 'Total Quality' is the target in the whole chain of customer-supplier relationships which exist not only between a firm and both its suppliers and customers, but also within the firm between departments. The aim of Total Quality Management (TQM) is to achieve zero defects, rather than simply an acceptable level of waste and failure. The whole of a business (including 'non-production' departments like sales, or administration) is seen as a process, translating inputs into outputs for 'customers'. This is illustrated in Fig. 20.5.

Total quality is the aim; zero defects is the target.

Zero defects appear to be an impossible target, but travelling in that direction is more important than arriving and requires the total commitment of top management.

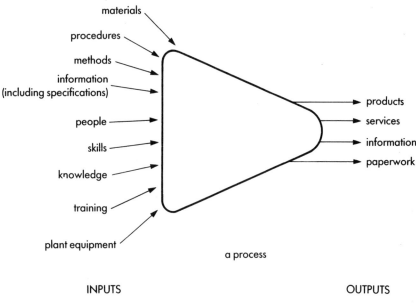

Fig. 20.5 The production process

source: J.S. Oakland 'Total Quality Management'

A quality policy

The key requirement is a *quality policy*, including the following ingredients:

Essential ingredients for a successful policy.

- an organised system for achieving quality.
- a system to identify the customer's perceived needs.
- a system to assess the ability of the firm to meet these needs economically.
- a system to ensure that suppliers of 'bought out' materials and services meet required standards.
- a system for preventing failure, scrap, rework and waste by measuring the 'costs of non-conformance' and the 'costs of achieving quality' (internal failure costs, appraisal costs and prevention costs). (See Fig. 20.6)
- educate and train all workers to measure and monitor quality and seek improvement.
- a system for reviewing quality management techniques to maintain progress.

The measurement of costs of non-conformance and quality is critical. It can be shown that waste and rework cost 10% plus in manufacturing and account for a startling 40% at times in service activities.

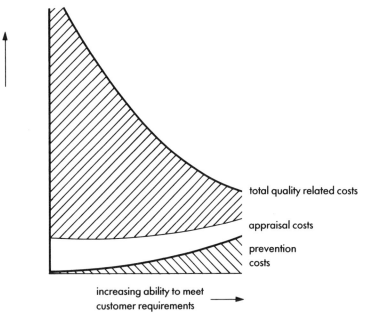

total quality related costs

appraisal costs

prevention costs

increasing ability to meet customer requirements

1 **failure costs**
waste, scrap, rework and seconds (downgraded)

2 **appraisal costs**
costs of inspection, measurement, calibration and the necessary systems

3 **prevention costs**
training of workers in quality monitoring

NB   as costs **2 & 3** increase, cost **1** declines disproportionately

relationship between direct costs of quality and organizational capability

Fig. 20.6 Costs of quality

Once the costs of quality have been established, the company must systematically seek continuous improvement in the direction of zero defects. In other words, it must always seek to 'get it right first time'. The achievement of this objective depends on the development of a flatter hierarchy, middle management as coaches not controllers, an intelligent and trained workforce, able and willing to accept responsibility for their own work. The change in corporate culture involved in setting up such a quality programme is very substantial and difficult; however, the rewards are great. One major advance which is made possible is the introduction of JIT (just in time inventory management). The arrival on the line of the necessary inputs, in exactly the right quantities, of perfect quality, just when needed, enables much greater flexibility of production and makes enormous savings in inventory costs. For example when Rover introduced JIT, they saved £40m in the first year, which goes straight through to the 'bottom line'.

❝Reduction in stock costs.❞

The concept of total quality management was originated by an American consultant, W.E. Deming, in the 1950s, ignored in the USA but taken up by the Japanese. Since that time the success of Japanese companies, and their increasing influence through outward investment, has caused the concept to be taken up by US and UK companies as an essential kit for survival. Major UK companies which have benefited enormously from an ongoing TQM programme include British Steel; British Gas; British Telecom; Rover, whilst service sector companies have now followed suit, e.g. TSB, British Rail.

EXAMINATION QUESTIONS

1 a) What are the objectives of stock management?   (*10*)
     b) How might each of these objectives be achieved?   (*15*)
                                                                    (UCLES 1985)

2 a) Differentiate between job and batch production systems.   (*5*)
     b) How might a biscuit manufacturer benefit from changing production processes from batch to flow?   (*10*)
     c) Discuss the potential problems that might arise from such a change.   (*10*)
                                                                    (UCLES 1989)

OUTLINE ANSWER

Question 1

a) In this section it is important to stress that good stock management is not just about minimising the cost of stocks held but also about ensuring sufficient stocks are kept to satisfy requirements. The cost of running out of stock is just as important as the cost of holding stock. To optimise the balance between stock levels and requirements, a stock policy must provide a means for bringing and holding stock at a target level. Finally, good stock management should be flexible so that stocks adapt to changing circumstances.

b) The first objective to be achieved is the establishment of the cost of holding stocks. This will include storage, handling, insurance, deterioration costs and most importantly the cost of tying up financial resources. This last part could be emphasised by a short numerate example showing the calculation of average stock and its cost by using the firm's return on assets. These costs increase with the level of stock held and must be balanced by the cost of running out of stock. The combination of the two costs gives the overall stock cost and the minimum point will determine the optimum stock level. The second objective of establishing stock targets can be achieved by calculating the economic order quantity, the re-order level and the safety stock level. This will give a minimum and maximum stock level. A linear graph would be a suitable diagram to include. Finally some discussion is required about the firm's objectives and its views about risk. An example of how stock policy would alter following a change in the market would be a suitable inclusion, e.g. stock of oil reserves after the invasion of Kuwait by Iraq.

STUDENT'S ANSWER

> Illustrate each type with several examples.

Question 2

a) Job production is usually associated with a particular customer who requires a unique item whereas batch production is concerned with producing a standardised item aimed at the general market. Job production tends to use general purpose machinery which is operated by a high-skilled and flexible workforce. The longer runs of batch production allows the use of special purpose machinery and labour need not be as versatile but more specialist. The layout for the production process may also be different as job production tends to be static, e.g. building of an off-shore oil-rig whereas batch production requires movement from one process to another, e.g. pottery making.

b) The major benefit to be derived from switching to flow production would be the reduction in unit costs. Flow production would allow a greater quantity of biscuits to be made without a similar proportional increase in the inputs used, particularly labour. The firm could then take advantage of economies of scale. Larger discounts may be available from suppliers for bulk purchases so that raw material costs are reduced. Technical economies could be made by introducing a greater degree of mechanisation and automation. Instead of moving the biscuits from one process to another a flow method would allow continuous movement on a conveyor type system. This would entail less handling and therefore a reduction in labour costs. A more mechanised system should also produce a more uniform product with less waste through breakage in handling.

   The end product should be more standard which could lead to greater consumer satisfaction and fewer complaints. With a flow system quality management can be built into the production method rather than requiring inspection at each stage. This should also reduce waste and guarantee a more marketable product. A standard product of good quality and produced in large quantities may allow the firm to enter markets previously denied it, e.g. to supply a national chain of supermarkets.

The reduction in handling and the constant movement of the product should ensure a greater level of hygiene and perhaps better working conditions for the operatives who would no longer have to handle hot materials or goods. The continuous flow process would no longer require storage between processes. The extra space can be used for storage of the finished product.

If the economies outweigh the initial investment it would be worthwhile financially for the company to switch production methods.

> A good description of the many advantages of flow production in terms of cost, product and the market.

c) It is no use switching to flow production unless there is a high level steady demand for the end-product. The product life-cycle should indicate a long-term life for the biscuit. This is required to justify the expense of the investment in new, automated capital equipment.

Another problem associated with flow production is the risk of breakdown. Any halt in one part means down-time for the whole process and consequently a high associated cost.

If change results in lost jobs then a problem may arise with labour relations in deciding who is to be made redundant, how much compensation to be paid and the general effect on morale. Previously skilled labour may no longer be needed or skills of a different order are required. The move between methods must have the support of the workforce.

The production of large quantities of particular items may require the firm to review its marketing mix. A large variety may no longer be possible because of the need for longer production runs. There may well be a loss of flexibility in the scheduling of products.

> The timing of the investment is also important.

The shareholders or owners of the firm may also view the increased financial commitment as a problem. Initially a large investment will be required which may not produce improved profits for a considerable time. The type of finance chosen may also be a problem if it significantly alters the firms gearing, making it more prone to interest rate changes.

Finally, the overall reaction to change may present problems. Suppliers, management, workforce and distributors will all have to adopt new measures with new demands on their time and energy. The natural reluctance to accept change may cause some parts of the company to drag their feet. The change will only succeed if it is well co-ordinated, well resourced and explained to a motivated workforce.

Tutor's comments

A well-thought out essay, delivered in a concise and direct manner.

FURTHER READING

Powell, *Production Decisions* Longman 1987:
   Chapter 9, Types of Production.

PRODUCTION II

GETTING STARTED

The aim of the business is to produce a range of goods and services which can be marketed and sold at an acceptable level of profit. The task of management is to organise the firm's limited resources in the most effective manner in order to achieve the firm's agreed objectives. This requires good and efficient decision-making. *Operations Research* (OR) is designed to help management determine their strategic and tactical decisions in a more scientific manner. Operations research is concerned with the construction and manipulation of mathematical models in order to analyse and study business problems. The OR approach to problem-solving incorporates seven key steps:

- Identify the problem
- Define the problem
- Represent the problem in model form
- Manipulate the model
- Test the solution
- Select the optimum solution
- Implement the solution

N.B. Where the pre-implementation test proves unsatisfactory management should return to manipulate the model again to identify a better solution.

OR techniques include the following:

- *Critical path analysis (CPA):* designed to help businesses to plan and control complex activities.

- *Linear programming:* designed to compare a given number of alternatives in order to extract the best option, e.g. the least cost or most profitable level of production.

- *Simulation:* designed to imitate what happens in practice and to take account of the unpredictability and variability of real-life events.

Operations research is a logical and scientific approach to problem solving which is largely, but not always, quantitative in its methods. This must be allied with, and complementary to, qualitative approaches to management.

❝❝ An aid to planning and control. ❞❞

ESSENTIAL PRINCIPLES

The main objective of *critical path analysis* (CPA) is to produce a network model of a complex project in order to help management effectively plan and control its operations. An alternative title is network analysis, as the technique revolves around the production of a 'network diagram' which represents visually all stages of the project. It helps planning by requiring management to list all activities in sequential order, to determine activity time, to assess resources required and to calculate the project duration and the critical path. CPA also helps to control a project once it is under way. It does this by comparing actual performance to that of the planned network. When delays occur or work is completed ahead of schedule the network diagram can be used to assess the consequences, allowing management to re-direct resources accordingly. Critical path analysis requires the following steps to be undertaken:

- Define the objective of the project.
- Identify the individual tasks.
- Draw the network diagram.
- Determine the project duration and the critical path.

❝❝ The end product or goal. ❞❞

DEFINING THE OBJECTIVE OF THE PROJECT

The *objective* must be clearly stated, together with any constraints such as time, finance or resources. An example could be the construction of a four-bedroom detached house and gardens within a prescribed budget and in a time period of 52 days.

IDENTIFY THE INDIVIDUAL TASKS

Each task must be accurately described and an estimate made of the time and resources required. Some of the tasks for the house project might include:

❝❝ Sequence and duration. ❞❞

- Digging of foundations
- Building of walls
- Erection of garden fence
- Roof construction
- Interior plastering
- Central heating installation
- Landscaping of gardens, etc

These could be broken down further into sub-tasks, each with their own duration and order sequence.

DRAW THE NETWORK DIAGRAM

A *network diagram* is based on the premise that some jobs can be done simultaneously whereas others must run consecutively. A logical sequence must be followed to show the interdependence of the individual tasks. A network diagram is made up of three components; activities, nodes and dummies.

❝❝ Components of the network. ❞❞

- An *activity* is a task which consumes time and/or resources. It is represented by an arrow from left to right (→) (the length of the arrow has *no* significance). For example, digging the foundations is an activity which requires a given quantity of materials, machines and labour for 8 days.
- A *node* indicates the start and finish of an activity and is represented by a circle (○).
- A *dummy* is an activity of zero duration which indicates a logical sequence and is represented by a dotted line (- - - →).

For example, the house project could be represented by the following tasks:
From the table it can be seen that activities A, B and C can start together but activity D must await the completion of Activity A and so on. The completed network is given in Fig. 21.1. N.B. Each activity is an integral part of the project and must be joined to the network.

Fig. 21.1 A network diagram

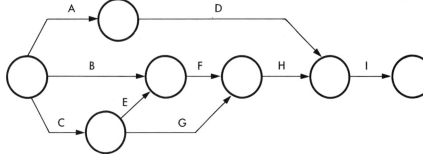

Fig. 21.2 Network diagram with node numbers

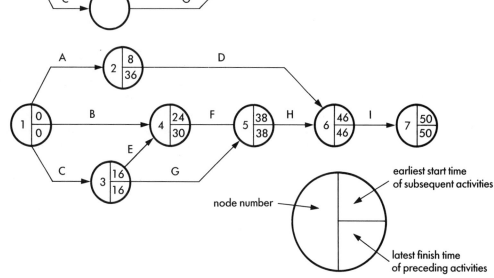

Activity	Preceded By	Estimated Duration (Days)
A	–	8
B	–	14
C	–	16
D	A	10
E	C	8
F	B, E	8
G	C	22
H	F, G	8
I	D, H	4

> No unattached lines allowed.

Instead of identifying the activity by means of a letter, the nodes could be numbered thus allowing the activity to be described by its start and finish node number. For example, Activity A would be 1–2 and Activity D would be 2–6 (see Fig. 21.2). The node is also used to indicate the Earliest Start Time (EST) and the Latest Finish Time (LFT). The EST figures are calculated from left to right, taking account of all preceding activities. They are written in the top right-hand side of the circle. For example, Activity D cannot start until Activity A has finished; therefore its EST is Day 8.

The LFT is calculated from right to left backwards through the network and written in the bottom right-hand sector. The LFT shows, for each activity, how late it can be completed without delaying the total project. For example, the estimated project time is 50 days; therefore all activities before Activity 'I' must be finished by Day 46 to enable 'I' (duration 4 days) to be completed by Day 50. The procedure is to subtract the duration time from the previous activity's LFT.

> Often required in examination questions.

N.B. The mechanical rule where there is more than one activity into a node is to take the 'highest' value when calculating the EST and the 'lowest' value for the LFT. For example, the EST of Activity F is Day 24 as it can only start when Activity B (14 days) is finished and Activity C (16 days) followed by Activity E (8 days) is complete.

DETERMINE THE PROJECT DURATION AND THE CRITICAL PATH

> Critical activity where EST = LFT.

The 'critical' activities are those where no delay is possible, i.e. the EST and the LFT are the same. In every project there will be 'at least' one sequence of activities that is critical. This critical path is denoted by cross hatching the relevant activity lines. The completed network is shown in Figure 21.2.

The critical path sequence is given by Activity C, G, H, I or activity numbers 1, 3, 5, 6, 7 which indicated that the project can be completed in a duration of 50 days (two days inside the maximum time limit). The non-critical activities are A, B, D, E and F. These activities have a certain amount of *float*; that is, the time they can over-run before affecting the project as a whole. There are two principal types of float:

1 *Total float:* the longest the start of an activity can be delayed from its EST without delaying the project's duration is calculated using the equation:

   Total Float = LST – EST

   where the LST (Latest Start Time) is given by LST = LFT – duration.

Therefore the equation can be rewritten as

Total Float = LFT – duration – EST

2   *Free float:* the maximum period of delay from the EST of an activity which will not affect the EST of any subsequent activities. It is calculated using:

Free float = EST at end – duration – EST at beginning.

For example, the non-critical Activity E (Nodes 3–4) would have a total float of $22 - 15 = 6$ days (LST = $30 - 8 = 22$ days) and a free float of $24 - 8 - 16 = 0$ days. In other words, Activity E can be delayed up to 6 days without affecting the project duration as a whole, but cannot be delayed at all without also affecting the EST of the subsequent activity (Activity F).

> 'Float' allows the re-allocation of resources.

The importance of float time is that resources such as labour and machines could be re-allocated, thus reducing costs. It may be worthwhile diverting resources to critical activities in order to reduce the project duration. This is particularly worthwhile where bonuses are paid for early completion or where penalties are incurred for overrun. Each activity will have a cost-slope that is the cost of reducing an activity by one day or the savings made by delaying the activity (by not devoting as many resources to it). Management could use the network diagram to experiment with different solutions, diverting resources to critical activities in order to reduce overall total costs. For example, if landscaping was a non-critical activity some labour could be released to help in a critical area such as wall erection in order to reduce the overall project time. If this were successful, expensive skilled labour such as brick-layers could be reduced.

SUMMARY

> A more scientific form of decision-making.

CPA or network analysis is both a planning tool and a control tool. It is an invaluable management technique for complex projects where hundreds of diverse activities have to be dovetailed in the most cost-effective manner. It also allows managers to deal efficiently with unforeseen events such as delays or early completions. The logical sequence and complex nature of the technique lends itself to computer application so that intuitive on-site guesswork is replaced by informed objective analysis.

LINEAR PROGRAMMING

Linear programming is a technique which can be used to compare a number of alternatives and to determine the optimum choice. It can be applied to problems which exhibit the following characteristics:

- The problem can be expressed in numerical terms.
- All factors involved have a linear relationship, i.e. a change in one factor brings about a proportional change in another, e.g. costs and revenue are proportionately related to the volume of activity.
- There are choices between alternative courses of action, e.g. the product mix of a company producing several different items.
- There are constraints on some of the factors, e.g. on resources or time or the market available.

The alternative name for linear programming is *blending*, which indicates its principal use. That is, one problem, the solution of which requires a mixture of factors. These factors may be components, such as in the production of animal feed, steel manufacturing and food processing.

> Used to solve problems of choice.

Alternatively they may be a mixture of products which have different profit contributions. Whatever the problem, a linear programming model is formulated in three stages:

1   Determine the key variables
2   Define the objective functions
3   Formulate the constraints

This process is best illustrated through an example.

EXAMPLE

A manufacturer produces two types of table: a standard model and a deluxe model. Both types are assembled from pre-manufactured kits and then finished by sanding and varnishing. The production details are given below.

PRODUCTION DETAILS	*Standard*	*Deluxe*
Production time (hrs per unit)		
Assembly	3	4
Finishing	2	4
Contribution (£/unit)	80	120
Maximun potential sales (units/per week)	30	20

Production capacity is limited to 120 hours in the assembly shop and to 100 hours in the finising shop.

The manufacturer wants to find the combination of products which will give the maximum contribution towards overheads and profits.

Determine the key variables

The problem is to determine the mixture of standard and deluxe tables which will produce the maximum contribution.

> Let x = the number of standard tables
> Let y = the number of deluxe tables
> where x and y are the *key variables*.

Define the objective function

Since the contribution on a standard table is £80 and on a deluxe table is £120, the total contribution produced by a combination of the two types will be given by

> $C = 80x + 120y$

The *objective function* is to maximise the contribution, C.

> **"The best combination of tables."**

Formulate the constraints

The amount of contribution which can be realised per week is limited by the following constraints

> **"All production is limited in some way."**

Assembly	$3x + 4y \leqslant 120$
Finishing	$2x + 4y \leqslant 100$
Sales of y	$y \leqslant 20$
Sales of x	$x \leqslant 30$

In addition, since we cannot have a negative number of tables then

> $x \geqslant 0$
> and $y \geqslant 0$

These are the non-negativity constraints.

Solving the problem

The constraints can be expressed in graph form as in Fig. 21.3.
  The assembly constraint is $3x + 4y \leqslant 120$. Therefore

> when $x = 0$ $y = 30$
> and when $y = 0$ $x = 40$

These points when plotted produce line AB. In a similar way, the finishing constraint $2x + 4y = 100$ produces points

> $x = 0$ $y = 25$ and line CD
> and $y = 0$ $x = 50$

> **"All combinations inside the boundaries are possible."**

The sales constraints are the lines $y = 20$ and $x = 30$. The shaded area indicates levels of production which are not feasible given the existing constraints. Any point inside the boundaries is feasible.

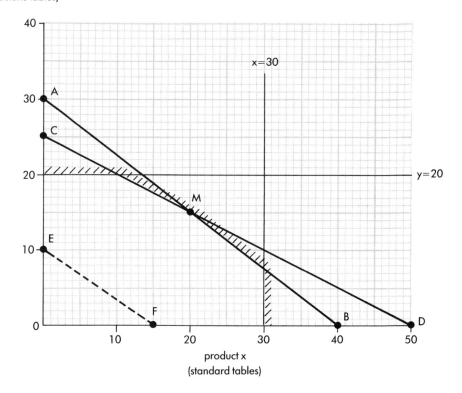

Fig. 21.3 Constraints to
contribution

The optimum solution always occurs along the boundary of the feasible region and for contribution maximisation it will be as far to the right as possible. This point can be determined by graphing the objective function C = 80x + 120y. Assume any given level of contribution (e.g. 1200). For example:

Let C   = 1200
therefore   1200 = 80x + 120y
When   x = 0   y = 10
and when   y = 0   x = 15

This contribution line is shown as EF in Fig. 21.3. As the contribution increases, the line will shift to the right, parallel to EF and is maximised at point M, i.e. a combination of 20 standard tables and 15 deluxe tables. This produces a total contribution of:

C = 80x + 120y

C = 80 × 20 + 120 × 15
C = 1600 + 1800
C = £3,400

> It may change in the long-run with the addition of further production capacity in one of the three areas.

This is the maximum contribution subject to three constraints of assembly, finishing and market potential. If any of these factors change, then the optimum solution will also change but in the short term it is the best alternative.

SUMMARY

Linear programming is a good short-term decision-making tool which can be used when relations are linear and constraints exist. The essential steps are:

- Write the problem in mathematical form
- Graph the constraints
- Determine the feasible region
- Graph the objective function and move it parallel to find the optimum point
- Identify the optimum combination
- Substitute solution into the objective function to find the best combination

SIMULATION

In the previous section the manager was faced with variables which behaved in a *linear* manner which made decision-making somewhat easier. However, in many cases the manager faces conditions of uncertainty. *Simulation* or *queuing theory* is a technique which allows evaluation about decisions under such conditions and takes account of the unpredictability and variability of real-life situations. It does this by creating a model which duplicates the essential features of the system under investigation, including the essential ingredient of variability. The arrival pattern of customers at a supermarket check-out, cars at a petrol station or components at an assembly point provide good examples of random behaviour.

INFORMATION REQUIRED

Knowing whether a queue will form is extremely important because it informs the manager about

- Resources not being fully utilised
- Inadequate resources to deal with 'customer' demand

Both of these involve cost which could be minimised. To do this, a model is created which requires four factors to be known:

1 *The pattern of arrivals*: i.e. the arrival interval between 'customers' who are demanding a service, e.g. aircraft wanting to use airport facilities.
2 *The service time*: i.e. how long it takes to service each customer, e.g. the turnaround time for a Boeing 737 with over 300 passengers compared to a light aircraft carrying a handful of people.
3 *The number of service points available*: i.e. how many loading bays exist at the airport terminal.
4 *The queue discipline*: this is what determines the order in which customers are served, e.g. first come, first served or in order of importance (aircraft size).

	Observed frequencies of customer arrivals and service times.				
	CUSTOMER ARRIVAL INTERVAL			CUSTOMER SERVICE INTERVAL	
(minutes)	*Frequency (%)*	*Cumulative Frequency (%)*		*Frequency (%)*	*Cumulative Frequency (%)*
0	8	8		–	–
1	20	28		10	10
2	36	64		28	38
3	18	82		42	80
4	12	94		18	98
5	6	100		2	100

CONSTRUCTING THE MODEL

Step 1: identify the problem

Example: A new manager is appointed to a busy curio shop in a sea-side resort and wants to know whether or not to install a second check-out point.

Step 2: information gathering and presentation

Gather the relevant information about customer arrivals and service times and present in the form of a percentage frequency table with a cumulative frequency column.

ALLOCATION OF RANDOM NUMBERS					
Customer Arrivals (mins.)	*Cumulative Frequency (%)*	*Allocation of Random Numbers*	*Customer Service Intervals (mins.)*	*Cumulative Frequency (%)*	*Allocation of Random Numbers*
0	8	01–08	0	0	0
1	28	09–28	1	10	01–10
2	64	29–64	2	38	11–38
3	82	65–82	3	80	39–80
4	94	83–94	4	98	81–98
5	100	95–00*	5	100	99–00*
					* represents 100

Table 21.1 Allocation of Random Numbers

Step 3: allocate random numbers

The allocation of the random numbers is done according to the cumulative percentage frequency so that the number of random numbers accurately reflects the frequency of each class interval. For example, numbers 9 to 28 are allocated to those customers with an arrival interval of one minute and numbers 29 to 64 to those customers with a two minute interval and so on. The same is done for service times as shown in Table 21.1.

Random Numbers									
Arrivals	20	35	16	74	58	72	79	98	09	47
Service	07	98	82	69	63	23	70	80	88	86

> Learn to use a random number table or the random number function on a scientific calculator.

Step 4: simulate the imaginary event

To create imaginary customers we use random numbers taken sequentially from a random number table. N.B. In an examination, the numbers will be provided as shown below.

Customer Number	Arrival Interval		Service Time		Arrival Time	Service Begins	Service Ends	Idle Time	Queue Time
	Random Number	Simulated Value (mins)	Random Number	Simulated Value (mins)					
1	20	1	07	1	08.01	08.01	08.02	1	–
2	35	2	98	4	08.03	08.03	08.07	1	–
3	16	1	82	4	08.04	08.07	08.11	–	3
4	74	3	69	3	08.07	08.11	08.14	–	4
5	58	2	63	3	08.09	08.14	08.17	–	5
6	72	3	23	2	08.12	08.17	08.19	–	5
7	79	3	70	3	08.15	08.19	08.22	–	4
8	98	5	80	3	08.20	08.22	08.25	–	2
9	09	1	88	4	08.21	08.25	08.29	–	4
10	47	2	86	4	08.23	08.29	08.33	–	6
								2	33

Table 21.2 Simulated event

Customer number one is allocated random number 20 to simulate arrival interval, and random number 07 to simulate service time. Using Table 21.1 the number 20 equates to an arrival interval of one minute and the number 07 to a service time of one minute. This process is repeated to simulate as many customers as is needed. Table 21.2 shows the likely situation for the first ten customers, assuming that the shop opens at 08.00 hours.

Step 5: analyse the results

The simulation investigates what could occur in practice. The first customer arrives one minute after opening and is served straight away, as is the second customer. However, from 08.04 onwards a queue of two or three people develops, each waiting between 2 and 6 minutes to be served. The manager must now assess the likely effects of this such as

> Analyse the results.

- customers not returning to the shop because of poor service
- impatient customers leaving the queue and not purchasing goods, i.e. lost sales
- the cost in terms of labour and equipment to open a second checkout
- the effect of the workload on service staff

The manager could then test any suggested changes by running another simulation. Possible alterations could be:

- opening a second check-out (re-run the simulation with a different queue discipline).
- using a different type of till, e.g. automatic bar code reader to speed up service times.

- employ extra staff to read prices and package goods, again to reduce service times.

Each alternative can be simulated, examined and fully costed before being implemented.

ADVANTAGES OF SIMULATION

Simulation has four major advantages:

- It is an inexpensive method for analysing the behaviour of a system.
- It creates what is likely to happen in real-life.
- It allows alternative courses of action to be studied.
- It is simple to operate and easily adapted for computer use.

N.B. The only disadvantage to be borne in mind is that the benefits of the simulation must always outweigh the cost of its undertaking.

EXAMINATION QUESTIONS

1 a) Briefly explain the advantages and limitations of Critical Path Analysis as a control tool for management. (5)

   b) Use the critical path diagram below Fig. 21.4 to calculate the earliest and latest start times of each activity, the critical path and the minimum possible duration of the whole project. Show your workings. (7)

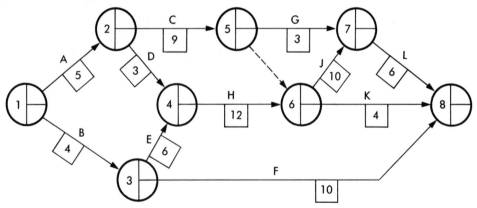

Fig. 21.4 Critical path diagram

   c) Six days must now be cut from the minimum project duration. No single activity can be reduced by more than 2 days. Using the information given, find the cheapest way of achieving this. What is the new critical path? (7)

FURTHER INFORMATION

Activity	Cost of reducing by one day (£)
A	4
B	4
C	1
D	4
E	3
F	1
G	2
H	4
J	2
K	4
L	1

d) Assume that the cuts in question c) are NOT introduced. Activities C, D, E and F require labour of skill X as below:

Activity	Units of skill X needed per day
C	10
D	12
E	10
F	8

 i) Assuming each activity starts at its earliest time, draw a histogram to show the total utilisation of X.   (3)

 ii) What are the implications if only 17 units of X are available?   (3)

                  (UCLES 1990)

2 a) What assumptions typically underlie queuing simulations?   (3)

b) The manager of a small port, which has two quays, has asked for your help in determining whether a third quay should be built. You have the following data.

Interval between boat arrivals		Time boats spend at quayside	
Days	Frequency %	Days	Frequency %
0	5	4	30
1	10	5	40
2	20	6	30
3	40		
4	15		
5	10		

 i) Show, on the basis of a single simulation, that if 10 boats arrive, only 2 boats will each have to wait one day.   (6)

  N.B. Use the Random Numbers below. Use Row 1 to simulate arrival times and Row 2 to simulate time spent at quayside. Work from left to right.

 ii) Is a single simulation adequate as a decision aid? Give your reasons.   (4)

c) Each day of waiting costs £100 in penalties paid by the port manager to the boat owners. The port manager has just been offered £10,000 to hire out the 2nd quay exclusively to a shipping firm for 31 days.

 i) Show that if only one quay is available a queue of boats seems certain to form. Explain why this is so.   (3)

 ii) Assume the arrival of 10 boats. Would it pay the port manager to hire out the second berth?   (5)

 iii) Explain *two* additional problems the port manager would incur if he were to accept the offer.   (4)

Random Numbers

Row 1	20	84	27	38	66	19	60	10	51	20
Row 2	30	41	26	14	82	17	21	32	43	90

                  (UCLES 1989)

TUTOR'S ANSWER

Question 1

a) Advantages of CPA as a control tool:

- allows managers to experiment without spending vast amounts of time, money or resources
- allows 'what if' analysis
- allows continuous up-date of the network once the project has started
- can be computerised
- probabilities can be built in
- is proactive rather than reactive.

Disadvantages include:

- costs time and money if applied incorrectly
- only as accurate as the data input
- can result in on-site human resistance to the recommend changes

b)

Activity	Duration	E.S.T.	L.F.T.	L.S.T.*	Total Float (LST–EST)
A	5	0	7	2	2
B	4	0	4	0	0
C	9	5	22	13	8
D	3	5	10	7	2
E	6	4	10	4	0
F	10	4	38	28	24
G	3	14	32	29	15
H	12	10	22	10	0
J	10	22	32	22	0
K	4	22	38	34	12
L	6	32	38	32	0

*LST = LFT – duration

Where there is no total float the activity is critical. Therefore the critical path is B, E, H, J, L.

c) Cut J by 2 days which costs £4
   Cut L by 2 days which costs £2
   Cut E by 2 days which costs £6
      Total cost is £12
   N.B. To cut project duration, only critical activities need to be reduced.

   From the Total Float column a reduction of six days in the project duration will make activities A and D critical as well.

d) i) See the histogram in Fig. 21.5.
   ii) If only 17 units of skill X are available, then activities from Day 4 will be affected. Management must either re-schedule activities, if possible, or attempt to acquire more units of X. Activity F has enough float for delay, but unless extra skill is found the total project-duration will be affected.

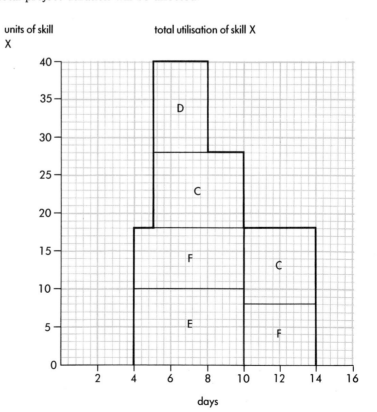

Fig. 21.5 Histogram

OUTLINE ANSWER

Question 2

a) The assumptions are based on the four key factors, i.e. the pattern of arrivals, the service time, the number of service points and the queue discipline. It is used when the variables are non-linear and unpredictable.

b) i) Create a simulation similar to that in the chapter but remembering there are two service points.

   ii) It is best to run a number of simulations to ensure the result is not a freak one. The average of several simulations would then be a good guide.

c) i) Calculate the average service times and arrival intervals. The mean service time of 4.7 days is greater than the mean arrival interval of 2.5 days, therefore a queue is likely to form.

   ii) Calculate the number of days ships are queuing (77 days) and multiply by the penalty (£100 per day). In financial terms the hire charge of £10,000 is greater than the total penalties of £7,700 to give a net gain of £2,300.

   iii) Accepting the order would create a backlog into the next month and, even more importantly, it may deter regular customers from using the port because of poor service.

FURTHER READING

Harris and Powell, *Quantitative Decision Making* Longman 1987:
  Chapter 14, Network Analysis.
  Chapter 15, Blending.
  Chapter 17, Simulation.
Martin, *Statistics* Mitchell Beazley 1983:
  Chapter 8, Further Topics.
Francis, *Business Mathematics and Statistics* DP Publications 1988:
  Chapter 44, Linear inequalities.
Harrison, *Operational Research* Mitchell Beazley 1983:
  Chapter 3, Mathematical Programming.
  Chapter 4, Queuing Theory.

INDEX